Y0-CAN-799

THE SCIENCE OF MANAGING ORGANIZED TECHNOLOGY

Edited by

MARVIN J. CETRON

and

JOEL D. GOLDHAR

VOLUME 3

GORDON AND BREACH, SCIENCE PUBLISHERS

New York London Paris

150 Fifth Avenue, New York, N.Y. 10011

Library of Congress Catalog Card Number: 79-106646

Editorial office for Great Britain:
Gordon and Breach, Science Publishers Ltd.
12 Bloomsbury Way
London W.C. 1

Editorial office for France:
Gordon & Breach
7-9 rue Emile Dubois
Paris 14e

Printed in the United States of America

FOR

GLORIA AND LAURA

PREFACE

The need for a book of this nature became evident to the authors during the process of developing a course in R&D Management for students at the Industrial College of the Armed Forces and in their day-to-day work of developing and managing an R&D program. No single authoritative text was available to cover the broad spectrum of data, techniques, and problems; apropos R&D Management, to which we felt both practicing managers and students of management should be exposed. In addition, we wanted to teach general managers and administrators about the research and development function, and about the important characteristics of science and technology; rather than attempting to teach management to scientists and engineers within the confines of a one-semester course. We expect that in the future more and more managerial responsibilities for R&D will be given to non-scientists owing to the need for efficient use of scientific and technical manpower. We hope this book will contribute to the technical "literacy" of such administrators. In addition, many technical people working in their own specialities have little understanding of the overall role and process of R&D; this collection is edited with them in mind as well.

Because of the increasing rate of growth of R&D Management literature, we felt that the time was ripe for a critical review and synthesis of the available materials. The final product is intended to be a total package for teaching and review covering all the aspects of the R&D Manager's environment. It was a difficult task to select the works in each area which would be most meaningful and useful to current and future R&D Managers from the extensive bibliography of excellent material available. In many cases, our final decision was based upon "Teachability" and usefulness of the article in a classroom situation rather than specific technical criteria.

We chose to compile and edit a collection of articles rather than write a more typical text in order to be able to reflect contributions being made by current practitioners and by recognized authorities in a wide range of academic disciplines.

The purpose of this book was to provide a complete and up-to-date collection of materials on the subject of R&D management in a format and framework useful for the classroom as well as individual study. The book offers a survey of the R&D manager's macro and micro environments, his problems and some possible solutions. The material was selected for its relevance to the unique properties of the R&D functional area and offers background to managers. The book is *not* intended to be a scientist's introduction to the elementary principles of management. Rather we intended it to be a substantive offersing to individuals engaged in the study and practice of RD&E management.

Since the book is addressed to the individual R&D manager, we first looked outward at his surroundings and environmental influences and than turned inward to a broad coverage of his tasks as a decision-maker and administrator. In other words, we dealt with the manager's two principle environments; the external which he can usually only observe and adapt to and the internal which to some extent he can control and change. The R&D manager's job is to balance the conflicting demands of these two environments. Diagramatically:

In summary, this book is intended to aid the manager in reducing the uncertainty under which he must make his decisions in the R&D environment.

Each "part" and chapter has an introduction and conclusion written by the editors and covering:

—overall purpose of the part
—Focus of each chapter
—Specific contribution of each article
—Summary overview of the total picture presented in the part

Part I: Background for R&D Management

A selection of readings to set the manager's philosphical background and illustrate the variety of forces which affect his managerial decisions in the R&D area. These forces and pressures may act as either opportunities or constraints and his job is to discriminate among them and adapt his internal environment for optimal performance or flexibility in the face of an uncertain future.

Part II: R&D Decision Making

A switch in focus and perspective to the "controllable" internal environment. In the last section the frame of reference was the outside world and the R&D manager's place in that world. We now look at how he allocates his own scarce resources consistent with the opportunities and constraints presented by the external environment. This part surveys the most important tools which he can use. The material is offered in a logical task sequence; goal setting, Technological Forecasting, Projection Evaluation and Selection, and the Systematic approach to technical planning.

Part III: Administering the R&D Process

This part relates the unique features of R&D activities to the reader's background of management principles and highlights the difference between traditional administration and the administration of an R&D activity.

Part IV: Tying the Pieces Together

A summary and overview of the problem of managing organized technology for effective and efficient results. A look at the possible future environment for R&D managers. A systems approach to the manager's understanding of technological change and its effect on his organization's long term growth and continuity.

We hope that we have achieved a balance between the theoretical and the practical, and between the external and the internal. We have tried to compile a "package" (or a "total system" to use the vernacular) useful for both teaching and self-instruction, and of interest to both managers of R&D and general managers who desire a better understanding of the Research and Development process.

Our most important debt is naturally to the many contributors and publishers who have made this volume possible. Complete acknowledgement is made on the title page of each contribution. We also owe a debt of gratitude for the encouragement and helpful comments of Professors Charles Bartfeld, Ralph Cole, Lowell Hattery and Nikos Photias of American University. And to Professors Burt Dean of Case Western Reserve, Ed Roberts of MIT, Dan Roman of the George Washington University, Al Rubenstein of Northwestern, and other pioneers in research-on-research. Special acknowledgement is due to Jim Duda and Lee Pagano, and to Bill Sproull who aided in the preparation of the book reviews and the Dig Deeper Sections, respectively, and to Miss Barbara Miranov, our secretary, who typed the manuscript.

A special tribute must go to our wives, Gloria and Laura to whom this volume is dedicated; who have helped us with patience, encouragement, and not a small amount of critical commentary. Naturally, we assume responsibility for all errors, both of commission and omission, and hope that users of this book will feel free to give us their reactions to the collection of material offered herein.

November 1970

Marvin J. Cetron
Joel D. Goldhar

TABLE OF CONTENTS

VOLUME ONE

Marvin J. Cetron and Joel D. Goldhar	Preface Managing Organized Technology: An Introduction	1

PART I

BACKGROUND FOR R&D MANAGEMENT 13

Chapter 1: Science and Technology in Perspective 19

Derek J. deSolla Price	The Difference Between Science and Technology	21
Morris C. Leikind and Wyndham Miles	The Nature of Science and Technology	37
Alain Pons	Research Management	51
Aaron Gelman	A Model of the Innovative Process in a Non-Science-Based Fragmented Industry	65
J. A. Morton	A Model of the Innovative Process in a Science-Based Integrated Industry	81
Emmanuel G. Mesthene	How Technology Will Shape The Future	101

Chapter 2: The Economic Environment 125

Joel D. Goldhar	Dimensions of R&D Activity	127
National Science Foundation	Research and Development in Industry, 1967	211
Bureau of the Budget	Federal Research, Development, and Related Programs	229
Richard Nelson, Merton J. Peck & Edward Kalachek	Industrial R&D Concentration: Causes and Significance	243

Chapter 3: Social and Political Environments 265

Ithiel de Solla Pool	The Social Environment for Sustained Technological Growth	269

George L. Dickey — The Political Environment for National Defense R&D: Organizational Setting and General Concepts 283

Krishnan D. Mathur — Science and the Federal Government 203

Harold P. Green — The New Technological Era: A View From the Law 319

William S. Beller — Decision-Making in Washington ... 335

Alvin M. Weinberg — Scientific Choice, Basic Science and Applied Missions 376

Carl Pfaffman — Behavioral Sciences 377

Preston E. Cloud, Jr. and V. E. McKelvey — The Environmental Sciences and National Goals 413

Daniel S. Greenberg — The New Politics of Science 443

Richard Nelson, Merton J. Peck & Edward D. Kalachek — False and Real Concerns About Technological Progress 467

VOLUME TWO

Chapter 4: R&D Entrepreneurship 483

Edward B. Roberts — Entrepreneurship and Technology .. 485

Albert Shapero — Management of Technical and Intellectual Resources 505

Gerald Gordon and Edward J. Morse — Creative Potential and Organizational Structure 517

Herbert A. Wainer and Irwin M. Rubin — Motivation of R&D Entrepreneurship Determinants of Company Success 533

John H. Dessauer — Xerography—A Single Idea Transforms a Company 547

Chapter 5: The Future Environment

David M. Kiefer — The Futures Business 559

Herman Kahn and Anthony J. Weiner — The Next Thirty-Three Years: A Framework for Speculation 593

Dennis Gabor — Technological Forecasting in a Social Frame 619

Chapter 6: The Economics of Technological Change 643

Edwin Mansfield — Technological Change and Productivity Growth 645

Jacob Schmookler — Technological Change and The Law of Industrial Growth 681

Fritz Machlup — The Supply of Inventors and Inventions 695

John Jewkes, David Sawers and Richard Stillerman — The Instutitionalization of Research 721

PART II

R&D DECISION MAKING 731

Chapter 7: Setting Goals and Corporate Strategy 735

Ram Charan — A Concept of General Management. 739

Robert E. Seiler — The Formulation and Application of Research Objectives 751

Vladimir Haensel — Lucky Alva 761

Donald L. Pyke — TRW's PROBE II 765

H. Igor Ansoff and John M. Stewart — Strategies for a Technology-Based Business 781

Chapter 8: Technological Forecasting 803

Marvin J. Cetron — Forecasting Technology 807

Ralph Lenz, Jr. — Practical Applications of Technical Trend Forecasting 825

William L. Swager — Effective Technological Forecasting 855

Marvin J. Cetron and Thomas I. Monahan — An Evaluation and Appraisal of Various Approaches to Technological Forecasting 857

Edward B. Roberts — Exploratory and Normative Technological Forecasting: A Critical Appraisal 891

VOLUME THREE

Chapter 9: Project Evaluation and Selection 911

Burton V. Dean and S. S. Sengupta — Research Budgeting and Project Selection 913

C. K. Buell — When to Terminate a Research and Development Project 941

Marvin J. Cetron and Harold Davidson — Macro R&D 949

Marvin J. Cetron, Joseph Martino and Lewis Roepcke — The Selection of R&D Program Content—Survey of Quantitative Methods 965

Chapter 10: A Systematic Approach to Technical Planning 991

Joseph P. Martino — The Use of Technological Forecasts for Planning Research 993

Marvin J. Cetron — Prescription for the Military R&D Manager: Learn the Three Rx's. 1005

William J. Abernathy & Richard S. Rosenbloom — Parallel and Sequential R&D Strategies: Application of a Simple Model 1041

PART III

ADMINISTERING THE R&D PROCESS 1063

Chapter 11: Organization of R&D Activities 1067

Albert H. Rubenstein — Organization Factors Affecting Research and Development Decision-Making in Large Decentralized Companies 1069

David W. Conrath — The Role of the Informal Organization in Decision Making on Research and Development ... 1089

Gerald Gordon — Preconceptions and Reconceptions In the Administration of Science. 1113

Hendrick W. Bode — The Systems Approach 1121

Irwin Mordka — A Comparison of a Research and Development Laboratory's Organization Structures 1145

Chapter 12: Technology Transfer 1161

Hendrick W. Bode — Reflections on the Relation Between Science and Technology 1163

William J. Price and Lawrence W. Bass — Scientific Research and The Innovative Process 1203

Thomas J. Allen — Performance of Information Channels In the Transfer of Technology 1217

Charles Kimball	Technology Transfer	1235
Harold Davidson	Coupling of Research and Development	1245
Bodo Bartocha, Francis Narin and Clinton A. Stone	TRACES—Technology in Retrospect and Critical Events in Science	1268

Chapter 13: Management of Scientific Personnel 1273

Harold Guetzkow	The Creative Person in Organizations	1275
Gerd D. Wallenstein	Fundamentals of Technical Manpower Planning	1285
C. W. Churchman, C. E. Kruytbosch and P. Ratoosh	The Role of the Research Administrator	1307

VOLUME FOUR

Chapter 14: Creativity and Creative Organizations 1317

Donald C. Pelz and Frank M. Andrews	Creativity	1321
Albert H. Rubenstein	Studies of Idea Flow in Research and Development	1343
William P. Hettinger, Jr.	Creativity and Idea Generation	1363

Chapter 15: Budgeting and Control 1369

Russell L. Ackoff	Specialized vs. Generalized Models in Research Budgeting	1371
G. T. Gmitter	Towards a Better Understanding of Industrialized R&D Cost Control	1385
Peter V. Norden	Resource Usage and Network Planning Techniques	1395
Daniel D. Roman	The PERT System: An Appraisal of Program Evaluation Review Technique	1417
Jack Moshman, Jacob Johnson and Madalyn Larsen	RAMPS—A Technique for Resource Allocation and Multi-Project Scheduling	1429

Contents

PART IV

TYING THE PIECES TOGETHER 1451

Chapter 16: Research Effectiveness 1453

Robert E. Seiler — Techniques for an Overall Evaluation of the Research Effort 1457

Raymond S. Isenson — Factors Affecting the Growth of Technology—As seen Through Hindsight 1469

Howard Vollmer — Evaluating Two Aspects of Quality in Research Program Effectiveness 1487

Joseph Martino — Citation Indexing for R&D Management 1503

Chapter 17: Final Ideas 1515

Murray L. Weidenbaum — Arms and The American Economy: A Domestic Convergence Hypothesis 1517

Marvin J. Cetron & Alan L. Weiser — Technological Change, Technological Forecasting and Planning R&D—A View From The R&D Manager's Desk 1529

Edward B. Roberts — The Problem of Aging Organizations 1557

Edward Teller — The Evolution and Prospects for Applied Physical Science in the U.S. 1569

Harold Linstone — A University for the Post Industrial Society 1605

Charles Williams — Setting National Research Goals for the U.S. 1631

Marvin J. Cetron and Joel D. Goldhar — Managing Organized Technology: Overview with Modest Conclusions 1653

Marvin J. Cetron and James L. Duda — Book Reviews 1653

CHAPTER NINE

PROJECT EVALUATION AND SELECTION

Every R&D Manager spends a large portion of his time allocating (or arguing for the allocation of) resources to specific research or development projects. This is a difficult task in light of the great uncertainties inherent in the creative processes and many approaches and attempts to synthesize and routinize the problem have been presented in the literature. On the other hand, many R&D managers argue that the only reasonable method is their own "best judgment", "guesstimation" or "knowledgeable hunch". We agree with these managers to a large extent; however, as the organization grows in size and complexity some systematic efforts must be made to allocate limited resources efficiently and effectively.

In reality, the mental process of most R&D decision-makers using "hunch" methods are very similar to the more vigorous quantitative techniques—except they are implicit rather than explicit. The four selections in this chapter have been chosen as representative of the available literature and useful in stimulating the reader's thinking on the problem of economic resource allocation. Essentially the techniques are the familiar financial analysis, probability and uncertainty, linear programming, break-even and present value techniques used in all areas of management. These articles suggest how they may be adapted for use in the R&D situation.

In the first article in this chapter Dean and Sengupta present a summary of decision-making in the area of research budgeting and project selection. Their prime objective was to determine if scientific analysis could be utilized to derive objective and quantitative procedures in this area dominated by "mature judgment" and intuition. Buell then discusses the agonizing question of, "When do I terminate an ongoing research and development project?" After asking the R&D administrator to answer some 21 questions on why the current projects should not be canceled, he concludes by hoping that these questions do not make the administrator lose his courage to initiate new projects.

Cetron and Davidson in their article entitled "MACRO R&D" outline elements of a quantitative resource allocation technique for allocating applied research funds. MACRO R&D which stands for *M*ethodology for

*A*llocating *C*orporate *R*esources to *O*bjectives for *R&D* is perhaps one of the most sophisticated systems developed. It is based on the concept of marginal utility of each piece of technology.

MACRO, as well as the other 30 techniques mentioned in the last article in this chapter, is intended not to yield decisions but rather to furnish information that might facilitate decision making. *Indeed, the principal value of the technique is derived from its providing a thinking structure to force methodical, meticulous analysis.* Data plus analysis generate information. Information couples with judgment to render decisions.

The final article in this chapter by Cetron, Martino and Roepcke presents a summary of methods for evaluating and selecting R&D projects. Approximately thirty methods, which have appeared in scattered places in the literature, are described briefly, and a bibliography is provided for further information. The various methods are compared and contrasted with each other relative to a standard set of features which they may possess, to a standard set of characteristics relating to ease of use, and to scientific or technological area of applicability.

For individuals planning to introduce quantitative project selection into their organization we would suggest that the first step is to thoroughly review the basic quantitative and economic methods (a good reference is *Technical Resource Management: Quantitative Methods* by Cetron et. al. MIT Press, 1970.) Then they should decide how they can be applied to the specific situation.

RESEARCH BUDGETING AND PROJECT SELECTION*

B. V. Dean
and
S.S. Sengupta
Case Western Reserve University

A summary is presented of a study of decision-making in the area of research budgeting and project selection. Data were obtained from three major chemical companies. The objective of the study was to determine if scientific analysis could be employed to derive objective and quantitative procedures in these areas, currently dominated by a mixture of intuition, judgment, and experience. A two-fold classification of R&D is used—"product research" and "process research." A solution is presented for the general R&D budgeting problem, involving a budgeting model. A computational procedure for this general problem is illustrated. The special problem of allocation of the budget to specific projects is treated briefly in this paper.

INTRODUCTION

The importance of R&D in the development of the national economy in general, and in the growth of industries and firms in particular, is widely recognized. This recognition is manifested by the increasing effort to develop procedures for improving the quality of managerial decisions in the area of R&D. Here we summarize one such effort.

Our objective has been one of determining whether scientific analysis could be employed to derive objective and quantitative procedures that might improve results obtained by the current mixture of intuition, judgment and experience. Three major chemical companies served as a laboratory in which this study was performed. In spite of differences in structure and operations they had had two features in common: 1) each had long experience in research and development, and 2) each had grown principally by the introduction of new and improved products. These basic facts are

* Reprinted from the *IRE Transactions on Engineering Management, December, 1962.*

reflected in the procedures developed here. We emphasize, therefore, that the analysis presented is *not* a general theory of R&D budgeting applicable without change to any company in any industry. The specific features of a company's experience and operations must be carefully studied in order to arrive at a procedure appropriate to that company. It cannot be emphasized too strongly that the usefulness of the results obtained depends critically on the validity of the assumptions in the particular context in which they are applied.

One final introductory observation: the concepts and measures used in this study are the outcome of a series of compromises between what would have been ideal from a theoretical point-of-view and what could be practically obtained with reasonable effort within the framework of company practice. As R&D record-keeping and accounting practices are changed, a change that may well be accelerated by such studies as this one, it will be increasingly possible to bring the ideal requirements of theory and the requirements imposed by current practices into closer agreement.

THE PROBLEM

The management of research-oriented industrial organizations is concerned with allocating some of its available funds *to* and *within* R&D activities. Three questions are involved in such budgeting decisions:

1) How much to allocate to R&D over a planning period (*e.g.*, one year)?

2) How to divide these funds between different types of R&D (*e.g.*, basic and applied)?

3) How much to allocate to which specific R&D projects?

In the course of this study we found that the companies which served as a laboratory do not keep R&D project records in such a way as to yield accurate cost data on past expenditures in basic and applied research. Consequently we looked for an alternative classification that would be both useful and feasible. The distinction between "offensive" research (that directed toward new products and processes) and "defensive" research (that directed toward improving existing products and processes) was used in these companies, but it too led to some difficulty in distinguishing between expenditures of these types. Practical considerations, therefore, lead to adapting a simple division of R&D into

1) Product Research: research directed toward creating new or improving old products.

2) Process Research: research directed toward reducing the cost of production processes.

Projects are classified according to the original intention behind them. If a particular project failed to accomplish its objective this would be reflected in the estimates of the return from projects with the same objective. In the three companies involved in this study there were only a very few instances of projects succeeding in a way other than that anticipated. For this reason it was not necessary to treat this possibility separately. That is, for proposed projects it could be assumed with little cause for concern that if a project succeeds, it will succeed in the way intended.

It is apparent that if the question—How much to allocate to Product and Process Research?—is answered, the question—How much to allocate to R&D?—is also answered, since all R&D can be classified as either Product or Process Research. We shall refer to this question as the *general* budgeting question.

The third question—How much to allocate to which specific R&D projects?—will be referred to as the *special* budgeting question. It involves the initiation, continuation, or termination of specific R&D efforts.

LOGIC OF SOLUTION TO THE GENERAL PROBLEM

The General R&D Budgeting Problem

The principal steps performed in solving the "general" problem can be briefly described as follows:

1) *Analysis:* constructing a quantitative explanation of the way investments R&D, Physical Plant, and Selling and Administration interact to affect the growth of a firm;

2) *Solution:* using this analysis to estimate the sizes of these investments which maximize the rate of return on investment in capital equipment (the ratio of net profits to gross Value of the planned level of Plant), the total amount invested being restricted to the amount available, including loans;

3) *Control and Adjustment:* setting up a procedure a) for determining when the relevant characteristics of the firm or its competitive environment have changed significantly, and b) for adjusting the budgeting procedure appropriately when such changes occur.

Prerequisites for Developing the Budgeting Procedure—The method to be described for developing an R&D budgeting procedure has two basic requirements:

1) Knowledge of the total amount of funds available for allocation to different *functions* within the company.[1]

[1] In the event that divisions do not coincide with functions, each division's require ment has to be negotiated after the available Corporate funds have been determined.

This study has *not* been concerned with determining what portion of a company's annual income should be budgeted for expenditure over all functions in the succeeding year. It is assumed that this decision has been explicitly made and the results are available to those responsible for R&D budgeting.

2) A record of past R&D effort.

The procedures developed here are not applicable to companies which are either initiating an R&D activity or are in the very early stages of such an effort. The measures which play a central role in this procedure are all essentially extrapolations from past to future performance.

The Measure of Effectiveness.—The most common measures of performance used by companies are, of course, profit and return on investment. We found in the three companies involved in this study, and in the many other companies for which we have done research in the last decade, a wide divergence of accounting methods used to obtain these measures. It was critical for our purposes to use a measure that could be applied in different companies in essentially the same way. Consequently we have employed as a measure of company performance the following ratio:

$$\frac{\text{Sales Revenue} - \text{Production Costs} - \text{Sales, Administration and General Expenses} - \text{R\&D Costs.}}{\text{Gross Value of Plant}}$$

Although the procedures developed are directed toward maximizing this ratio for the coming year, these procedures can be easily modified to accommodate any measure of performance which is composed of the same income and cost factors contained in the ratio we have employed. If, however, other income and cost factors are used, fundamental modification in our procedure would be required.

The Budgeting Model.—By a "model" we mean a mathematical representation of the activities of the firm and their relationship to its performance. The model takes the form of an expression which equates the firm's performance to some specified relationship between cumulated Product Research, Process Research, the level of Production Cost and Sales, Administrative and General Expenses. This relationship is shown schematically in Fig. 1.

Product Research, it will be recalled, is that research which is directed toward the development of new and improved products. To the extent that it succeeds it will tend to increase the proportion of sales that will be derived from the new and improved products. The amount of increase in this proportion depends on the amount spent in Product Research. Now, clearly, it

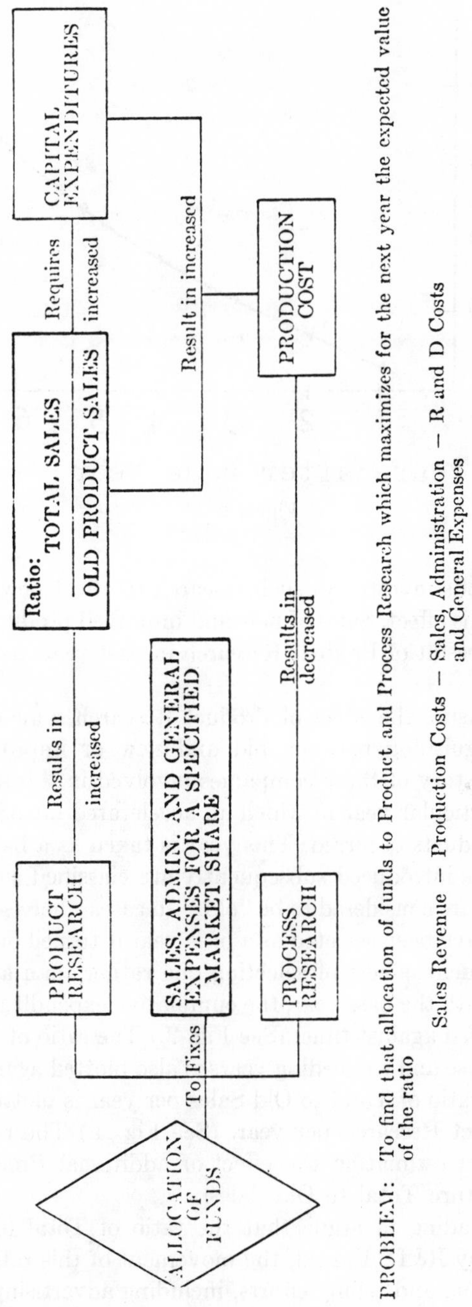

Figure 1—Schematic diagram of budgeting model.

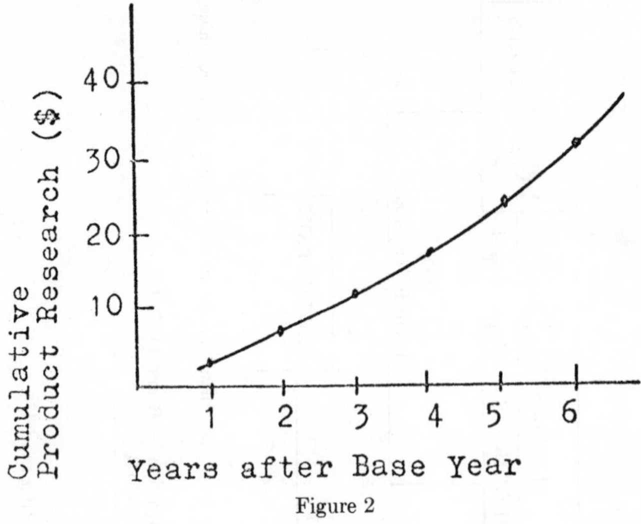

Figure 2

takes time for funds invested in such research to affect new sales; that is, there is a lag in this effect. Sales of new and improved products obtained in this year are the result of Product Research in past years as well as in the current year.

In order to measure the effect of Product Research some criterion is required for distinguishing between old and new or improved products. Analysis of the history of three companies involved in this study revealed in each case a particular year in which an accelerated introduction of new and improved products occurred. This year is taken as a base and new or improved products introduced subsequently are classified as "new," those introduced earlier are considered to be "old." In cases where several alternative years could have been selected as a base year it turned out there are no significant subsequent effects of selecting one rather than another.

Then starting with the base year, the cumulative expenditures in Product Research are plotted against time. (See Fig. 2.) The ratio of Total Sales to Old Sales in the base and succeeding years is also plotted against time. (See Fig. 3.) Now the ratio of Total to Old Sales per year is plotted against the cumulative Product Research per year. (See Fig. 4.) The resulting curve provides a basis for estimating the effect of additional Product Research on the ratio of future Total to Old Sales.

It will be misleading to argue that the ratio of Total to Old Sales is influenced solely by R&D. Indeed, the movement of this ratio is governed also by 1) marketing and selling efforts, including advertising, 2) plant ex-

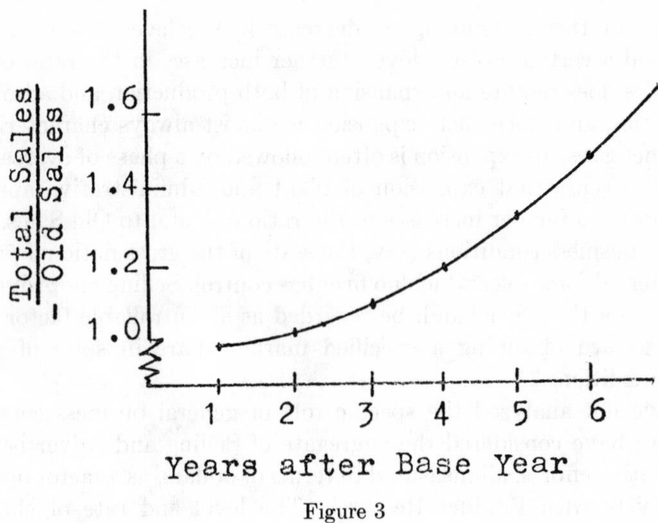

Figure 3

pansion, 3) administration and, finally, 4) the state of the national economy.[2] Although each of these factors is important in itself, the impact of each on the ratio of Total to Old Sales is different. Plant expansion, for example, is a *supporting* activity, and so is increased Administration. Increases in the ratio of Total to Old Sales is possible only up to a certain

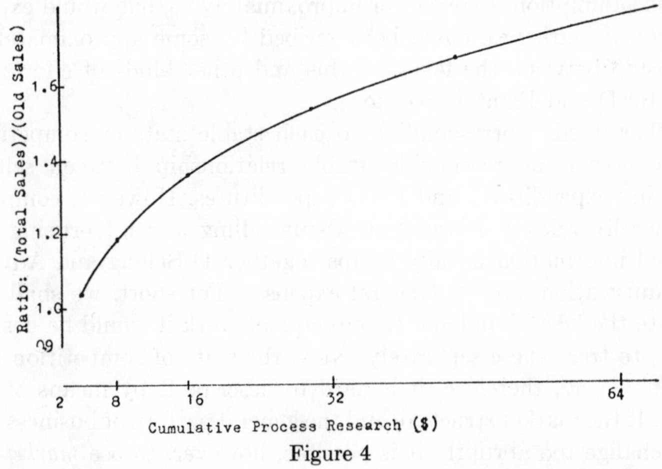

Figure 4

[2] This is often conveniently summarized by the level and, perhaps, the rate of change of gross national product or of disposable personal income.

point without these, assuming no decrease in the level of sales revenue. But beyond a certain critical level, further increases in the ratio of Total to Old Sales does require an expansion of both production and administrative facilities; and since such expansion is almost always characterized by discrete increases, an expansion is often followed by a phase of overcapacity. It is in this sense that expansion of plant and administrative apparatus lends support to further increases in the ratio of Total to Old Sales.

General business conditions (say, the state of the gross national product) are an external force over which no firm has control. Selling and Advertising effort may, on the other hand, be regarded as a controllable factor that is directed toward obtaining a specified market share in spite of general business conditions.

We have not analyzed the specific role of general business conditions. Instead we have considered the aggregate of Selling and Advertising and administrative efforts, all measured in terms of dollars, as a factor operating co-extensively with Product Research. The level and rate of change of Selling and Advertising expenditures of a company reflect the state of competition and the strategy chosen by the company. The process of interaction of strategies that ultimately determines the levels and changes of the market shares of competitors is too complex to have been analyzed in this study. Since we are primarily interested in the *outcome* of market conflict, we have assumed that *the nature of competition is not very likely to change significantly over a short period.*

If this assumption is correct or approximately so, one would expect that the effect of marketing could be described by some approximately stable relationship between the levels of this and other kinds of efforts (for example, R&D and Plant Expansion).

In other words, corresponding to each stable state of competition one would expect some reasonably stable relationship between selling and advertising expenditures and R&D expenditures. However, companies do not generally release information about selling and advertising outlays; published information usually lumps together 1) Selling and Advertising, 2) Administration, and 3) General expenses. For short, we shall call this aggregate the "SAG" dollars. In subsequent work it would be desirable, if possible, to treat these separately. Now, the state of competition is multidimensional and, therefore, it is hard to describe it by means of a single number. If the market structure and the general pattern of business strategy do not change too abruptly it is possible, however, to use *market-share* as an measure of competitive position. If the preceding argument is valid, one would expect a stable relationship between R&D and SAG expenditures for each level of market-share. This expectation was fulfilled.

TABLE I
RELATIONSHIP BETWEEN R&D AND SAG EXPENSES*
(16 chemical companies, 1947–1957)†

Average Fraction of Chemical Industry Sales	Average Value of Ratio $p = \dfrac{\text{Cumulative R\&D Expenditures}}{\text{Cumulative SAG Expenditures}}$	Value of Factor = $1 + 1/p$
0.002–0.005	0.20	6.00
0.005–0.020	0.22	5.54
0.020–0.040	0.27	4.70
Greater than 0.040	0.36	3.78

* SAG are the Annual Selling, Administrative, and General Expenses.
† "Survey of business," U. S. Department of Commerce, Washington, D.C.; 1958 (value of output of chemical companies).
"Moody's Industrial Index;" 1947–1957 (R&D and SAG expenditures).

For 16 chemical companies over the period 1947–1957 it was observed that when these companies are grouped according to their Average Share of the Market (ASM) for chemicals over this period, they are characterized by significantly different[3] average values of the ratio, R&D ($)/SAG ($). This is shown in Table I.

It appears, then, that if a company belongs to one of these market-share groups, we may expect the ratio of R&D to SAG to be approximately equal to that shown in Table I. Consequently, the combined outlay on R&D and SAG can be expressed by applying a "factor" of 1 + 1/(ratio) to the R&D dollars, where the ratio corresponds to the average market share a company currently enjoys. We emphasize again that this is a very crude (although very plausible) approximation, and we suggest that a company should independently explore the specific functional interdependence between R&D, SAG and market-share that is appropriate to its own situation.[4]

While New and Improved Products account for an increase in the ratio of Total to Old Sales they also have two other important effects:

Firstly, their introduction generally requires increased capital invest-

[3] Variation of ASM within a market-share group was found to be significantly smaller than between the groups.

[4] To be sufficiently realistic, such functional relationship should be sought between the levels *and* rates of change of these variables.

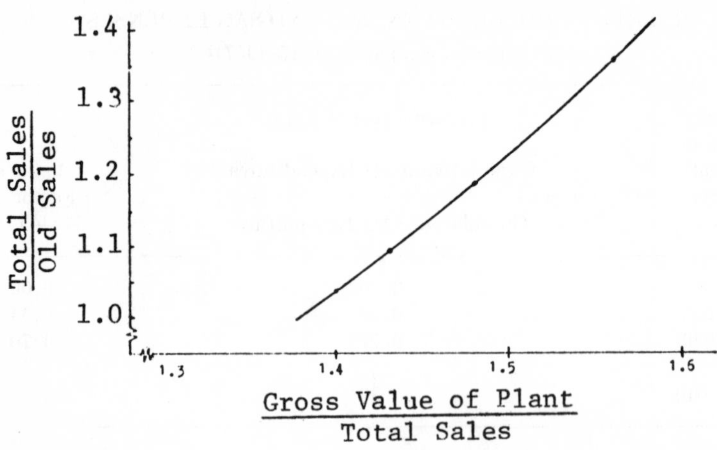

Figure 5

ment in additional plant and equipment to support the expansion and diversification of the product-line. In other words, the amount of capital investment per dollar of sales increases with increases in the ratio of Total to Old Sales, but in most instances it does so at a decreasing rate. Specifically, we found an average relationship between the Total to Old Sales ratio and the Gross Value of Plant required to support a dollar's worth of total sales: The ratio Gross Value of Plant/Total Sales increases at a diminishing rate as the ratio Total Sales/Old Sales increases. This is shown in Fig. 5.

Secondly, increase in the ratio of Total to Old Sales ratio were also found to be accompanied by increases in the ratio:

$$\frac{\text{Production Cost}}{\text{Sales Revenue}}$$

The chief reason for this appears to be that an attempt to develop and market new products and processes forces the firm initially into inefficient methods of production and plant utilization. If a company starts expanding when it is already making full use of its production facilities, it is very likely that the new facilities acquired are not utilized economically in the initial stages. It is the semiactive plant and the necessary unplanned diversification of products that appears to account for the increasing ratio of Production Cost to Sales Revenue.

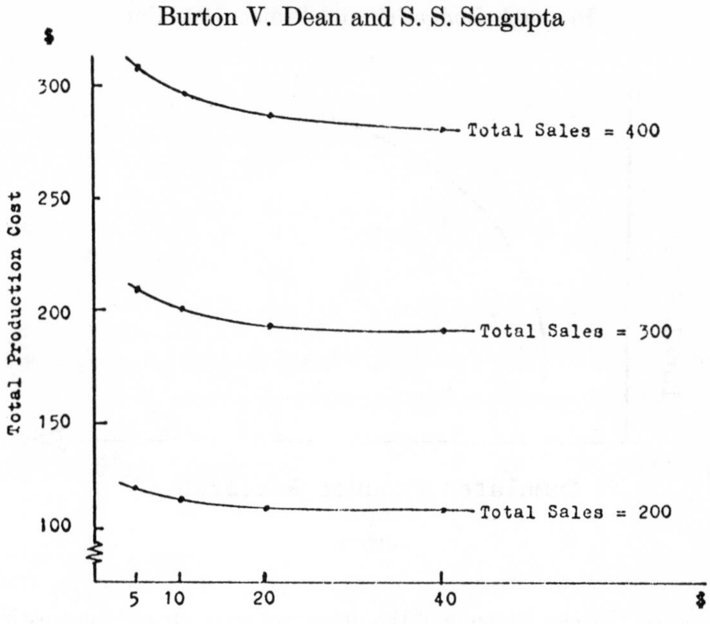

Figure 6

This phenomenon may be alternately described as follows: The increase in the level of aggregate production costs will be accociated with increase in the level of sales, such that an increase in sales will cause a more than proportionate change in the aggregate costs. But, through its Process Research, the firm makes an effort to hold down the tendency of costs to increase more than proportionately to sales. Therefore, residual variations in aggregate costs, after one takes into account the impact of rising sales, should be related to the (cumulated) level of Process Research. One would normally expect that as Process Research gets under way, the residual variations in costs would tend to diminish. This conjecture was verified in all the cases we examined. This is illustrated in Fig. 6 for different level of Total Sales.

The relationships summarized in Figs. 4–6 constitute the essential building blocks for the budgeting procedure we have developed. It is important, then, to understand all the implications of these relationships.

Fig. 4 depicts the relationship between Cumulative Product Research and the ratio of Total Sales to Old Product Sales. In any year a company can prepare an estimate of next year's sales from old products. In fact, it can prepare several such estimates in any one year and these will vary from

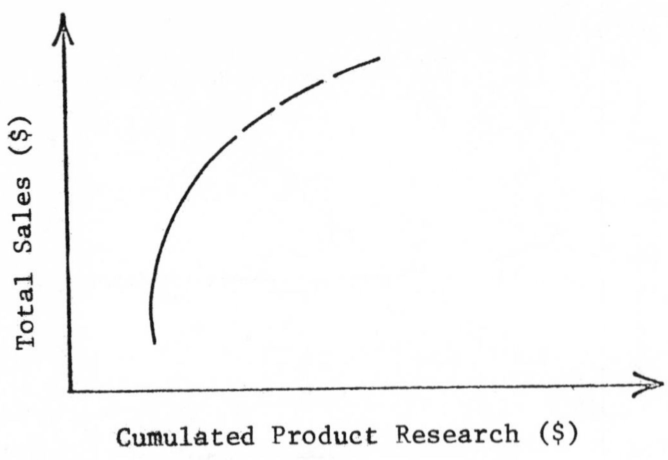

Figure 7

year to year. Use can be made of the uncertain character of these estimates. We may express the relationship shown in Fig. 4 as one between Cumulated Product Research and Total Sales, *given* a particular estimate of Old Product Sales. In other words we say that

Given an estimate of Old Product Sales, Cumulative Product Research determines Total Sales.

This transformed relationship is shown in Fig. 7.

Next, we may interpret the relationship shown in Fig. 5 as one between Total Sales and Gross Value of Plant *given* an estimate of Old Product Sales. It would be wrong to interpret this as a causal one-directional relation because, as we warned earlier, the reasons that control plant-investment decisions are far too complex to be described by one variable such as Total Sales; but

Given an estimate of Old Product Sales, Gross Value of Plant can be associated with Total Sales.

This transformed relationship is shown in Fig. 8.

One may start, then, with some trial estimate of Old Product Sales and determine the levels of Total Sales and Gross Value of Plant associated with a particular level of Cumulated Product Research. But once the level of Total Sales has been determined, Fig. 6 indicates the relationship between Production Costs and Cumulated Process Research expenditures. Fig. 6 can then be conveniently transformed into Fig. 9.

Observe that all the quantities appearing in the measure of performance (Total Sales, Production Costs, Sales-Administration-General Expenses,

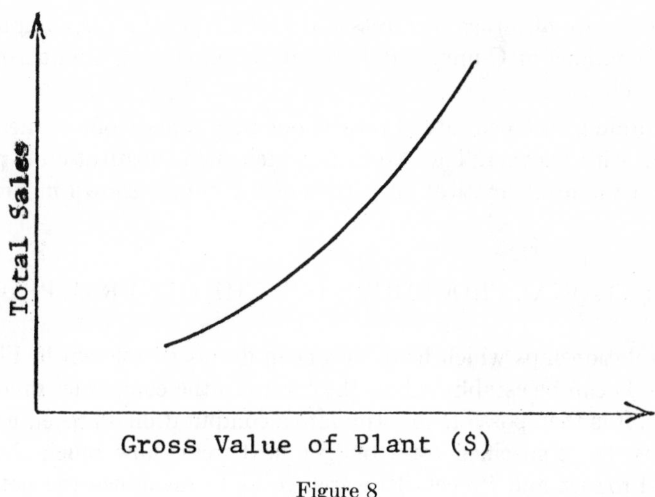

Figure 8

and Gross Value of Plant) are now measurable in terms of Cumulated Product Research and Cumulated Process Research expenditures. We have already seen that for a specified market share there is a relationship between Cumulative SAG and Cumulative total R&D expenditures; and, as we have just demonstrated, Total Sales, Production Costs, and Gross Value of Plant are all measurable in terms of the two kinds of Cumulated research expenditure, *given* the estimate of Old Product Sales. Therefore,

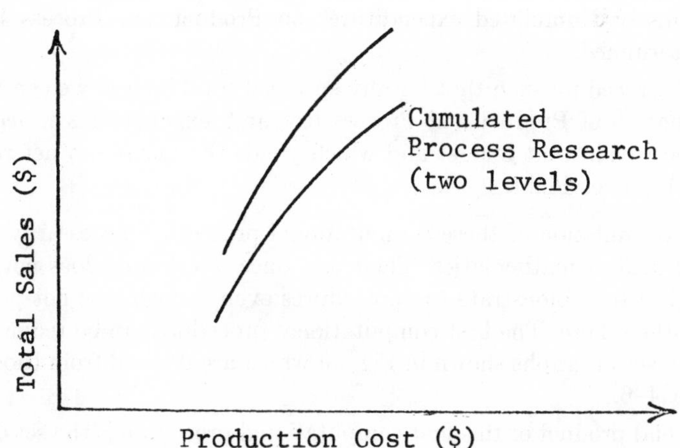

Figure 9

any specified rate of return on Gross Value of Plant, one can compute possible combinations of Cumulated Product Research and Cumulated Process Research.

To maintain a specified rate of return, one may replace one of these types of research with another. The extent to which such substitution is possible depends on the mathematical properties of the curves shown in Figs. 4–6.

COMPUTATIONAL PROCEDURE FOR THE GENERAL PROBLEM

If the relationships which have just been discussed (shown in Figs. 4–6 and Table I) can be established, as they were in the companies involved in this study, it is then possible to formulate a computational procedure which determines, for a specified total budget next year, how much should be spent on Product and Process Research so as to maximize the net return on Gross Plant Investment.

The computational procedure has three parts:

1) A procedure such that for a specified share of market next year, one can determine all combinations of Cumulated expenditures on Product and Processes Research which will yield a specified net return on Gross Plant Investment. Then for each of a variety of values of net return on Gross Value of Plant, all these Cumulated R&D expenditure-combinations can be determined.

2) A procedure such that for any specified total budget all possible combinations of Cumulated expenditures on Product and Process Research are determined.

3) A procedure such that for any specified total budget we can find that combination of Product and Process Research expenditures which will be possible within that budget and which yields the maximum net return on Gross Value of Plant.

The formulation of these computational procedures necessarily involves a good deal of mathematics. Their use, once developed, does not. It may be helpful to demonstrate the procedures even though it is not possible to derive them here. The first computational procedure can be reduced to the use of a set of graphs shown in Fig. 10 which are derived from those shown in Figs. 4–6.

The end product of this first computational procedure is the set of graphs shown in Fig. 11. Fig. 11 (c) shows the possible combinations of Cumulative expenditures of Product and Process Research which yield various

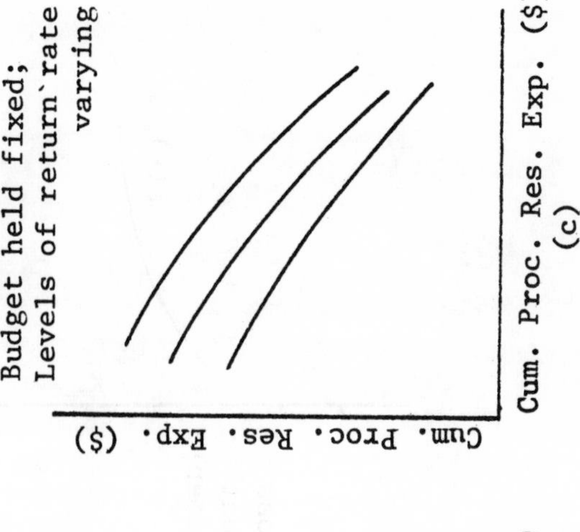
Budget held fixed;
Levels of return rate
varying
Cum. Proc. Res. Exp. ($)
Cum. Proc. Res. Exp. ($)
(c)

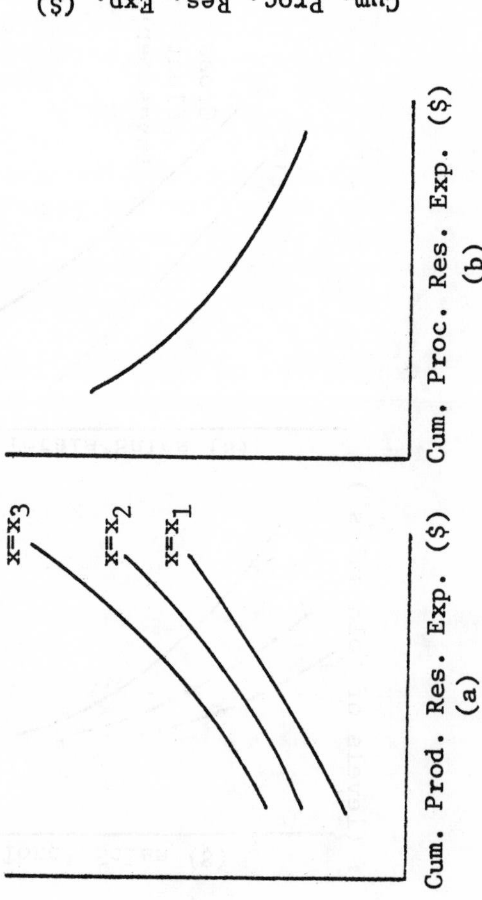
Cum. Proc. Res. Exp. ($)
(b)
x=x3
x=x2
x=x1
Cum. Prod. Res. Exp. ($)
(a)

Figure 10

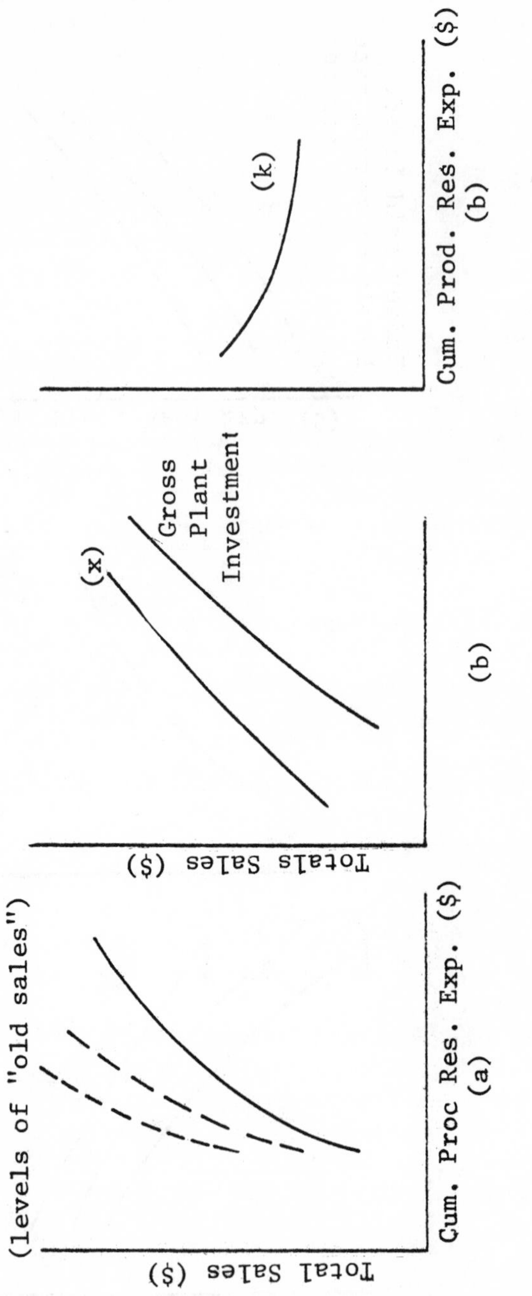
Total Sales ($)
(levels of "old sales")
Cum. Proc Res. Exp. ($)
(a)
Totals Sales ($)
(x)
Gross
Plant
Investment
(b)
(k)
Cum. Prod. Res. Exp. ($)
(b)

Figure 11

rates of net returns on Gross Value of Plant, three of which are shown. The procedure for generating this graph is as follows:

1) From Table I select a value of the factor (F) corresponding to current market share.[5]

2) Select a trial value of Cumulative Product Research Expenditures.

3) Calculate the product of 1) and 2).

4) Prepare an estimate of next year's Old Products Sales.

5) Using the estimate from 4) and the trial value from 1) determine from Fig. 10 (a) the Total Sales.

6) Using the Total Sales from 5) determine from Fig. 10 (b) the Gross Value of Plant.

7) Select a trial value of net return on Gross Value of Plant from a preselected set of trial values.

8) Multiply the results of 6) and 7).

9) Add the results of 3) and 8).

10) Subtract the result of 9) from that of 5). Call the result A.

Repetition of these ten steps for various trial values of Product Research expenditures yields Fig. 11 (a).

11) Select a trial value of Cumulative Process Research Expenditures.

12) Multiply the value selected from Table I in step 2) by the trial value selected in 11).

13) Using the value of Cumulative Process Research Expenditures selected in 11) determine from Fig. 10 (d) the value of the intermediate variable k.

14) Using the value of Total Sales from 5) determine from Fig. 10 (b) the value of the intermediate variable x.

15) Multiply the value of k obtained in 13) by the value of x obtained in 14): xk.

16) Add xk 15) to the result of 12). Call this result B.

Repetition of the last six steps for various values of Cumulative Process Research Expenditures, grouping the results by values of x obtained in 14), yields Fig. 11 (b).

17) For each trial value of Cumulative Product Research Expenditures used in 1) list the corresponding value of x used in 14).

18) Using the value of Cumulative Product Research Expenditures from 17) determine from Fig. 11 (a) the corresponding value of A.

---

[5] If a company desires a higher share of the market than it now has, it is necessary to carry out the computations for the "ratio" appropriate to whatever market-share is planned for. We should like to emphasize, however, that such an extrapolation is very likely to be of little value unless supported by more detailed analysis of the total situation.

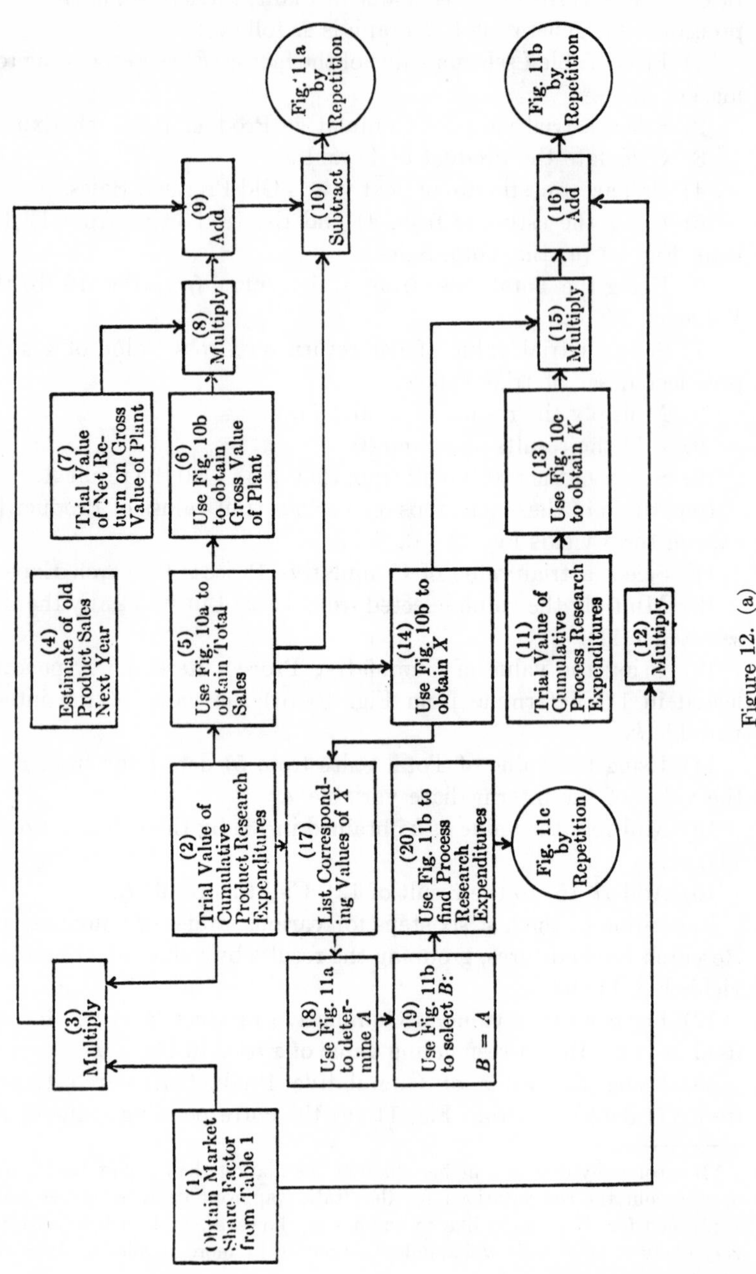
(1) Obtain Market Share Factor from Table 1
(2) Trial Value of Cumulative Product Research Expenditures
(3) Multiply
(4) Estimate of old Product Sales Next Year
(5) Use Fig. 10a to obtain Total Sales
(6) Use Fig. 10b to obtain Gross Value of Plant
(7) Trial Value of Net Return on Gross Value of Plant
(8) Multiply
(9) Add
(10) Subtract
Fig. 11a by Repetition
(11) Trial Value of Cumulative Process Research Expenditures
(12) Multiply
(13) Use Fig. 10c to obtain K
(14) Use Fig. 10b to obtain X
(15) Multiply
(16) Add
Fig. 11b by Repetition
(17) List Corresponding Values of X
(18) Use Fig. 11a to determine A
(19) Use Fig. 11b to select B:
B = A
(20) Use Fig. 11b to find Process Research Expenditures
Fig. 11c by Repetition

Figure 12. (a)

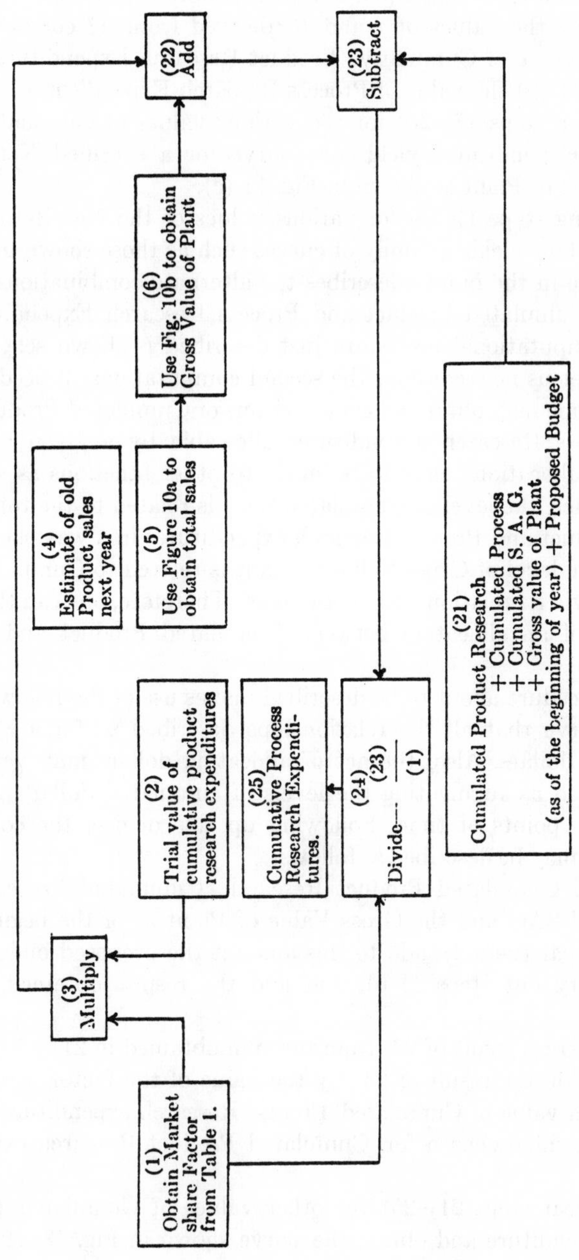
(1) Obtain Market share Factor from Table 1.
(2) Trial value of cumulative product research expenditures
(3) Multiply
(4) Estimate of old Product sales next year
(5) Use Figure 10a to obtain total sales
(6) Use Fig. 10b to obtain Gross Value of Plant
(21) Cumulated Product Research
+ Cumulated Process
+ Cumulated S. A. G.
+ Gross value of Plant
(as of the beginning of year) + Proposed Budget
(22) Add
(23) Subtract
(24) Divide— (23)/(1)
(25) Cumulative Process Research Expenditures.

Figure 12. (b)

19) Select a value of B equal to that of A obtained in 18).

20) Using the values of x and B (derived from A) corresponding to a particular value of Cumulative Product Research Expenditures determine from Fig. 11 (b) the value of Process Research Expenditures.

Repeating steps 17)–20) for the various values of Cumulative Product Research Expenditures yields one curve for a specified Net Return on Gross Value of Plant as shown in Fig. 11 (c).

Repeating steps 1)–20) for various values of the Net Return on Gross Value of Plant yields a family of curves such as those shown in Fig. 11 (c). Each curve in the family describes the alternate combinations of required levels of Cumulated Product and Process Research Expenditures.

The computational procedure just described is shown schematically in Fig. 12. Let us now consider the second computational procedure, the one by which one may obtain all combinations of Cumulated Product Research and Process Research expenditures allowable by a given budget. It is true that allocations have to be made to other functions as well. But, as noted earlier, the level of Cumulated SAG is related to the total of Cumulated Product and Process Research expenditures in a way shown in Table I. Also, the level of Gross Value of Plant is related to Cumulated Product Research via its relation with Total Sales. Therefore, one can think entirely in terms of an allocation between Cumulated Product and Process expenditures.

The procedure about to be described makes use of the following outlook. First observe that all the relationships described so far are in terms of *cumulated* dollars. Also, the act of allocating dollars may very naturally be described as augmenting the levels of cumulated dollar quantities between two points of time. Following up this device, the computational procedure may be described as follows:

21) Add Cumulated Product Research, Cumulated Process Research, Cumulated SAG and the Gross Value of Plant as of the beginning of the planning year (period); add to this amount the proposed budget.

22) Carry out steps 1)–6), and add the results obtained at steps 3) and 6).

23) Subtract result of 22) from the sum obtained in 21).

24) Divide the result of 23) by the value of the factor used in step 1); this gives a value of Cumulated Process Research expenditure corresponding to the value chosen for Cumulated Product Research expenditure in step 2).

25) Repeat steps 21)–25) for other values of Cumulated Product Research expenditure and obtain the curve shown in Fig. 13. If several proposed budgets are available, generate one such curve corresponding to

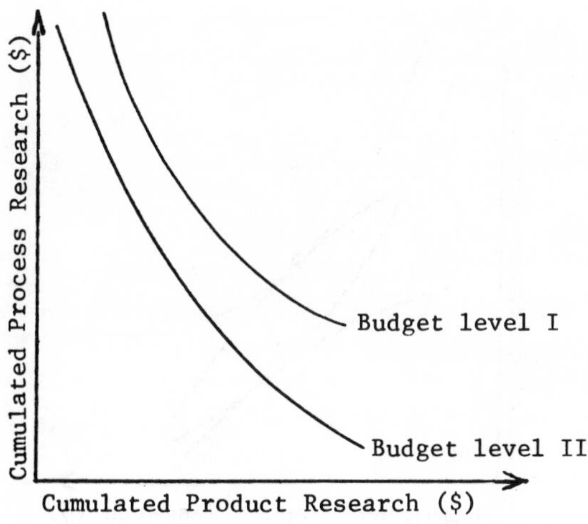

Figure 13.

each budget. (The two curves shown in Fig. 13 correspond to two different levels of proposed budget.)

The computational Procedure, steps 21)–25), is shown schematically in Fig. 12 (b).

The final step is now one of determining the allocations that would maximize the rate of return on Gross Value of Plant. This is schematically indicated in Fig. 14, where the budget possibility curve (of Fig. 13) has been superposed on the iso-return curve (of Fig. 11 (c)). The point where the former touches one of the family of iso-return contours is the point of interest: this combination of Cumulated Product Research and Cumulated Process Research expenditures is feasible (on account of budget restrictions) and, at the same time, holds out the possibility of the highest rate of return on the Gross Value of Plant. In other words, these are the levels to which the Cumulated Product and Process expenditures have to be adjusted. The detailed procedure may be conveniently expressed by the following sequence of steps:

26) Subtract the initial amount of Cumulated Product Research expenditures from the value read off from Fig. 14; the difference is the desired allocation to Product Research for the planning period.

27) Substract the initial amount of Cumulated Process Research expenditures from the value read off from Fig. 14; the difference is the allocation to Process Research for the planning period.

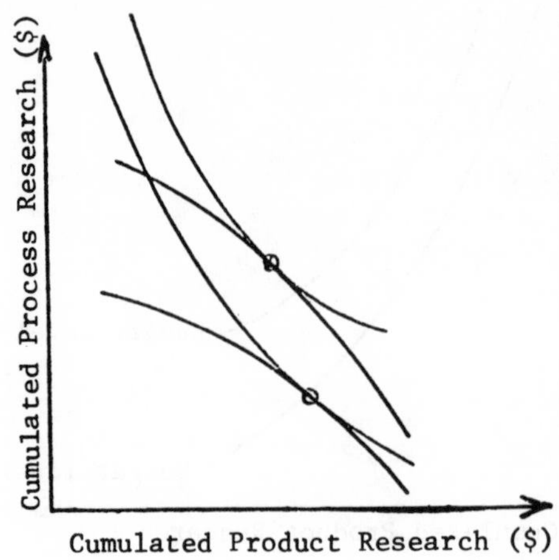

Figure 14.

28) Add the two amounts read off from Fig. 14.

29) Multiply the result of 28) by the factor used in step 1).

30) Add the initial amount of Cumulated SAG expenditure to result of 28) and subtract 29) from the sum; the result gives the allocation to SAG expenditure for the planning period.

31) Determine allocation to Gross Value of Plant as a residual; that is, subtract 29) from the sum obtained in 21) and subtract the initial Gross Value of Plant from the difference so obtained.

THE SPECIAL PROBLEM: ALLOCATION TO PROJECTS

For the solution to this problem, it is assumed that the allocation of the R&D budget to Product and Process Research has been made. We also assume the availability of the following kinds of information:

1) A list of continuing and proposed R&D projects.

2) Information on the expenditures to date of the current projects.

3) Information, concerning a number of completed and abandoned projects, on annual costs and subsequent returns.

A method has been developed which uses this information for selecting projects for continuation, termination, or initiation, *if* we can assume that no significant changes in the business environment and competitive behavior will take place in the foreseeable future. Thus, pricing and selling policies of the firms assumed to be given.

Project Payoff

A research project can be classified according to the objective it is intended to obtain. The expected outcome of R&D projects may be a) additional new sales in subsequent periods, b) additional sales of existing products through quality-improvement or c) savings in production costs, or d) some combination of these. In any event, one or more of these benefits will accrue only if the project yields a usable result and if the result is exploited (commercialized) by the company,

It is possible to estimate the relative performance (*i.e.*, "worth") of any two projects by comparing their respective "payoff indices:"

$$\frac{\text{present value of expected future returns from the project}}{\text{present value of expected future efforts required for the project}}$$

Determination of the value of this payoff index of a project requires the following estimates:

1) probability of success of the project;
2) probability that it will be commercialized if successful;
3) the incremental return from the project if successful and commercialized;
4) the time pattern of this return;
5) the total future cost of the project;
6) the time pattern of these expenditures.

Each of these is considered below.

In addition, an appropriate discount rate must be selected. The discount rate chosen for arriving at the estimates of *present* value of future income and expenditures is left for the company to decide; in most instances, this can be taken as the average (actual or desired) rate of return on aggregate company funds. It is interesting to observe that if the R&D environment is assumed to be unstable this situation can be roughly taken care of by setting the level of the discount factor appropriately. For example, if one expects a change for the worse, a high discount factor can be selected to insure against overestimation of returns.

Probability of Success and Commercialization

The probability that a project will lead to a commercialized result is the product of a) the probability that the project is technically successful, and b) the probability that a successful project is commercially exploited.

It is absolutely essential to understand that we cannot talk meaningfully about the probability of any unique project succeeding or being exploited.

The concept of probability applies only to members of a class of like things, and the same probabilities must apply to all members of the class. Hence, project classification is critical.

R&D projects must be classified into the same basic classes as are used in the general budgeting problem (*e.g.*, Product and Process Research). These classes should be further subdivided until groups of projects are formed which satisfy two conditions:

1) Any further subdivision of these groups fails to yield subgroups in which the past proportions of successful projects differ significantly. That is, there should be no objective basis for distinguishing between members of the same project group with respect to probability of success.

2) The past proportion of successful projects in each group should be significantly different; groups which are not significantly different should be combined.

Grouping of projects, then, should take into account such factors as their age, expenditures to date, the technology involved, the type of product or process involved, and the availability of required skill, knowledge, and equipment. Once satisfactory groups are formed, the proportion of past projects in a group which were successful provides an estimate of probability of success of projects in that group. The proportion of past successful projects in a group which were commercialized provides an estimate of probability of commercialization of successful profects in that group. This probability of commercialization may be influenced by such things as subsequent capital availability and requirements, competitive R&D efforts, other investment opportunities, and changing external factors over which the company has no control. Anticipation of any of these or simular conditions may require adjustment of estimates of probability of commercialization which are based exclusively on past history.

Conceivably, for the continuing and proposed projects, personnel in R&D and Marketing will have their own estimates of the probabilities of success and commercialization. If a record of past estimates of this type are available their accuracy can be compared with estimates prepared in the way described above. The better of the two estimating procedures can then be used.

Estimating Costs and Returns

The procedure outlined here requires that R&D, and Production and Sales personnel can generate reasonably good estimates of annual research costs and benefits. In many instances, however, this task will have to be taken up almost from scratch. Nevertheless, while effort should be directed

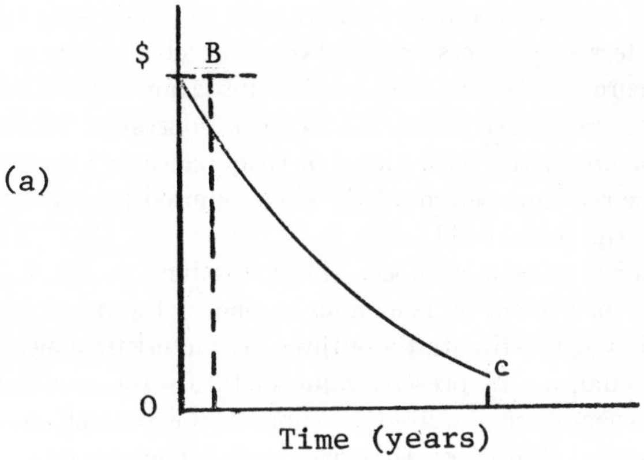

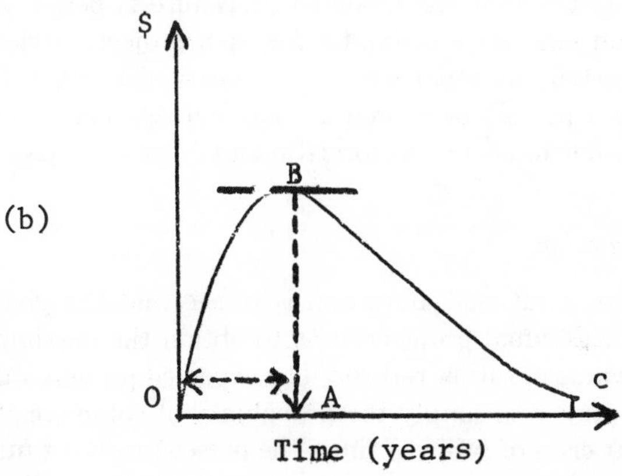

Figure 15—Patterns of annual outlays. (a) *OB*: Maximum annual outlay (occurring in first year). Area under curve: total outlay. (b) *AB*: Maximum annual outlay. *OA*: Time to reach this. Area under curve: total outlay.

to setting up such an organization of information flow, it is still possible—with minor modifications—to make use of the procedure we have described above. The nature of these modifications is described below.

Our experience indicates that in growing companies the overwhelmingly large proportion of project-expenditures and product-sales obey one or the other of the two broad time-patterns shown in Fig. 15.

The pattern of Fig. 15 (a) refers to projects (products) for which the largest annual expenditure (sale) occurred *in* the first year; the pattern of Fig. 15 (b) refers to projects (products) for which the largest expenditure (sale) was recorded *after* the first year of initiation (introduction). These patterns are characterized by certain intrinsic constants. More specifically, these constant are 1) the initial level of costs (sales), or the total cost (returns) over the relevant period, 2) the time required to reach the peak, and 3) the level of the peak itseld.

If the technical personnel of the R&D, Production and Sales divisions can identify each profect as belonging to one or the other historical pattern, and if they can estimate these three characteristic constants, then, it is possible to compute a) present value of future returns, and b) annual amounts of expenditure required to support the project till completion. It will be observed, therefore, that we are replacing realistic year-by-year estimates of annual costs and returns by idealized quantities based on certain broad group-characteristics derived from past data.

It is not suggested that the modified procedure is better than the one based directly on individual estimates for each project; obviously, we are leaning rather heavily on reliability of classification. Further, they may be occasions where a project or a product may entirely defy a classification, so that we may not have any historical parallel from the past.

Optimization Criterion

The purpose of a rational allocation is to see that the given budget is divided among individual projects so as to obtain the maximum total expected present value of future returns. The expected present value of future returns from a project is simply the probability of commercialization (appropriate to that class of project) times the present value of future benefits expected of the project. Summing these products over all projects, we obtain the quantity to be maximized.

Therefore, if in any one year, there is available a set of estimates of expenditures required in future years for the current and proposed projects, and if the R&D manager has available to him an expected total amount he can spend, the decision problem can be stated as follows: *Choose projects and, consequently, be prepared to grant the corresponding request for funds so that the total expected present value of future benefits from the projects so selected is as large as possible.*

It should be noted that the amount to be spent on a particular project in the next period is here assumed to be given. Obviously, in actual practice the R&D manger must also decide how much ought to be spent on each project. This decision in turn affects the probability of success. Ultimately, this decision, how much to allocate to a project, should be incorporated into the special budgeting procedure. The procedure suggested here, however, assumes that this decision has been made and hence does not include it in the optimization procedure.

A Simple Method of Solution

The solution to this problem may be obtained by the method of Linear Programming. Because of the special character of the desired solution (saying "yes" or "no" to each project), a nearly optimal solution can be obtained by a simple ranking procedure:

1) Tabulate projects in descending order of magnitude of the expected present value of future benefits.

2) Select projects (to be continued or initiated) from the top of the list down to the point where the budget is allocated.

3) Terminate or do not initiate the remaining projects.

CONCLUSION: ASSUMPTIONS AND LIMITATIONS

Since the study reported here is among the first efforts at a comprehensive solution to a very complex problem it can hardly be considered to have put the problem to rest. To the contrary, this study was intended to stimulate intensive research in this important problem area, research which will undoubtedly improve the results obtained here.

Despite the temptation to claim more for a study than one has a right to it is important to reemphasize the three basic assumptions on which the results obtained here are predicted:

1) It is assumed that general business and competitive conditions will remain relatively stable over the foreseeable future.

2) It is assumed that there is very little chance that a project intended to produce one kind of result will produce a very useful outcome of an entirely different kind.

3) It is assumed that the share of market that the company realistically expects (in contrast to what is hoped for) in the next period is essentially the same as it had in the past.

In brief the procedures developed here can be applied where these assumptions hold and where

1) Graphs such as those shown in Figs. 4–6 can be drawn and mathematical expressions for the resulting curves can be obtained.

2) Projects can be classified into groups which have different probabilities of success.

3) The necessary estimates of costs and return can be obtained with an acceptable degree of accuracy.

It should also be reemphasized that the procedures presented have been applied successfully and hence are not merely "theoretical." On the other hand, the number of applications has as yet been relatively small. Whatever generality can be claimed for the results must be based on theoretical rather than practical considerations.

A company which attempts to use the procedure outlined here can be assured of at least this much: It can improve its R&D budgeting because it will develop the kinds of data and ask the kind of questions that are necessary for systematic improvement of such budgeting.

WHEN TO TERMINATE A RESEARCH AND DEVELOPMENT PROJECT*

C. K. Buell
President, Applied Automation, Inc.
Bartlesville, Oklahoma

A survey made by the Board of Editors of *Research Management* disclosed that a substantial number of subscribers would like to see papers written on the difficult problem of deciding when to terminate a research and development project that seems to be getting nowhere. Guidelines are conspicuous by their absence. Subsequently, the writer was asked to present his views from the standpoint of an industrial corporation's research and development department.

I suspect that the reason so little information has been published on this subject is because it is most difficult to set down specific and reasonably incontestable guidelines of widespread applicability. Indeed, one might well ask how any guidelines whatsoever can be advanced when the projects in question may be so diverse, complex or of such a pioneering nature that decisions as to their fate are based upon subjective areas such as intuitive judgment, educated guesses, hunches, or even hopeful aspirations. Furthermore, at some stage almost every project involving relatively large R&D expenditures comes under not only the scrutiny and evaluation of R&D but also top management and key personnel of other corporate departments, all of whom have widely divergent technical and business backgrounds, viewpoints, and objectives. When one considers all the multitudinous risk factors that must be weighed in advancing a new process or product from test tube to commercialization, it is impossible to even approach unanimity within the company on a given project's fate.

Doubtless all of us would like to base our decisions at any point in time as a project proceeds down the research and development path, on precise scientific, technological, and marketing knowledge, all translated into realistically projected, business venture economics. Ideally, we would like to wrap up everything in a neat set of quantitative mathematical expressions, the net result being some kind of a numerical rating that would

---

* *Research Management*, Vol. X, No. 4 (1967).

indicate we should temporarily shelve, terminate, or accelerate a project. However, at our present level of sophistication, and even employing the lightning-fast computers now at our disposal, I am convinced that we are still a long way from this Utopia. I believe that most R&D administrators in decision-making positions, if they honestly look back, will concede that they were sometimes dead wrong when they based decisions to terminate a project on a numberical rating that did not have superimposed upon it the varied and mature judgment of top management and other knowledgeable segments of the company's organization. On the other hand, corporate management can make drastic mistakes if it "over-exercises" its prerogatives (particularly at early stages of R&D work) in deciding to terminate a project. None of the foregoing comments are intended in any way to imply that the writer is not a strong advocate of judiciously using every numerical project evaluation tool, including "subjective" probability analysis, which will assist R&D and other corporate personnel in making better decisions.

Certainly, without corporate management's wholehearted support of R&D programs, along with its business skills, judgment, foresight, and courage to aaume the risks inherent in commercializing many projects, no R&D department can be truly effective. However, R&D should be in a somewhat favored position to exercise the best judgment as to ultimate probability of success of most projects. The more echelons of higher management committees that must successively pass judgment on the importance and merits of R&D findings and recommendations, the greater the chance a good project might be "killed." This results from the fact that other pressing demands for the time of the men on such committees oftentimes precludes their looking into and assaying all the pertinent technical and business ramifications of the project. Further, if committees made up of other corporate departments (such as manufacturing and marketing) rather than top management exercise *dominant* control over R&D's broad planning and programming, other deleterious effects can result. The responsibilities of other corporate departments are of an entirely different type than those of R&D. They are primarily responsible for the profitable operation of the physical facilities already in existence, whereas R&D is primarily responsible for developing new technology that will help ensure the long-term profitable growth of the company. If R&D is controlled too tightly by other corporate departments, it can easily degenerate into a technical service organization of a troubleshooting nature working on day-to-day problems. Now that I have tried to explain why it is most difficult, perhaps inadvisable, and certainly presumptuous on my part to write on this subject, nevertheless, I hope the reader will forgive my temerity if I try. Certainly this subject deserves increasing attention, particularly in view of rapidly rising R&D costs and the ensuing cost-productivity squeeze. Also, I believe that terminating a research and development project is one of the most agonizing decisions that confronts R&D administrators because those working on a problem are invariably sure that success is just around the corner. However, like drilling oil wells, it is not practical to keep on drilling forever. If one does not strike oil, a decision must be made to stop drilling.

Before delving deeper into this subject, I would like to reiterate that this paper will only address itself to the question of terminating a project from an industrial (not government or university) point of view. The sole purpose for the existence of an industrial research and development organization is to increase the company's growth and earnings, even if it engages in basic research without regard to how such knowledge might specifically be used. I would also like to qualify my remarks by adding that when I use the word "terminate," it does not necessarily imply that a project should be buried forever. Situations can and do arise where it may be advisable to reinstate work on a project that has been "terminated" within a few years or even within a few months. For example, new science or technology may be developed in some unrelated areas of research and development that is applicable to the project in question and thereby the feasibility and economics are suddenly improved. Perhaps changes in a company's raw material position or marketing capabilities will have a favorable bearing on the project. Or, perhaps, the top management's goals may shift toward greater diversification and thereby have a salutary effect on a project's status. Obviously, R&D administrators should constantly keep such considerations in mind when working on project planning and programming.

Against the above background, and after careful consideration, I have decided that it would be extremely inadvisable and dogmatic on my part to set forth specific and rigorous guidelines. In my opinion, the subject matter we are dealing with is too subjective to make "hard and fast" guidelines; at some later date we can hopefully take much of the present "art" of such decision-making into the realm of science. Rather, I shall attempt to raise a number of "warning flags" having to do with the question of when to terminate a project. If one or more of the questions raised by the "warning flags" indicate that there *may be* valid reasons for terminating a project, then every project evaluation tool and technique, and every corporate channel of communication at our disposal, should be fully and rapidly used to reach a final decision. A list of such "warning flags" (along with an explanatory note, if needed, that elaborates on the underlying reasons or circumstances for raising the questions) follows:

(*1*) *Is there any doubt that the project is related to the present general ob-*

jectives or goals of the company, or is responsive to the immediate or long-term needs of the company? Most companies have certain primary appraisal tests set by corporate management that are applied to any project to make certain that it conforms to broad company policies, spheres of activities, and economic goals. These tests, including profitability indices, may vary considerably depending on the size of the company, amount of capital currently available for expansion, its raw material position, extent to which it wishes to diversify, its particular background of skills and know-how, its patent position, and other competitive factors and considerations. As a company's resources and technical background grow, or perhaps as its management shifts its viewpoints, the company's broad policies, objectives, and lines of activities change, thus oftentimes necessitating a different set of appraisal tests. Although, for most effective results, R&D should have considerable latitude in programming its own activities, projects should continuously be scrutinized as they progress from research to commercial scale to make certain that they continue to meet the company's basic tests. (Even pure research projects may have to pass these tests depending upon management's degree of permissiveness or insistence that even basic research work be conducted in fields very closely connected with the company's present spheres of activities.)

If in doubt on this question, R&D should periodically review with corporate management the status and objectives of work on majos projects. Such reviews, for maximum effectiveness, should also cover (with the assistance of other departments) the market outlook patent position, raw material supplies, projected economics, and other related subject matter.

(2) Does the project have a practical goal? An industrial research and development department's goals are to develop new processes, products, markets or services, or improve existing ones, to ensure the company's continued progress. Industrial research and development is effective only when it succeeds in maintaining or increasing profits and assets. No matter how successful an accomplishment might be from a scientific point of view, it is worthless to the corporation unless we can find ways and means of exploiting it in the market place.

(3) Is there any doubt that management, as a major project proceeds from test tube toward commercialization, is enthusiastic enough to support the increasing research and development effort with the necessary funds, men, physical facilities, and working environment—whatever it takes to get the job done when it should be done? This question is particulary important if the project happens to involve work in a major new field of business that the company heretofore has not engaged. In this situation it is imperative that R&D frequently point out to top management both the attractive profit

potential and the technical and economic hazards that exist and solicit their help and advice in evaluating and passing judgment on the opportunities for commercialization.

(*4*) *Is there any doubt that the over-all scope of a major project is compatible with the company's ability to finance and commercialize the project when the technology is presumed to be ready?*

(*5*) *Considering the research and development department's budget and the company's over-all needs and objectives, do any projects within the R&D department raise questions as to whether or not R&D has a "balanced program" in all areas of the company's interest?* Any good research and development organization has more ideas than it can possibly handle. Some of these ideas may relate to current operational problems in some phase of the company's engineering, manufacturing or marketing business. Other ideas may anticipate radically new departures in the more distant future. Each of these ideas or prospective programs (particularly those of a break-through nature waiting in the "wings") should be carefully analyzed in light of probability of timely and successful solution and that the profitability will well exceed the cost. Since R&D funds of any company are not unlimited, we cannot afford to work on all new ideas or discoveries. To allocate our man-power and budget funds most wisely, we must be selective in choosing the "horses" we will ride, whether in basic, applied, or service areas.

(*6*) *If the project involves a new or improved product, process, of service of immediate or near term interest to the marketing, manufacturing, or other corporate departments, does it have the support of those departments?* The best research and development efforts may be doomed to failure unless we gain the confidence and support of other corporate departments. Although top management can certainly help, by and large the research and development organization itself must sell its new ideas and projects. This involves staying in close and constant communication with key personnel in other interested departments and taking maximum benefit of their comments, suggestions, and constructive criticism. Such contacts are invaluable in helping program and expedite R&D's work.

(*7*) *Because of manpower, dollar, or other constraints, does it appear that research and development effort is being spread so thin on too many projects such that it appears likely that none of them will get "over the hump" in a reasonable time?* If this situation pertains, decisions obviously should be made to concentrate on and expedite the potentially most important projects. The reason is obvious—accomplishments are the best measure of success of any research and development endeavors.

(*8*) *Because of budgetary or other reasons, are research and development efforts spread too thin on a single project?* If too few men are assigned to a given project, they can do little more than keep up with the literature, much less forge ahead of the competition.

(*9*) *Does it appear that research and development efforts on a project are producing technology too far ahead of the time when company might reasonably expect to commercialize upon such technology?* Research and development must keep abreast of new scientific discoveries, new industrial developments, economic trends, and other factors with a view toward anticipating effect of such things on the company's operations, how their company may profit thereby, and instituting new research and development projects well ahead of the time when the information will be actually needed. However, if R&D efforts too far out race a company's ability to finance and commercialize a given project, then the manpower on that project might temporarily be better utilized elsewhere.

(*10*) *Does the research and development administrator have a feeling that the group working on a project is "playing minor variations on the same tune," or that the men working on the project have run out of new ideas and are "grasping at straws?"* There is a tendency for a group working on a project to get stale. If work were stopped for a year or so and then reinstated, new ideas or technology might be generated major improvements achieved. This technique helps overcome the tendency to always justify "just one more experiment." Many of these experiments are in reality of minor economic importance and the manpower could be much better utilized on "breakthrough" research.

Altrenatively, the project might be temporarily shelved until a new team having different disciplinary backgrounds and fresh ideas can be organized and assigned to the project.

(*11*) *Does it appear that work on a project has little chance of the company's developing a substantial patent or know-how position, but that industry as a whole may need the kind of technology expected to come out of the project to improve its operation?* Perhaps this kind of research and development should be "farmed out" to an industry-supported cooperative or "non-profit" research organization.

(*12*) *Does the project involve service work that can be handled just as well by other segments of the company's organization or farmed out?* If so, R&D should consider terminating its work and concentrating on its basic mission of producing new science and technology. As a corollary, R&D professional groups will function most effectively when they are relieved of service functions so they can be free to concentrate on their primary responsibilities. Before passing judgment on this question too hastily, however, I would like to point out that some service work is desirable to keep in contact with operating departments and thus avoid becoming an "ivory tower" type of R&D organization.

(*13*) *Is the project staffed with the right kind of people?* If there is serious question that the men on the project do not have the proper multi-disciplinary technical knowledge and experience, a genuine enthusiasm for their work, will accept responsibility for their actions, and have the courage of their convictions, perhaps the project should at least be temporarily shelved until the project organization can be strengthened.

(*14*) *After research and development has expended every effort to sell its new ideas and projects, does it still encounter a great many negative reactions to doing research in particular fields from top management, marketing, manufacturing or other corporate departments?* Normally, a selling function is not associated in most people's minds with a research and development organization. This is far from the true situation. Doubtless, most all R&D organizations can look back at some wonderful business opportunities that were missed simply because someone up or down the line in the R&D organization did not do an effective job of selling. Technical ability counts greatly in our business, but this ability will be largely wasted and the company's future progress impeded if R&D cannot sell its achievements and overcome obstacles that may force project terminations because of lack of support on the part of top management or other corporate departments.

(*15*) *What is the longevity of the current projects?* Ideally there should be a distribution of project ages with some very new, the majority of intermediate age, and only a few very old projects. If an R&D organization finds itself in the position where the distribution is skewed and a large portion of the projects are very old, it is probably slipping on creativity or its management is not sufficiently risk-minded.

(*16*) *What is the relationship between efforts on product research and process research?* This factor will vary from industry to industry. In some industries it is fatal to concentrate too much effort on improvement of products made by existing processes and ignore the possibility of improvements in the process itself.

(*17*) *Is it necessary to continue research in a process field of great importance to the company but one which has been "thoroughly plowed?"* In general, most major technological investment fields should be backed up by continuing research and development effort to effect technological improvements and improve economics. However, long-established processes probably justify little work.

(*18*) *Has the company lost the services of a key man or men who are the "spark plugs" on a project?* If this situation arises, the project might best be temporarily shelved until remedial measures can be taken.

(*19*) *Are the men responsible for (working on) the project enthusiastic about their chances of success?*

(*20*) *Considering the time value of money, have the possibilities been explored of purchasing the desired technology from others rather than developing it ourselves?*

(*21*) *As a project advances from bench scale through pilot-planting, do continuously projected economic analyses show every reasonable expectation that the project will meet whatever minimum profitability index guidelines top management has set?* R&D management must recognize good ideas and research discoveries at the earliest possible time and put the wheels into motion to aggressively pursue potentially profitable projects. On the other hand, R&D's basic drive and desire to create, develop, and commercialize new science and technology must be tempered with good economic judgment. Consequently, the research and development administrator should continuously scrutinize the economics from research to projected commercial plans to make certain that the project will contribute substantially to the company's future growth and earnings and therefore be expected to have the support of top management when it reaches a commercialization appropriation request stage.

In conclusion, I hope that I haven't posed so many questions bearing on reasons why we, as R&D administrators, should consider terminating current projects that will lose our courage to initiate new ones. Doubtless, we will continue to make mistakes, but we will also continue to produce profitable achievements.

MACRO R&D*

Marvin J. Cetron
Naval Material Command
Harold F. Davidson
Army Research Office

Quantitative techniques are of proven value in the solution of a variety of problems within the spectrum of managerial interests. Their most obvious application is to production problems, where operations research initially gained recognition from the business community. Since, then, managers in other areas, including finance, marketing, and research and development, have begun applying quantitative methods. Such applications have become very much the fashion. Nonetheless, controversy has developed over the applicability of some of these techniques to the management of technical efforts. A recent article by Professor Edward B. Roberts, "Facts and Folklore in Research and Development Management" (IMR, Spring 1967), contained a rather harsh appraisal of quantitative decisionmaking tools being advocated in some circles. Subsequent comments appearing in this journal justified attempts to deal more rationally with R&D resource allocation decisions.

The reader may very well be familiar with the arguments for and against the use of quantitative tools for making resource allocation decisions without being familiar with any of the tools themselves. In this paper, Marvin Cetron and Harold Davidson, active practitioners in the area, outline elements of a quantitative resource allocation technique for exploratory development funds. The reader can evaluate the relevance of methods such as MACRO to decision requirements of his organization.

INTRODUCTION

A series of developments during the past two decades have greatly changed the character of Research and Development management. The

* The authors are indebted to Mr. Patrick Caulfield, Dr. Harold Liebowitz, Dr. Joseph Martino, and Mr. Lewis Roepcke, other members of the interservice team, for their valuable assistance in preparing the methodology, and to Mr. Ben Nutt for his efforts in testing the technique. This article was originally published in *Industrial Management Review*, Winter 1969, Vol. 10, Number 2.

most obvious change is in the magnitude of the management problem. In 1949, resources devoted to R&D amounted to less than $2 billion. Currently, annual expenditures on R&D in the United States are roughly $25 billion. Concomitantly, the entire character of general management has changed. Long-range corporate planning, an unknown phenomenon in 1950, is now commanding a recognized position among corporate activities. Operations research, with the advent of computer systems, has transformed many decisions that were at one time "vest pocket decisions" into rational choices among systematically evaluated alternatives. Finally, management in the scientific and technical community, meshed as it is with the government in general and the Department of Defense in specific, has been profoundly influenced by the "McNamara era." These developments have generated a large number of analytical techniques for dealing with problems of R&D management. On such technique is MACRO: Methodology for Allocating Corporate Resources to Objectives for R&D.

THE PROBLEM

The need for a scientific approach to the problem of resource allocation, especially the allocation of funds, has been plaguing the research and development community for years. The critical need for a management decision tool to facilitate the allocation of funds has become increasingly pressing as the resources devoted to research and development have soared. The recognition of this need by numerous industrial and government leaders led to much work on project selection and appraisal in the United States. Thirty different techniques for quantitative resource allocation are listed in an article that appeared recently in the *IEEE Transactions on Engineering Management*.[1] Although most of the techniques listed are American developments, interest is far from limited to the United States. Numerous Western European nations are exploring various resource allocation rationals with a view toward initial experimental evaluation on a small scale and eventual implementation. The British Ministry of Technology, in particular, is actively pursuing resource allocation studies.[2]

The orientation of most quantitative methods for R&D decisions is to the public sector, particularly defense efforts. MACRO, however, was developed to supplement the decision processes of corporate management. The technique provides an analytical framework within which corporate management can deal systematically with the problem of achieving balance in the allocation of applied research and development funds.[3]

[1] See Cetron [1].

[2] See [2], p. 7.

[3] MACRO does not deal with problems of allocation for basic or fundamental research, nor does it deal with development beyond the prototype stage.

MACRO facilitates simultaneous consideration of most management judgments and decisions that impact on the development program. It does *not* replace informed judgments, nor can it operate in the absence of these judgments. The required judgments come from individuals expected to be the most knowledgeable, and the conclusions flow from a consistent, objective, analytic process. Each step is fully identified. Any contested conclusions can be examined readily, and corrected if necessary.

An organization invests in scientific and technical investigations because of a need for the findings of these investigations. The amount of money spent in advancing some area of science or technology reflects the interest of the organization in that area. Similarly, the relative amounts spent in several areas reflect the varying degrees of corporate interest in those areas. Because total resources are limited—and obviously will never be able to support all potentially useful investigations—some prospects must be denied. No area of science or technology can be advanced as rapidly as its proponents might desire without affecting other areas. The problem of allocation—or of achieving balance—becomes a matter of determining how much an additional advance in one field is worth compared with an advance in some other field which might be obtainable with the same money. The resultant problem of balance creates the need for a good scientific resource allocation methodology.

MACRO is a technique for assisting in the distribution of a specified aggregate budget to exploratory development programs in various technologies. Given a budgeted amount, MACRO proposes to clarify the matter of "balance" by requiring that the following information be provided for each area of science or technology:

1. What achievements are desired?
2. What is the relative worth of each?
3. When are the achievements needed?
4. What will each cost?

The bases for the analysis are: (1) judgments and policy decisions by the top management, and (2) systems and technological analyses from throughout the customer and RDT&E community.

In any technology, a variety of levels of sophistication can be realized in a set of time periods (i.e., years). Given any more than a few technologies, a myriad of combinations of exploratory efforts from which the decision maker must select an optimal allocation strategy present themselves. This complexity generates a need for quantitative methodology.

Two general goals can be assigned to the development efforts of an organization. First, the larger portion of the effort and funds is directed specifically toward generating technology needed to support the development of product ideas or concepts. Where R&D effort is motivated by such an end-product application, a systematic method of relating magnitude of effort to urgency of need is of obvious value. Second, some effort is, and always should be, expended to seek and capitalize on unexpected developments in science or technology. MACRO is intended for use in balancing those efforts designed to fulfill the first goal, while placing no arbitrary restrictions on expenditures related to the second goal.

THE TECHNIQUE

MACRO utilizes collective judgments and policy decisions from three levels within the organization: corporate planning and policy staffs, interdisciplinary teams of marketing and engineering personnel, and teams of specialists within given technologies (see Figure 1). The input data emanating from these sources are processed consistent with certain assumptions to derive utility measures. A MACRO program then determines the optimal allocation of an aggregate development budget to specific technologies based on this utility measure. The process which MACRO incorporates is described below.

Corporate Planning and Policy Staffs

The members of the corporate planning and policy staffs are given responsibility for setting out the broad priorities of the organization. Constraints with respect to the extent of desired government business, expected investment returns, and growth objectives are outlined for MACRO as Corporate Capability Objectives (CCO's). Associated with each CCO is a numerical weighting which reflects the relative emphasis top management desires to place on the goal. Examples of CCO's are:

Weight	*Corporate Capability Objective*
12	To be in a low volume, high margin business.
15	To maintain a minimum share of 10 per cent of the market.
18	To realize an annual growth of 12 to 15 per cent.
14	To maintain a product of high versatility.
10	To develop products needing no more than 5 years to reach maximum profits.
12	To develop no more than 25 per cent government business.
19	To have a minimum discounted cash flow of 20 per cent of investment.
100	

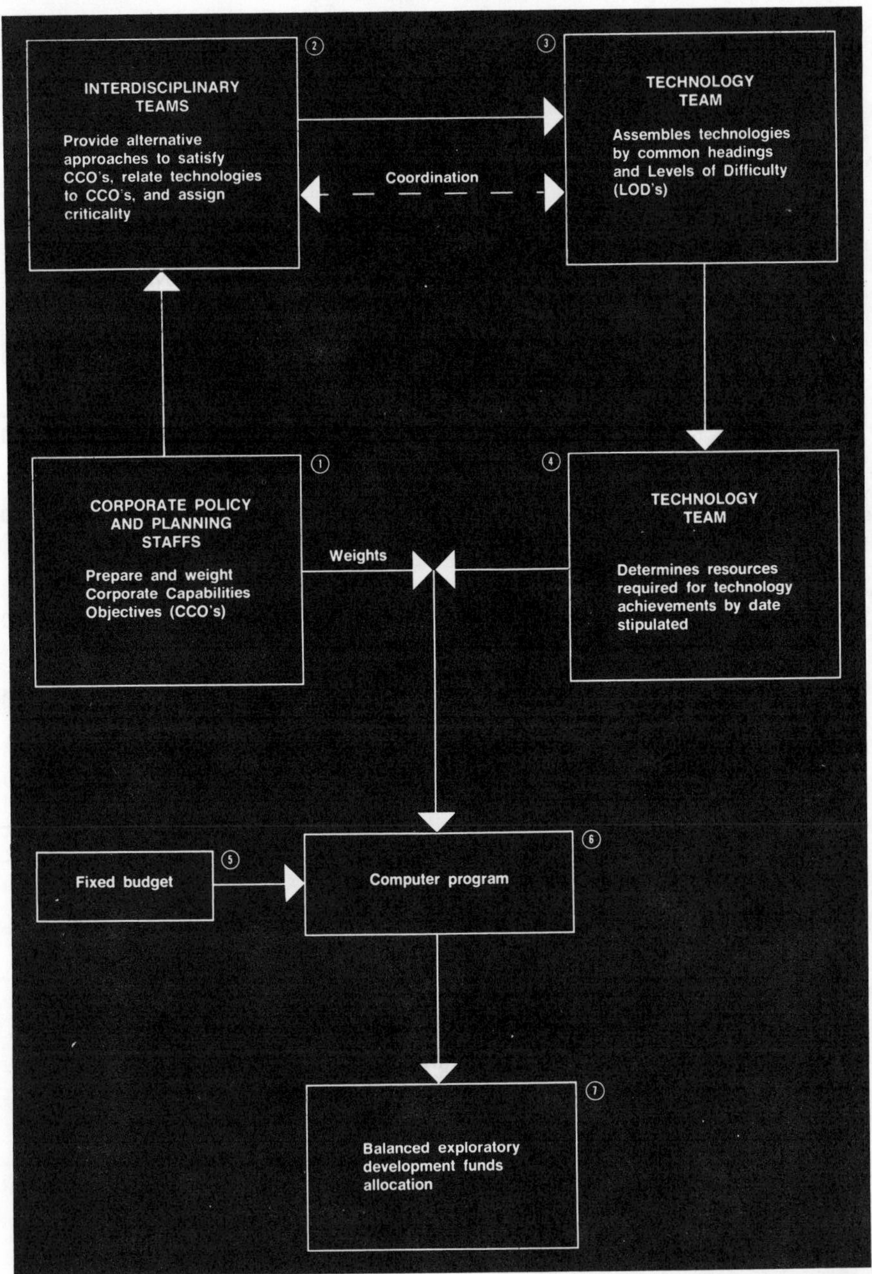

1 Macro Simplified Operational Diagram

Category		Criticality Index
Absolutely Essential	Failure to have this technology will absolutely prevent the attainment of the capability desired	1.0
Major Contribution	Failure to acquire this technology will result in a significant decrease in one or more of the major performance parameters. Such degradation probably would not prevent a favorable decision for development of the product or service	0.7
Cost Reduction	Success in achieving this technology will provide a major reduction in the cost of achieving the capability desired	0.5
Substantial Contribution	Failure to achieve this technology will result in the loss of a highly desirable but not essential capability	0.4
Refinement of Capability	Achievement of this technology will result in some refinement of the present capability but it can be achieved without this effort	0.3
Indirect Contribution	Achievement of this technology will be only an indirect contribution to the capability desired	0.2
Remote Association	This effort has only a remote association with the capability desired	0.1
No Contribution		0.0

Table I Criticality of a Technical Effort to a Desired CCO

Interdisciplinary Teams

Once these broad objectives have been outlined, interdisciplinary teams of marketing and engineering personnel analyze alternative approaches for meeting corporate objectives. The teams, comprised of marketing personnel, design and systems engineers, and consulting technologists, examine systems and subsystems related to product concepts, specific projects, or product ideas which contribute to corporate capability objectives. For example, a corporation defining itself as being in the power source business might consider development of the concept of a parametric system for a thermoelectric device. A product for this organization might be a fuel

	1969	1970	1971	1972	1973	1974	1975
LOD A	150	100	—	—	—	—	—
LOD B	—	50	100	100	—	—	—
LOD C	—	—	—	50	100	50	—
TOTAL	150	150	100	150	100	50	—

Table II Technology Costing (Thousand of Dollars)

cell or a dry cell battery. A new project would involve the development of a new type of wet cell for use in a specific product. The team states the level of technological capability required to meet the needs of each subsystem component and technology.

The next step is to assign a number representing the criticality of the technological capability to the objective. This may range from a low number, representing a capability that contributes only minimally, to a high number implying that the objective cannot be attained without this technological achievement. Table I contains this criticality index. Finally, the interdisciplinary team must assign to each level of technological capability the earliest date needed and the latest date by which the achievement can still be used with full effectiveness in realization of the objectives listed in the CCO's.

Technology Team

The technological capabilities desired are collected in packages representing single areas of technology. In many cases these will cut across objective lines. A team of specialists in a given technology then arranges the technologies in order of increasing Levels of Difficulty (LOD's) and estimates the cost of achieving each capability by the required date. The cost for a given Level of Difficulty reflects but does not include LOD's which have to be achieved first (see Table II). The current year's budget represents a fraction of the total cost of achieving the highest LOD. Provided the technology leading to accomplishment of the LOD is funded at the level specified by the technology team, the LOD under the procedure is expected to be achieved when needed. Worth of the LOD will be decreased if the achieve-

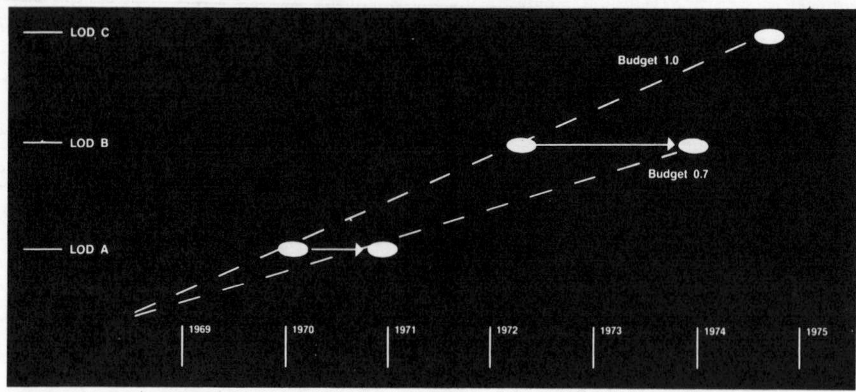

2

ment date is retarded by budget reductions. (For instance, a 30 per cent budget reduction would slip the completion dates of the LOD's as shown in Figure 2.) A tardiness penalty is assessed if substantial delays result.

Under the MACRO system, the worth of having each LOD achieved is evaluated as a function of its weighted objective, its criticality number modified by a timeliness factor, and the specific LOD cost fraction (for example, 0.7 cost fraction as a 30 per cent reduction of budget). The utility of a budget level allocated to a technology is the sum of the worths of each of the LOD's in that technology.

Utility can be computed separately for several possible budget levels for the current year. The computer program selects the combination of allocation levels in each of the various categories that, with a given budget, will buy the maximum utility. The aggregate budget will be allocated so that each technology will be advancing at the maximum rate consistent with the worth of its products and the funds available. An understanding of this general concept allows us to illustrate the precise functioning of the MACRO system.

Assumptions

The data obtained from the various teams are sufficient to permit allocating the available budget to various technologies, given some assumptions about the consequences of program reductions. Each of the technology teams has given an estimate of the budget required to achieve its objectives, including an estimate of the budget for the forthcoming fiscal year (FY)

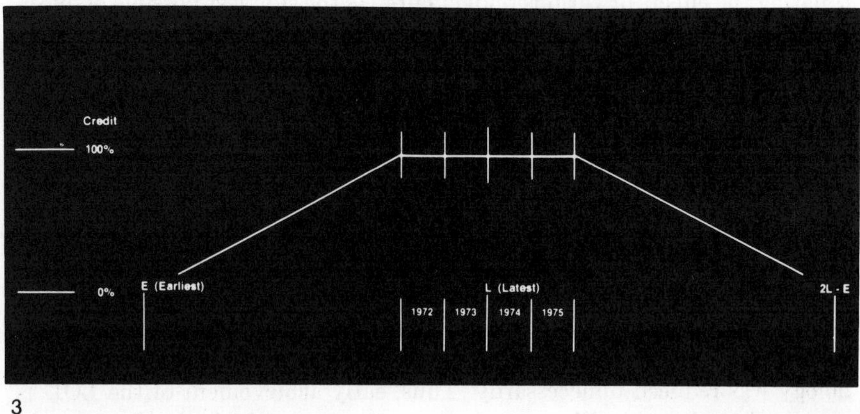

3

MACRO Information Processing The MACRO computer program[4] maximizes a utility function through the MACRO algorithm (simulation model):

$$\text{Technology Utility} = \sum_{j}^{N_s} S_j \; C_i \; \frac{F_i + S_1}{T_j + S_2} \; t_j$$

where

N_s = Systems Supported

S_j = System Relative Value

C_i = Technology Criticality to System

F_i = Current Year (CY) Funds

S_1 = Sum of CY Funds for Previous LOD's

T_j = Total LOD Funds

S_2 = Sum of Funds — Previous LOD's

t_j = Time

(here assumed to be 1969). It is almost certain, however, that the total of all the estimates for FY 69 will exceed the FY 69 budget available. What happends to both the total cost of achieving an LOD and the date at which it is achieved if the rate of expenditure per year is changed from that given by the technology teams? Some assumption must be made to permit es-

[4] The program can be obtained from the authors.

timating the effects of various budget cuts. As the simplest possible assumption, it will be assumed that the total cost of each achievement remains fixed and that the time required is inversely portional to expenditure rate. That is, cutting the budget in half doubles the time to achievement and the total cost remains constant. It is emphasized that this assumption is not essential. Any other rational assumption desired can be made and used in the allocation method.

Another factor which must be considered is the effect of achieving an LOD earlier or later than the "latest" date specified by the interdisciplinary team. For simplicity, if an achievement is late, its worth will be assumed to decrease with time, using the time function described below. If an LOD is achieved too early, the rate of progress of some other technology was reduced unnecessarily. Thus, early achievement of the LOD is penalized as shown in Figure 3. It is accepted that the latest date is only an estimate, and an LOD should not be penalized if it misses the latest date by a short time, either early or late. Achievement of an LOD will be penalized for missing the latest date according to a "timeliness function" of the shape shown in Figure 3. No penalty is assessed for being within two years of the latest year. For being early, the slope of the timeliness function is linear from the "earliest" year. For simplicity, the slope for the "late" side of the timeliness function is made the same as for the "early" side. Again, this particular timeliness function is not essential to the method. Any other timeliness function could be used.

Possibly a numerical illustration of the MACRO system as applied to a particular technology budget would be useful. Suppose that the corporate capability objectives have been provided and analyzed by the interdisciplinary team; information relevant to any department will be of the form and content shown in Table III.

The dates refer to years when CCO/technology links associated with the CCO's require the technology in question. Here the LOD's are assumed to have been ordered in increasing difficulty. In practice, the first action may be to perform this ordering.

The timeliness function for the LOD's, derived as described above, is given in Table IV. For instance, LOD B is stated to be required by the end of FY 74. It receives full credit for achievement in any of the years FY 73, 74, 75, or 76. It receives zero credit for achievement before its earliest year of FY 70. Its credit for achievement between the beginning of FY 70 and the end of FY 72 increases linearly, as shown.

Now let us consider the year in which the LOD's will be achieved for various budget levels. The levels considered will be 1.0, 0.8, 0.7, and 0.6

LOD	Criticality	Earliest Date	Latest Date	CCO
A	1.0	1969	1973	V_3
B	0.5	1970	1974	V_5
C	0.7	1971	1975	V_1
D	0.3	1971	1976	V_4
E	0.2	1972	1977	V_3
F	0.4	1973	1978	V_6

Table III

LOD	Year of Achievement (FY) 69	70	71	72	73	74	75	76	77	78	79	80	81	82	83	84	85
A	$\frac{1}{4}$	$\frac{1}{2}$	$\frac{3}{4}$	1	1	1	1	$\frac{3}{4}$	$\frac{1}{2}$	$\frac{1}{4}$	0						
B	0	$\frac{1}{4}$	$\frac{1}{2}$	$\frac{3}{4}$	1	1	1	1	$\frac{3}{4}$	$\frac{1}{2}$	$\frac{1}{4}$	0					
C		0	$\frac{1}{4}$	$\frac{1}{2}$	$\frac{3}{4}$	1	1	1	1	$\frac{3}{4}$	$\frac{1}{2}$	$\frac{1}{4}$	0				
D		0	$\frac{1}{5}$	$\frac{2}{5}$	$\frac{3}{5}$	$\frac{4}{5}$	1	1	1	1	$\frac{4}{5}$	$\frac{3}{5}$	$\frac{2}{5}$	$\frac{1}{5}$	0		
E			0	$\frac{1}{5}$	$\frac{2}{5}$	$\frac{3}{5}$	$\frac{4}{5}$	1	1	1	1	$\frac{4}{5}$	$\frac{3}{5}$	$\frac{2}{5}$	$\frac{1}{5}$	0	
F		0	$\frac{1}{7}$	$\frac{2}{7}$	$\frac{3}{7}$	$\frac{4}{7}$	$\frac{5}{7}$	$\frac{6}{7}$	1	1	1	1	$\frac{6}{7}$	$\frac{5}{7}$	$\frac{4}{7}$	$\frac{3}{7}$	$\frac{2}{7}$

Table IV

of those requested. The results are shown in Table V. It must be remembered that a budget level of 0.6 means that the budget is reduced to 60 per cent of that requested and that the program is stretched to 1/0.6 times as long.

	Budget Level			
	1.0	0.8	0.7	0.6
LOD				
A	1972*	1973	1974	1975
B	1973	1975	1976	1977
C	1974	1976	1977	1979
D	1975	1977	1978	1980
E	1976	1978	1980	1982
F	1977	1979	1981	1984

Table V Effect of Stretching Programs

* Year of achievement.

The FY 69 budget represents a certain proportion of the total costs of achieving each of the LOD's. The proportion is shown in Table VI. If, for example, the FY 69 estimate were $50,000 and it were 1/12 of the total cost of achieving LOD A, or 0.0833 of the total cost, the table could have been developed utilizing the same procedure.

The data shown in Table VI must now be combined into a measure of utility to be associated with each of the possible budget levels for FY 69. That is, we want to answer the question, "What is the utility of a given budget level, in terms of achievement of the various LOD's at some time in the future and in terms of their worth?" Each LOD is associated with CCO's. CCO's have weights associated with them. The criticality of the LOD to a CCO is a number between 0 and 1 which gives the proportion of the weight "earned" by achieving the LOD. The worth of achievement is further modified by the timeliness function according to the date at which the LOD will be achieved at a given budget level. Finally, the FY 69 budget represents a certain proportion of the ultimate cost of achieving each LOD. The worth of achievement is further modified by this "cost fraction" to get the measure of utility of an LOD which is "earned" by a budget level: Utility = Weight × Criticality × Timeliness × Cost Fraction. The

	Budget Level			
	1.0	0.8	0.7	0.6
LOD				
A	.0833	.0666	.0584	.0500
B	.0555	.0445	.0388	.0353
C	.0435	.0349	.0305	.0261
D	.0345	.0276	.0242	.0207
E	.0270	.0216	.0189	.0162
F	.0217	.0182	.0152	.0130

Table VI Cost Fractions

sum of these products for each LOD toward which a budget leads is the measure of utility of the technology package for that budget level.

MACRO's OUTPUT

For information output, MACRO generates a set of budgets for technology areas maximizing the exploratory development program in terms of corporate objectives. *The technique is intended not to yield decisions, but rather to furnish information that might facilitate decision making. Indeed, the principal value of the technique is derived from its providing a thinking structure to force methodical, meticulous analysis. Data plus analysis generate information. Information couples with judgment to render decisions.*

MACRO techniques have been applied in three industrial firms, two in the chemical industry and one in the electronics industry. In two of these firms, management goes through the "drill," and compares the results with those obtained by "seat of their pants" decisions. When there are significant differences in resource allocations, management then decides on the appropriate budget for each technological area. In the third firm, the company allocates funds directly from computer results. In the authors' opinion this is wrong, but the company planner defended his approach: "How else am I going to allocate money to more than 1000 pieces of R&D

work? This system is better than just plain 'guestimates' or what I gave each project last year."

One problem arising in implementation has been that collecting considerable information on corporate strategy at one point creates security difficulties because of the mobility of the members of the technostructure. Further, the technique is susceptible to "gamesmanship": trying to test the system. It should also be pointed out that the technique offers no panacea to the ever changing problem of achieving the most effective balance in the allocation of exploratory development funds. One complicating factor is that MACRO does not take into account the effects of competitors' research and development on the corporate posture.

Another limitation is that it does not account for the inability to work in some areas of science or technology due to lack of qualified personnel or ceiling limitations, problems of technical risk, and problems of one firm's doing work which benefits another. Additional considerations for which it offers no formula include the obvious need to allot some proportion of the total funds for use in high-risk, high-payoff efforts of apparently low relevance which may lead to significantly improved corporate capability. The validity of the system's applicability to non-material areas, such as the behavioral sciences, also is open to conjecture.

These short-comings should not prevent the successful testing and possible eventual use of MACRO in the many firms where it is applicable. A quantitative, quality management tool, with some constraint, is more valuable than a tool that is at best limited in view and in scope or than no tool at all.

APPENDIX

The following statements define terms used in this paper which may be unfamiliar to some readers. The terms are listed in alphabetical order.

Alternate Approaches to Meeting Corporate Objectives

Conceptual descriptions of systems, subsystems, etc., which are the means for achieving the ability to carry out an objective.

Balanced Resources Allocation

An allocation which, based upon contribution to desired corporate capabilities, determines the relative utility of a technology, its criticality, cost, and appropriate time phasing, thus providing an input toward rational funds allocations.

Corporate Capability Objective (*CCO*)

A description of a portion of the role or mission of a corporation. It is a broad statement of a desired operational function rather than a precise statement of how or with what equipment the function is to be carried out.

Criticality (*of a Technology to an Objective*)

A method for indicating the importance of a Level of Difficulty (LOD) of a technology to a Corporate Capability Objective (CCO). The criticality is expressed as a numerical value from 0 to 1.0 and is obtained from a pre-defined criticality scale.

Interdisciplinary Team

A team comprised of users, long-range planners, systems analysts, preliminary design groups, and consulting technologists who propose methods for carrying out the Corporate Capability Objectives. It also estimates the technologies required to support the alternatives and the criticality of the technologies to the achievement of the alternatives proposed.

Level of Difficulty (*LOD*)

A quantitative statement of a technological capability required to achieve a CCO. A technology package is comprised of one or more similar LOD's at different levels.

MACRO (*Methodology for Allocation of Corporate Resources to Objectives for R&D*)

A resources allocation system that applies analytical techniques to the determination of a balanced corporate applied research and exploratory development budget for a corporation.

Technology Package

A set of one or more related levels of technical capability (LOD's) stated in quantitative terms. When more than one level of capability is sought, the levels represent homogeneous technological capabilities, and the lowest capability is required before any higher level can be attained.

Technology Team

A group of scientific and engineering personnel who are knowledgeable in a given area of technology. It is responsible for rationally arranging LOD's within a technology and for stipulating the annual expenditure of resources required to achieve the LOD's (and consequently technologies) in the given number of years stipulated by the interdisciplinary team.

Utility of a Funding Level

A quantitative determination of the importance of each of several levels of funding in a technology package.

REFERENCES

1. Cetron, M. J., Martino, J., and Roepcke, L. "The Selection of R&D Program Content-Survey of Quantitative Methods," *IEEE Transactions on Engineering-Management,* Vol. EM-14, No. 1 (March 1967), pp. 4–13.
2. *New Technology,* No. 7. Published by British Ministry of Technology (July 1967).

THE SELECTION OF R&D PROGRAM CONTENT—SURVEY OF QUANTITATIVE METHODS*

Marvin J. Cetron
Advanced Concepts Branch
HQ. Naval Material Command
Washington, D. C.
Joseph Martino
Office of Scientific Research
Office of Aerospace Research
Washington, D. C.
and
Lewis Roepcke
Directorate of Developments
U. S. Army Materiel Command
Washington, D. C.

This paper provides a summary of a number of known techniques for quantitative evaluation of R&D projects. Successful application of quantitative methods to problems such as inventories, queueing, transportation, and other problems requiring decisions on resource allocation or scheduling, has at least made it conceivable to raise the question of whether comparable quantitative evaluation methods could also be applied to research and development projects. The advent of the computer has made such applications appear feasible, where the R&D efforts are large in number. The desired outputs from such quantitative methods would be an evaluation of a prescribed selection of projects, or better yet, a procedure for scheduling projects or allocating resources among competing projects.

Interest in such quantitative methods, especially within the Department of Defense, has become quite high within the past few years. As a result of this interest, the authors have conducted a survey of methods, both completed and on-going, which have been devised in industry and in the government, and have evaluated those methods against a fixed set of factors.

---

* Reprinted from the *IEEE Transactions on Engineering Management*, Vol. EM-14, No. 1, March 1967.

While the original purpose of this survey and evaluation was to form a basis for recommending a system for application within one of the military services, the results of the survey may well be of interest to others, and are therefore presented here.

II. FEATURES OF THE METHODS

The various methods uncovered in our survey took into account various items of information about the R&D projects to be evaluated, and provide various items of information as output from the evaluation. A total of 15 different features were found which could describe the items of input and output of the various methods. No single method possessed all the features. The various features are described in some detail below.

1) *Utility Measure:* Does the method take into account some measure of the utility or value of success of a particular R&D project? This measure may be share of a market, profitability, some measure of military worth, etc.

2) *Probability of Success:* Does the method explicitly take into account an estimate of the probability of success of each individual R&D project?

3) *Orthogonality of Criteria:* Are the criteria used by the method mutually exclusive (orthogonal), rather than being highly correlated or having a high degree of overlap?

4) *Sensitivity:* Has the sensitivity of the output to small changes in the input been checked? A high degree of sensitivity to small variations in input is undesirable, since the output then becomes unstable in the presence of minor perturbations in the input.

5) *Rejected Alternatives Retention:* When a project is rejected for funding, is it retained for later consideration in the event of a budget increase or other adjustment, rather than being rejected completely?

6) *Classification Structure:* Does the method provide a structural relationship between the R&D project and a hierarchy of higher-level goals of the organization?

7) *Time:* Does the method take into account scheduling requirements, or provide scheduling information as an output?

8) *Strategies:* Does the method permit the user to take into account several possible scenarios, world environments, market situations, etc.?

9) *System Cross Support:* Does the method give a system development credit for support which it provides to another system development?

10) *Technology Cross Support:* Does the method give a project for advancement of technology credit for support which it provides to the advancement of other technologies?

11) *Graphical Display:* Is the output amenable to presentation in some graphical form which gives the user a condensed picture of the evaluation of various projects?

12) *Flagging:* Does the method flag problem areas, to bring them to the attention of the responsible management?

13) *Optimization Criteria:* What criterion for optimization does the method use, and what constraints are considered? All methods used either a composite score from a number of factors, to obtain a ranking, or used some form of maximum (discounted) net value.

14) *Constraints:* Constraints considered by the methods were: budget, skills available, facilities available, competitor efforts, and raw materials available.

15) *Computerized:* Is the method implemented in a computer program, and is it a linear program or a dynamic program? Those marked as computerized are known to the authors to have been programmed for some machine. It should be noted that most of the techniques could be computerized if desired.

III. EASE OF USE

Each method was evaluated according to several criteria bearing on ease of use. The criteria considered are described below.

1) *Data Requirements:* While in general the more data a method uses as input, the more information it provides as output, nevertheless, the ease of use is affected by the amount of data required. Two factors enter into the amount of data required: the level of organization at which data is obtained, i.e., individual work unit, subsystem, system, etc.; and the amount of data required on each effort on which data is gathered.

2) *Manual:* Is manual operation of the method possible or reasonable to consider?

3) *Computer Program:* If a computer is required, has the method been programmed for some computer?

4) *Running Time:* If the method has been programmed, what is the running time for one cycle of evaluation or allocation?

5) *Updating:* What is the ease of updating the system to take into account new information, whether the new information is developed periodically or new items come in on an unscheduled basis?

6) *Proficiency Level:* What level of proficiency is required of the operator (not the manager who is using the output)? Can it be handled by a clerk? Does it require a skilled technician? Does it require a degreed professional?

7) *Outside Help:* Is help or information required from persons outside the R&D organization, in evaluating goals set by others, environments not under control of the R&D organization, etc.?

IV. AREA OF APPLICABILITY

Few of the systems appeared to be applicable throughout the entire R&D spectrum. Some were more applicable to one portion of the spectrum than to others. The methods are rated as being applicable to research, to exploratory development, to advanced development, or to engineering development.

V. DESCRIPTION OF METHODS

Each method surveyed is described briefly below. The methods are identified with the name or names of the originators, unless some acronym or title has been used to designate the method. Methods 1 through 10 and their descriptions are from the Baker-Pound article "R&D Project Selection: Where We Stand," printed in IEEE TRANSACTIONS ON ENGINEERING MANAGEMENT, vol. EM-11, no. 4, December 1964.

1) *Mottley-Newton, 1959:* "A decision theory approach. Project proposals are rated with respect to a number of evaluation criteria. An overall score is computed and used to rank the alternatives. Selection criteria are considered with respect to constraints including research budget, risk, and overall program balance."

2) *Gargiulo et al., 1961:* "A decision theory approach. Project proposals are rated with respect to a number of evaluation criteria. An overall score is computed and used to rank the alternatives. Constraints such as research budget, skills available, facilities available, and competitor efforts in the area are considered."

3) *Pound, 1964:* "A decision theory approach. Project proposals are rated with respect to a number of weighted selection objectives. An overall score is computed and used to rank the alternatives. The budget constraint is considered."

4) *Sobelman, 1958:* "An operations research approach. For each alternative project, estimates are made of average value per year, economic life, average development cost per year and development time. Selection is accomplished by maximizing discounted net value, perhaps subject to constraints."

5) *Freeman, 1960*: "An operations research approach. For each alternative project, an estimate is made of the probability distribution of net

value. Selection is accomplished by maximizing expected discounted net value subject to constraints on the total budget, facilities, and personnel. A linear programming formulation is used."

6) *Asher, 1962:* "An operations research approach. For each alternative project, estimates are made of the discounted net value of the project and probability of success. Selection is accomplished by maximizing expected discounted net value subject to constraints on the man hours available and on the raw materials available. The optimal manpower allocation is indicated by the result. A linear programming formulation is used."

7) *Hess, 1962:* "An operations research approach. For each alternative project, estimates are made of the discounted gross value as of several points in time. Probabilities of success are also estimated. Selection is accomplished by maximizing expected discounted net value subject to a budget constraint for the first period. The optimal allocation to each project is indicated for each period. A dynamic programming formulation is used."

8) *Dean-Sengupta, 1962:* "An economic analysis and operations research approach. The optimal research budget is first determined. Then for each alternative project, estimates are made of the discounted net value and the probability of technical and commercial success. Selection is accomplished by maximizing expected discounted net value subject to a budget constraint. A linear programming formulation is suggested."

9) *Disman, 1962:* "An economic analysis approach. For each alternative project, an estimate is made of the discounted net value (not including R&D costs). This estimate, perhaps modified by a probability of technical and/or commercial success is considered to be the maximum expenditure justified. The ratio of the maximum expenditure justified to estimated project cost is an index of the desirability of the project."

10) *Cramer-Smith, 1964:* "An economic analysis and operations research approach. An application of portfolio selection and utility theory to the problem of research project selection. For each alternative project, estimates are made of net values and probabilities of occurrence. Utility curves are also obtained. Projects may be ranked on the basis of expected value or expected utility. Lack of project independence is also mentioned."

11) *Esch, "PATTERN," 1963:* Combination decision theory approach and operations research approach. Project PATTERN is a continuing, large-scale, corporate effort to assign quantitative, relative values to the importance of conducting R&D on the various technology deficiencies which now stand in the way of the achievement of the national security objectives for the decade from 1968 to 1978. The model considers national survival, threat force structure, capability, prestige, cost effectiveness,

requirements, scientific implications, feasibility, effort, risk, capability improvement, and operational advantages. This technique is the first full-scale application of the heuristic "relevance tree" concept development in 1958 by H. Wells in his Ohio State University Master's thesis.

12) *Blum, 1963:* A mathematical treatment leading to a methodology of ranking R&D events in the project by their cost, risk, time, and value. The methodology sequences the efforts by a version of the DOD and NASA PERT-cost technique.

13) *Bakanas, 1964:* A model to aid in the selection of applied research and development tasks for inclusion in a long-range R&D program. The model consists of a structure relating the conceptional elements of the R&D program; formats for delineating the characteristics of the conceptional elements; mathematical relations between the expected program value and military prior to probability of task success, task cost, and program cost; and a rank-ordering procedure to select a program of maximum expected value. A computer program aids in formulating the R&D program.

14) *Dean, 1964:* An operations research approach. Mathematical models consider the relevant resource variables, noncontrollable variables, parameters, and constraints that are responsive to corporate goals and yield solutions for allocating technical resources to projects. The scoring model permits determination of important factors in a profitability model.

15) *Hill-Roepcke, 1964:* An operations research approach. A mathematical model considering the military value of the objective for technology, the technical probability of success, the expected value of the individual efforts, and a method to select the optimum program from many such efforts.

16) *Nutt, 1965:* An operations research approach. A deterministic model which quantifies the value or technical payoff of each research task. The model developed considers the world environment; the Air Force missions; future weapons systems configurations; laboratory technical objectives; and the timeliness, complexity, and scope of each research effort. The result consists of recommended funding levels of efficient tasks along with suggested tasks for close scrutiny or possible elimination. A modified linear program.

17) *Cetron, "PROFILE," 1965:* Decision theory of approach designed to aid in exploring (a) the total structure of project selection decision problems in the context of the R&D manager, and (b) R&D processes which are relevant to the design and implementation of management systems for planning, appraising, and controlling resource allocation among various projects. PROFILE's nine quantified criteria (value to warfare, task re-

sponsiveness, timeliness, long range plan, probability of success, technological transfer, manpower facilities, and funding) are used in developing a task "Profile" as well as in determining the military utility, the technical feasibility, and the application of resources for each project.

18) *Rosen & Saunder, 1965:* An operations research approach. A modification of Hess' dynamic programming approach by discussing it in the context of different optimization criteria for obtaining optimum expenditure patterns. The optimization criteria are: expected profit; total expected output; life expected output; and a minimum fixed percent return on nondiscounted expenditure.

19) *Sacco, 1965:* An operations research approach. A refinement to the Hill-Roepcke model that permitted dynamic programming to be used and thus achieving a more nearly optimum R&D program.

20) *Albertini, 1965:* An operations research approach. A methodology for the evaluation and selection of research and development tasks directed toward the determination of materiel development objectives. A mathematical choice model to assist management in the synthesis of pertinent information for the purpose of selection, within applicable constraints, of a maximum expected value program of research and development effort. Specifications, in the form of flow charts, are included for the computerization of the model.

21) *Berman, 1965:* An economic analysis and decision tree approach. The approach considers the incremental cost of the project in R&D resources; the incremental production and operating and manning costs of introducing the new technology, and the incremental military value of the technology.

22) *Sobin-Gordon, 1965:* A comparative method which will analyze alternative applications of resource allocation techniques and attempt to evaluate the value of these techniques against various frames of reference. The analytical method thus developed (basically using ordinal values converted to relative value made up of interdependence of different proposals, definiteness of applications, capability values, probability of success, and military utility) will be used to optimize the selected principles of resource allocation in the dynamic multiple project environment. Linear programming will be used. Principal application to laboratory selection of efforts.

23) *Albertini, 1965:* An operations research approach to synthesize information pertinent to the planning procedure for the purpose of determining which long-range technical plan tasks to recommend for funding. This technique begins with given major barrier problem areas (MBPA's), operations on these MBPA's using the following criteria: expected technical value, annual cost of a configuration, annual monetary quota cost of a con-

figuration. A computer program helps formulate the recommended R&D program.

24) *Wells, 1968:* A decision theory approach to store, track, and properly relate judgments concerning systems; to show the impact of these judgments; to permit real-time iterations of planning problems to facilitate the assessment and selection of system candidates for development. Criteria are: threat, types of war, policy objectives, functions, systems contributions, force structure, technical feasibility, schedule & cost, and budget.

25) *Cetron, "QUEST," 1966:* An operations research approach. QUEST utilizes a double set of matrices, consisting of the sciences, technologies, and missions, developed with the "technology" parameter common to both. By having "figures of utility" assigned to each mission and by determining the value of the contribution of each technological area to each mission, a cumulative quantified value for each technological area is then related to each scientific area and the relevant impact of each of the scientific disciplines is identified with each technological area.

26) *Dean-Hauser, 1966:* An economic analysis and operations research approach. An application of project selection under constrained resource conditions. By using mathematical models, computer programs, and available information concerning costs, uncertainties, and military values, it is possible to obtain optimum solutions. The Case study has developed a mathematical model for handling the large number of alternatives through the use of a series of simpler computerized methods, where the results of one stage are used in the succeeding stage. A dynamic programming formulation is used.

27) *Belt, 1966:* A decision theory approach based on quantified subjective judgments on the predicted value of a successful laboratory project outcome, the likelihood of success of the project in terms of its technological achievability, the specific plan of attack and the suitability of the proposed performers of the work, and the predicted cost. This technique stops short of producing a single numerical rating of project value, but gives the decision maker the opportunity to select from a group of alternative projects.

28) *De L'Estoile, 1966:* A decision theory approach. This refined rating scheme uses a formula including four factors: military utility, probability of technical success, possibility of realization in France, and direct and indirect economic impact (including the cross support to the civilian sector of the economy). This total system, because of the large number of projects involved, will be computerized in 1967.

29) *Martino et al., 1967:* An operations research approach. Factors taken into account are importance of military missions, criticality of technological effort to mission, and level of technology required. Funds are allocated

	Utility Measure	Prob. of Success	Orthog. Criteria	Sensi-tivity	Retain Rej. Alt.	Class Struc.	Time	Strategies	Sys. Cross Support	Tech. Cross Support	Graph. Displ.	Flag.	Optimize* Criteria	Constraints**	Computerized
1. Mottley–Newton, 1959	X	X	X	X			X	X					1	1, 6, 7	X
2. Gargiulo et al., 1961	X	X	X				X		X	X			1	1, 2, 3, 4	
3. Pound, 1964	X	X				X							7	1	
4. Sobelman, 1958	X	X					X						7		
5. Freeman, 1960	X	X	X					X					7	1, 2, 3	X
6. Asher, 1962	X	X	X										7	2, 5	X
7. Hess, 1962	X	X					X						7	1	X
8. Dean–Sengupta, 1962	X	X			X	X							7	1	X
9. Disman, 1962	X	X	X										7		
10. Cramer–Smith, 1964	X	X			X	X							7	1	
11. Esch, "PATTERN," 1963	X	X	X	X		X	X	X	X				1, 2		X
12. Blum, 1963	X	X	X		X	X							6	6	
13. Bakanas, 1964	X	X	X	X		X							3	1, 6	X
14. Dean, 1964	X	X	X	X	X	X							4		
15. Hill–Roepcke, 1964	X	X	X			X							2	1, 6, 7	
16. Nutt, 1965	X	X	X	X	X	X	X	X		X	X		1, 2, 3	1, 2, 3	X
17. Cetron, "PROFILE," 1965	X	X	X	X	X	X	X	X		X	X	X	1, 2	1, 2	
18. Rosen–Saunder, 1965	X	X											3, 3, 4, 7	1	X
19. Sacco, 1965	X	X	X			X			X				3		
20. Albertini, 1965	X	X				X			X	X			2	1, 6, 7	X
21. Berman, 1965	X	X				X	X	X					5		
22. Sobin–Gordon, 1965	X	X		X	X								1	1, 2, 3, 7	X
23. Albertini, 1965	X	X	X			X								1, 6, 7	
24. Wells, 1966	X	X	X	X	X	X		X			X		2	1, 7	X
25. Cetron, "QUEST", 1966	X	X			X	X	X	X		X		X	1, 2	1, 7	
26. Dean–Hauser, 1966	X	X	X	X	X	X		X				X	2, 3	1, 6	X
27. Belt, 1966	X	X			X					X		X			
28. De l'Estoile, 1966	X	X								X			3		X
29. Martino et al., 1967	X		X		X	X	X	X					3	1, 7	
30. Caulfield–Freshman, 1967	X	X			X	X	X	X	X	X	X	X	1, 2, 3	1, 7	

* Optimization Criteria
1. Ordinal Ranking
2. Expected Value
3. Cost-Benefit
4. Profitability
5. Incremental Costs
6. Composite Score
7. Discounted Net Value

** Constraints
1. Budget
2. Skills Available
3. Facilities Available
4. Competitor Efforts
5. Raw Materials Available
6. Risk
7. Program Balance

Figure 1. Features of the methods.

	Data Req'ts	Manual Oper'n Poss.	Comp. Prog. Avail.	Comp. Run Time	Diffic. of Updating	Operator Profic. Level	Need for Outside Help
1. Mottley–Newton, 1959	L	X	X		L	T	L
2. Gargiulo et al., 1961	M	X				T	L
3. Pound, 1964	C	X				T	L
4. Sobelman, 1958	M	X					
5. Freeman, 1960	C	X	X			T	
6. Asher, 1962	C		X			T	
7. Hess, 1962	C		X			T	
8. Dean–Sengupta, 1962	C					T	
9. Disman, 1962	C						M
10. Cramer–Smith, 1964	M	X					M
11. Esch, "PATTERN," 1963	C		X	C	C	P	C
12. Blum, 1963	M	X			L	T	
13. Bakanas, 1964	C		X	M	L	T	
14. Dean, 1964	M	X			L	P	L
15. Hill, Roepcke, 1964	C			M	L	T	L
16. Nutt, 1965	C		X	L	L	P	C
17. Cetron, "PROFILE," 1965	L	X			L	P	M
18. Rosen–Saunder, 1965	C		X			T	
19. Sacco, 1965	C			L	L	P	L
20. Albertini, 1965	C		X	M	L	T	
21. Berman, 1965	C			C	L	T	
22. Sobin–Gordon, 1965	M		X	M	L	P	L
23. Albertini, 1965	C		X	M	L	T	L
24. Wells, 1966	M		X	L	L	P	C
25. Cetron, "QUEST," 1966	C	X			M	P	C
26. Dean–Hauser, 1966	C		X	L	L	P	L
27. Belt, 1966	M	X			M	P	L
28. De l'Estoile, 1966	C		X	C	C	P	C
29. Martino et al., 1967	C	X			M	P	C
30. Caulfield–Freshman, 1967	C	X			M	P	C

Symbol Keys

Computer Running Time
L—little
M—moderate
C—considerable

Difficulty of Updating
L—low
M—moderate
C—considerable

Need for outside help
L—little or none
M—moderate
C—considerable

Operator Proficiency
C—clerk
T—technician
P—degreed professional

	Rsch.	Expl. Devel.	Adv. Devel.	Engr. Devel.
1. Mottley–Newton, 1959	X	X	X	
2. Gargiulo et al., 1961		X	X	X
3. Pound, 1964		X	X	
4. Sobelman, 1958			X	
5. Freeman, 1960				X
6. Asher, 1962			X	X
7. Hess, 1962				X
8. Dean–Sengupta, 1962				X
9. Disman, 1962		X	X	X
10. Cramer–Smith, 1964	X			
11. Esch. "PATTERN," 1963		X	X	X
12. Blum, 1963		X	X	X
13. Bakanas, 1964		X	X	
14. Dean, 1964		X	X	X
15. Hill–Roepcke, 1964		X	X	
16. Nutt, 1965		X	X	
17. Cetron, "PROFILE," 1965		X	X	
18. Rosen–Saunder, 1965				X
19. Sacco, 1965		X	X	
20. Albertini, 1965		X	X	
21. Berman, 1965		X	X	X
22. Sobin–Gordon, 1965	X	X	X	
23. Albertini, 1965	X			
24. Wells, 1966			X	X
25. Cetron, "QUEST," 1966	X	X		
26. Dean–Hauser, 1966		X	X	X
27. Belt, 1966		X	X	
28. De l'Estoile, 1966		X	X	X
29. Martino et al., 1967	X	X		
30. Caulfield–Freshman, 1967			X	

Figure 2. Ease of use. Figure 3. R&D areas of applicability.

among technical projects on the basis of maximum marginal payoff per dollar, within a budget total.

30) *Caulfield-Freshman, 1967:* A decision theory approach. Development project proposals are rated with respect to a number of weighted selection categories. These six categories consist of progress of program, military utility, technical risk, resources, management environment, and technological transfer; an overall score is computed and used to rank the alternatives. This technique is used to develop a task "Profile" which serves as an aid in the allocation of resources.

VI. COMPARISON OF METHODS

The various methods are compared as to features, ease of use criteria, and area of applicability in Figs. 1, 2, and 3, respectively. The various methods and features, criteria, or areas are displayed in matrix form. An entry of X in the matrix indicates that the method has the feature, satisfies the criterion, or is applicable to that area. For level of information or data required, the methods are coded L for little or none, M for moderate amount, and C for considerable amount. These evaluations are subjective, of course, but will provide some guidance as to the ease of use.

VII. SUMMARY

Several methods for appraisal of R&D programs have been evaluated against a set of criteria. The capabilities and limitations of each of the methods have been indicated. Each method, within its capabilities and limitations, can provide assistance to the management of an R&D enterprise in appraising the worth of its R&D effort. In particular, the use of quantitative methods tends to eliminate bias, provide a degree of consistency, and force managers to render their judgments more explicit in evaluating R&D programs. While some of the techniques described lack certain features, these usually can be added with some modification, if desired.

The value of any of the appraisal methods is further limited by two factors:

a) the validity of input information supplied by the laboratory workers and management staff;

b) the effective support and use of the system by higher management. If management supports a method, and makes proper use of it, and furthermore insures that the input information is as valid as humanly possible, the methods can provide a very valuable tool for improving the management of an R&D organization.

Considering the limitations of the methods described, there is clearly much room for further refinement and improvement of quantitative methods for appraisal of R&D programs. However, even in the absence of these refined methods, the spectrum of existing methods can provide the R&D manager with considerable assistance in appraising his program.

BIBLIOGRAPHY

Ackoff, R. L., *Scientific Method: Optimizing Applied Research Decisions.* New York: Wiley, 1962.

——, Ed., *Progress in Operations Research,* vol. 1. New York: Wiley, 1961.

——, "Specialized versus generalized models in research budgeting," presented at the 2nd Conf. on Research Program Effectiveness, Washington, D. C., July 1965.

Ackoff, R. L., E. L. Arnoff, and C. W. Churchman, *Introduction to Operations Research.* New York: Wiley, 1957.

Adams, J. G., and H. R. E. Nellums, "Engineering evaluation—tool for research management," *Indust. Engrg. Chem.*, vol. 49, p. 40A, May 1957.

Albertini, J., "The QMDO planning process as it relates to the U. S. Army Materiel Command," Cornell Aeronautical Lab. Rept. VQ-2044-H-1, USAMC Contract DA-49-185 AMC-237(X), August 31, 1965.

——, "The LRTP planning process as it relates to the U. S. Army Materiel Command," Cornell Aeronautical Lab. Rept. VQ-2044-H-2, USAMC Contract DA-49-186 AMC-237(X), October 30, 1965.

——, "LRTP mathematical model brochure," Cornell Aeronautical Lab. Rept. VQ-2044-H-3, USAMC Contract DA-49-186 AMC-237(X), October 30, 1965.

Amey, L. R., "The allocation and utilization of resources," *Operations Research Quart.*, vol. 15, June 1964.

Andersen, S. L., "Venture analysis, a flexible planning tool," *Chem. Engrg. Prog.*, vol. 57, pp. 80–83, March 1961.

——, "A 2 × 2 risk decision problem," *Chem. Engrg. Prog.*, vol. 57, pp. 70–73, May 1961.

Anderson, C. A., "Notes on the evaluation of research planning," presented at the 2nd Conf. on Research Program Effectiveness, Washington, D. C , July, 1964.

Ansoff, H. I., "Evaluation of applied research in a business firm," in *Technological Planning on the Corporate Level,* (Proc. Conf. at Harvard Business School), J. R. Bright, Ed. Cambridge, Mass.: Harvard University Press, 1962, pp. 209–224.

Andrew, G. H. L., "Assessing priorities for technical effort," *Operations Research Quart.*, vol. 5, pp. 67–80, September 1954.

Anthony, R. N., and J. S. Day, *Management Controls in Industrial Research Organizations.* Cambridge, Mass.: Harvard University Press, 1952.

Asher, D. T., "A linear programming model for the allocation of R&D efforts," *IRE Trans. on Engineering Management*, vol. EM-9, pp. 154–157, December 1962.

Aumann, R. J., and J. B. Kruskal, "Assigning quantitative values to qualitative factors in the naval electronics program," *Naval Research Logistics Quart.*, vol. 4, p. 15, March 1959.

Asher, D. I., and S. Disman, "Operations research in R&D," *Chem. Engrg Prog.*, vol. 59, pp. 41–45, January 1963.

Bakanas, V., "An analytical method to aid in the choice of long range study tasks," Cornell Aeronautical Lab. Rept. VQ-1887-H-1, USAMC Contract DA-49-186 AMC-97(X), May 19, 1964.

Baker, N. R., and W. H. Pound, "R and D project selection: Where we stand," *IEEE Trans. on Engineering Management*, vol. Em-11, pp. 124–134, December 1964.

Barmby, J. G., "The applicability of PERT as a management tool," *IRE Trans. on Engineering Management*, vol. EM-9, pp. 130–131, September 1962.

Battersby, A., *Network Analysis for Planning and Scheduling.* New York: St. Martins Press, 1964.

Baumgartner, J. S., *Project Management.* Homewood, Ill.: Richard Irwin Press, 1963.

Beckwith, R. E., "A cost control extension of the PERT system," *IRE Trans. on Engineering Management*, vol. EM-9, pp. 147–149, December 1962.

Belt, J. R., "Military applied R&D project evaluation," Master's thesis, U. S. Navy Marine Engineering Lab., Anapolis, Md., June 1966 (unpublished).

Bensley, D. E., "Planning and controlling a research and development program: A case study." Master's thesis, Mass. Inst. Tech., Cambridge, Mass., 1955.

Berman, E. R., "Research allocation in a PERT network under continuous activity time-cost functions," *Management Science*, vol. 10, 1964.

——, Draft: "Theoretical structure of a methodology for R&D resource allocation," Research Analysis Corp., May 26, 1965.

Bernstein, A., and I. de Sola Pool, "Development and testing an evaluation model for research organization substructurs," presented at the 2nd Conf. on Research Program Effectiveness, Washington, D. C., July 1964.

Blinoff, V., and C. Pacifico, *Chem. Processing,* vol. 20, pp. 34–35, November 1957.

Blood, J. W., Ed., *The Management of Scientific Talent.* New York: American Management Association, 1963.

Blum, S., "Time, cost, and risk analysis in project planning," U. S. Army Frankford Arsenal Rept., August 22, 1963.

Bock, R. H., and W. K. Holstein, *Production Planning and Control.* Columbus, Ohio: Merrill Books, 1963.

Bonini, C. P., R. K. Jaedicke, and H. M. Wagner, *Management Controls: New Directions in Basic Research.* New York: McGraw-Hill, 1964.

Boothe, N. et al., *From Concept to Commercialization, A Study of the R&D Budget Allocation Process.* Stanford, Calif.: Stanford University, 1962.

Brandenburg, R. G., *A Descriptive Analysis of Project Selection.* Pittsburgh, Pa.: Carnegie Inst. Tech., July 1964.

——, "Toward a multi-space information conversion model of the research and development process," Carnegie Inst. Tech., Pittsburgh, Pa., Management Sciences Research Rept. 48, August 1965.

Bright, J. R., Ed., *Technological Planning on the Corporate Level* (Proc. Conf. at Harvard Business School). Cambridge, Mass.: Harvard University Press, 1962.

Busacker, R. G., and T. L. Saaty, *Finite Graphs and Networks: An Introduction With Applications.* New York: McGraw-Hill, 1965.

Bush, G. P. *Bibliography on Research Administration, Annotated.* Washington, D. C.: University Press, 1964.

Carroll, P., *Profit Control—How to Plug Profit Leaks.* New York: McGraw-Hill, 1962.

Caulfield, P., and R. Freshman, "Technology evaluation workbook," HQ Research and Technology Div., AFSC, Bolling AFB, Washington, D. C., January 1967.

Cetron, M. J., "Programmed functional indicies for laboratory evaluation, 'PROFILE,'" presented at the 16th Military Operations Research Symp. (MORS), Seattle, Wash., October 1965.

Cetron, M. J., "Quantitative utility estimates for science & technology 'Quest,'" presented at the 18th Military Operations Research Society, Fort Bragg, N. C., October 1966.

Cetron, M. J., and R. Freshman, "Some results of 'PROFILE,'" presented at the 17th MORS, Monterey, Calif., May 1966.

Charnes, A., "Conditional change-constrained approaches to organizational control," presented at the 2nd Conf. on Research Program Effectiveness, Washington, D. C., July 1964.

Charnes, A., and A. C. Stedry, "Optimal real-time control of research funding," presented at the 2nd Conf. on Research Program Effectiveness, Washington, D. C., July 1965.

Churchman, C. W., *Prediction and Optimal Control.* Englewood Cliffs, N. J.: Prentice-Hall, 1960.

Churchman, C. W., C. Kruytbosch, and P. Ratoosh, "The role of the research administrator," presented at the 2nd Conf. on Research Program Effectiveness, Washington, D. C., July 1965.

Clark, W., *The Gantt Chart.* London: Pitman and Sons, 1938.

Clarke, R. W., "Activity costing—key to progress in critical path analysis," *IRE Trans. on Engineering Management,* vol. EM-9, pp. 132–136, September 1962.

Combs, C. E., "Decision theory and engineering management," *IRE Trans. on Engineering Management,* vol. EM-9, pp. 149–154, December 1962.

Cook, E. F , "A better yardstick for project evaluation," *Armed Forces Management,* pp. 20–23, April 1958.

Cramer, R. H., and B. E. Smith, "Decision models for the selection of research projects," *The Engineering Economist,* vol. 9, pp. 1–20, January-February 1964.

Crisp, R. D., "Product planning for future projects," *Dun's Review and Modern Industry,* March 1958.

Dantzig, G. B., *Linear Programming and Extensions.* Princeton, N. J.: Princeton University Press, 1963.

Daubin, S. C., "The allocation of development funds: An analytic approach," *Naval Research Logistics Quart.,* vol. 3, pp. 263–276, September 1958.

Davidson, H. F., "Surveys as tools for acquisition of research management information," presented at the 2nd Conf. on Research Program Effectiveness, Washington, D. C., July 1964.

Davis, K., "The role of project management in scientific manufacturing," *IRE Trans. on Engineering Management,* vol. EM-9, pp. 109–113, September, 1962.

Dean, B. V., Ed., *Operations Research in Research and Development* (Proc. Conf. at Case Inst. Tech.). New York: Wiley, 1963.

——, "Allocation of technical resources in a firm," presented at the 1st Conf. on Research Program Effectiveness, Washington, D. C., July 1964.

——, "Stochastic networks in research planning," presented at the 2nd Conf. on Research Program Effectiveness, Washington, D. C., July 1965.

——, "Scoring and profitability models for evaluating and selecting engineering projects," Case Inst. Tech., Operation Research Group, 1964.

Dean, B. V., and Glogowski, "On the planning of research," ONR-AMC Project NOOR1141(19), July 1965.

——, and L. E. Hauser, "Advanced materiel systems planning," Case Inst. Tech., Cleveland, Ohio, Operations Research Group Tech. Memo. 65, ONR-AMC Project Nonr-1141(19) September 15, 1966.

Dean, B. V., and S. Sengupta, "On a method for determining corporate research development budgets," *Management Sciences, Models and Techniques,* vol. 2, C. W. Churchman and M. Verhulst, Eds. New York: Pergamon Press, 1960.

Dean, J., *Managerial Economics.* Englewood Cliffs, N. J.: Prentice-Hall, 1951, pp. 249–610.

——, "Measuring the productivity of capital," *Harvard Business Review,* vol, 32, January-February, 1954.

DeL'Estoile, "Resource allocation model," French Ministere Des Armees, Paris, France.

DeVries, M. G., *A Dynamic Model for Product Strategy Selection.* Ann Arbor, Mich.: The University of Michigan, 1963.

——, "The dynamic effects of planning horizons on the selection of optimal product strategies," *Management Science,* vol. 10, pp. 524–544, April 1964.

Disman, S., "Selecting R&D projects for profit," *Chem. Engrg.,* vol. 69, pp. 87–90, December 1962.

Dooley, A. R., "Interpretations of PERT," *Harvard Business Review,* vol. 42, pp. 160–171, March–April, 1964.

Drucker, R. F., "Twelve fables of research management," *Harvard Business Review,* vol. 41, January–February, 1963.

——, *Managing for Results.* New York: Harper & Row, 1964, pp. 25–50.

Easton, D., *A Systems Analysis of Polictical Life.* New York: Wiley, 1965.

Eisner, H., "Generalized network approach to the planning and scheduling of a research program," *Operations Research,* vol. 10, pp. 115–125, 1962.

——, "The application of information theory to the planning of research," presented at the TIMS American Internat'l Meeting, September 1963.

Elmaghraby, S. E., "An algebra for the analysis of generalized activity networks," *Management Sciences,* vol. 10, pp. 494–514, April 1964.

Emlet, H. E., "Methodological approach to planning and programming Air Force operational requirements," Research and Development (MAPORD), Analytic Services Rept. 65-4, October 1965.

Esch, M. E., "Planning assistance through technical evaluation 'pattern' " presented at the 17th Nat'l Aerospace Electronics Conf., Dayton, Ohio, May 1965.

Ewing, D. W., Ed., *Long-Range Planning of Management*. New York: Harper & Brothers, 1958.

Flood, M. W., "Research project evaluation," in *Coordination, Control, and Financing of Industrial Research*, A. R. Rubenstein, Ed. New York: Columbia University and King's Crown Press, 1955.

Fong, L. B. C., "A visual method of program balance and evaluation," *IRE Trans. on Engineering Management*, vol. EM-8, pp. 160–163, September 1961.

Ford, L. R., Jr., and D. R. Fulkerson, *Flows in Networks*. Princeton, N. J.: Princeton University Press, 1962.

Freeman, J. R., "A survey of the current status of accounting in the control of R&D," *IRE Trans. on Engineering Management*, vol. EM-9, pp. 179–181, December 1962.

Freeman, R. J., "A generalized network approach to project activity sequencing," *IRE Trans. on Engineering Management*, vol. EM-7, pp. 103–107, September 1960.

——, "An operational analysis of industrial research," Ph.D. dissertation, Department of Economics, Mass. Inst. Tech., Cambridge, Mass., 1957.

——, "A stochastic model for determining the size and allocation of the research budget," *IRE Trans. on Engineering Management*, vol. EM-7, pp. 2–7, March 1960.

——, "Quantitative methods in R&D management," *California Management Review*, vol. 11, pp. 36–44, 1960.

Fry, B. L., "SCANS—system description and comparison with PERT," *IRE Trans. on Engineering Management*, vol. EM-9, pp. 122–129, September 1962.

Galbraith, J. K., *The Affluent Society*. New York: Mentor Books, 1958.

Gargiulo, G. R., J. Hannoch, D. B. Hertz, and T. Zang, "Developing systematic procedures for directing research programs," *IRE Trans. on Engineering Management*, vol. EM-8, pp. 24–29, March 1961.

Gloskey, C. R., "Research on a research department: An analysis of economic decisions on projects," *IRE Trans. on Engineering Management*, vol. EM-7, pp. 166–172, December 1960.

——, M.A. thesis, Mass. Inst. Tech., Cambridge, Mass., 1959.

Goldberg, L. C., "Dimensions in the evaluation of technical ideas in an industrial research laboratory," M.S. thesis, Northwestern University, Evanston, Ill., 1963.

Guy, K., *Laboratory Organization and Administration.* London: Macmillan, and New York: St. Martin's Press, 1962.

Hackney, J. W., "How to appraise capital investments," *Chem. Engrg.*, vol. 68, pp. 146–167, May 1961.

Hahn, W. A., and H. D. Pickering, "Program planning in a science-based service organization," presented at the 2nd Conf. on Research Program Effectiveness, Washington, D. C., July 1965.

Hansen, B. J., *Practical PERT Including Critical Path Method.* Washington, D. C.: American House, 1964.

Harrel, C. G., "Selecting projects for research," in *Research in Industry: Its Organization and Management*, C. C. Furnas, Ed. New York: Van Nostrand, 1948, ch. 7, pp. 104–144.

Heckert, J. E., and J. B. Willson, *Business Budgeting and Control.* New York: Ronald Press, 1955.

Henke, R., *Effective Research & Development for the Smaller Company.* Houston: Gulf Publ. Co., 1963.

Hertz, D. B., *The Theory and Practice of Industrial Research.* New York: McGraw-Hill, 1950.

Hertz, D. B., and P. G. Carlson, "Selection, evaluation, and control of research and development projects," in *Operations Research in Research and Development*, B. V. Dean, Ed. New York: Wiley, 1963, pp. 170–188.

Hertz, D. B., and A. H. Rubenstein, *Costs, Budgeting and Economics of Industrial Research* (Proc. 1st Ann. Conf. of Industrial Research). New York: Columbia University Press, 1951.

Hertz, D. B., and A. H. Rubenstein, Eds., *Proc. 3rd Ann. Conf. on Industrial Research: Research Operations in Industry.* New York: Columbia University Press, 1953, esp. pp. 55, 153.

Hess, S. W., "A dynamic programming approach to R&D budgeting and project selection," *IRE Trans. on Engineering Management*, vol. EM-9, pp. 170–179, December 1962.

——, "On research and development budgeting and project selection," Ph.D. dissertation, Case Inst. Tech., Cleveland, Ohio, 1960.

Heyel, C., Ed., *Handbook of Industrial Research Management.* New York: Reinhold, 1959.

Hickey, A. E., Jr., "The systems approach: Can engineers use the scientific method?" *IRE Trans. on Engineering Management*, vol. EM-7, pp. 72–80, June 1960.

Hildenbrand, W., "Application of graph theory to stochastic scheduling," presented at the 2nd Conf. on Rresearch Program Effectiveness, Washington, D. C., July 1965.

Hill, F. I., and L. A. Roepcke, "An analytical method to aid in the choice of long range study tasks," presented at the U. S. Army Operations Research Symp. at Rock Island Arsenal, May 1964.

Hill, L. S., "Toward an improved basis of estimating and controlling R&D tasks," presented at the 10th Nat'l Meeting of the American Association of Cost Engineers, Philadelphia, Pa., June 1966.

Hitchock, L. B., "Selection and evaluation of R&D projects," *Research Management*, vol. 6, pp. 231–244, May 1963.

Hodge, M. H., Jr., et al., "Basic research as a corporate function," Stanford, Calif: Stanford University, 1961.

Honig, J. G., "An evaluation of research and development problems," presented at the 1st Conf. on Research Program Effectiveness, Washington, D. C., July 1964.

Horowitz, I., "The economics of industrial research," Ph.D. dissertation, Mass. Inst. Tech., Cambridge, Mass., 1959.

Janofsky, L., and S. Sobelman, "Balancing equations to project feasibility studies," presented at Operations Research Society of America, Detroit, Mich., October 1960.

Johnson, E. A., and H. S. Milton, "A proposed cost-of-research index," *IRE Trans. on Engineering Management*, vol. EM-8, pp. 172–176, December 1961.

Johnson, R. A., F. E. Kast, and J. E. Rosenzweig, *The Theory and Management of Systems*. New York: McGraw-Hill, 1963.

Karger, D. C., and R. G. Murkick, *Managing Engineering and Research*. New York: Industrial Press, 1963, pp. 193–253.

Kelley, J. E., Jr. and M. R. Walker, "Critical-path planning and scheduling," *Proc. of the Eastern Joint Computer Conf.*, 1959; see also, *Operations Research*, vol. 9, pp. 296–320, 1961.

Kiefer, D. M., "Winds of change in industrial chemical research," *Chemical Engineering News*, vol. 42, pp. 88–109, March 1964.

Klein, B., and W. Meckling, "Applications of operations research to development decisions," *Operations Research*, vol. 6, pp. 352–363, May–June 1958.

——, "The decision-making problem in development," in *The Rate and Direction of Inventive Activity*. Princeton, N. J.: Princeton University Press, 1962, pp. 477–508.

Kliever, W. R. and R. Z. Bancroft, "Choosing and evaluating research projects," *Product Engrg.*, June 1953.

Koontz, H., *Toward A Unified Theory of Management*. New York: McGraw-Hill, 1963.

Landi, D. M., *A Model of Investment Planning for Research and Development*. Evanston, Ill.: Northwestern University, 1964.

Leermakers, J. A., "The selection and screening of projects," in *Getting the Most from Product Research and Development*. New York: American Management Association, 1955, pp. 81–94.

Levy, F. K., G. L. Thompson, and J. E. Wiest, "Multiship, multishop, workload-smoothing program," *Naval Research Logistics Quart.*, vol. 11, March 1962.

Lipetz, B.-A., *Measurement of Effectiveness of Science Research*. Carlisle, Mass.: Intermedia, 1965.

Lytle, A. A., "The yardsticks for research success," *Product Engrg.*, vol. 30, pp. 34–37, October 1959.

Magee, J. F., "How to use decision trees in capital investment," *Harvard Business Review*, vol. 42, pp. 79–96, September–October 1964.

Manning, P. D., "Long range planning of product research," in *R&D Series #4*. New York: American Management Association, 1957.

Marples, D. L., "The decisions of engineering design," *IRE Trans. on Engineering Management*, vol. EM-8, pp. 55–71, June 1961.

Marquis, D. G., "Organization and management of R&D," presented at the 1st Conf. on Research Program Effectiveness, Washington, D. C., July 1964.

Marschak, T. A., "Models, rules of thumb, and development decisions," in *Operations Research in Research and Development*, B. V. Dean, Ed., New York: Wiley, 1963, pp. 247–263.

——, "Strategy and organization in a system development project," in *The Rate and Direction of Inventive Activity*. Princeton, N. J.: Princeton University Press, 1962, pp. 509–548.

Marshall, A. W., and W. H. Meckling," Predictability of the costs, time and success of development," in *The Rate and Direction of Inventive Activity*. Princeton, N. J.: Princeton University Press, 1962, pp. 461–475.

Martino, J. P., Caulfield, M. Cetron, H. Davidson, H. Liebowitz, and L. Roepcke, "A method for balanced allocation of resources among R&D projects," USAF Office of Scientific Research, Tech. Rept., February 1967.

Massey, R. J., "A new publication: Department of the Navy RDT&E management guide," presented at the 1st Conf. on Research Program Effectiveness, Washington, D. C., July 1964.

McMaster, S. B., "Study of project selection techniques in an R&D organization," Master's thesis, Northwestern University, Evanston, Ill., 1964, (unpublished).

McMillian, C., and R. F., Ganzalez, *Systems Analysis: A Computer Approach to Decision Models*. Homewood, Ill.: Richard D. Irwin, 1965.

Mees, C. E. K., and J. A. Leermakers, *The Organization of Industrial Scientific Research*, 2nd ed. New York: McGraw-Hill, 1950, esp. ch. 11.

Mellon, W. G., *An Approach to a General Theory of Priorities: An Outline of Problems and Methods*, Princeton University Econometric Research Program, Memo. 42, Princeton, N. J.: Princeton University Press, 1962.

Miller, D. W., and M. K. Starr, *Executive Decisions and Operations Research*. Englewood Cliffs, N. J.: Prentice-Hall, 1960.

Miller, R. W., *Schedule, Cost and Profit Control with PERT*. New York: McGraw-Hill, 1963.

Miller, T. T., "Projecting the profitability of new products," American Management Association, New York, N. Y., Special Rept. 20, pp. 20–33, 1957.

Morgenstern, O., R. W., Shephard, and H. G. Grabowski, "Adaption of graph theory and an input-output model to research description and evaluation," presented at the 2nd Conf. on Research Program Effectiveness, Washington, D. C., July 1965.

Moshman, J., J. Johnson, and M. Larson, "RAMPS—A technique for resource allocation and multi-project scheduling," *Proc. of the Spring Joint Computer Conf.* Baltimore, Md." Spartan Books, 1963, pp. 17–27.

Mottley, C. M., and R. D. Newton, "The selection of projects for industrial research," *Operations Research*, vol. 7, pp. 740–751, November– December 1959.

National Science Foundation, Washington, D. C., "Science and Engineering in American Industry," Final Rept. on 1953–1954 Survey, October 1956.

Norden, P. V., "Curve fitting for a model of applied research and development scheduling," *IBM J. Research and Development*, vol. 2, pp. 232–248, July 1958.

——, "Some properties of R&D project recovery limits," presented at the 2nd Conf. on Research Program Effectiveness, Washington, D. C., July 1965.

——, "The study committee for research, development and engineering (SCARDE): A progress report and an invitation to participate," *IRE Trans. on Engineering Management*, vol. EM-8, pp. 3–10, March 1961.

Norton, J. H., "The role of subjective probability in evaluating new product ventures," *Chem. Engrg. Prog. Symp.*, Ser. 42, vol. 59, pp. 49–54, 1963.

Nutt, A. B., "An approach to research and development effectiveness," *IEEE Trans. on Engineering Management*, pp. 103–112, September 1965.

Nyland, H. V., and G. R. Towle, "How we evaluate return from research," *Nat'l Association of Cost Accountants Bull.*, May 1956.

Olsen, F., "The control of research funds," in *Coordination, Control and Financing of Industrial Research*, A. H. Rubenstein, Ed. New York: King Crown Press and Columbia University, 1955, pp. 99–108.

Pacifico, C., "Is it worth the risk?," *Chem. Engrg. Prog.*, vol. 60, pp. 19–21, May 1964.

Pappas, G. F., and D. D. MacLaren, "An approach to research planning," *Chem. Eng. Prog.*, vol. 57, pp. 65–69, May 1961.

Pound, W. H., "Research project selection: Testing a model in the field," *IEEE Trans. on Engineering Management*, vol. EM-11, pp. 16–22, March 1964.

Quinn, J. B., *Yardsticks for Industrial Research: The Evaluation of Research and Development Output.* New York: Ronald Press, 1959.

Quinn, J. B., and J. A. Mueller, "Transferring research results to operations" *Harvard Business Review*, vol. 41, January–February 1963.

Rae, R. H., and Synnott, "Project RDE, a framework for the comprehension and analysis of research and development effectiveness," USAF Flight Dynamics Lab., Dayton, Ohio TM 63-22, October 1961.

——, "A systems development planning structure," ABT Associates Inc., November 1955.

——, "An Automated Scenario Generator," ABT Associates, Inc., January 1966,

Raiffa, H., and R. Schalaifer, *Applied Statistical Decision Theory.* Boston, Mass.: Harvard University Press, 1957.

Roberts, E. B., *The Dynamics of Research and Development.* New York: Harper & Row, 1964.

Roberts, C. S., "Product selection—witchcraft or wisdom," *IRE Trans. on Engineering Management*, vol. EM-6, pp. 68–71, September 1959.

Roman, D. D. "Organization for control," *J. Academy of Management* (Proc. of the Annual Meeting, Pittsburgh, December 1962).

——, "The PERT system: An appraisal of program evaluation review technique," *J. Academy of Management*, vol. 5, April 1962.

——, "Project management recognizes R&D performance," *J. Academy of Management*, vol. 7, pp. 7–20, March 1964.

Roman, D. D., and J. Johnson, "On the allocation of common physical resources to multiple development tasks," presented at the 18th Military Operations Research Society, Fort Bragg, N. C., October 1966.

Roseboom, J. H , C. E. Clark, and W. Fazer, "Application of a technique for research and development program evaluation," *Operations Research,* vol. 7, pp. 651–653, September-October 1959.

Rosen, E. M., and W. E. Souder, "A method for allocating R&D expenditures," *IEEE Trans. on Engineering Management,* vol. EM-12, pp. 87–93, September 1955.

Rubenstein, A. H., Ed., *Coordination, Control, and Financing of Industrial Research.* New York: King's Crown Press and Columbia University, 1955.

——, "Evaluation of the possibilities of research effort in a new field of technology, Sweden,'. vol. 6, pp. 239–251, 1965.

——, "Setting criteria for R&D," *Harvard Business Review,* pp. 95–104, January-February 1957.

Rubenstein, A. H., and I. Horowitz, "Project selection in new technical fields," *Proc. Nat'l Electronics Conf.,* vol. 15, 1959.

——, "Studies of project selection behavior in industry," in *Operations Research in Research and Development,* B. V. Dean, Ed. New York: Wiley, 1963, pp. 189–205.

Rubenstein, A. H., and C. W. Haberstroh, Eds., *Some Theories of Organization.* Homewood, Ill.: Richard D. Irwin, 1960.

——, "Some common concepts and tentative findings from a ten-project program of research on R&D management," presented at the 2nd Conf. on Research Program Effectiveness, Washington, D. C,, July 1965.

Saaty, T. L., *Mathematical Methods of Operations Research.* New York: McGraw-Hill, 1959.

Sacco, W. J., "On the choice of long range study tasks," Ballistic Research Lab. Memo Rept. 1963, August 1965.

Savage, J. J., *The Foundation of Statistics.* New York: Wiley, 1954.

Scherer, F. M., "Time-cost tradeoffs in uncertain empirical research projects," *Naval Research Logistics Quart. ONR,* vol. 13, March 1966.

Schweyer, H. E., "Graphs can reveal project feasibility," *Chem. Engrg.* pp. 175–178, September 1961.

Seiler, R. E., *Improving the Effectiveness of Research and Development.* New York: McGraw-Hill, 1965.

Shank, R. J., "Planning to meet goals," in *Optimum Use of Engineering Talent, AMA Rept. 58.* Cambridge, Mass.: Riverside Press, 1961.

Shaller, H. I., "An exploratory study in research planning methodology," Dept. of the Navy, Washington, D. C., ONR Tech. Rept. ACR/NAR-27, September 1963.

Sher, I. H., and E. Garfield, "New tools for improving and evaluating the effectiveness of research," presented at the 2nd Conf. on Research Program Effectiveness, Washington, D. C., July 1965.

Silk, L. S., "An optimal method for selection of product development projects," presented at the 15th Nat'l Meeting of the Operations Research Society of America, Washington, D. C., May 1959.

S. Herbert, *The New Science of Management Decisions.* New York: Harper & Row, 1960.

S. Herbert, *The Research Revolution.* New York: McGraw-Hill, 1960.

Sobelman, S. A., "Modern dynamic approach to product development," Picatinny Arsenal, Dover, N. J., December 1958.

——, "An optimal method for selection of product development projects," presented at the 15th Nat'l Meeting of the Operations Research Society of America, Washington, D. C., May 1959.

Sobin, B., and A. Proschan, "Search and evaluation methods in research and exploratory development," presented at the 2nd Conf. on Research Program Effectiveness, Washington, D. C., July 1965.

——, "Proposal generation and evaluation methods in research and exploratory developments," Research Analysis Corp., Paper RAC-P-11, November 1965.

Special Projects Office, *PERT Summary Report I.* Washington, D. C.: Bureau of Naval Weapons, 1959.

Spencer, M. H., and L. Siegelman, *Managerial Economics.* Homewood, Ill.: Richard D. Irwin, 1964, pp. 461–567.

Stanley, A. O., and K. K. White, *Organizing the R&D Function.* AMA Research Study No. 72. New York: American Management Association, 1965.

Steiner, G. A., *Managerial Long-Range Planning.* New York: McGraw-Hill, 1963.

Stilian, C. N. et al., *PERT—A New Management Planning and Control Technique.* New York: American Management Association, 1962.

Stoessl, L., "Linear programming techniques applied to research planning," Master's thesis, U. S. Naval Post-Graduate School, 1964.

Stoodley, F. H., "A Study of methods which could improve the relevance of naval applied research and exploratory development," Office Naval Research Rept., June 1, 1966.

Sullivan, C. I., "CPI management looks at R&D project evaluation," *Indus. Engrg. Chem.*, vol. 53, pp. 42A–46A, September 1961.

Taylor, F. W., *Scientific Management.* New York: Harper & Brothers, 1947.

Theil, H., "On the optimal management of research; a mathematical approach," presented at the Conf. of the Internat'l Federation of Operations Research Societies, Oslo, Norway, July 1963.

Thompson, R. E., "PERT—Tool for R&D project decisionmaking," *IRE Trans. on Engineering Management*, vol. EM-9, pp. 116–121, September 1962.

University of California, Berkeley, "A system engineering approach to corporate long-range planning," Department of Engineering, Rept. EEP-62-1. June 1962.

Walters, J. E., *Research Management: Principles and Practice*. Washington, D. C.: Spartan Books, 1965.

Wasson, C. R., *The Economics of Managerial Decision*. New York: Appleton-Century-Crofts, 1965, pp. 147–218.

Wells, H. A., "Systems planners guide," presented at the 18th Military Operations Research Society Meeting, Fort Bragg, N. C., October 1966.

——, "The allocation of research and development resources," Wright Air Development Center, August 1958 (unpublished).

Wachold, G. R., "An investigation of the technical effectiveness of a government research and development test and evaluation organization," Navy Missile Center, Pt. Mugu, Calif., July 1965 (unpublished).

CHAPTER TEN

SYSTEMATIC APPROACHES TO TECHNICAL PLANNING

We can no longer afford the luxury of developing everything. Traditionally, our country's products and services are based on what *happens to be available* technologically, and not upon technology that *could have been* available to produce superior products or services if the product's parameters had been available to the planners.

The subject of this chapter then is the integration of environmental analysis and corporate strategy into operational plans for the R&D function. By doing so we are saying that the future is amenable to analysis, and susceptible to shaping. Certain eventualities can be encouraged and that whatever will be is to a large extent affected by what you want it to be—provided you plan and commit resources to that purpose.

We have chosen articles which will help to emphasize the required explicitness of technical planning. Joseph Martino discusses the task in terms of integrating explorative and normative technological forecasting. By combining estimates of future needs with technological forecasts of capabilities, the R&D manager will be in a position to evaluate the feasibility of his goals, examine competitive technologies and their cost and performance implications, and select the best research avenues for reaching his objectives.

Some of the most advanced managerial techniques are being practiced by the military—a natural result of the size of military R&D budgets. Cetron's article "Learn the three Rx's" discusses the integration of forecasts and goals into R&D planning and illustrates the specific techniques being tested by the U. S. Navy. These specific methodologies are applicable to any large R&D effort, especially those with a variety of different technologies and many multi-disciplinary projects.

Abernathy and Rosenbloom, in the last article in this chapter, discuss the difference between parallel and sequential R&D strategies. This is an important subject because different projects will require differing strategies. The principle focus in this article, based on studies of 14 R&D projects, is the information requirements for a sound choice between the two strategies and the consequences of choosing a strategy on the basis of incomplete information.

THE USE OF TECHNOLOGICAL FORECASTS FOR PLANNING RESEARCH*

Joseph P. Martino
Office of Aerospace Research
U.S. AIR FORCE

The planning of research is a broad field and many articles have already been written on the subject,[1] but little has been written about the influence of technological forecasting on research planning. Air Force experience has shown that technological forecasts are useful for planning research, including choosing research areas, selecting projects within these areas, and formulating sound personnel policies. However, to do this effectively one must have a clear understanding of categories of technical effort.

DEFINITIONS

The term "research" is defined here as an attempt to acquire new knowledge about some phenomenon in the universe, or about some phenomenon in an abstract model of a portion of the universe, which is not necessarily made with an application in mind. The definition makes no distinction between basic and applied research, since the difference between the two terms is usually in the motivation of the researcher, and this is not an objectively measurable quantity. Although an application may well be in the researcher's thoughts, no inference is made here about what is going on in his mind while he is doing his research.

There is, however, a meaningful distinction between research and development: development is an attempt to construct, assemble, or prepare for the first time, a device, material, technique, or procedure, meeting a prescribed set of specifications or desired characteristics and intended to

* Published originally in *Technological Forecasting for Industry and Government* by James Bright (Editor), New York: Prentice-Hall, 1968.

[1] J. B. Quinn, and R. M. Cavanaugh, "Fundamental Research Can Be Planned," *Harvard Business Review*, January-February, 1964; W. L. Swager, "Improving the Management of Research," *Business Horizons*, Vol. 2, No. 4, Winter, 1959, and E. D. Reeves, "Industrial Research: A Kind of Business Strategy," *Chemical and Engineering News*, Vol. 43, No. 43 (Oct. 25, 1965), 92–97.

Figure 1. A Common "Research-to-Product" Model.

solve a specific problem. This definition includes not only mechanical devices and hardware, but such things as computer programs, chemicals, and other materials. The essence of this definition is that development is intended to meet some set of specifications in order to solve a specific problem.

The interaction between research and development is shown in Figure 1, which depicts a common model of the way research progresses into products. This is usually phrased in such terms as "getting an idea out of the laboratory and into production." The kindest thing one can say for this model is that it is erroneous. Research and development are two entirely different categories of activity, and there is no neat linear progression from one into the other, as this model would imply.

Figure 2 shows a more nearly correct model in which research feeds a pool of knowledge which is drawn upon for exploratory and advanced development, and for systems engineering. This model recognizes that additional knowledge is added to the pool at each of these stages. It was originated by Al Shapero[2] and has received support from the recent report of the Materials Advisory Board.[3]

Companies perform research for the following reasons:

1. To say competitive in present areas of business;
2. To produce new products to enter new areas of business;

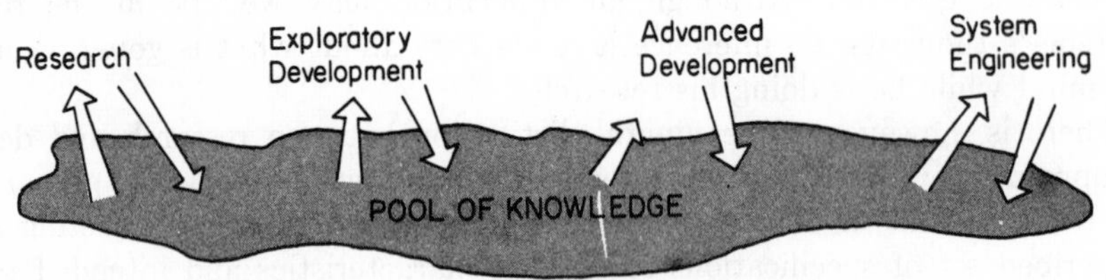

Figure 2. Correct "Research-to-Product" Model.

---

[2] A. Shapero, *Diffusion of Innovations Resulting from Research*, Stanford Research Institute, 1965.

[3] *Report of the Ad-Hoc Committee on Principles of Research Engineering Interaction*, National Research Council, Washington, D.C., July, 1966.

3. To maintain a pool of talent which can be used for problem solving or advising management;
4. To exploit outside discoveries which occur elsewhere in the field of science;
5. To anticipate outside threats to present markets from discoveries elsewhere in science;
6. To avoid an adverse patent or know-how situation which might erode present business or freeze a company out of a new area of business;
7. To give a firm an image of progressiveness.

Research can be divided into three main categories—connecting, supporting, and pioneering.

Connecting Research is the research an organization does for the purpose of remaining in touch with the world of science—to see what is going on. In order to keep up with the latest activities in any field of science a company has to have a ticket to the club. The ticket is being able to say something which is of interest to the other researchers in the field. In short, if an organization is to keep in touch with the latest activities in any field of science, it must have at least one man who is doing high-quality research in that field of science.

Supporting Research is the research a company does to support its present products and markets. This, too, must be high-quality research, on the frontiers of the area of science in which it is done. However, the purpose of this research is to find answers to problems encountered while improving products in order to keep abreast of competition. It should not be confused with "quick-fix" efforts to cure some immediate production or application problem. The problem which provides the initial motivation for a piece of supporting research must be one which is going to be around for some time, because there will be a considerable time lag, of the order of years, between initiation of the research and incorporation of the results into products. The problems must be chosen so that they will still be of interest when the answer is found.

Pioneering Research is undertaken in order to enter new fields and create new products and markets. Like the other two types of research, it must be of high quality, and it must be on the frontiers of the area of science in which it is done. Choices of research areas and projects for pioneering research will be discussed later.

Figure 3 shows the requirements for performing each of these categories of research. Connecting research requires approximately one fulltime man who will do 1 per cent or less of the research being done in that field. Re-

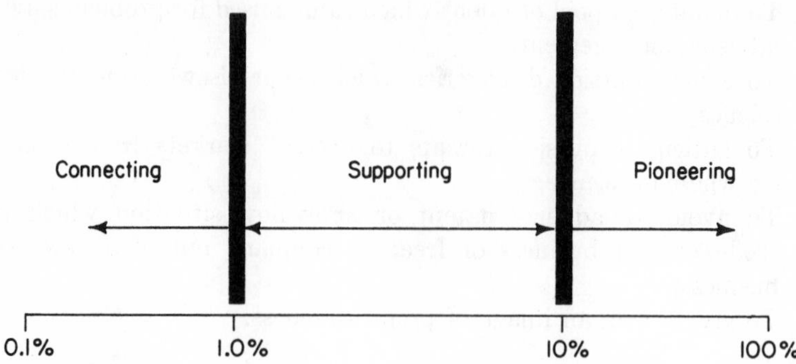

Figure 3. Research Efforts Required for a Company to Perform Each of the Three Categories of Research (As a Percentage of Industry-wide Activity).

search to support present markets requires the performance of 1 per cent to 10 per cent of all the research in the pertinent field. To pioneer in some field, a company must plan to do over 10 per cent of all the research in that area. These percentages tend to vary with the field of science, and with the number and activity of competitors.

Figure 4 shows the relationship between the goals of research and the kinds of research. In order to stay competitive, a company clearly has

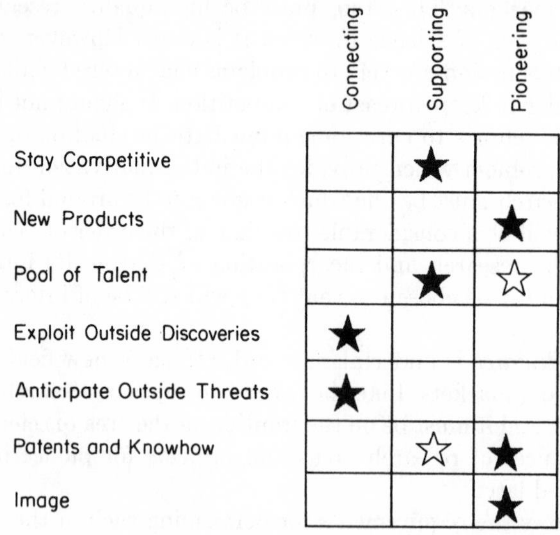

Figure 4. Relationship Between Goals of Research and Types of Research.

to do supporting research. To get new products, it needs to do pioneering research. A poor of talent is provided primarily by supporting research although pioneering research also accomplishes this objective. Exploiting outside discoveries and anticipating outside threats are facilitated by connecting research. Protecting and generating a patents and know-how position are aided somewhat by supporting research but are achieved primarily through pioneering research. Finally, producing a company image for progressiveness requires pioneering research.

RESEARCH PLANNING

If a company is going to plan for research, it must plan:

1. The goals and strategy of the research organization;
2. The choice of research areas;
3. The choice of projects within research areas;
4. The research personnel (their recruitment, career development, and purging);
5. The organization of the research program (discipline vs. project research, and organizational and physical barriers between the research group and the rest of the organization);
6. The communication patterns with the rest of the organization (the researcher with his peers, with the users of his research, and with the executives who make decisions about his research);
7. The motivation and incentives for the researchers; and
8. The research facilities.

APPLICATION OF TECHNOLOGICAL FORECASTING

Figure 5 shows a schematic of a manufacturing process. From suppliers, companies receive raw material, intermediate products, and components. These are processed into a final product. From the standpoint of research planning it is necessary to consider each of the four items as sets of performance characteristics, not just as physical items. Similarly, the processes by which this transformation takes place must be considered as generalized rather than detailed assembly processes. This approach makes it possible to inquire how research can lead to improvements in both the materials and the processes involved in the manufacture of products.

Performance characteristics include such things as:

1. The function(s) performed by the product;
2. Factors (such as time, distance etc.) of function performance;

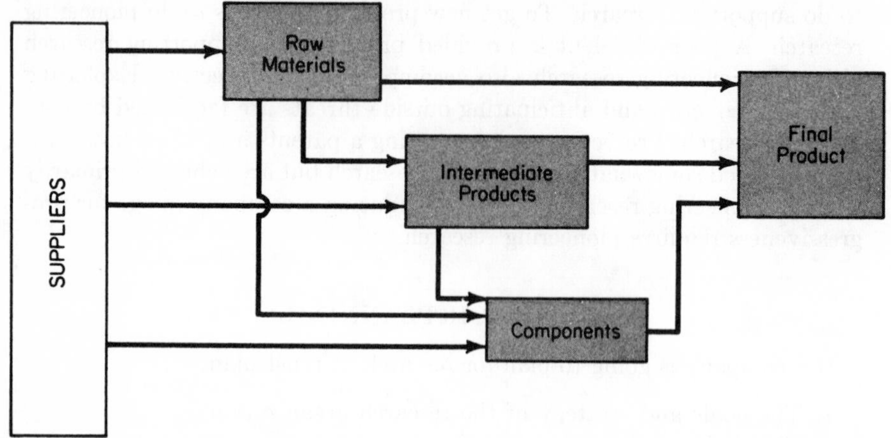

Figure 5. Schematic of Manufacturing Process.

3. Size and weight;
4. Dollar cost;
5. Other problems relating to handling, storage, manufacturing operations, lifetime, etc..

The idea of viewing a product as a set of performance characteristics may be clarified by some examples. The performance characteristics of the whale oil lamp were also satisfied by both the kerosene lamp and the electric light. The performance characteristics of vacuum tubes in portable radios were also satisfied by transistors. The performance characteristics of plant-derived dyes, such as indigo, were also satisfied by synthetically produced chemical dyes. The key point is to avoid getting bogged down in detailed questions of a product's composition and how it is made, and, instead, to look at what it does and how well it does it.

Similarly, the transformation processes involved in converting raw materials, intermediate products, and components into final products must be viewed from a more generalized aspect. Are they chemical concentration processes? Are they heat transfer or mechanical assembly processes? If an open-hearth steel furnace is viewed only as an assemblage of bricks, pipes and so forth, it is easy to overlook the fact that steel making involves a heat transfer process which can also be performed by an electric arc furnace, or, perhaps in the future, by a solar furnace operating in space or on the moon. As another example, the assembly of electronic components into a radio set, either manually or mechanically, is a mechanical assembly process which can also be performed by methods which produce printed circuits.

The reason for looking at a manufacturing process in terms of the performance characteristics of the intermediate and final products, and the transformation processes used, is to make it clear that a product may be replaced by another product which has the same performance characteristics, but is based on an entirely different field of science. The indigo industry was overturned, not by a better species of indigo-producing plant, but by developments in the field of chemistry. The kerosene lamp industry was overturned, not by better petroleum-refining methods, but by developments in the field of electromagnetics. The radio manufacturing industry is undergoing a revolution brought about by advances in solid state physics which have nothing to do with vacuum tubes.

One of the major functions which a research organization performs is to warn a firm of the possibility that a field of science which is unrelated to its product or the processes by which it manufactures can provide performance characteristics which would permit substitution for the company's components or intermediate products, transformation processes, or worse yet, final products. Another function, of course, is to permit the firm to take advantage of these advances before competitors do.

Here, then, is a very important role for technological forecasting. Research planning staffs must evaluate the possibility that any given area of science could provide a threat or an area which might be exploited. In those areas where such a possibility exists, a technological forecast is needed. Such a forecast should estimate the performance level to be expected and the probability that this performance level will be achieved by a certain time. Figure 6 illustrates the type of forecast which should be used.

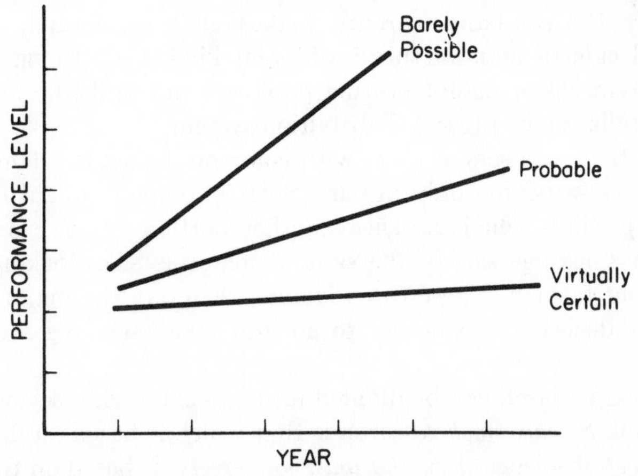

Figure 6. Forecast of Performance Obtained from a Field of Science.

Companies then have to decide whether they want to ignore that field of science completely, connect with it, or do supporting research in that field. If the probability of the field's development is extremely low, the company may decide it can ignore the field. If the likelihood of an advance is small, but still too big to ignore, the company may want to hire a man to do nothing but keep in touch with the field and warn the firm of any pertinent developments. Finally, if the likelihood of an advance is sufficiently high, a company may wish to do supporting research in that field rather than become boxed in by competitors who may gain a patent or know-how position.

PIONEERING RESEARCH

Most important is the field of pioneering research. The primary purpose of pioneering research is to give a company new products. The industrial function consists of three parts: a set of manufacturing processes and skills; a distribution system geared to reach a certain set of users; and a set of users with a common demand. These users are not really a part of the organization and, in fact, a company and its competitors are competing for them, but they are essential to operations.

If a company is to manufacture a new product, it should take advantage of at least one of these three areas. It might decide to manufacture a new product which uses current manufacturing processes and skills, but is aimed at a different market; e.g., if it manufactures automobile radios, it might decide to go into the business of making portable radios. Or it might wish to capitalize on a distribution system which is set up to reach a certain set of users. If a company currently makes one type of kitchen appliance, it might decide to manufacture a different kind, even though this called for a different set of manufacturing processes and skills, because the firm could capitalize on its present distribution system.

Finally, there are sets of users with common demands—demands which a company is satisfying only in part. Such a company might decide to go to a new product which satisfies another portion of the same demand; e.g., nylon stockings satisfy the same demand as silk stockings although in a different fashion. These three factors, then, are the major constraints on a firm's decision on whether to go into manufacturing a specific new product.

Pioneering research can be divided into two categories: science push and demand pull. *Science push* research is that which is based on developments within a field of science. *Demand pull*, conversely, is based on the discovery or realization that there is a demand for a certain product or service but that pioneering research will be needed in order to make that product or service possible.

In science push research, the major role of technological forecasting is that of forecasting instrumentation technology. New instrumentation almost always makes possible advances in various fields of science. By way of examples from the past, the computer has tremendously speeded up old fields such as differential equations and statistics, and has even created new fields of science, such as computational linguistics. Two new techniques, nuclear magnetic reasonance and electron spin resonance, both originally developed out of research in physics, have had a tremendous impact upon the field of chemistry. In some cases they make it possible to cut chemical analysis time to one-tenth or one-twentieth of that required by previous methods. A new device—the laser—is currently having a major impact on on the field of aerodynamics by making it possible to examine transient flow fields and shock waves in much more detail than was previously possible.

All of these developments have had and are having tremendous impact upon many fields of science. Other devices can be foreseen which will have similar impact in the future. For instance, within the next few years, the improvements in clocks for scientific research should permit time measurements which are accurate to a resolution of one picosecond (i.e., it will be possible to divide one second into a million parts and then divide each one of those parts into a million parts). Clocks with this resolution will make it possible to test the general theory of relativity for the first time.

Another upcoming development is that of an electron microscope with a beam of energy of ten million electron volts and a resolution of about half an Angstrom unit. Since atoms have a diameter of about one to two Angstrom units, this new electron microscope will literally make it possible to take a snapshot of a molecule, showing the position of all the atoms in that molecule. The impact of this capability on the field of chemistry will be tremendous.

In a similar way, forecasts of the technology of scientific instrumentation will show which fields of science can be expected to advance most rapidly. It then becomes necessary to estimate what new products can be derived from advances in these fields. If the potential new products are of interest to an organization, then it would be desirable for the firm to do pioneering research in these fields.

Demand pull research starts at the other end. Through such things as demographic and economic analyses, demands are derived which would be difficult or impossible to satisfy without technological and scientific advances. The need for such advances may result from shortages of certain required materials, side effects of current technology, or deficiencies in current technology.

An example of a clearly predictable shortage which will call for substitutes is animal protein. It is reasonably clear that, before the end of this century, there simply will not be enough animal protein available to provide an adequate diet for all the people of the world. Some substitute is going to be necessary.

To cite another example, by the mid-1980's there will not be enough animals slaughtered to provide sufficient leather for shoes for all the people who are going to be living at that time. Some substitute for shoe leather is going to be required.

Also, as the population increases and as the literacy rate increases, within a few years there will not be enough newsprint available to print all the books and newspapers which will be required. Some substitute for newsprint will be needed.

A side effect of current technology which is clearly going to demand alternative technologies is environmental pollution. The combustion process in the automobile engine is so inefficient that we simply cannot live in an environment containing large numbers of automobiles. Some changes in the technology of automobile engines are going to be required.

Probably the classic example of inefficiency in technology is that of the manually operated telephone system. If the telephone system that we have in the United States today, handling as many calls as it now handles, had to be run with the manual operation of the 1920's, there simply would not be enough women in the United States to supply all the operators needed. Clearly, here was a demand which, in fact, was foreseen by the telephone system and the demand was met by improved technologies.

Once demands have been identified, they must be reduced to research opportunities. Figure 7 shows how this is done. First, it is necessary to lay out broad alternative approaches. For instance, if the demand to be filled is the supply of adequate protein, direct synthesis of protein, improved fishing, or breeding of plants which have adequate quantities of the necessary proteins in them might be considered.

For each of these broad alternative approaches it is necessary to define one or more processes and methods by which the approach might be realized. For instance, if it were decided that "improved methods of fishing" was a worthwhile approach to a solution for the protein problem, then possible processes and methods might include deliberate fish farming, new ways of catching fish in the open sea, or methods for attracting fish to a place where they could be caught.

The performance and cost objectives would have to be determined for

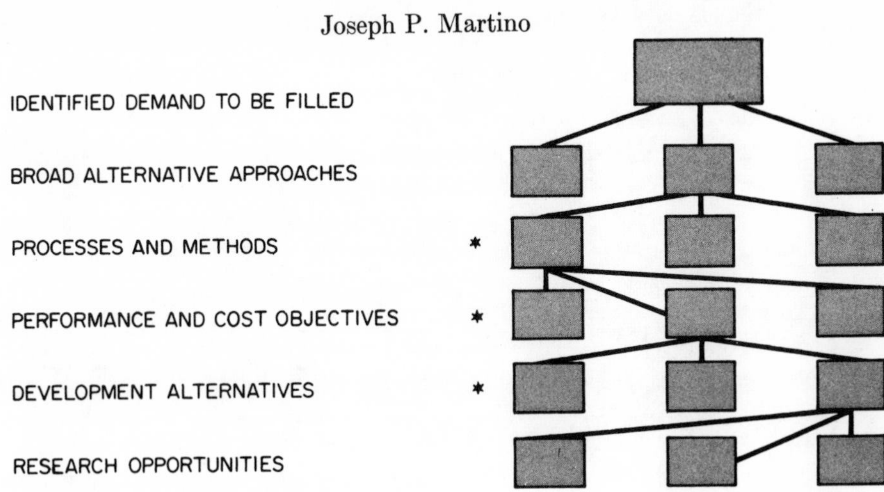

Figure 7. Reduction of Demands to Research Opportunities.

each of these processes and methods. Clearly, high cost can be tolerated only if it is accompanied by high performance. Low performance may be tolerated if it can be obtained at low cost.

The next step is the determination of development alternatives for each of the performance and cost objectives. For instance, it might be decided to develop an electronic fish locator which would make it possible to locate fish on the open sea. In order to provide adequate performance characteristics at acceptable cost, certain technological barriers may have to be removed. This will, in turn, give rise to further research opportunities. The role of technological forecasts in this process is to forecast: (1) the cost and performance of various processes and methods, and (2) the performance of the components and materials which can be considered in development alternatives for these performance and cost objectives.

SUMMARY

The use of technological forecasts in the planning of research has a very definite concrete objective. That objective is to determine what research a firm should be doing this year, next year, and perhaps the year after, based on the products, markets, needs, and possibilities for five, ten or more years in the future. For most institutions, there is no point in forecasting the research that might be done at the end of the century or what the technology of the year 2050 will be. Primary concern is with making decisions today, for immediate research goals. These, however, must be based on a reasonable forecast of the technology that will be available or required at the time a company is interested in going into a market.

A PRESCRIPTION FOR THE MILITARY R&D MANAGER: Learn The Three R_x's

Marvin J. Cetron
Technological Forecasting and Appraisal Group
Exploratory Development Division
Headquarters, Naval Material Command

R_{x1}—Learn How to Forecast Technology;

R_{x2}—Learn How to Set Military Goals for Technology;

R_{x3}—Learn How to Integrate these Concepts into R&D Planning.

INTRODUCTION

Government and industry are developing many new ways to forecast future technical developments, but the payoff comes when these projections are incorporated as part of the R&D planning process. This is done on two levels: when deciding on future work in a specific development project and when assigning priorities to the overall R&D effort. Systems being developed in the Navy and other branches of the federal government, are able to integrate technological forecasts with data on future needs, probabilities of success, and potential funding levels. The computerized result is a complete ranking of all on-going and potential projects according to their overall worth. But care must be taken to ensure that the computer printout retains its role as a servant and not a ruler of managers.

One of many Normative (goal-oriented) Technological Forecasting Techniques currently being examined by the Navy will bé discussed in this paper. It is hoped that this technique will accomplish two interrelated purposes: (1) to explore the structure of project selection decision problems in the context of the information and organization environment of the R&D manager and (2) to explore characteristics of the R&D process which are relevant to the design and implementation of management system for planning and controlling resource allocation among various R&D projects.

BACKGROUND

Over the past five years, both government and industry have become fascinated with the potential of technological forecasting as an aid in planning R&D budgets. As laboratories expanded and budgets grew, managers found that many of the traditional ways of allocating their resources of men and money seemed inadequate. But most attempts to build better allocation systems foundered on two basic questions: Which research areas are most likely to be the source of significant technical breakthroughs? Which breakthroughs are most likely to bring an important new development?

The realization that technological forecasting methods could help answer these questions was catching hold slowly when many R&D planners were rudely shaken by a new reality: a leveling-off or even a cutback in most government-sponsored research efforts. With NASA's post-Apollo projects whittled back, the United States DOD research budgets cut extensively, and other usually expanding budgets on a shorter rein, the need to make hard choices in funding became more critical than ever. Now many planners are turning to technological forecasting to help them make their difficult selections.

In my previous presentation to the NATO Defense Research Group,[6*] I discussed many of the specific techniques used to make a technological forecast. Additionally, I, as a U. S. participant, have had distributed to the DRG a *Report on Technological Forecasting.* Based on the foregoing, many requests for further information were forthcoming. However, most requests were not for further information on how Technological Forecasting could be made, but how Technological Forecastings once made could be integrated into R&D planning efforts. In this paper, I will explain some of the approaches being examined within the United States Department of the Navy as well as some of the directions being actively explored in U. S. industry. The truth is, however, this field is still in an evolutionary phase and most work now being done in one organization cannot be modified enough for adoption in others. At best, what is being done can provide many helpful hints for planners grappling with their own problem of using technological forecasts in allocation problems.[4,5]

It is vital to remember that a technological forecast is not a picture of what the future will bring. Instead, it is a prediction, with a level of confidence, in a given time frame, of a technical achievement that could be expected for a given level of budgetary and manpower support.

---

* The supernumerals refer to the references, which are listed at the end of the paper in alphabetical order.

The foundation underlying technological forecasting is the tenet that individual R&D events are susceptible to influence. The times at which they occur—if they can occur at all—can be modulated significantly by regulating the resources allocated to them. Another basic tenet of technological forecasting is the belief that many futures are possible and that the paths toward these futures can be *mapped*.[7]

In use, a technological forecast can be looked at from two vantage points. One, in the present, gives the forecast user a view which shows the path that technological progress will probably take if it is not consciously influenced. In addition, the user will see critical branch points in the road—the situation where alternative futures are possible. He will also gain a greater understanding of the price of admission to those branching paths.

The second vantage point is in the future. The user selects or postulates a technical situation he desires. Looking backward from the point, he can then discern the obstacles that must be overcome to achieve the result he wants. Once again, he is brought up against the hard realities of what he must do to achieve a desired result. As one user has said: "The process substitutes forecasting for forecrastination."

MAKING BASIC FORECASTS

At this point, it is worth reviewing some of the basics of making technological forecasts. Let me hasten to say that the idea is not new. Leonardo da Vinci is probably the prime example of the scientific and technical forecaster whose knowledge and imagination enabled him to foresee many developments far in the future. Science fiction writers from Jules Verne to Arthur Clarke have also peered into the future, often with great success.[7] As long as one remains within the general bounds of knowing natural laws, he is safe in forecasting almost any technical achievement and enjoying some success. But a highly developed imagination offers little help for the technological planner—the odds aren't good enough.

To reduce the odds, most technological forecasts, today, fall into four categories: intuitive, trend-extrapolating, trend-correlating, and growth analogy.[11]

In intuitive forecasting, an individual may make an educated guess, or he may call on polls or panels of experts for advice. A technique which promises to produce more objective intuitive forecasts is the Delphi method, developed by Olaf Helmer of the Rand Corporation. In one version, a group of experts in a chosen field might be asked to name technical breakthroughs or inventions urgently needed and realizable within the next 50 years. The experts are polled by written questionnaires, eliminating the open debate generally found in panel decision-making. As a result, the influence of certain psychological factors is reduced: a persuasive speaker, unwillingness to abandon publicly expressed opinions, or the bandwagon effect of majority opinion. In a second round of questionnaries, participants are asked to give a time scale for achieving each of the items selected. They are also asked the reasons for their earlier opinions. These data are correlated and fed back to each with a request that he reconsider his earlier beliefs and submit new estimates. The result is usually some sort of a consensus.[12]

The strength or weakness of Delphi or other polling systems rests upon the knowledge or intuition of selected experts. It assumes that the consensus estimate is generally correct without an examination of basic data. Most other forecasting methods are tied directly to basic technical data. The trend extrapolation technique, for example, is based on two fundamental assumptions: (1) the forces that created the prior pattern of progress are more likely to continue than to change; (2) the combined effect of these forces is more likely to extend the previous pattern of progress than it is to to produce a different pattern.

One difficulty in using this technique, however, is that the longer the period of the forecast, the greater the probability that one or more of the assumptions made will become invalid. The yield strength of a material, for example, will go up as its density is increased, but there is a theoretical limit.

The trend correlation method, on the other hand, uses two or more identifiable trends in a technical field and tries to determine the probable relationship of one to the other. Plotting the speeds of military and transport aircraft indicates that the transports lag by a predictable amount. Therefore, looking at current—or future—military aircraft gives a good insight into the future of airliners.

Finally, forecasting by growth analogies recognizes that progress in a specific technical development has an exponential characteristic initially, then changes its slope and tapers off toward a horizontal asymptote. This approach, however, is good only for a short term—ten years at the most. In many cases, a new development will take over the improvement rate as the old one is running out of steam. Mercury vapor lamps, for example, started improving dramatically just as incandescent lighting had reached its limit.

The four techniques discussed have one common aspect: They depend on historical data and projection. There is no provision in them for the systematic introduction of management plans and actions. To take these into account, the forecaster must still rely on intuitive judgment. Newer and more sophisticated attempts at forecasting, however, include a systems analysis and a mathematical modeling approach. Basic to these methods is the interaction of human awareness of economic, social, and geopolitical needs with the technical state of the art. The technical inputs are formulated by methods like those mentioned above, but they are then examined for nontechnical feasibility.

PUTTING FORECASTS TO WORK

In most cases, a manager does not have a total system to work with. Instead, he has the results of trend extrapolations or other regular technological forecasting projections. How does he use these data? While there are many approaches, the following is one which the Navy Department is examining to determine which techniques can best help decide which R&D projects to fund.

We begin with a technical planning flow chart (Figure 1) that shows the "shredding out" of all the bits and pieces that comprise the makeup of a new vehicle. Assume that we have a technological forecast for each and every parameter of the shred-out. The forecasts, at each level of the breakdown, are the probable paths that various technologies will take. Armed with this type of data, a meaningful discourse can ensue between the user and producer. For a given set of operational requirements and performance characteristics called for by the user, the technical planners can respond with data that tell the user by what alternative means his needs can be satisfied, and when he can expect these to be accomplished. Many of the trade-offs—between steam, diesel, and nuclear energy, for example—become clear.

Operations officers, however, are not usually quite so acquiescent in accepting what a planner sees ahead. When faced with a military threat, or an anticipated threat, they want an effective answer to that threat by a specified date. The same holds true if they wish to create a new force of their own. In these situations, planners are taking a vantage point at some time in the future and are trying to discover if they will have the technology they need by that time.

Quite likely an examination of the technological forecasts to that point in time will reveal that the users are not likely to get what they want. Now, this is useful information in itself, and represents an approach that is not yet widely used in industry.

However, this view of the technological forecasting task is not the only one. There is the question of which path we should take to achieve a desired result. By deciding on our needs in the future and looking at the forecasts, we can spot the principal obstacles standing in our way, and the magnitude of those obstacles. The inference is clear: If the given goal is to be achieved in a given time, the efforts must be applied in the areas containing the major obstacles. Or, we can settle for something less with clear knowledge of what that something less will be. Often, this analysis will show that two or more paths may be taken to achieve the needed or acceptable capabilities. The point here is that an environment of flexible choice is engendered—choices of which the user was not previously aware. A truly comprehensive technological forecast is backed up not only by material and data which were used in generating the specific forecasts but also by supplementary analysis of various subfactors that could influence each technological forecast. Forecasts like these help indicate the future posture of an enemy or competitor. While you don't know what he *will* do, you at least have a better idea of what he *could* or *could not* do.

MECHANICS OF DECISION-MAKING

Now let's turn to an example and see how a specific decision can be analyzed, based on the forecasting techniques utilized at the Annapolis Division of the Naval Ship Research and Development Center.[15] Forecasts for ship propulsion systems are given in terms of specific weight, reliability, noise, etc. The next level of consideration takes us into the area of subsystem segments—transmission, energy converter, thrust producer, etc. Each of these key into an associated set of parameters which, in turn, key into specific forecasts. In this fashion, we can work our way down the chart, (Figure 1), eventually going into any degree of detail we wish.

This information is used for very practical decisions. Marine gas turbines, for example, have a tremendous potential for development. The possibilities for highpower, lightweight, compact power plants are unmatched in any other type of unit. These characteristics are particularly vital for powering new-concept vessels such as hydrofoils and air-cushion craft. In the last few years, there has been a rapid growth in the horsepower capacity of gas turbine units. Engines as large as 43,000 horsepower have been built, and units exceeding 50,000 horsepower are projected. This growth trend will probably continue but at a lesser rate as limitations of mechanical, thermal and ducting size are approached. However, much larger power outputs will be built by using multiple gas generators to drive a single turbine engine. Power outputs as high as 150,000 horsepower have already been attained by this method. The R&D manager's problem is to decide which aspects of turbine development are most critical.

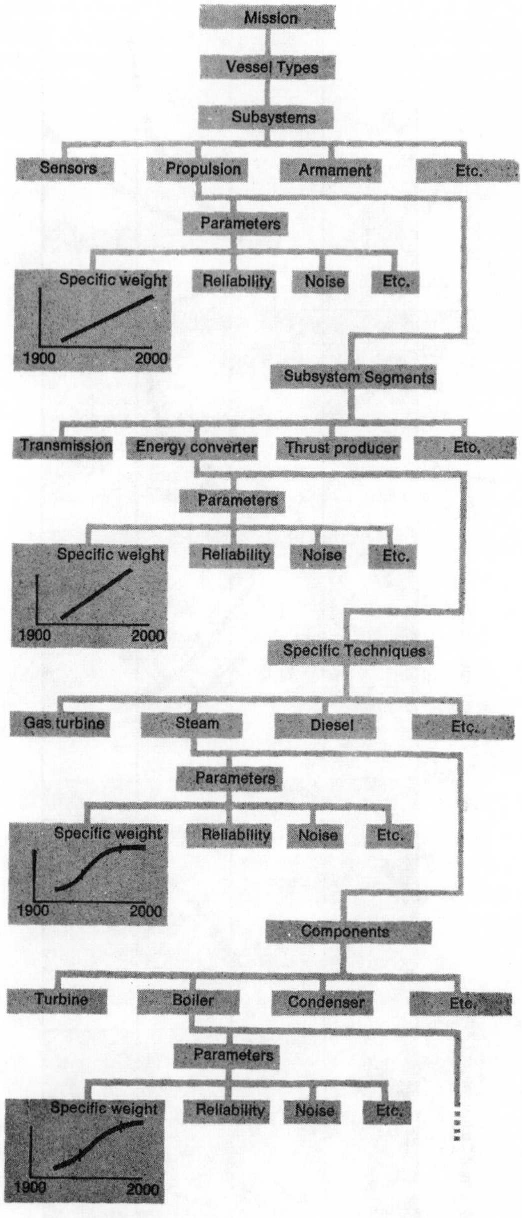

Figure 1. Technical Planning Flow Chart.

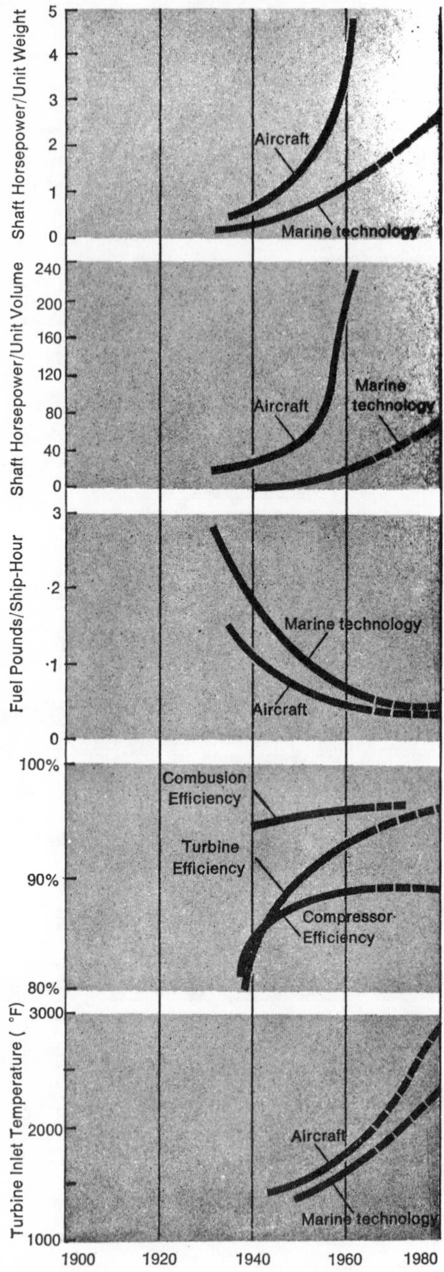

Figure 2. Gas Turbine Characteristics.

The development trends for the specific weight, volume, and fuel consumption for a simple cycle gas turbine are shown in the graphs (Figure 2). In all of these the trend correlation (lead-follow relationship) was used in the study. Aircraft gas-turbine technology has been the leader not only because of the greater aircraft speed payoff, but also because the marine environment led to problems of corrosion. Now that materials and other problems are being overcome, the curves are coming together—the aircraft experience gives some indication of what can be expected in future naval turbines.

As shown in the efficiency graph in figure 2, the compressor, combustion, and turbine efficiency have reached a plateau according to a growth—analogy study. Any future improvement will be limited. Consequently, these component efficiencies will have an insignificant effect on future engine characteristics. Recent improvements, moreover, have resulted from an increase in the compressor-pressure ratio. But any further increase will be small. Because of improvements in blade loading, compressors are now designed to an optimum pressure ratio determined by turbo inlet temperature. And this blade loading, which has enabled engines to obtain pressures with fewer stages, appears to be approaching a limit.

This combination of forecasts shows that the addition of more heat energy within the same basic engine configuration—the major contributing factor to recent engine improvement—is likely to be the key factor in future improvement. Extrapolation of the curve to temperatures in excess of 2500° F is based on laboratory tests in which operating temperatures as high as 4000° F have been achieved—another trend correlation forecast.

As a result of this forecasting approach we now know where our R&D efforts should be concentrated. These are the high payoffs:

(1) Cooling of turbine blades and other components in high-temperature ambients. This will allow higher turbine inlet temperatures.

(2) New materials and protective coatings for these high-ambient components. This will increase high-temperature capabilities by increasing resistance to high-temperature oxidation and sulfidation. An increased resistance to thermal fatigue and creep is also required.

(3) Improved materials, designs, and fabrication techniques for regenerative gas turbines to reduce their cost, weight, and bulk.

(4) Further application and adaption of aircraft gas turbines and technologies to ships.

(5) Attempts to improve efficiency of combustion, compressor, and turbine.

(6) Attempts to increase significantly the blade loading or compressor-pressure ratio if accompanied by major design changes.

THE OVERALL PICTURE

Up to this point we have been discussing the technological forecasting needed for one problem in a laboratory. But any organization has many such problems.[13] Here the question becomes one of allocation of resources of men, money, and materials. The evaluation scene therefore shifts from the technical specialist to the department manager, the head of research, and the overall planners. The forecast data must be fitted into their overall planning approach if it is to be really useful.

When management problems are simple, decision-maker can examine the various factors he must consider with relative ease. One man, such as the hermit in a cave, the individual homeowner, the small businessman, or the teacher in a one-room school, may be able to interrelate all of the necessary information and succeed in his endeavors.

As the management scope becomes larger and the complexity of problems increases, more and different factors must be considered to reach a decision. Soon, staff and management procedures are needed to assist in all phases of management. Eventually, the point is reached where any one decision affects many facets of the operation; all efforts become interrelated to an alarming degree.

Increasing complexities are particularly true with programs or projects which must operate within a fixed government or corporation resource ceiling. Choices must be made on alternative approaches, specifically, which efforts should proceed and which should be dropped or delayed. Since numerous efforts are interrelated in time, resources required, purpose and and possible technical transfer one to another, choices must be made with consideration of the total effect. Whether he be a manufacturer, a service industry director, government administrator, or university professor, every manager seeks the greatest payoff resource investments.

What alternatives does a manager have for developing resource-allocation approaches? The resource allocation problem is usually too big to keep in one man's head and often inputs come from levels completely outside of his control. Hundreds of inputs can be involved when the alternatives are examined in depth.

A familiar resource allocation approach is termed the *squeaking wheel* process. One can cut resources from every area (one can be sophisticated and cut some areas more than others) then wait and see which area complains the most. On the basis of the loudest and most insistent squeaking, the manager can then restore some of the resources previously withdrawn until he reaches his ceiling budget.

Another common approach develops the minimum noise level and results in fewer squeaks by allocating this year's resources in just about the same manner as last year. The budget perturbations are minimized and the status quo maintained. If this *level funding* approach is continued very long within a rapidly changing technological field, the company, group, or government agency will end up in serious trouble.

An effortless version of the preservation of management security approach to resource allocation seeks to perpetuate the *Glorious Past.* Last year, or the year before, or perhaps several years ago, a division or organization had a very successful project, therefore why not fund the unit for the next five years on any projects that they advocate? The premise is "once successful, always successful." This method really means that no analysis should be made of the proposed project or its usefulness; instead, projects will be assigned resources solely upon the basis of past record of an individual or organization.

Still another way to allocate resources is called the *white charger* technique. Here the various departments come dashing in to top management with multi-color graphs, handouts, and well-rehearsed presentations. If they impress the decision-maker, they are rewarded with increased resources. Often the best speaker or the last man to brief the boss wins the treasure.[2]

Finally, consider the *committee approach,* which frees the manager from resource allocation decisions. The committees tell the manager to increase, decrease, or leave all allocations as they are. A common danger is that the committee may not have enough actual experience in the organization or sufficient information upon which to base its recommendations. If the committee is ad hoc or from outside the organization, the members can also avoid responsibility in not having to live through the risky process of implementing their recommendations.

Obviously, the described allocation methods are neither scientific nor objective, though they are utilized quite extensively. These naive approaches point up the need of the manager and his staff for an aid to bring information into a form upon which judgment may be applied. It is a common experience for an organization to have numerous reports on specific technical subjects which recommend increased resources for the particular area. But the direct use of this data only compounds the manager's problem when he tries to allocate resources among the many technical areas. If he is operating under a fixed budget ceiling, to increase funding for one technical area requires that either one or more technical areas must be correspondingly decreased.

TECHNOLOGICAL RESOURCE ALLOCATION SYSTEM

A more sophisticated alternative approach involves the use of staff or specialists in operations research. Information they assemble can be used to significantly assist managerial judgment. This is the point where quantitative evaluation techniques enter the picture. Each major aspect of a program can be examined, first separately and then as it is interrelated to competing factors. Items such as timeliness, cost utility or payoff, confidence level or risk, personnel, facilities, etc., can be evaluated by specialists in each field and the total picture made available as a basis for decision. Greater payoff areas can be identified and problems can be highlighted. Inputs can be accurately recorded, made clearly visible and analyzed for assisting the final decision.

The use of quantitative techniques permits input factors and possible outcome to be reexamined readily and different managerial emphasis applied. The manager can still hedge his "allocation selections" by allocating resources through such criteria as increased resources to previously successful groups, backing a high-risk effort—i.e., a high cost project with slim chances of success which might yield gigantic results. The decision-maker can incorporate any desired additional criteria—such as the politics of selection, competitive factors, or technological barriers.

The question now becomes one of allocation of the resources of men, money, and materials. Figure 3, the long-range planning diagram, which is really a broad allocation diagram, shows the interactions of numerous managers from the technical specialist to the department manager, the head of research, and the corporate planners. The data must be fitted into an overall planning approach if it is to be really useful. Corporate goals are the main topic and occupy the central position in the chart. In order to establish corporate goals, the preliminary steps of systems analysis, needs analysis, and deficiency analysis must be accomplished. After the goals and technical objectives are established, technology assessment and R&D Programming take place to complete the R&D resources allocation process. Each of these steps will be explained in greater depth.

System Analysis

Corporate policy must be considered and involves philosophic and strategy questions, including these: Shall I be the industry leader? Shall I keep abreast of the industry technically and see if a major market develops? In the overall environment, competitors' actions must be followed closely, but there are other factors such as interest rates, business expectation,

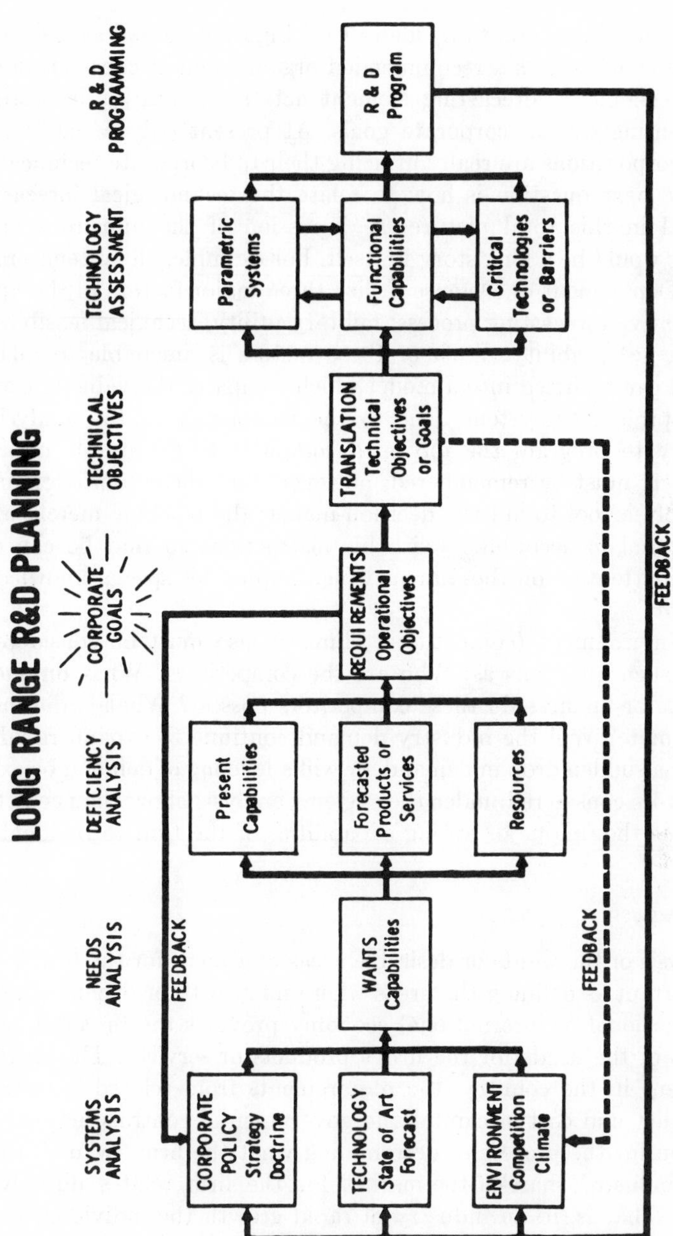

Figure 3. Long Range R&D Planning.

economic forecasts, etc. to be identified.[1] Figure 3 viewed as the corporate planning chart, shows a recommended organization of considerations.

The technology forecasting element acts as a catalyst in setting and implementing overall corporate goals. At present only a handful of the largest corporations are really utilizing their full corporate technical potential. The next question is how to relate the technological forecasts with appraisal in this total picture. A discussion of the numerous appraisal methods would be a long story in itself. For example, all systems employed by the Department of Defense utilize three major factors in the appraisal or normative forecasting process: military utility, technical feasibility, and financial acceptability. Each of these factors is amenable to quantification and can be fitted into a model which compares the value of each component project or system. Due to the complexity of the analysis, it is necessary to program the job on a computer to get usable information quickly. It must be remembered, however, that these computer processes are simply a tool to aid the decision-maker; the machine merely arranges the material in accordance with his instructions so that he can quickly focus his attention on those areas which require his special knowledge and judgment.

The environment (competition, climate) also must be considered, and include such questions as: Who are the competitors? What unique skills, products, or finances do these competitors possess? What is the industry-wide climate? Will the industry demand continue to expand rapidly, will there be a sudden drop in demand, or will a leveling of demand be expected. The factors considered under the systems analysis allow the needs (wants) as well as the unique or strong capabilities of the firm to be identified.

Need Analysis

Analysis of the wants or desirable areas of growth for the firm is equally as important as defining the areas where no growth or decline is expected.

The national or international economy provides the broadest scope for analysis of the needs for the firm's products or services. The stage of development in the country, the requirements from related industries, the availability and cost of capital and governmental controls may all require attention for the process of determining what the firm "wants" to do.

The industry share-of-the-market for the firm relates directly to its volume. That is, in an industry of rapid growth the individual firm may grow while remaining constant relative to its competitors. Conversely, the share-of-the-market may need to be greatly increased to remain at a level stage in a declining industry.

Finally, the desire of the firm and of the individual groups within the firm can be assessed. However, these desires may not be attainable within the capability of the firm. Thus, the wants need to be balanced against the firm's capabilities.

Deficiency Analysis

After the wants of the organization have been established, the capabilities available must be delineated in order that areas of deficiency can be identified. Ordinarily, the present capabilities of an organization will be known, but often effort is required by management to obtain a comprehensive statement of its technological capabilities in terms of men, money, and machines. Because we are dealing with futures, the products and services such as new manufacturing methods, new materials, and advanced skills that are forecasted to be available must also be carefully identified. Other resources available to the organization will also be important information. Skills or manufacturing processes or equipment, etc. may exist that could be available from outside the organization when and if required.

By identifying and analyzing the present capabilities, forecasted products and services along with other resources available, the deficiencies and excesses will become evident. The analysis now permits management to focus upon realistic corporate goals.

Corporate Goals

The most important phase of the resource allocation system may now be brought into focus—the corporate goals (objectives). These goals may be viewed by top management from the wants (desires or needs) of the organization which have been carefully considered for feasibility against the present or potential capabilities of the organization. Several passes through the analysis described above usually are required before acceptable goals are achieved by top management.

These corporate goals will be translated into requirements for performance of the organization, or as operational objectives.

Technical Objectives

The idea of applying quantitative approaches to resource allocation has too long been suspect by management. Currently, both industry and government are seeking tangible improvements in the results from use of available resources. Economy drives and or cost/benefit analyses have resulted in pared budgets with the need more critical than ever to make hard choices among alternative programs. The application of objective measurements to resource assignments has too long been classified as visionary and impractical.

For example, how does a corporation decide whether its allocation this year for research and technology is adequate? And how does it decide the right balance between the research and development or manufacturing projects?

A prime example of lack of quantitative data exists in the area of assessing technological effort. Querying the scientist or engineer and requesting a justification of his selection of a program or a task (including projected benefits to a mission or product-oriented organization) has often been construed as an assault against the scientific professionals' prestige and prerogatives. Today, scientists and engineers are beginning to realize that they are accepted at the highest organization levels and that one of the signs of this ascendancy is their high visibility and responsibility to the interrogation of criteria and rational judgments. The technical managers intuition can no longer be accepted as infallible and beyond managerial review.[2]

Several project evaluation and selection techniques have as their basis a belief in the efficacy and acceptance of Bayesian statistics and theories of probability.[4,5 & 13] Bayesians believe that it is correct to quantify feelings about uncertainty in terms of subjectively assessed numerical probabilities. Thus, assessments are made of probabilities for events that dctermine the profitability or utility of alternative actions open to the decision-maker.

For example, there is a necessity to assess the criterion of whether a piece of research is technically feasible (Technological Forecasts) or what is the probability that it will be successfully accomplished (level of confidence criterion). Bayesian theory believes that it is possible for an "expert" in the field being assessed to assign a figure of merit or "subjective" probability number that the event will actually occur. This theory states that on this very subject matter an expert can assign a "subjective" probability number from a scale, for example, between 0 and 10. Men of considerable experience in a field usually have no difficulty in utilizing a Bayesian probability scale. In a like manner, other criteria, such as the utility of the research to the objectives of the organization, or relevance to desired priority systems or corporation products, are assessed (criterion of utility).

The use of Bayesian subjective probabilities makes feasible the incorporation into the decision process, in a formal and visible way, many of the subjective and objective criteria and variables previously taken into account by the decision-maker informally and without visibility.

The probability assignment, a number between 0 and 10 to each facet, factor, criterion, or parameter inherent to a rational decision, reflects the degree of belief held by the individual expert(s) that the above objective will be met.

Thus the experience, knowledge of the subject, and judgment of the various experts are summarized by the subjective probabilities that they assign against the respective criteria. The final or top decision-maker then has a clear view of the alternatives and can use the results of the probability assignments of the different experts. A computer can be used to summarize the choices or probabilities of the experts. The computer can also be used to determine "consequences" if the probability assignments are changed or if the final decision-maker adds new information or weighting factors, etc.

Advocates of allocation and selection procedures are accused of assuming that the myriad of quantitative estimates of scientific relevance, importance, feasibility and the like should and can be collected and manipulated.[14] Apparently the academic community also believes in the above assumption. For example, in the field of education, the university admission policy is based on a "myriad of quantitative estimates."

Mr. Robert Freshman, one of the U. S. Air Force Laboratory planners who was previously a professional educator, relates the following example:[2] High school students are admitted to universities based on the quantitative judgments of teacher grades as the key criterion. These teachers grade about 5 subjects a year, for 4 years of high school—thus, 20 teacher judgments. Different teachers, different subjects, different tests, different subject matter taken in high schools throughout the nation, are fused into one. Teacher opinions on how to grade, biases and prejudgments, oral recitations, grades on nonstandardized, unstructured subject matter and tests are all injected into the above conglomeration to form the individual teacher's final grade in one subject.

High school grades for the four years are averaged to come up with one number—the high school average—the *magic number* which has great influence in college admission. More miraculous is that there is a good, positive correlation between this magic number and success in college. It is recognized that this "quantitative estimate" of many judgments is the best single criterion or indicator of success in *college*; but again it is just an aid to the decision-maker. The personal interview, college boards, or extra curricular activities also effect his judgment prior to making a final decision.

Opinions and judgments can be and should be weighed by every decision-maker in his final decision. Several quantitative techniques gather and summarize the opinions and judgments to enable the final decision-maker (like the university dean of admissions utilizing teacher judgments) to visualize and weigh, as one input to his decision, the judgments of numerous people on diverse factors.

Two main points on quantitative decision making should be emphasized:

(a) The quantitative management techniques discussed *do not make decisions,* but provide a basis of information upon which decisions can be made.

(b) A validity check can not be made since once the resources are allocated, the plan becomes self-fulfilling.

Subsystem Analysis or Technology Assessment

Assessment of technology or subsystem analysis is employed to answer the question: which, when and how many resources should be allocated among the alternative projects: Since the topic is multi-faceted it is necessary to draw information from a variety of sources including operations research, project selection techniques, and technological forecasting.

Technology assessment is not oficial jargon. The expression"assessment of technology" is not found listed in the table of contents or indexes of texts on management. Nor is it identified and found in the general literature of management or in official planning, programming and policy documents of the government agencies.

Assessment is commonly considered to mean "setting a value to." Assessment of technology, then, means setting a value to technology. Technologies include areas of special knowledge such as gas turbines, diesels, thermionics, thermoelectrics, fuel cells, and energy conversion as opposed to the areas of science which include items such as alloy theory, surface physics, cryogenics, and magnetism. The kinds or measures of value attributed to technologies will be discussed later. Also, it can be demonstrated that the nature of the assessment of technology depends on who assesses, why the assessment is performed, and the nature of the technology, itself.

How is Technology Assessed?

One simple technique of assessing technology uses an analogy and a rather trivial example. To assess the value of two baskets of fruit with contents as listed in Table I, first assess or determine the value of the baskets in one of many respects such as weight (a critical criteria for submarines), volume (a critical criteria for space craft), calories (a critical criteria for weight-watchers), and cost (a critical criteria for budgeteers). For this

TABLE I

Basket #1	Fruit Cost (¢/unit)	Basket #2
5 apples	10	10 apples
8 oranges	20	2 oranges
6 bananas	30	9 bananas

example, assessment can be readily done in terms of financial cost with monetary cost values assigned to the individual items as follows:

10 cents per apple
20 cents per orange
30 cents per banana

$$\begin{aligned}\text{Value (\#1)} &= (5 \times 10) + (8 \times 20) + (6 \times 30)\\ &= 50 + 160 + 180\\ &= \$3.90\end{aligned}$$

$$\begin{aligned}\text{Value (\#2)} &= (10 \times 10) + (2 \times 20) + (9 \times 30)\\ &= 100 + 40 + 270\\ &= \$4.10\end{aligned}$$

The analogy is made by having the baskets of fruit represent technologies, the fruits to represent characteristics of parameters of the technologies, and the cost values of the fruit to represent their "relative importance factors." The value for each basket can be represented by the formula:

Value

= summation of [(relative importance factor) × (criteria or parameter)]

This illustration introduces the terms "importance factors" and "parameters" and demonstrates (assuming that the analogy is valid) that the parameters, while different from each other, provide measures of technology that can be taken collectively to determine a single numerical value which can be compared to a similarly derived value of another technology. Note again that the assessment could have been made for the purpose of comparing other importance factors—values of weight, volume, calories, etc. It is easy to see that the selection of the relative importance factors is dependent upon the parameters (kinds of fruit, in the example), and ugon the purpose of the assessment. This latter dependency will be discussed further in addressing the question: Why (or for what purpose) assess technology? Please note that the above example does not add together

TABLE II

Boat #1	Importance Factor	Boat #2
25 K		20 K
80 db		50 db

apples and oranges, rather importance factors have been constructed so as to cancel the different units of fruit in the multiplications, and does add like units of cost associated with each different fruit.

Another *hypothetical* example of technological assessment is provided by Keith Ellingsworth of the Annapolis Division of the Naval Ship Research and Development Center, Division Planning Office.[8] This one is not in the form of an analogy nor is it trivial. It concerns the design of a boat for river warfare use in Vietnam. The design has proceeded to the point where a choice must be made between two parameters of two boats, as illustrated in Table II.

The two boats respectively have speeds (knots) and noise levels (decibels) of 25K, 80db and 20K, 50db. Here it appears difficult to assign relative importance factors, but there are methods which can be used. In this case a mission analysis can allow us to determine the relative importance factors. Imagine the boat patrolling a river "looking" up and down the river with its radar. Its mission is to prevent enemy junks from crossing the river. The more noise the boat makes, the further up the river the enemy can hear the boat. The farther away the boat can be heard, the more time the enemy has to escape by crossing the river or by ducking back into a shallow creek where our boat can't go, and the faster our boat must be to catch the enemy. It is simply a matter of physics and geometry to determine, say for a given boat noise, the speed required to achieve a stated level of mission effectiveness. The results of a mission analysis might be stated as for every 16 decibels of noise, 4 knots of speed are required in order to be able to intercept those junks up to a mile away and in the middle two-thirds (width) of the river. In other words, 4 decibels of noise are equivalent to 1 knot of speed, and these are the relative importance needed. The boat is then selected as illustrated in Table III. Calculations

TABLE III

Boat #1	Importance Factors (db/kts)	Boat #2
25 K	4	20 K
80 db	1	50 db

of value from data follows:

$$V(\#1) = (25 \times 4) - (80 \times 1) = 20$$
$$V(\#2) = (20 \times 4) - (50 \times 1) = 30$$

Note that speed adds to the boat's value, noise subtracts. The above assessment indicates the choice of Boat #2. It's a slower boat but its reduced noise makes it more effective by the criteria established. This sort of assessment might be done to determine operational capabilities, to determine design criteria, or in resource allocation determine the appropriate levels of effort in the two technological areas of boat power and noise reduction.

Who Assesses Technology and Why—Or For What Purpose.

Intuitively, nearly everyone assesses technology at some time, for some purpose, and to some degree of sophistication. The "man on the street" for example may essentially assess the aggregates of the technologies of color versus black and white television. He may consider the collective value of parameters such as cost, picture quality, repair frequency, and pressure from his wife in order to choose which, if either, to buy. That nearly everyone has different values was pointed out by William D. Guth and Renato Tagiuri which emphasized the following points:[9]

—The personal values that businessmen and others have can be usefully classified as theoretical, economic, aesthetic, social, political, and religious.

—The values that are most important to an executive have profound influence on his strategic decisions.

—Managers and employees often are unaware of the values they possess and also tend to misjudge the values of others.

—The executive who will take steps to better understand his own values and other men's values can gain an important advantage in developing workable and well-supported policies.

Earlier it was stated that the assessment of technology depends on who assesses, why the assessment is undertaken, and on the nature of technology itself. A hypothetical situation which provides some illustration of the range of assessors, and how assessment might vary over this range is provided in the following example. This example also illustrates one of the difficulties in assessing technology which results from variations of people and purposes involved.

Consider the technology of batteries and three of its parameters: volume, cost and time between recharging. A broad range of assessors might be the following in the situations described.

Technology Involvement	*Situation*
User	LT USN: Commanding Officer of a boat, which contains batteries; drifting on a Vietnamese river on night patrol.
R&D Manager	Chief of Naval Development; responsible for Navy's total Exploratory Development Program (Applied Research) considering each year's fiscal budget.
Boat designer	Naval Architect, Naval Ship Systems Command, designing a boat for use in Vietnam
R&D Engineer	Project engineer; working in a Navy R&D lab to improve the general performance of batteries

These four people might assess battery technology using the same quantitative techniques, where 10 is the highest value that may be assigned and 0 the lowest, as shown in Table IV.

Table IV shows the relative importance factors that the four persons might assign to the parameters based on intuition. The differences shown by the variations of relative importance are possibly true, while perhaps exaggerated. The importance factors were chosen considering the following rationalizations.

The boat operator's life depends to a large extent on his boat. He's probably very concerned when, in the situation described, he must start-up his *loud* engines to charge the batteries. He therefore considers the necessity and the time between recharging very important. He's probably not too concerned with the volume of the batteries so long as they don't infringe significantly on ammo storage space. He probably doesn't care what the batteries cost, much less the cost of the battery R&D effort.

The R&D manager is likely to place more importance on cost and less importance on individual performance characteristics. This is probably due to his responsibility for a large number of R&D programs and proposed programs involving many different parameters of many different technologies and the common element among these is cost.

TABLE IV

Parameter	Technology: User	Batteries Manager	Designer	Engineer
Volume	3	2	10	8
Cost	0	10	2	2
Time between Recharging	10	2	4	1

The boat designer is concerned with the overall performance of the boat. He must assure that all components required fit onto the boat, and he therefore considers volume relatively more important than cost or time between recharging.

The project engineer is concerned with many characteristics of batteries; he is concerned with the improvement of batteries in general. It is not particularly required of him that he produce a profit. Therefore he may not be particularly cost conscious. It is not required of him, perhaps, that he produce the smallest possible boat battery, and therefore he places less importance on volume than the boat designer does.

The above considerations suggest that the selection by a person of relative importance factors for parameters describing a technology is highly influenced by the environment in which the person is involved. Key expressions taken from the above for the persons described are:

User:	life, Vietnamese river (warfare)
Manager:	total R&D program; command
Designer:	performance of boat (system made up of many technologies); engineering center
R&D	many characteristics of one technology; laboratory

A difficulty in assessing technology, illustrated above, is the problem of obtaining and maintaining an alignment of relative importance factors between the users of technologies and those responsible for improving the capabilities of technologies.

In the *hypothetical* example, the R&D engineer may not have been aware of the degree of importance of a particular parameter to a particular user. In other words, an R&D engineer may not recognize the need for a particular technological improvement. The importance of such need-recognitions as it contributes to the successful development of weapon systems is well illustrated by the comprehensive technology source study Project HINDSIGHT conducted by Col. Raymond Isenson and Dr. Chalmers Sherwin of the Department of Defense.[10]

R&D PROGRAMMING

To reiterate three factors used by the U. S. Department of Defense to evaluate systems programs are "military utility," "technical feasibility," and "financial acceptability." These factors are also important when planners evaluate research and development. However, it is necessary to quantize these factors so that they may be compared for different Research and Development programs.

One of the simplier techniques being investigated by the Navy utilizes Appraisal Sheet No. 1 which addresses the problems of military utility. Military utility with respect to development atmosphere is a measure of R&D work in terms of its usefulness in meeting U. S. Navy's General Operational Requirements (GOR). To be useful, hardware or information must provide a new or improved capability in the shortest possible time after its need is recognized. Thus, military utility is made up of three interdependent criteria: value to naval warfare, responsiveness, and timeliness. In this condensed version, we will consider "value to naval warfare."

This criterion considers the extent of the contribution of a task area objective (TAO), a unit of work, in terms of its inherent value as well as its military operational value. The importance of a task is measured by its relative impact on any individual naval warfare category as well as the number of categories receiving a contribution from the task objective. This is done by multiplying the assigned value of the warfare category by the impact value of the contribution to arrive at a value for each individual category. The sum of these values will determine the value of the task area objective.

Note: The figures of merit, or point values assigned to each naval warfare category (Column 1) are dummy figures; they were assigned for this example only. The actual total number of points assigned these 29 naval categories are equal to 100, and they are assigned for test purposes on the basis of the importance of each of these categories in the 1975 and 1980 time frame since this is when most of our current exploratory development work will find its way into the Fleet. The operational users provided the test figures based on the present world situation and their estimates of the most probable future situations.

When the warfare area specialist filled in Column 2, the impact of the task area objective contributions, he considered the descriptors at the bottom of the page (Scale of Definitions). In some cases the 4 descriptors do not adequately describe the contribution; in those cases he interpolates between these numbers.

The credibility of the ratings of technical feasibility and the probability of success increase if they are rated by personnel who have the necessary technical expertise and competence, as they can best judge these factors on the basis of the ability and experience of the individuals and/or organizations carrying on the development efforts under consideration.

The top half of Appraisal Sheet No. 2 solicits the opinion of the technical specialist regarding the probability of achieving the total task area objective that is being undertaken. It considers whether the task could be suc-

APPRAISAL SHEET NO. I

VALUE TO NAVAL WARFARE

Column I - Categories General Operational Requirements (GORs)		Column 2 Impact of Task Contributions										Column 3 Value to Individual Category
		1.0	.9	.8	.7	.6	.5	.4	.3	.2	.1	
31	STRIKE WARFARE											
6	Airborne Attack											
3	Surface Attack											
5	Submarine Attack											
4	Amphibious Assault											
7	Sea Based Strategic Deterrence											
3	Airborne Anti-Air Warfare											
3	Surface Anti-Air Warfare											
31	ANTISUBMARINE WARFARE											
5	Airborne ASW				✓							3.5
4	Surface ASW						✓					2.0
5	Submarine ASW						✓					2.5
10	Undersea Surveillance								✓			3.0
2	Mining											
3	Mine Countermeasures											
2	ASW Ancillary Support									✓		0.4
23	COMMAND SUPPORT											
3	Command and Control											
4	Naval Communications											
4	Electronic Warfare											
1	Navigation											
4	Ocean Surveillance											
5	Reconnaissance & Intelligence											
1	Environmental Systems											
1	Special Warfare											
15	OPERATIONAL SUPPORT											
2	Logistics											
4	Personnel											
2	Astronautics											
2	Aviation Support											
2	Ship Support											
2	Ordnance Support											
1	NBC Defense											

4. TOTAL VALUE TO NAVAL WARFARE = 11.4

Scale of Definitions for "Impact of Task Contribution" (Column 2):

Points - Descriptors

1.0 Creation of radically new mission concepts (meets overriding critical need)
.7 Revolutionary extension of capabilities
.4 Incremental or marginal improvement of capabilities
.2 Increase in economy

APPRAISAL SHEET NO. I

APPRAISAL SHEET NO. 2

Probability of Success

☐ 80 - 100% Chance of Meeting TAO

☑ 30 - 80% Chance of Meeting TAO

☐ 0 - 30% Change of Meeting TAO

Number of Different Concurrent Approaches

☐ 1	☐ 3	☐ 5	☐ 7	☐ 9
☐ 2	☑ 4	☐ 6	☐ 8	☐ 10 or more

Sacred Cow? Who Says?

S-1 ☐ President

S-2 ☐ Congress

S-3 ☐ DOD (Department of Defense)

S-4 ☐ ASN (R&D) (Assistant Secretary of Navy for Research and Development)

S-5 ☐ JCS (Joint Chiefs of Staff)

S-6 ☐ CNO (Chief of Naval Operations)

S-7 ☐ CND (Chief of Naval Development)

S-8 ☐ Other ________

Appraisal Summary

No. of GOR's 5

Value (V) 11.4

Probability of Success (P_S) 0.9375

Expected Value (EV) 11.4 x 0.9375 = 10.7

Optimum Funding $2 million

Desirability Index (D) 5.35

APPRAISAL SHEET NO. 2

cessfully accomplished from a scientific and technical feasibility point of view. Technical risk also takes into consideration the degree of confidence or prediction that the remaining portion of the total objective can be attained. The degree of confidence or prediction that the remaining portion of the total task objective can be attained usually assesses the factors of the present state-of-the-art, either implicit or explicit. This technical appraisal is naturally based on technical forecasts and includes time factors and resource levels, as well as the competence of the investigating team.

Therefore, the technical specialist checks the box that best describes his opinion regarding the task area objective being evaluated, as well as the number of different concurrent approaches being taken which are also a measure of probability of success.

The area called "sacred cow?" and "who says?" was also considered in what we call the "management environment." This section solicits opinions on the acceptability of the effort in the management structure. Here, the evaluator is asked to give what he believes to be "the Washington environment" considerations concerning this effort, and he checks the applicable box.

The bottom of Appraisal Sheet No. 2 is then analyzed. The total program is calculated by Value, Expected Value, and Desirability Index for three funding levels, by the computer. The inputs for military utility come from Appraisal Sheet No. 1.

For example: Suppose the proposed task area objective (TAO), or R&D effort, is to devise a system able to detect submerged submarines a given distance away from a sensor, say 20 miles. We shall consider the criterion "Value to Naval Warfare." Of the 29 naval General Operational Requirements shown in Column 1 of Appraisal Sheet No. 1, the TAO would be of value and contribute only to five GOR's: Airborne ASW, Surface ASW, Submarine ASW, Undersea ASW, and ASW Ancillary Support.

With respect to airborne ASW, the success of the R&D venture in this hypothetical example is considered a "revolutionary extension of capabilities, and is accorded 0.7 point. At the same time, airborne ASW is said to contribute 5 out of the 100 units assigned to all the GOR's. Thus, the value of the TAO to naval warfare with respect to airborne ASW is $0.7 \times 5 = 3.5$. The other categories can be similarly evaluated for their contributions, and the total value of this TAO to naval warfare is summed at 11.4, as shown on the appraisal sheet.

For our calculation of the Probability of Success (P_s) in meeting the TAO, we use the probability chart shown on Table V. In this chart, n is the number of concurrent approaches used to accomplish the TAO, and *C*

TABLE V
TABULATION OF P_s

C / *n*	*0.8*	*0.5*	*0.2*
1	0.80000	0.50000	0.20000
2	0.96000	0.75000	0.36000
3	0.99200	0.87500	0.48800
4	0.99840	0.93750	0.59040
5	0.99968	0.96875	0.67230
6	0.99993	0.98438	0.73786
7	0.99997	0.99219	0.79029
8	0.99999	0.99609	0.83223
9	0.99999	0.99805	0.86578
10	0.99999	0.99902	0.89263

is a number arbitrarily assigned to the chances of succeeding in a given approach. We use:

80–100% chance of success: $C = 0.8$

30–80% chance of success: $C = 0.5$

0–30% chance of success: $C = 0.2$

We assume that all approaches n have the same chance of success, and therefore the same value of C. If each n were to have a different C, a more involved calculation would have been necessary.

The number assigned to the probability of one approach failing is then $(1 - C)$.

The number assigned to the probability of n approaches failing is $(1 - C)^n$.

Further, if we assume that at least one of the approaches taken will succeed, then the number assigned to the probability of success Ps is $1 - (1 - C)^n$.

This figure for Ps is filled in on Appraisal Sheet No. 2 under the Probability of Success column.

Example: On an Appraisal Sheet No. 2, we might have had 4 approaches ($n = 4$) with a 30–80% chance of meeting TAO ($C - 0.5$). Then the number corresponding to the probability of success is 0.93750 or 93.75%. From our previous example we calculated the total value of a given TAO to be 11.4. Therefore, the expected value is $11.4 \times 0.9375 = 10.7$.

The preceding has been a discussion of concurrent approaches. If the task area were made up of phased or sequential operations, these probabilities would be handled in a different manner.

Three funding levels are utilized in the "concurrent" approach: the actual/optimum, maximum, and minimum.

The actual/optimum consists of the latest approved fiscal data. For each subsequent year, funds are entered based on what is estimated as necessary to achieve the completion date if the task area is supported at an optimum rate. An optimum rate is one which permits aggressive prosecution using orderly developmental procedures—not a crash program.

The maximum consists of what could effectively be expended in advancing task area completion data. Maximum funding is the upper limit in which unlimited resources are assigned in order to accelerate the accomplishment of a task area.

The minimum consists of what could be effectively utilized to maintain continuity of effort and some progress toward fulfilling the task area objective. Minimum funding is the threshold limit below which it would not be feasible to continue further efforts in the task area.

The simplified formula is:

$$\text{VALUE (V)} \times \text{PROB OF SUCCESS } (P_s) = \text{EXPECTED VALUE (EV)}$$

$$\frac{\text{EXPECTED VALUE (EV)}}{\text{FUNDING LEVEL (C)}} = \text{DESIRABILITY INDEX (D)}$$

Finishing up the analysis of the rating sheet, "GORs" represent the number of general operational requirements affected by the project; "Ps" as previously stated, is read off a probability chart; and the optimum funding level is determined according to the resources needed to complete the project in the time span of the study. The final desirability index numbers now provide a way to compare a great multitude of current and proposed R&D projects. By carrying out similar evaluations on the basis of responsiveness to expected needs, the timeliness of the projects, and other criteria, it is possible to combine all the information about the project and come up with its "total warfare value."

NAVMAT PROGRAM EVALUATION REPORT
(RANKING OF 6924P012 BY TOTAL WARFARE VALUE MR. CETRON 6YTPG)

PAGE 33
26 APR 1967

TASK AREA NUMBER	TITLE	SC	EXP. VALUE	FUNDING MAX	CUM	OPT	CUM	MIN	CUM	RANKING*
WF11511781 WF0190101	(U)SPACE SYSTEMS ENGINEERING		26.446875	300	300	300	300	300	300	27.3
XF03229001 YF0190208	(U)COMMUNICATIONS SATELLITE SUPPORT		22.050000	2000	2300	1375	1675	1000	1300	25.2
WF03227781 WF0190101	(U)SATELLITE COMMUNICATIONS		16.350000	350	2650	350	2025	0	1300	21.8
WF12552781 WF0190202	(U)SATELLITE OCEANOGRAPHIC DATA COLLECTION		9.375000	900	3550	700	2725	150	1450	12.5
WF12551782 WF0190202	(U)SOLAR RADIATION MONITORING SATELLITE		8.000370	3000	6550	2800	5525	1200	2650	11.9
WF03232781 WF0190101	(U)SATELLITE NAVIGATION			2250	8800	2250	7775	0	2650	10.2
WF12551781 WF0190202	(U)METEOROLOGICAL SATELLITE DATA READOUT		8.750000	600	9400	200	7975	150	2800	10.0
WF02112781 WF0190102	(U)ADVANCED TECHNIQUES FOR SPACE OBJECT DETECTION AND IDENTIFICATION		2.800000	850	10250	850	8825	0	2800	5.6
WF02111782 WF0190202	(U)OCEAN SURVEILLANCE SYSTEMS ANALYSIS			5500	15750	5000	13825	4000	6800	4.8
WF05311781 WF0190102	(U)SATELLITE INTERCEPTER SYSTEMS ANALYSIS			500	16250	500	14325	200	7000	1.0
WF05372781 WF0190102	(U)ASTRO-DEFENSE THREAT STUDIES			300	16550	200	14525	100	7100	1.0

Figure 4

EXAMPLE: COMPUTER PRINTOUT RANKED BY WARFARE VALUE AND EXPECTED VALUE

860801260001
C

NAVMAT PROGRAM EVALUATION REPORT
(RANKING BY OPT DESIRABILITY)

TASK AREA NUMBER	TITLE	SC	MAX	CUM	FUNDING OPT	CUM	MIN	CUM	RANKING*
SF08452002	(U)ACOUSTICAL SILENCING (INTERNAL SHIPS SYSTEMS)	S6	320	320	220	220	185	185	.266477
SF08452004	(U)ACOUSTICAL SILENCING, SHIP ISOLATION DEVICES	S6	535	855	435	655	333	518	.181034
XF10532001	(U)TEST EQUIPMENT	S3	2400	3255	1300	1955	770	1288	.124614
SF08452005	(U)ACOUSTICAL SILENCING, HULL VIBRATION AND RADIATION	S6	955	4210	680	2635	610	1898	.093750
SF02132001	(U)DIRECT VIEW IMAGE INTENSIFIER TECHNIQUES	S4	400	4610	300	2935	65	1963	.080000
SF08452001	(U)SHIP SILENCING MEASUREMENTS, ANALYSIS AND PROBLEM DEFINITION	S6	1360	5970	1095	4030	860	2823	.072602
XF02132601	(U)IMAGING RECONNAISSANCE SENSOR DEVELOPMENT	S3	1000	6970	750	4780	200	3023	.056666
RF08412002	(U)DEEP RESEARCH VEHICLE PROGRAM	S6	1700	8670	1510	6290	1180	4203	.048344
SF01121003	(U)DOMES AND SELF NOISE	S6	600	9270	550	6840	540	4743	.041236
XF10545001	(U)ADVANCED ACTIVE DEVICES AND TECHNIQUES	S3	4000	13270	2600	9440	2000	6743	.039711
PF11521004	(U)IMPROVED NAVY STAFFING CRITERIA	S6	500	13770	500	9940	253	6996	.036400
SF01121007	(U)SYSTEM ANALYSIS AND ENGINEERING	S6	1000	14770	850	10790	500	7496	.037058
SF08452003	(U)ACOUSTICAL SILENCING. EXTERNAL SHIP SYSTEM	S6	1920	16690	1735	12525	1412	8908	.033789
TF10531001	(U)CARGO MOVEMENT AND DISTRIBUTION	S6	700	17390	550	13075	300	9208	.018039
SF01121004	(U)TRANSDUCERS AND ACOUSTIC POWER GENERATORS	S6	4500	21890	4009	17084	2700	11908	.011785
SF01121002	(U)SONAR SIGNAL PROCESSING AND CLASSIFICATION	S6	7000	28890	6520	23604	5800	17708	.007246
SF01121001	(U)UNDERWATER SOUND PROPAGATION	S6	6400	35290	6000	29604	4800	22508	.005250
SF09443004	(U)NUCLEAR PROPULSION PLANT MATERIALS DEVELOPMENT	S4	1100	36390	1100	30704	0	22508	
SF09443001	(U)NUCLEAR PROPULSION PLANT TECHNOLOGY	S4	1000	37390	1000	31704	0	22508	
SF09442003	(U)SURFACE SHIP REFUELING EQUIPMENT AND PROCEDURES DEVELOPMENT	S4	2200	39590	2200	33904	0	22506	

Figure 5

EXAMPLE: COMPUTER PRINTOUT RANKED BY DESIRABILITY

The end results of a research and development planning effort like this are computer printouts (Figures 4 and 5) which rank every project according to its value in the overall program. In the Navy, this comes to over 700 separate R&D projects. It would be a mistake, however, to think that the impressive-looking computer printouts are taking over the final decision-making job. Most of those who design and work with information systems like the one described, fully realize that technological forecasts and quantitative estimates of project value are no more or less than a planning tool—and only one of many that a manager must use in making final decisions.

CONCLUSIONS

I am well aware of many of the omissions and weaknesses of these quantitative selection or resource allocation techniques. It should be stressed again that they were not intended to yield decision, but rather information which would facilitate decision. Indeed, these techniques are merely thinking structures to force methodical, meticulous consideration of all the factors involved in resource allocation. *Data* plus *analysis* yields *information. Information* plus *judgement* yields *decisions.*

$$\text{Data} + \text{Analysis} = \text{Information}$$

$$\text{Information} + \text{Judgement} = \text{Decision}$$

I am firmly convinced that if I had to choose between any machine and the human brain, I would select the brain. The brain has a marvelous system that learns from experience and an uncanny way of pulling out the salient factors or rejecting useless information. It is wrong to say that one must select intuitive experience over analysis or minds over machines; really they are *not* alternatives, they complement each other. Used together, they yield result far better than if used individually.

A close look at a few "facts" concerning the quantitative resource allocation methods shows these approaches to be merely experimental management techniques. The fact that a computer or an adding machine may be used to facilitate data handling should, in no way distract from the basic fact that human subjective inputs are the foundation of these systems. Accurate human calculation, as opposed to use of a computer for the calculations of all the interrelationships considered would not alter the basic principles of these management tools in any respect. Yet, I often hear the reactionary complaint that quantitative measurements cannot be applied to management processes because human judgement cannot be forsaken and machines cannot replace the seasoned experience expertise of the manager.[14]

The real concern should be directed toward using the collective judgement of technical staffs (technological forecasts) and decision-makers in such a manner that logically sound decisions are made, greater payoff is achieved for the resources committed, and that less, not more, valuable scientific and engineering time expended. To make an incorrect decision is understandable, but to make a decision and not really know the basis for the judgement is unforgivable. The area of good resource allocation certainly must have advanced beyond this point; otherwise, a pair of dice could replace the decision-maker.

Most of the managers who design and work with information systems fully realize that technological forecasts, quantitative estimates of project value, and other aids to resource allocation are merely a planning tool—and only one of a brand new kit of advance decision-making devices.

Even this caveat, however, does not defuse critics of the whole idea—and there are some very vocal ones around in government and business. Some of the criticism is in reaction to the fear of "mechanization" of a task felt to be rightfully in the province of human evaluation. Other critics claim that building up a logical system, computerizing the output, and quantifying what are essentially intuitive and judgement decisions may insulate some managers with a false sense of security. The validation of the process will not be continued and management responsibility will be abandoned. Another criticism stems from the use of estimates as basic figures in the analysis. This kind of objection can also be applied to decision based on "experience" and made without a quantitative approach.

Technological forecasting and systematic analysis tend to force managers to consider their resource allocation tasks more comprehensively and highlights problem areas that might easily be overlooked by more traditional approaches. However, regardless of the high degree of sophistication being attributed to these planning devices, managers should use them with caution.

REFERENCES

1. Ansoff, H. I. and J. M. Stewart, "Strategies for a Technology-Based Business, *Harvard Business Review*, Cambridge, Mass., Nov.–Dec. 1967 P.P. 71–83.
2. Cetron, M. J., P. H. Caulfield and R. D. Freshman, "Facts and Folklore in R&D Management Revisited'. Submitted to *Management Science* (TIMS) for publication in the Winter of 1969.

3. Cetron, M. J., H. Darracott and H. Wells, *Report on Technological Forecasting* sponsored by the Joint Commanders of the Army Materiel Command, Navy Material Command, and Air Force Systems Command, (AD 664108); CFSTI, Springfield, Va. 22151, May 1967.

4. Cetron, M. J., R. Isenson, J. Johnson, A. B. Nutt & H. Wells, *Quantitative Methods for Technological Resource Management* accepted for publication by MIT Press, Cambridge, Mass., in the Spring of 1969.

5. Cetron, M. J., J. Martino and L. Roepke, "The Selection of R&D Program Content—Survey of Quantitative Methods." *IEEE Transactions on Engineering Management,* Vol. EM-14, No. 1 March 1967, PP 4–12.

6. Cetron, M. J. and T. Monohan, "An Evaluation and Appraisal of Various Approaches to Technological Forecasting", *Technological Forecasting for Industry and Government* edited by J. R. Bright, Prentice-Hall, Inc.; Englewood Cliffs, New Jersey, May 1968 PP 144–179.

7. Cetron, M. J. and A. L. Weiser "Technological Change, Technological Forecasting and Planning R&D—A View from the R&D Manager's Desk" *George Washington Law Review,* (Technology Assessment and the Law) Vol. 35 No. 5 George Washington University, Washington, D. C. July 1968.

8. Ellingsworth, K. "Technology Assessment", an unpublished masters paper in R&D Management, American University, Washington, D. C. June 1968.

9. Guth, W. D. and R. Tagiuri, "Personal Values and Corporate Strategy," *Harvard Business Review*—Cambridge, Mass. Sept–Oct 1965.

10. Isenson, R. S. & C. W. Sherwin, *Project Hindsight* (Interim Report), Office of the Director of Defense Research and Engineering, CSTI (AD 642 400) Springfield, Va. June 30, 1966 (Revised, Oct. 13, 1966).

11. Lenz, R., *Technological Forecasting,* CSTI (AD 408 085) Springfield, Va. 1962.

12. North, H. Q. and D. L. Pyke, "Technology, the Chicken-Corporate Goals, the Egg", *Technological Forecasting for Industry and Government,* edited by J. R. Bright, Prentice-Hall, Inc.; Englewood Cliffs, New Jersey, May 1968, PP 412–425.

13. Nutt, A. B., "An Approach to Research and Development Effectiveness" *IEEE Transactions on Engineering Management,* September 1965 PP 103–112.

14. Roberts, E. B., "Facts and Folklore in R&D Management" *Industrial Management Review,* Sloan School of Management, Cambridge, Mass., Spring 1967.

15. Smith, D. F. and F. A. Hansen, "Long Range Research and Development Planning" (MEL 395/66) Naval Ship R&D Center, Annapolis, Md. 1966.

PARALLEL AND SEQUENTIAL R&D STRATEGIES:
Application of a Simple Model*

William J. Abernathy
Assistant Professor
University of California
Los Angeles, California

and

Richard S. Rosenbloom
Professor of Business Administration
Harvard University
Boston, Massachusetts

It is common in technological development to identify and explore several approaches to a particular objective so that the best approach may be chosen. The outcome of any approach is uncertain; hence, it is difficult to choose the best one at an early date. To deal with this uncertainty, two or more approaches to the objective may be continued in parallel until a clear choice between them can be made, i.e., a parallel strategy. Such a strategy can provide better information for a decision, maintain options, or hedge against the occurrence of an unsatisfactory outcome. This paper addresses the manager's problem of deciding when to use or continue a parallel strategy. The principal focus is based on studies of 14 projects and illustrates the application, in one setting, of a general model appropriate to the structure of the decision as it is widely faced in practice. It discusses the information requirements for a sound choice between parallel and sequential strategies and the consequences of choosing a strategy on the basis of incomplete information.

The stream of technical choices made during the course of an R&D project will determine both the cost of the project and the value of its outcome. The men making these decisions—project managers, group leaders, and the like—face a common predicament. Within limits of time

* Reprinted from the *IEEE Transactions on Engineering Management*, Vol. EM-15, No. 1, March 1968.

and resources they must oversee both the systematic search for solutions to technical problems and the sequential accomplishment of specified goals. Decisions must be made in the face of substantial uncertainties about the consequences of possible courses of action. Yet although commitment to a specific problem-solving approach is risky, failure to do so may waste precious time. The essence of this problem is the need to find economical means of gaining sufficient information on which to base the major technical choices of the project.[1]

A strategy of parallel investigation or development is one means used by experienced managers to cope with the pressures of limited time and information.[2] By a parallel strategy is meant the simultaneous employment of two or more distinct approaches to a single task when successful completion of any one would satisfy the task requirements. By following more than one approach, the manager avoids the risks inherent in trying to discern a priori which of several uncertain approaches will prove to be the best. By this means he can purchase information that will permit a better choice between approaches, hedge against the risks of outright failure, and perhaps gain indirect benefits by stimulating competitive effort or building a broader technological competence for the organization.

The alternative to a parallel strategy is sequential, i.e., commitment to the best evident approach with other possibilities to be pursued only if the first proves unsuccessful. This, of course, is the most common practice. In most situations the benefits of a parallel strategy may seem obscure whereas its additional costs are quite evident. Yet use of the "usual" sequential strategy constitutes a decision against the alternative, a decision which might be reversed were it based on explicit evaluation of costs and benefits.

---

[1] The R&D planning problem has interested a number of other students of R&D management. Klein and Meckling,[7] in the early paper in this field, drew attention to the special characteristics of R&D. The works of Marples,[8] Eyring,[4] and Harlan,[5] among others, have offered systematic descriptions of the ways in which decision makers cope with uncertainty in R&D project choices. Bonini,[2] Rosenbloom,[15] and others have sketched primitive prescriptive models, which attempt to deal more formally with uncertain information.

[2] One must be wary of semantic confusion. Nelson[12] and Marschak[10] use this term in the same sense as the authors use it to refer to the simultaneous use of two or more approaches to the same task. Bonini,[2] on the other hand, employs the phrase "multiple approaches" to denote this strategy and reserves the term "parallel" for the situation when normally *consecutive* phrases of a project (e.g., design and tooling) are performed simultaneously. Allen,[1] in papers concerned with parallel projects, exploits the existence of such situations (in the authors' sense of the term) to study other questions in R&D administration. Allen has not been concerned with the decision to authorize a parallel strategy.

A parallel strategy should be used for an R&D task when it can be expected to increase the value of the task outcome by an amount commensurate with its expected increase in the cost of the task. In an early study of aircraft development, Schlaifer[16] found that parallel approaches in the form of competitive designs provided an important contribution to aircraft development in the United States. Nelson[12] has argued that parallel development makes good economic sense and has demonstrated in a hypothetical example of a single stage problem that a parallel strategy in the early stage of development can produce lower expected cost, or higher expected value, despite the apparently larger initial outlay.

Although it is evident that parallel strategies can enhance the effectiveness with which the resources of a project are utilized, the manager must decide whether a parallel strategy would have that consequence in his particular circumstances. The benefits of parallel development, if there are any, are uncertain and will be realized at some distant time. The immediate consequence of a parallel strategy is an increase in the rate of expenditure for the project or, alternatively, a dilution of the effort devoted to any given approach. Hence, the better course of action is seldom obvious beforehand.

This paper describes a simple analytical framework which may help managers to make better decisions about the use of parallel strategies of investigation and development. It is directed toward the decisions made on real organizations, rather than the theory of optimal choice. The authors believe that the logic of decision in most practical cases is, in fact, rather simple. Although ending an optimal rule for choosing among a large number of possibilities in an n-stage investigation is extremely difficult (see, for example, Marschak and Yahav[11]), most real problems involve a relatively small number of approaches and at most two or three stages of investigation.

The analytical framework is presented by decribing is application in a single situation, a million-dollar advanced development project (the SPS project). This method was chosen because the abstract concepts seem more readily understandable in relation to the concrete reality of a project and because the fact of its application illustrates the feasibility of obtaining appropriate data for the analysis within a real situation.

The framework itself was developed as part of a larger study.[14] The principal aims of the study were first, to construct a simple economic model for choice between parallel and sequential strategies which would have the potential for reasonably wide practical application, and second, to identify the information required for rational choice in these circumstances and to consider the feasibility of developing such information in real projects. The study began with the preparation of 14 case descriptions of situations (including the SPS project) in which explicit consideration had been given to a parallel strategy for an R&D task. This helped to develop a general statement of information requirements and to formulate a generalized though explicit statement of the precision problem. These ideas were then tested by intentive evaluation of the merits of a parallel strategy at a critical point in the SPS project.

THE SPS PROJECT

The silent power supply (SPS) project involved the engineering development of a technically advanced product which, if successful, would be marketed by the company in whose laboratories the work was being done. The technical phases of development were expected to cost more than $1,000,000 and to span several years. A key element in the design was a module which would require an advance in the state-of-the-art of fuel cell technology, a field in which the laboratory staff was among the leaders.

The project plan called for three phases of development of the fuel cell module: laboratory experimentation, development of engineering models, and system integration, leading to a manufactured prototype. Two fuel cell design concepts—ambient temperature and moderate temperature—had been identified. There was considerable uncertainty about the ultimate outcome of either design approach.

Management decided to carry both approaches through the first phase, at an added cost of $40,000. Having completed that work successfully, it had to decide whether to continue the parallel strategy through development of the engineering model, termed the XH1.[3] Since the company was firmly committed to developing the SPS system, failure in development of a single engineering model would lead to development of the alternative design. Management believed that there was one chance in four that either approach might fail to produce a satisfactory fuel cell design and asserted that the two approaches were independent.

Even under the assumption that these design approaches would turn out satisfactorily, considerable uncertainty remained about the specific nature of the project outcome. These uncertainties centered on the direct manufacturing cost (DMC) of the product and the completion time of the de-

[3] The possibility of carrying the development in parallel through a final stage, the development of a manufacturing prototype, was also a relevant consideration. The simulation model which the authors will subsequently discuss did include this final stage. The results suggest that a final stage was not an important element in this decision and for reasons of brevity they will not include this multistage description in this paper.

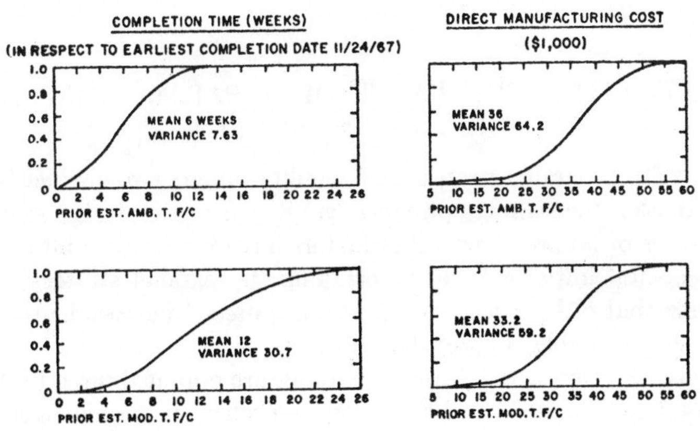

Figure 1. Judgemental cumulative probability distributions for principal outcome measures. These curves are based on the engineering manager's estimates of the probabilities of various outcomes with respect to both project completion and initial DMC of the developed product for the two technical approaches, ambient (Amb. T.F/C) and moderate (Mod. T.F/C) temperature designs.

velopment project. Management expectations about these two uncertain factors are shown in Fig. 1 in the form of cumulative probability distributions.

Both variables, manufacturing cost and completion time, would have an important impact on the economic value of the project. A delay in project completion would increase development expenditures at the rate of $11,000 per week. A loss of sales revenue could result from a significant delay in market introduction; although this is difficult to judge, a loss of four units was estimated as a consequence of a four-month delay. Studies conducted by the marketing department showed that sales revenues would be very sensitive to unit selling price. An annual volume of 10 units at a $30,000 price would be increased to 500 units at a $9,000 price. Total profit would be affected by both volume and the cost-price relationship. Direct manufacturing costs were expected to decline sharply in time; for example, an initial $30,000 DMC/unit was expected to fall to $3,000 within two and one-half years after project completion.

A decision to carry both designs through the XH1 phase would increase development costs by $15,000 beyond those that would be incurred if a single approach were followed and proved to be satisfactory. The question that must be answered is: "Do the economic benefits of a parallel strategy for the XH1 justify that cost?"

APPROXIMATING THE VALUE OF A PARALLEL STRATEGY FOR THE SPS PROJECT

In analyzing a parallel strategy one should evaluate two distinct benefits: the information the strategy provides and its worth as a hedge against the consequences of failure.[4] Two other factors have to be taken into account: the incremental initial cost of undertaking the parallel strategy and the probability that either technical approach, pursued independently, would provide an acceptable solution for the task.

For the SPS project, the latter two values are obtained directly. For the success probabilities, 0.75 in either case, one relies on the manager's judgment. It should be emphasized that considerable variation in outcome value is included within the definition of a "satisfactory" outcome. The incremental initial cost is given as $150,000. Ordinarily, when two approaches are to be undertaken, this value approximates the direct resource cost of the second approach since at least one must be undertaken anyway.

Gauging the magnitude of the benefits of the parallel strategy is a more difficult task. It is useful to evaluate these benefits in two categories. The authors proceed first through an approximate method of evaluation in order to provide an intuitive grasp of their meaning; then, they turn to more precise measures and a series of sensitivity tests which were obtained from a simulation model of the problem.

One set of benefits includes those whose magnitude depends on the time of completion of the task. These are *time-variant* costs to be saved by earlier completion. The symbol TV is used to represent their sum.

In the SPS project, if only one approach were undertaken and it failed, development of the engineering model for the alternative would be begun as soon as failure became evident. The mean estimate of the time that would be lost under these circumstances was approximately 15 weeks. The cost of that delay is the value that is assigned to TV. It comprises three types of cost. 1) The added cost of systems development. This is the additional cost of keeping the entire development effort intact during a delay period over and above fuel cell module development cost. 2) Profit contribution on lost sales. Management considered that with a delay, a

[4] Other benefits may be equally important in certain instances. Usually, however, these are related to the two that the authors have identified or that are not so directly concerned with the problem of dealing with the uncertainty in development.

few of the anticipated unit sales for which tentative delivery commitments were made will be lost to competitive types of power sources. 3) The financial cost of deferring the date at which the stream of revenues will begin. Any delay in development will mean that the future payoff from the development is also delayed, with a consequent loss in the returns which could otherwise be attained by reinvesting the fund flow earlier at the company's investment opportunity rate. The first is given as $11,000 per week, or $165,000 for the possible 15-week delay; the other two are more difficult to quantify. Very rough estimates suggest values of $100,000 and $160,000,[5] respectively, yielding a total of $425,000 (see Table I).

TABLE I

VARIABLES INFLUENCING THE CHOICE BETWEEN STRATEGIES

P: The probability of success for the given technical approach.

SPS Approximation: A three in four chance of success.

C: The incremental initial cost of a parallel strategy. (Usually the cost of the second approach)

SPS Approximation: $150,000

TV: The cost of failure. The cost when a sequential strategy is followed and the preferred approach is unsuccessful.

SPS Approximation:

1) Added cost of system development, at $11,000 per week for 15 weeks	$165,000
2) Foregone profit contribution,[5] on basis of four units lost in a 4-month delay	100,000
3) Financial cost of deferring[5] the date at which the stream of revenue will begin at 20 percent of 2M million dollars for 15 weeks	160,000
Approximate Total Value of TV:	$425,000

[5] With only a 2-month delay, no sales losses were anticipated, while ten units were the anticipated sales losses for a 10-month delay. Losses between 2 and 10 months were expected to be approximately linear with time. As a rough measure, the authors have used the loss of four units, at $25,000 each, as the consequence of the 15-week "most likely" delay. To get at the cost of deferring the receipt of revenue, the authors took a conservative calculated value of the development (about $2,750,000, which represents an unfavorable DMC outcome on Fig. 2) and determined a weekly opportunity cost of capital using a 20-percent discount rate. This cost for 15 weeks is very nearly $160,000.

Before turning to the other potential benefits, look at the logic of the situation so far. If management follows a sequential strategy and the first approach fails, it incurs penalties valued at about $425,000 and ends up paying $150,000 for the second XH1 anyway. But there is only one chance in four that this will happen, to the expected cost is 0.25 × $575,000, or not quite $145,000. To avoid this eventuality, a parallel strategy will cost $150,000. Thus, viewed strictly as insurance against the delay consequent on an initial failure, a paralled strategy in this case does not quite made sense.[6] These time-variant costs are often the only ones considered by managers evaluating a parallel strategy.

But there is another source of benefits, the value of information to be gained. This is a benefit whose magnitude depends on the conditional opportunity to choose the preferred design on the basis of better information; this is denoted by PREF. To illustrate the meaning of this concept and to develop an approximate measure of PREF, the authors simplify the problem and consider only the direct manufacturing cost outcome (DMC), the principal area of uncertainty in the dimensions of technical outcome.

Estimates of the DMC outcome (given in Fig. 1) are described approximately by means of the two normal distributions shown in Fig. 2. The distribution for the ambient temperature design has a mean of $36,000 and a standard deviation of $9,000. The comparable measures for the other approach are $33,000 and $8,000, respectively. The significance of these differences depends upon a stream of economic implications. A function that summarizes the economic consequences of any outcome as obtained by tracing the 4-year cost, price volume, and profit implications of three particular DMC outcomes. This function computes the discounted net present value for each outcome and fits a curve to those points, as shown above the distributions. Because the function is nearly linear over the relevant range, the point where the mean of the distribution intersects the economic function can be used as an estimate of the expected value of that choice. The value of the ambient temperature approach is $3,000,000 and that of the moderate temperature approach $3,300,000. Hence, the

[6] Stated alternatively, the authors are saying that conditional on the failure of the preferred approach and success of the second approach, they will incur the TV penalty with a sequential strategy and no such penalty with a parallel strategy. The suspected value of the insurance provided by the parallel strategy therefore, $(1 - P^1) \cdot P^2 \cdot \mathrm{TV}$. This is the expected value from one possible outcome. Expected costs and benefits from other out nes will be discussed subsequently.

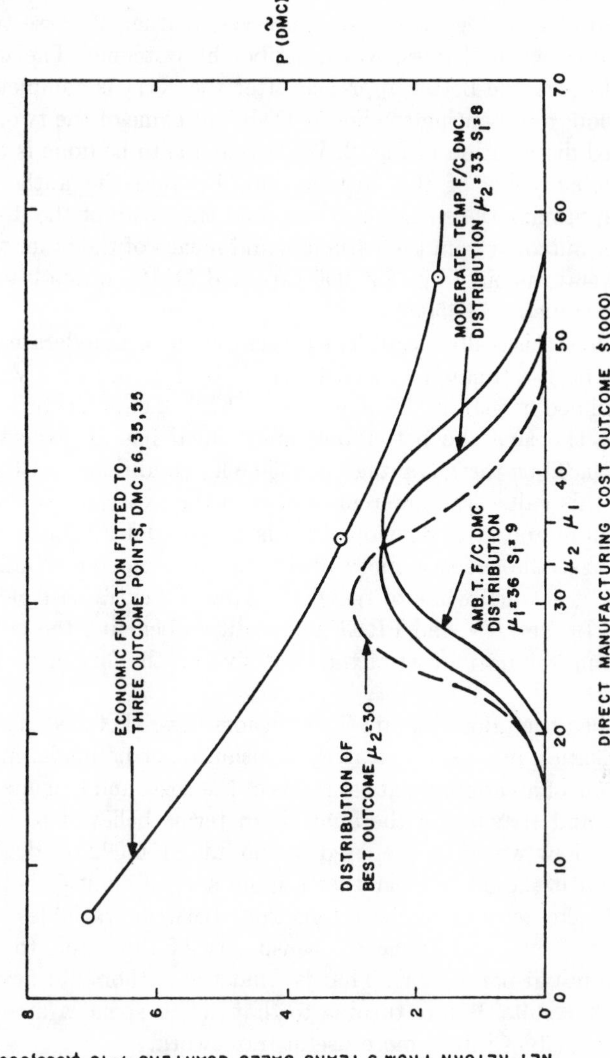

Figure 2. Approximate DMC distributions and an approximate economic function.

moderate temperature design would be the preferred first approach for a sequential strategy.

If a parallel strategy is chosen, however, neither of these two distributions, shown as solid lines, will describe the outcome. The manager will be able to pick the better approach after the XH1 is complete. This new distribution, representing the better DMC outcome of the two, is shown as the dotted distribution in Fig. 2. What remains to be done is to determine the expected value of this distribution. Because the authors are using normal approximations, they can compute the mean of the distribution of the better outcome from the variances and means of the other two distributions. This turns out to be $30,000 expected DMC, which is equivalent to a project value of $3,650,000.

What does this really mean? The present value of a moderate temperature XH1 has been estimated at $3,300,000. If both approaches would succeed (the likelihood of that is 0.75 × 0.75 or 0.5625), a parallel strategy gives the option of choosing the better outcome, which has an expected value of $3,650,000. Thus the advantage is $350,000, conditional on both succeeding, and this value (the difference between the expected worth of the best choice before and after development) is called PREF.[7] Since management believes that the event is more likely than the outcome "tails" on a flip of a coin, it is worthwhile to spend the $150,000 extra cost of the parallel strategy. In fact, TV and PREF are additive benefits, the latter by itself outweighing the initial cost of the strategy and the former coming close to equaling it.

What has been done so far? The authors have sketched the details of a single situation in which a strategy decision must be made, indicating the main points of an approximate analysis of the costs and benefits of a parallel strategy, and structuring the analysis in terms believed to be of general relevance. Few would be prepared to commit $150,000 on the basis of this sketch, but it should be clear that a more careful analysis is justified, one that will take account of the interactions between variables, reflect some secondary effects, and gauge the sensitivity of the result to errors of estimate in initial parameters. That is what the authors did next with some interesting results. Before turning to that, let us spend a moment putting the four variables into a more useful framework.

---

[7] Whereas $(1 - P^1) \cdot P^2 \cdot \mathrm{TV}$ was described in a previous footnote as the expected insurance benefit from one outcome state, PREF represents the benefits of a parallel strategy which occur in another outcome state. PREF is obtained only when both approaches turn out to be successful. It therefore was the expected value of $P^1 \cdot P^2 \cdot$ PREF.

A GENERAL ECONOMIC FRAMEWORK

Equation (1) expresses the situation where the costs and benefits of a parallel strategy are in balance, the left term giving its incremental expected cost, the right terms giving the expected benefits. This is a concise expression of the logic by which the authors compared costs and benefits. When the right-hand side exceeds the left, parallel strategy is attractive economically.[8]

$$P_1(C) = P_1P_2(\text{PREF}) + (1 - P_1)P_2(\text{TV}), \tag{1}$$

where P_i, $i = 1, 2$ is the probability that a given approach will lead to a satisfactory outcome and C is the incremental initial cost of the parallel strategy.

It should be clear that the absolute values of the cost and benefits are irrelevant; it is their relative magnitudes that count. Hence, the benefit figures can be normalized by dividing by the cost C giving

$$\text{TV/C} = \text{an "insurance cost" ratio}$$

and

$$\text{PREF}/C = \text{an "information cost". ratio.}$$

Equation (1), in these terms, defines a surface in three dimensions on which the economic factors are equal for parallel and sequential strategies. From this a characteristic graph is produced (Fig. 3)[9] showing a set of indifference curves as a function of P, PREF/C, and C/TV (using the reciprocal of TV/C to keep a 0, 0 origin). Any point on the 0.0 PREF/C

[8] With a parallel strategy, the additional cost C is incurred under all outcome states. With a sequential strategy, it is incurred only when the primary approach fails, having an expected cost of $(1 - P^1)\cdot C$. The difference, P^1C is therefore the expected cost of a parallel strategy. The right-hand side of the equation contains those terms described.[6, 7] They summarize the payoff of two possible outcome states: success of both approaches and failure of the preferred approach with success of the second approach. The other two of four possible outcome states, failure of both and success of the first with failure of the second, have no differential consequences which affect the choice between the two strategies. That is, the evidence suggests no differential benefits of consequence from one strategy choice or the other insofar as these two outcome states are concerned. Having zero differential value, the other two possible outcome states drop out of the equation.

[9] Figure 3 is simply a means of showing the relationships that are expressed by (1) It diagrams the values that $P(P = P^1 = P^2)$ and C/TV must take on when PREF/C is held constant at 12 different values, if the two strategies are to be equal in value. Because it represents the values for which the two strategies are equal, it may be used to indicate the direction of the inequality when the problem conditions are such that the two strategies are not equal in value.

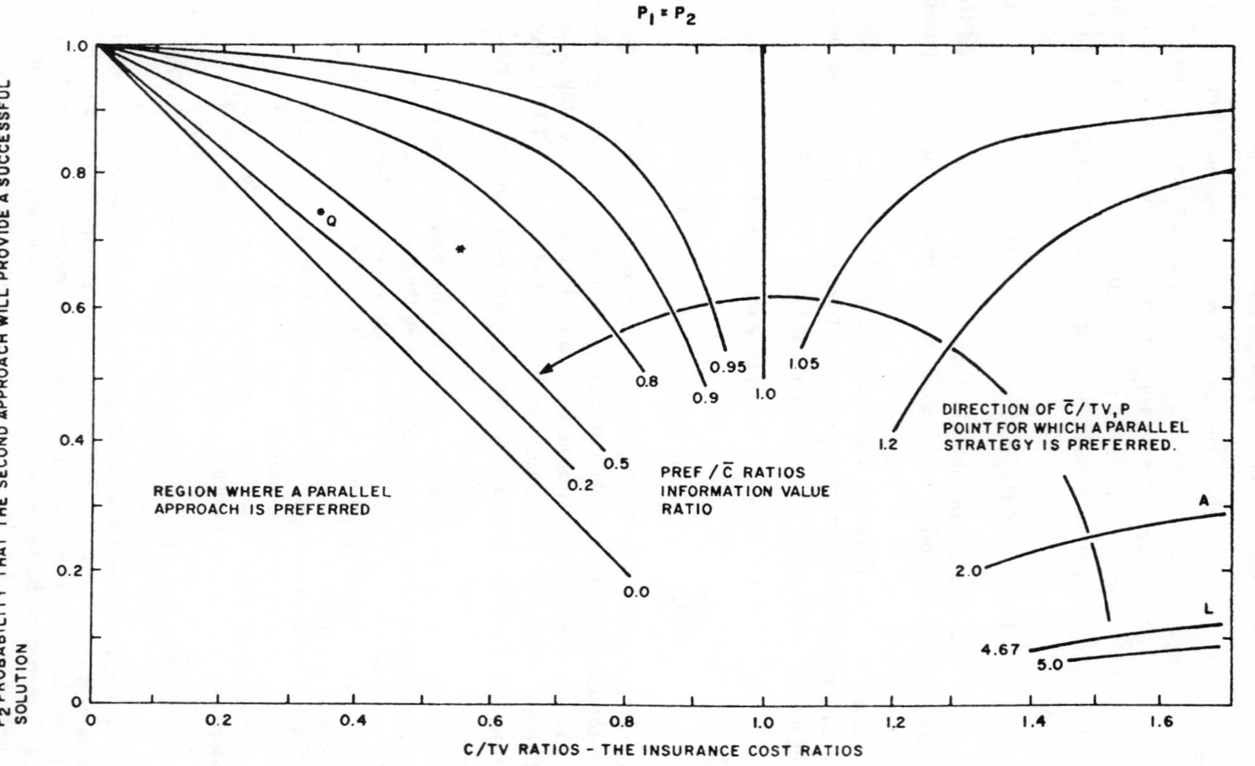

Figure 3. Characteristic graph.

ratio line, for instance, indicates the values which P and C/TV must take on when PREF/C is zero if the equality of (1) is to be maintained. On this graph, a project is represented by an insurance cost (C/TV) point and an information cost (PREF/C) line. If the point lies counterclockwise in relation to the relevant line, (1) is an inequality with the left-hand side smaller than the right and a parallel strategy is preferred.

MORE PRECISE VALUES FOR THE SPS DECISION

The analysis given earlier suggests the following approximate values for these variables in relation to the use of a parallel strategy for the XH1 stage of the SPS:

$$P_1 = P_2 = 0.75$$

$$C/\mathrm{TV} = \frac{150}{425} = 0.35$$

$$\mathrm{PREF}/C = \frac{350}{150} = 2.3.$$

In Fig. 3, comparison of the point Q (0.75, 0.35) and the line PREF = 2.0 (the nearest to the indicated value of 2.3) shows that this project is well within the area of preference for a parallel strategy. Use of the graph furthermore, permits certain simple kinds of sensitivity analysis. The graph shows that as long as PREF/C is estimated at more than 2.0, any reasonable P and TV values are still within the parallel region. But if PREF is, say, only \$120,000 rather than over \$300,000, and if either TV or the chance of failure is much smaller, one would get a different result.

The characteristic graph can be used to test sensitivity to variation in the summary measures. It is also desirable to test the underlying data from which the summary measures were derived. That requires more complex analysis.

A digital simulation model was constructed to develop more reliable measures of these benefits and to test their sensitivity to change in the original managerial estimates. Using Monte Carlo methods, this computer program "acts out" thousands of product life histories and summaries the technical and economic consequences in terms of frequency distributions and measures of expected value.

The simulation provided a means of evaluating the consequences of different management choices through the use of a model which brings together several different types of information relevant to strategy choices for the SPS project. It incorporates management's best estimates concerning the developmental results that will be achieved, information obtained through cost studies of development and manufacturing, market studies concerning the effects of manufacturing costs, and completion time on sales volume. A more complete explanation of the simulation model is contained in a report of this study, "Parallel and Sequential Strategies for R&D projects."[14] The general characteristics of the simulation, however, are as follows.

The duration, DMC, and time to assess success or failure of each approach through an initial stage of development, the XH1 stage, are drawn as samples from management's judgmental distributions (some of which are included in Fig. 1). The outcomes of a parallel or a sequential choice through this initial stage are retained for subsequent use. Given the simulated outcome of the initial stage, a second set of samples is drawn again, making to account the outcomes achieved and the uncertainty reduction of the first stage. Whereas the first simulation stage represents the outcome of the XH1 experimental model development, the second set of randomly determined outcomes represents the uncertain difference between the results achieved in an experimental model and those achieved in a manufacturing model. Again development outcome data concerning implications of following a parallel or sequential strategy through either the first stage only or both stages of development are retained for further processing.

From the simulated development outcome data, the post-development manufacturing and marketing consequences are traced for each of the possible strategy choices. A sales history for each is generated and evaluated over an 18-quarter period following development completion. A long-linear learning function whose parameters are determined by the development outcome is used to compute manufacturing cost improvement in each of the 18 quarters. Prices for each quarter are set so as to maximize profit in accordance with the expressed pricing policy of the company. The prices are set by a subroutine which takes the demand function, manufacturing costs, and growth constraints into account. Cash flows, netting R&D and manufacturing costs against sales revenues, are discounted at a specified rate and summed to yield the present worth. The procedure just described is repeated over and over, and the mean from many trials of net present worth of the project is computed for each strategy, as are summary measures of PREF and TV.[10]

Given management's estimates for the initial probability distributions,

---

[10] Other data which were computed but not reported in this paper include a frequency distribution of project value, and the payback period for alternative strategy choices.

demand curve, and progress function, plus an 18-period horizon and 20-percent discount rate, one obtains the following results:

Net Discounted Expected Project Value:

$4,884,000 Parallel strategy through the XH1 stage.
$4,511,000 Sequential strategy beginning with the ambient temperature fuel cell design.
$4,485,000 Sequential strategy beginning with the moderate temperature fuel cell design.

Summary Ratios:

0.34 C/TV—Insurance ratio for the XH1 stage.
4.67 PREF/C—Information cost ratio for the XH1 stage.

It may be recalled that a parallel strategy costs $150,000, whereas it offers a *net* return of approximately $370,000. Most of this value is provided by the information contribution of a parallel strategy, as indicated by the

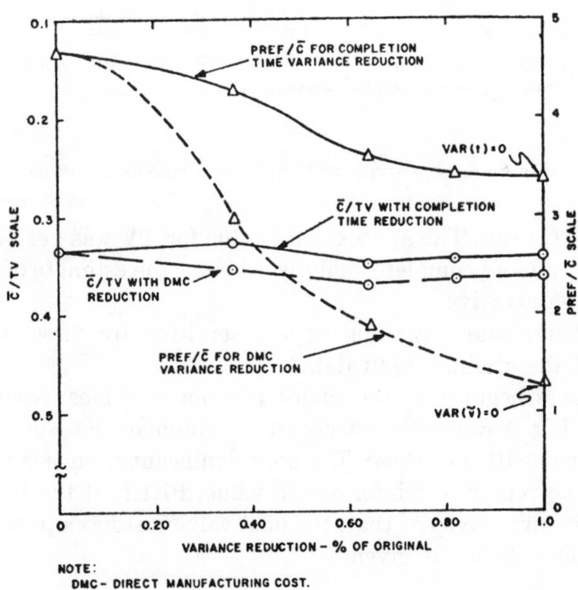

Figure 4. Sensitivity test of prior DMC and completion-time uncertainties.

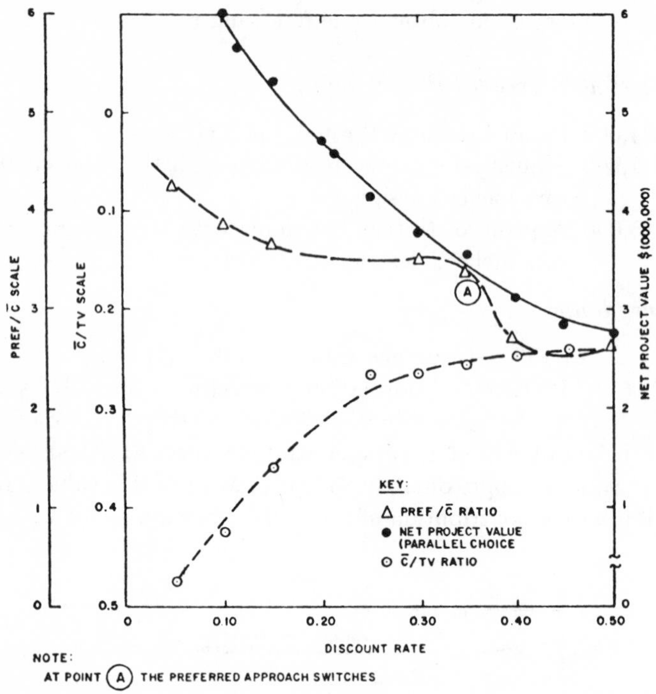

Figure 5. Sensitivity test of discount rate assumptions.

high PREF/C ratio. The approximate value for TV was very close to that produced by a more complete analysis, whereas the estimate of information value was conservative.

The next important question is, how sensitive are these results to the accuracy of the original input data?

The authors begin with the major random variables: completion time and DMC. Fig. 4 shows the effects on the summary measures of reducing the variance on either of these. The only significant change is the reduction of some 80 percent in the information value, PREF, if the DMC is taken as entirely certain. Even at that, the final value justifies a parallel strategy, all other things being as given.[11]

[11] Misestimating the relative differences in the two approaches (the relative positions of their means) has an effect on PREF that is similar to an error in assessing the variance in DMC and completion-time estimates.

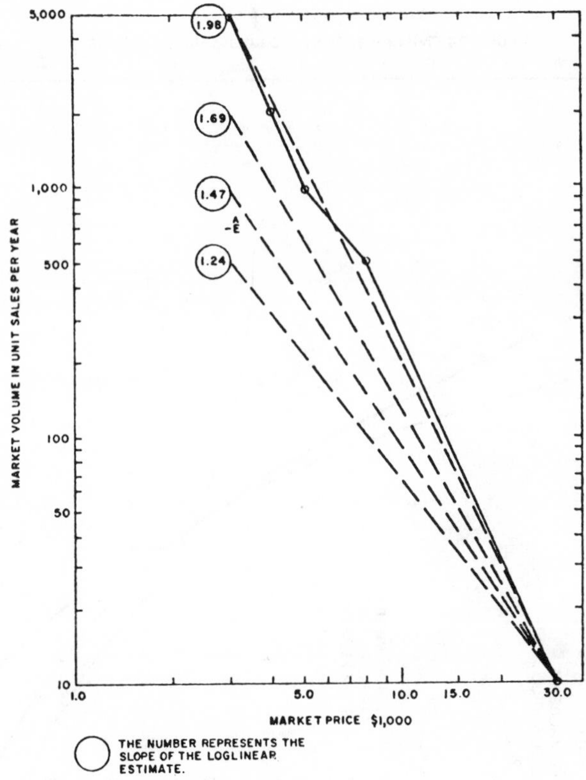

Figure 6. Estimated demand function, linear approximation, and alternative possible functions.

The discount rate is a measure of the scarcity of resources. A high rate implies a reluctance to commit current resources for distant returns. A parallel strategy, of course, does just that, increasing near-term costs for future benefits. Not surprisingly, the computed net project value turns out to be a declining function of discount rate, as shown in Fig. 5. This also shows that even the very high rate of 50 percent leaves a sizable indicated net gain from this strategy.

The influence of changes in market estimates is described by Figs. 6 and 7. The log-linear slope of the market demand curve has been systematically varied over an approximately 10 to 1 range. When the slope of the market demand curve is reduced below 1.34 (reflecting for a $3,000 sales price a decrease in unit sales from the expected 5000 to approximately 800

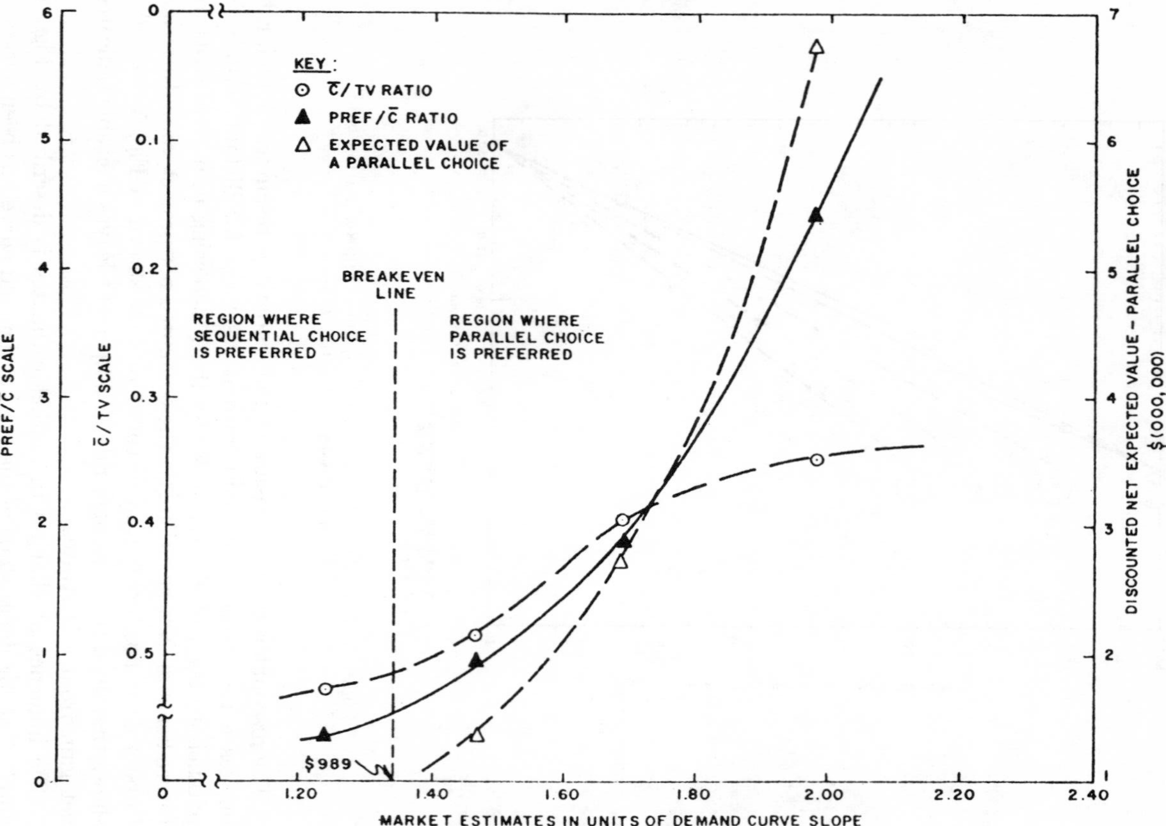

Figure 7. Sensitivity test of demand function slope assumption.

units), the preferred strategy choice switches. This severe change in market assumptions illustrates the relevance of user-market economic information to "technical" decisions made during the conduct of a development project.

The authors have been evaluating alternative development strategies for the SPS in terms of a simple economic model. Their analysis combined information concerning technical outcomes, resource costs, and the economics of use. The last is especially important, since the value of a new element of technology necessarily is derived from the circumstances of its use. Yet this factor is often overlooked in technical choices.

An explicit model not only serves to bring together these quite different considerations in a systematic way, but it also can be used to assess the value of improving the quality of the information available. In the SPS case, within an extremely wide range of judgments about technical uncertainties and resource costs, the indicated benefits for a parallel strategy continue to outweigh its costs. Only when one turns to the market data, which constitute the "circumstances of its use," does one find that plausible changes in estimates would indicate a different choice of strategy.

One frequently finds that decision makers are reluctant to use highly uncertain estimates, especially when they pertain to unfamiliar territory, as when an engineer confronts market data of the sort presented here. Yet when an engineer's choices will influence a firm's longer-run performance in a marketplace, as they often do, it seems much better to use bad data than to ignore potential market benefits. As is often true, the choice of a strategy is not very sensitive to reasonably large errors in the input parameters, but will be severely biased by the omission of some.

In addition, one can show that simple rules of thumb in common use may lead to unanticipated economic results. One manager in another firm, for example, would authorize parallel development when the cost of delay resulting from failure of the preferred approach exceeded five times the cost of the parallel approach; i.e., in the authors' terms when C/TV was less than 0.2. That rule leads to sequential development, a $370,000 inferior strategy, in this case. Use of a simple financial payback criterion, because it emphasizes the near-term at the expense of longer-term economic benefits, produces a similar distortion. A sequential strategy was actually used in the SPS case "because the payback period of the parallel strategy was too long."

CONCLUSION

A single situation, the SPS, has been used as a metaphor for exploration of the economics of parallel strategies. A few summary observations can be offered in conclusion.

A parallel strategy provides tangible economic benefits that are not always intuitively obvious or apparent. These benefits will be more readily recognized in any particular decision-making context if they are anticipated in advance. At a minimum, the potential benefits of a parallel strategy include its value as a means of providing information for the choice of an approach, its value as a hedge against the consequences of failure, and its value as a means of enhancing useful competition. The authors considered the first two benefits in this paper and have shown that at least these two may be assigned specific quantitative values.

The information that is relevant to the choice of a parallel strategy should be readily available to the decision maker. The relevant information includes the long-range implications of a decision, as well as project uncertainties and costs of the required resources. Decisions in the Department of Defense on development of operational systems are supposed to be made on the basis of consideration of the total "program package." In the same way, choices of development strategy should reflect consideration of the impact those choices have beyond the development phase, in any project whether the user is the military or a firm's own marketing department. In many instances some device similar to an incentive contract tradeoff structure might be quite useful in making resource- and market-related tradeoff relationships available to decision makers at various organizational levels. This information must be available in the early development phases of a program. Planning, control, and information systems that focus attention on cost minimization without regard to performance variation act to promote ineffectual use of development resources.

In other words, technical specialists are encouraged to be braver in their use of the slippery data of the world of economics. Although such data may be subject to wide errors of estimate, it is far more dangerous to ignore variables than to work with erroneous values for them, and better still to use an analytic framework that shows which estimates are most worth improving.

It is unfortunate that the specialization of modern organizations actually serves to isolate the required information from the decision maker. Firms have marketing or planning departments that develop marketing information for project approval and acquisition decisions. Frequently, this information is either not collected or not made available for decisions that occur during the conduct of a project. Although the technical man has a good understanding of the uncertainties that surround a particular course of action, he often has no effective means of communicating this information to others. All of this information is essential to the choice of a development strategy, but a special effort is required to bring it to bear effectively on the problem.

REFERENCES

1. T. J. Allen, "Studies of the problem-solving process in engineering design," *IEEE Trans. Engineering Management*, vol. EM-13, pp. 72–83, June 1966.
2. C. P. Bonini, "Information systems for decision making under uncertainity; an evaluation of research and development scheduling," Graduate School of Business, Stanford University, Stanford, Calif., Working Paper 83, October 1965.
3. C. E. Clark, "The greatest of a finite set of random variables," *Operations Research*, vol. 9, pp. 145–162, 1961.
4. H. B. Eyring, "Evaluation of planning models for research and development projects," unpublished D.B.A. dissertation, Harvard Business School, Cambridge Mass., 1963.
5. L. M. Harlan, "Structure and content of decision-making in engineering development projects," unpublished D.B.A. dissertation, Harvard Business School, Cambridge, Mass., 1965.
6. D. J. Hitch and R. N. McKean, *The Economics of Defense in the Nuclear Age*. Cambridge, Mass.: Harvard University Press, 1963.
7. B. Klein and W. Meckling, "Application of operations research to development decisions," *Operations Research*, vol. 6, pp. 352–363, 1958.
8. D. L. Marples, "The decisions of engineering design," *IRE Trans. Engineering Management*, vol. EM-8, pp. 55–71, June 1961.
9. W. E, Marshall and W. H. Meckling, "Predictability of the costs, time, and success of development," RAND Corp., Santa Monica, Calif., RAND Paper P-1 21, October 1959.
10. T. A, Marschak, "Models, rules of thumb and development decisions," in *Operations Research in Research and Development*, B. V. Dean, Ed. New York: Wiley, 1962, pp. 247–263.
11. T. A. Marschak and J. A. Yahav, "The sequential selection of approaches to a task," *Management Science*, vol. 12, pp. 627–647, May 1966.
12. R. R. Nelson, "The economics of parellel R&D efforts: a sequential decision analysis," RAND Corp., Santa Monica, Calif., RAND Research Memo. RN-242, 1959.

13. H. Raiffa and R. Schlaifer, "Applied statistical decision theory," Division of Research, Graduate School of Business, Harvard University, Cambridge, Mass., 1961.
14. R. S. Rosenbloom and W. J. Abernathy, "Parallel and sequential strategies for R&D projects," Graduate School of Business, Harvard University, Cambridge, Mass., February 1967.
15. R. S. Rosenbloom, "Information requirements for development decisions," in *Information System Sciences*, J. Spiegel and D. Walker, Eds. Washington, D. C.: Spartan, 1965, pp. 391–401.
16. R. Schlaifer, "Development of aircraft engines," Division of Research, Graduate School of Business Administration, Harvard University, Cambridge, Mass., 1950.

PART III

ADMINISTERING THE R&D PROCESS

Chapters 11–15 contain the "nuts and bolts" materials relating to R&D management. The phrase "nuts and bolts" should not be taken as demeaning—only as a reference to the operational level, day-to-day administrative tasks. Indeed, the final success of R&D efforts depend in large measure upon how well these administrative jobs are accomplished and with what regularity. In turn the ability to administer the R&D effort depends, we feel, upon an appreciation of the external environment and the concepts and techniques of R&D decision-making.

The articles in this part will discuss organizational structures, coupling research to technology and production—an expansion of the organization topic, management of scientific personnel, creativity and creative organizations, budgeting and control, and research effectiveness. These chapters are consistent with the implementation phase of the strategy formulation and implementation process discussed in Part II. Organizational structure must be consistent with and in support of the organization's goals and strategic plans. In turn the information control motivation systems must be consistent with the structure and in support of the organization's goals. Thus individuals will be forced for their own self-interest to make decisions which are in the total organization's best interests.

Generally the best practices of administration in any organization form the basis for policies and procedures in R&D activities modified by the unique characteristics of creative organizations:

— Extreme uncertainty of both costs and results
— High proportion of professional employees
— Little or no hierarchy in a matrix-type organization
— Need for a continual flow of new information and idea stimuli

Concepts and techniques of administration can be found in a variety of sources (see comment on Roman, *R&D Administration* in the Introduction). Part III will focus on information relating to the unique features of R&D activities in order to help the reader adjust and modify his management concepts and techniques to fit the needs of his specific creative organization.

TO DIG DEEPER

For readers interested in "Administering the R&D Process" the following annotated bibliography on organization structure, management of scientific talent and creativity is offered as a starting point.

Perhaps the best book to start with would be one that compares and contrasts the traditional and modern organizations. *Formal Organization: A Systems Approach*, by Rocco Carzo, Jr. and John N. Yanouzas (Homewood, Ill. Irwin, 1967) does exactly that, and does it well. They cover the basics of traditional organizational structure: Pyramid, Authority, Line and Staff, Span of Control, and Decentralization vs Centralization. The authors (both on the faculty at Penn State Univ.) also study the informal (social), formal structures and power structure in some detail. They develop a basic framework within which an organization is viewed as a system of interdependent components performing processes on flows of matter, energy, and information. This is similar to Industrial Dynamics expounded by Jay Forrester.

After digesting the framework for further analysis, the next reading should be case studies to show how practical situations can be considered within the structure. *Organizing the R&D Function* by A. O. Stanley, and K. K. White, (AMA Research Study #72, 1965. 223 pp) provides an overview of R&D organization, 42 case studies to show application of the theory and detailed job descriptions—a vital part of the organizational picture. The text material is based on an examination of some 200 industrial R&D organizations. A considerable portion of the research is devoted to the building block structure of R&D organizations observed frequently by the authors. The book is an excellent treatment on the theory and practical application of organization concepts.

Another valuable book on the administration of R&D is *Managers and Scientists* by R. M. Hower, and C. D. Orth, (Harvard University Press, Boston, 1963, 323 pp). This work, based on case studies of several R&D organizations examines what the authors call the two cultures of R&D, i.e. the "Management Culture" and the "Scientific Culture", each with its different values and motivations. The influence of these cultures are studied in situations involving both change in the R&D organization and in placement of key individuals. The book is an excellent treatment of the interplay that exists between management and performance of the R&D process.

The management of creativity is a relatively new subject in the study of R&D. Most of the good material on this subject has been published during the 1960's.

One of the outstanding books on creativity in R&D is *Essays on Creativity in the Sciences* by Myron A. Coler, (New York University Press, New York, 1963, pp 235). This book is a collection of the best essays on creativity presented to the Creative Science Seminar at New York University. Topics include the relationship between personnel selection and creativity, organization and creativity, group and individual creativity plus valuable analysis on the stages of the creative process and the means of improving individual creativity.

Anyone interested in learning more about creativity and improving the effectiveness of R&D, should read *Scientists in Organizations* by Donald Pelz and Frank Andrews (John Wiley and Sons, 1966, New York). This book contains one of the best quantitative analyses of the relationship between R&D effectiveness and the environmental, physical and social, aspects of the scientist's job. This outstanding book is reviewed in detail in the book reports section.

Another important contribution to the recent literature on creativity is *The Organization of Research Establishments* by Sir John Cockcroft, (Cambridge University Press, Cambridge, England, 1965, pp 275). In this book, the heads of 13 U. S. and U. K. research establishments discuss the problems involved in organizing research in a wide variety of fields, ranging from physics to psychiatry and from agriculture to transportation. The objective of this book is "... to discuss the factors which make for creativity and productivity in a wide variety of research establishments."

A comprehensive treatment of the human behavioral aspects of R&D management is provided in *Administrating Research and Development* by Charles D. Orth, Joseph C. Bailey and Francis W. Wolck, (Richard D. Irwin, Homewood, Illinois, 1964). The research studies and conceptual papers selected by the authors, who are all behavioral scientists at Harvard University, provide a broad treatment of the subject by drawing on the outstanding articles previously printed in the R&D management literature. The book is written as a case study guide in the human problems of administering Research and Development.

What might be called a job manual for engineering department managers and administrators is the book *Engineering Management and Administration* by Val Cronstedt, (McGraw Hill Book Co. Inc., New York, 1961, pp 345). The book is written primarily for the engineering manager concerned with the product design process and does not treat the subject of scientific or research activities.

An older but classic book on control of research activity is *Management Controls in Industrial Research Organization*, by Robert Anthony, (Harvard University Press, Cambridge, Mass., 1952). In this book, Anthony stated for the first time many of the concepts for the control of research activity. The book is further summarized in the book review section.

Another book of value to the operating manager is *Handbook of Industrial Research Management* edited by Carl Heyl (Reinhold Publishing Co., New York, 1960). This book is summarized in the book reports section.

A book by Robert E. Seiler, *Improving the Effectiveness of Research and Development,* (McGraw Hill Book Co. Inc., New York, 1965), provides an insignt into the various techniques available to the operating R&D manager. The book is further summarized in the book reports section.

An excellent book of readings on the subject of research effectiveness is *Research Program Effectiveness* by M. Yovits, D. Gilford, R. Wilcox and H. Lerner, (Gordon and Breach Science Publishers, New York, 1966). This book is also reviewed in the reports section.

The following additional references on the subject of administering R&D, not covered in the Book Review Section, will be of help gaining a comprehensive coverage of the field. They listed in alphabetical order.

REFERENCES

1. John S. Baumgarther, *Project Management,* Homewood, Illinois: Richard D. Irwin, Inc., 1963.
2. Carl E. Gregory, *The Management of Intelligence,* New York: McGraw Hill, 1967.
3. William H. Gruber and Donald G. Marquis (Editors), *Factors in the Transfer of Technology,* Cambridge: MIT Press, 1969.
4. Richard A. Johnson, F. E. Kast, and J. E. Rosenzweig, *The Theory and Management of System,* (2nd Ed), New York: McGraw Hill, 1965.
5. D. W. Karger and R. G. Murduck, *Managing Engineering and Research,* New York: Industrial Press, 1963.
6. W. Komhauser, *Scientists in Industry,* Berkeley, California: University of California Press, 1962.
7. James W. Kuhn, *Scientific and Managerial Manpower in Nuclear Industry,* New York: Columbia University Press, 1966.
8. C. Orth, J. Bailey and F. Wolek, *Administering Research and Development,* Homewood, Illinois: Richard D. Irwin, Inc., 1964.
9. A. Stanley and K. White, *Organizing the R&D Function,* New York: American Management Association, 1968.
10. David Willings, *The Human Element in Management,* New York: Gordon & Breach, 1969.

CHAPTER ELEVEN

ORGANIZATION OF R&D ACTIVITIES

Part III is concerned with operational level problems—essentially the implementation of corporate strategy/R&D planning. The first task of implementation is the organization of resources consistant with established goals and strategy. This idea has been explored earlier in Ram Charan's article in Chapter 7. The key point of this chapter and the rest of part III is that administrative policies and procedures must always be designed to support the organization's goals. In turn, the simple question—is it functional with respect to our goals—will serve to test the validity and feasibility of alternative arrangements.

Professor Albert Rubenstein of Northwestern University introduces the subject with a report on research done in large decentralized companies. He concentrates on formal organizational characteristics in a setting which will be familiar to many readers. The opposite end of the organization spectrum is presented by David Conrath who describes the role of informal groups in R&D decision-making. Understanding the "tone" informal patterns of communications and organization is essential to management of creative people. Dr. Conrath suggests that informal organizations are information processors which both compliment and hide the formal processes. Finally he offers some suggestions for making better use of the informal organizations.

A more general look at R&D administration is taken by Gerald Gordon in "*Preconceptions and Reconceptions in the Administration of Science.*" His guidelines for organization of R&D efforts can be considered in view of the material presented in the two previous articles in order to begin to develop the reader's own thoughts on organization of R&D activities.

A variety of specific organizational arrangements are well documented in the management literature. Their use in R&D activities has been discussed at length in the popular R&D management magazines. In the final two articles Hendrick W. Bode discussed the systems approach with emphasis on applied engineering and development. He illustrates his points with short case histories or microwave relay systems, the NIKE–AJAX and telstar. Finally Irwin Mordka illustrates and discusses the uses of four major types of organization structure found in R&D laboratories. As is true of all the articles presented in this chapter; the author reminds us that each structure has different characteristics, advantages and disadvantages, and usefullness which must be weighed against the needs of the situation.

ORGANIZATIONAL FACTORS AFFECTING RESEARCH AND DEVELOPMENT DECISION-MAKING IN LARGE DECENTRALIZED COMPANIES*†

Albert H. Rubenstein
Chairman, Dept. of Indust. Eng. and Management Sci.
Northwestern University

The design of a long term research program on the organization of R and D in decentralized companies is presented. The decentralized firm and the various deployments of R and D in such firms are described. Data is given on the incidence of the various organizational forms in five industry groups. The classes of decisions commonly encountered in R and D are indicated. Categories for describing and analyzing the assigned mission of an R and D lab are presented.

INTRODUCTION

The research and development process and its role in the industrial firm are extremely complex. Any attempt at a complete, systematic explanation or description is probably premature at this time. Our knowledge of how this process works and how it affects and is affected by the industrial environment is limited, based on a very small amount of systematic investigation in a few operating laboratories [1].

The opportunity to carry out organizational experiments in a manner analogous to those performed in physical science has been virtually non-existent. Other methods, more familiar to the social scientist and student of organization than to the physical scientist, must substitute for the rigor and reproducibility of physical science experimentation.

---

* *Management Science*, Vol. 10, No. 4, July, 1964.

† This is a report on one phase of a long term study of "Organization of Research and Development in Decentralized Companies". It was initiated by the author in the School of Industrial Management at M.I.T. and has been continued at Northwestern. Funds for the study have been provided by the School of Industrial Management, The McKinsey Foundation, two industrial companies, and the National Aeronautics and Space Administration.

As a consequence, our knowledge about the research process and its role in the industrial firm is not only limited, but is also not as well organized as is knowledge in many areas of physical science. In addition, the concepts and variables dealt with in this "research-on-research" are not as precise as one would like them to be and are not readily amenable to the formal manipulation required to transform them into respectable "theory."

For example, when we are dealing with concepts such as the "objectives" of a research and development (R and D) program or the "creative abilities" of researchers, we are not able to treat them as absolute, readily measurable, and subject to mathematical treatment.

As a result, investigations in this field are often of a scouting nature. One surveys a research and development laboratory or a group of laboratories, looking for some general relationships and some phenomena subject to careful description or crude measurement; e.g. recording of the frequency or general characteristics of "communication" or "decision-making."

The results are often strongly influenced by specific factors in the particular situation being investigated, which often cannot be described adequately enough to account for them in the analysis; e.g. the particular growth stage of the firm, the historical dependence on technology, organizational changes taking place, the influence of specific individuals. Generalization to "all" research and development organizations or even to another "similar" one is therefore difficult, if indeed it is feasible at all.

The investigation upon which this paper is based combines some aspects of the scouting survey and of other methods used in research on organizational processes. Wherever possible, attempts are being made to carry out quantitative analyses in relation to hypotheses and to fit the results into a coherent explanatory framework.

The framework is selective and does not attempt a complete explanation of how research and development laboratories operate and how they affect and are affected by their organizational environment.

THE DECENTRALIZED COMPANY

This investigation is concerned with a number of factors which appear to have particular relevance for R and D in the *decentralized* company, although they may also be relevant to R and D activity in any setting. Some of them derive directly from the very nature of the decentralized company, others appear to be accentuated by the specific circumstances of the decentralized company [2].

Rather than attempt, at this point, to "define" a decentralized company, a brief description will be given of top management's intentions in "decentralizing" their operations and the effects they hope to achieve through this decentralization. A partial structural description of the decentralized firm is given in Figure 6, where the prominent features may be recognized as a "Top Corporate Management," "Corporate Staff Activities" (e.g. "Research Management"), and a series of relatively autonomous "Operating Divisions" headed by Divisional Management which carry on the direct productive functions of the business such as production, engineering, and distribution.

The exact organization structure and distribution of functions varies between firms and between industries. The salient features for our purposes are the organization of the corporation's business into relatively "autonomous" operating units—generally along technological or market lines—and the establishment of measurements of performance for the purposes of control, incentive, and reward.

Top management intentions in "decentralizing" are epitomized in this statement from an IBM announcement to its employees, explaining the company's management decentralization some years ago [3]:

> . . . the new alignment of the various areas is based on products. Each of the product divisions will, within the framework of policy established by the Board of Directors and general management, operate almost as an individual company with its own manufacturing, sales, and service functions. Each of these divisions is equipped with special skills and product knowledge to concentrate on developing the full potential of a specific market.
>
> Further strength is given the organization with the creation of the Corporate Staff, which, being separate from the operating organization responsible for developing, producing, selling and servicing goods, can closely examine the special areas of the business and assist the operating executives in solving problems in these areas.

An instance of "extreme" decentralization is described in a popular article [4] on a company that has developed a decentralized corporate structure through acquisitions of existing companies:

> . . . at McGraw-Edison, only the top policy decisions, company-wide in import and usually financial, are made in the head office. Otherwise, the divisions handle their own affairs. And no memoranda and visitors from the home office tell the field how to do it.

A comment from a company [5] where ". . . decentralized or divisionalized corporate form does not reflect a recent innovation . . ." suggests the long term benefits that may accrue to this form of operation:

> A series of operating subsidiaries focused on lines of business, with production and sales, as well as research, handled by the subsidiaries

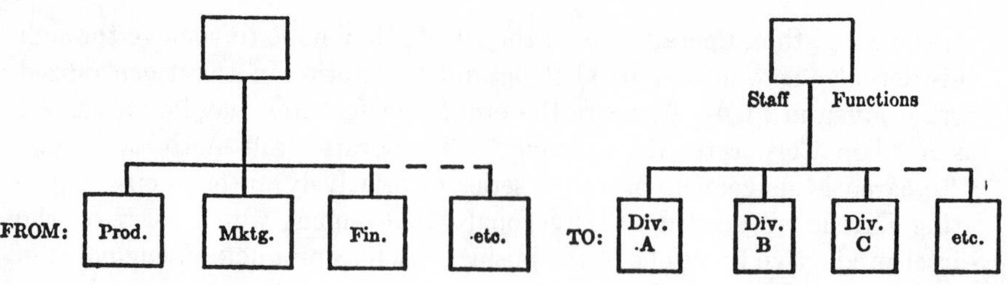

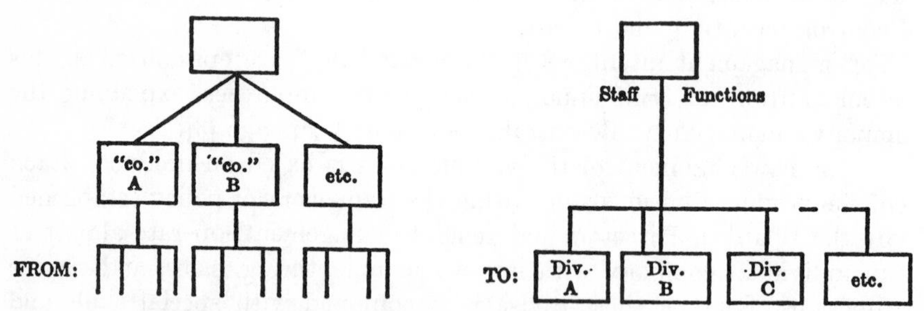

Fig. 1. Emerging patterns of company decentralization

A. *A functionally centralized company* decentralizes according to product line, customer, process phase, geography or other criteria.

B. *A loosely federated "holding company" operation* re-groups, combines certain non-operating functions, and decentralizes operating units. Recently, this has been frequently done through mergers of formerly nonassociated companies.

and major policy functions handled by the parent corporate staff, has been the prevailing pattern in our company for some time.

. . . our management has found the autonomous units to be profitable, stimulating and internally competitive forms of corporate government.

We believe that (our company) is a classical example of a successfully decentralized, highly diversified company with sufficient flexibility to cope adequately with economic drift across a broad range of consumer goods reaching to all areas of the free world.

Historically, we have observed two major patterns of management decentralization, with variations and combinations of both in specific companies. Both patterns tend toward the same general form, as indicated in Figure 1.

The speculative literature on management decentralization is voluminous. Only a few studies have been done, however, on the actual degree and effects of large scale delegation of decision-making which is supposed to accompany "true" decentralization [6].

Very little is known systematically, for example, of the way in which major organizational changes such as decentralization are perceived and

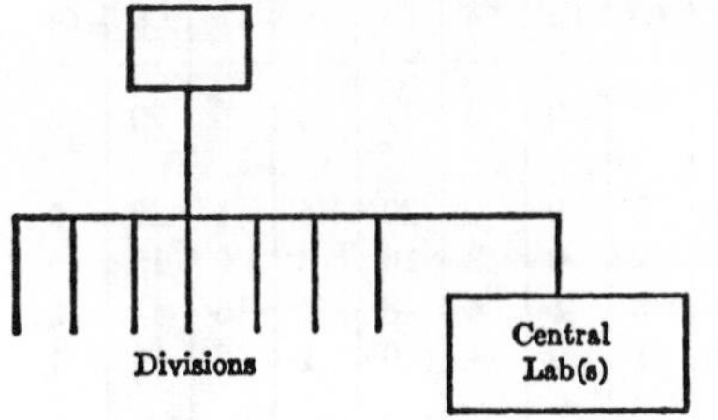

A. *"Pure" Centralized*
All work on new products and processes and all work on major improvements in products and processes are done in one central R and D facility. No work of this type is done within the divisions except, perhaps, an occasional major redesign job which approaches development proportions.

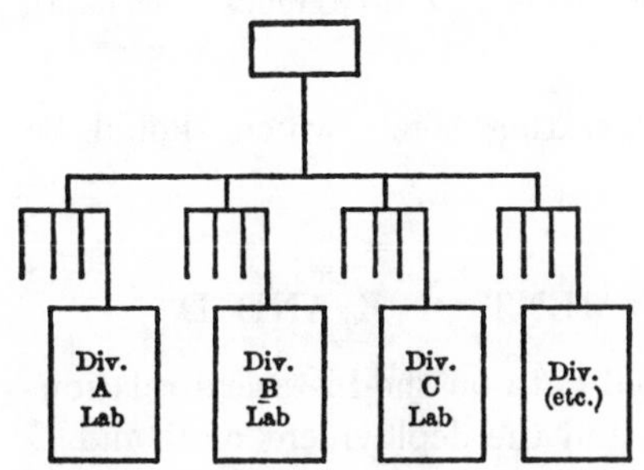

B. *"Pure" Decentralized*
All work on new products and processes and all work on improvements of products and processes are done within the operating divisions. In many large companies, a given division may have a number of labs concerned with different levels of R and D.

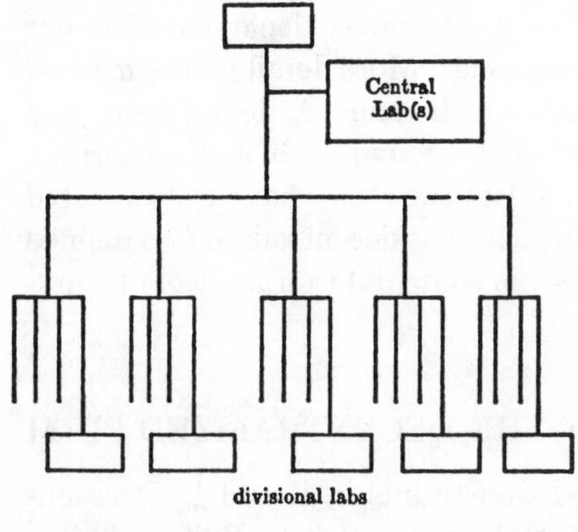

C. *"Pure" Combination*
The more general or long-range or basic or exploratory work is carried out in a central lab and the more specific, short-term, applied work is carried out within the divisions.

Fig. 2. Patterns of deployment of research and development in decentralized companies.

Industry Group	Corporate Organizational Form											
	Centralized (Ce)			Combination (Co)			Decentralized (De)			Total R & D Form		
	R & D Form			R & D Form			R & D Form					
	Ce	Co	De	Ce	Co	De	Ce	Co	De	Ce	Co	De
Chemical and Pharmaceutical (N = 32)	2	0	1	2	3	0	2	17	5	6	20	6
Electrical (N = 28)	1	0	0	0	2	0	0	20	5	1	22	5
Engineered Products (N = 30)	2	0	0	1	2	0	3	16	6	6	18	6
Food (N = 29)	7	0	0	5	3	1	4	8	1	16	11	2
Primary Materials (Glass, Paper, Rubber, Other Minerals) (N = 20)	2	1	0	2	1	0	4	0	1	8	11	1

Figure 3. Relation between company organizational form and depolyment of research and development in a sample of the largest companies in 5 industry groups (1960 data).

reacted to by people at the several operating levels which should be affected by the changes.

ORGANIZATIONAL DEPLOYMENT OF R AND D

Phase I of the investigation has yielded data on the historical relationship between corporate decentralization and the deployment of R and D between the operating divisions and a possible central research laboratory. Figure 2 indicates the three "pure" deployments encountered, with variations in specific industries and companies.

Figure 3 indicates the incidence of the three "pure" deployments in our sample of companies from 5 industry groupings. More detail on the method of analysis; definitions; relations between R and D deployment and decentralization, company size, etc.; will be found in a staff report on Phase I by Cotton [2]. Phases II and III of the study have concentrated only on the companies in our sample which are "decentralized" as defined in the preceding section. Figure 4 presents some data on multiple laboratory companies.

R AND D DECISION-MAKING IN THE DECENTRALIZED FIRM

In Figure 5 the "Chain of Perceived Constraints in R and D Decision-Making" is illustrated. The pattern of "Intentions, Beliefs, Philosophy"—

Approximate No. of Companies	Number of Laboratories
275	2 or more
180	3 or more
90	5 or more
30[c]	10 or more
5	25 or more

[a] Includes only those companies with 25 or more professional researchers.

[b] The number of labs includes multiple labs at one location (e.g. some companies operate a "research center" or "experiment station" for divisional labs), as well as labs at different locations.

[c] These 30 companies employed approximately 25,000 professional researchers in 1955, a significant proportion of the national total, at that time.

Figure 4. Distribution of multi-laboratory companies[a] by number of separately listed laboratories (1956 data)[b].

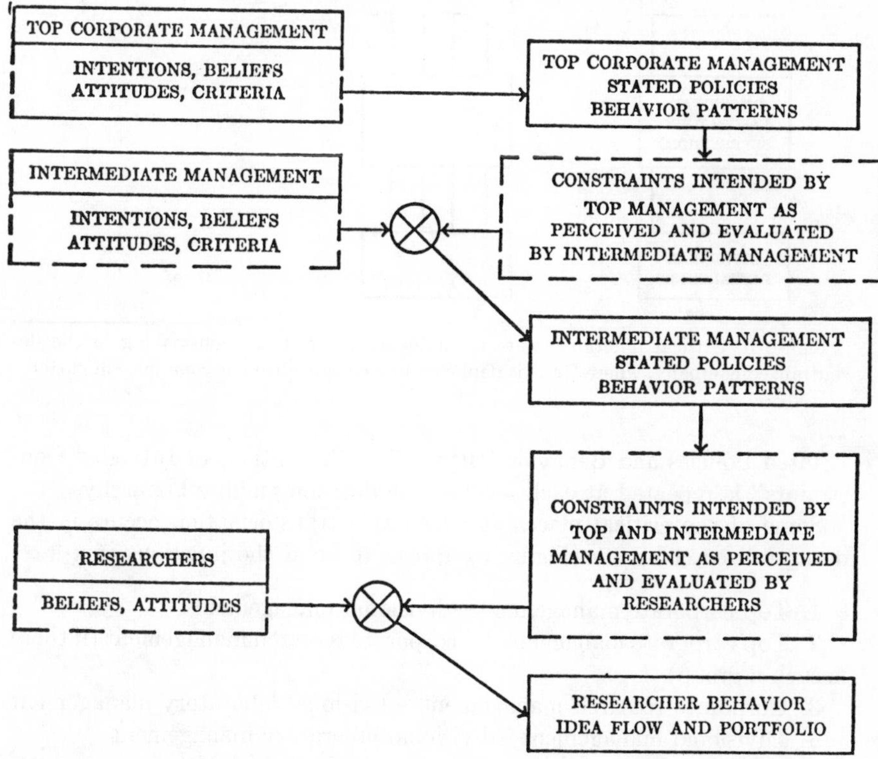

Figure 5. The chain of perceived constraints in R&D decision-making.

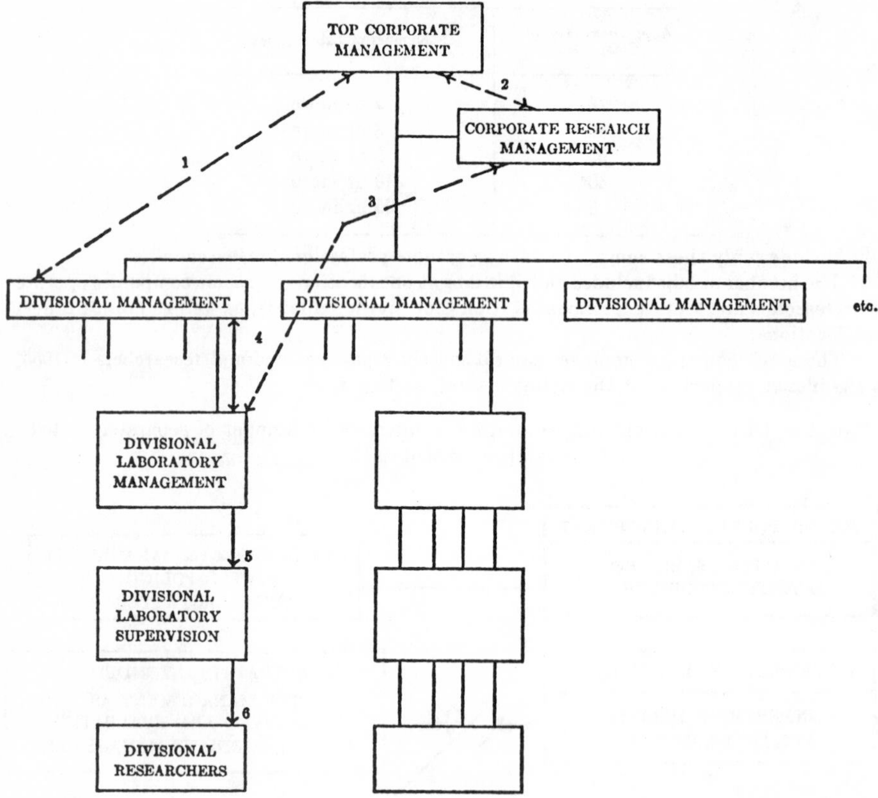

Figure 6. Critical junction points for influencing R&D decision-making in the decentralized company, where R&D is deployed in a decentralized or combination pattern.

"Stated Policies and Behavior Patterns"—"Perceptions of Intended Constraints" is repeated at each level of the decision-making hierarchy.

Some of the critical places at which this transformation occurs in the decentralized company (Figure 6) appear to be at the junctions of:

1. Top corporate management—divisional management
2. Top corporate management—corporate research management (if there is such a group)
3. Corporate research management—divisional laboratory management
4. Divisional management—divisional laboratory management
5. Divisional laboratory management—divisional laboratory supervision
6. Divisional laboratory supervision—working researchers.

In addition to these critical junctions in the company's vertical hierarchy, there are other points of contact which can have a significant effect on the decision-making process. These are points that involve any of the above groups with colleagues within the company or outside it. For example:

Top management may be influenced in their thinking about R and D by top managements in other companies. A number of the organizational changes observed during the investigation were reported to have been strongly influenced in this manner; i.e. "What works in ABC Co. ought to work (or at least be tried) in ours."

Corporate and divisional research management, through their many seminars, conferences, and workshops that have sprung up in the past ten years, have been learning the strategy and tactics used by their opposite numbers in other companies to influence top management and divisional management.

Working researchers often follow trends or styles of research current in their technical fields. The strength of this influence will depend on the degree of "enculturation" (see Avery [13]).

Division managers and division research managers will be influenced by the attitudes, ideas, and behavior of their colleagues in marketing, production, advertising, and other company activities.

An important task in this phase of the investigation is the cataloguing of the various classes of decisions made *by* R and D and *about* R and D which can have a significant effect on its contribution of economic results to the firm. Certainly each move by each researcher or member of the management hierarchy which relates to R and D can have some important effects on the outcome of specific projects, programs (related groups of projects), and the R and D activity as a whole. A chemist's decision to study material "A" first, rather than materials B, C, or D may have far-reaching consequences, as the history of science amply demonstrates [7]. These chance events, while important, are not subject to prediction except perhaps in the following fashion: if it could be demonstrated that the probability (empirical frequency) of their occurrence was in some way related to a particular pattern or a combination of circumstances or constraints (in our terminology), then an empirical relationship might be developed relating the particular pattern(s) to a rough "probability of the unusual event." There is an underlying faith among people who study the research process that there are certain environmental conditions under which unusual events, such as scientific discoveries, are more likely to occur. These environmental conditions are sometimes described as the research "milieu" or the general atmosphere in the laboratory or the organization in which the laboratory operates.

Although the results of the investigation thus far present strong evidence against a *unique* organizational form or set of specific constraints on the R and D activity in companies that have been technologically "successful," there is reason to expect that there exist a set of *sufficient* although not *necessary* patterns of constraints which are associated with "successful" R and D. That is, there may be a number of patterns or constraints which can, alternatively, provide the milieu or environmental conditions conducive to "chance" discovery [8].

Unfortunately, there is little chance that an investigation conducted at the level of the present one will yield quantitative data on this postulated set of patterns which are associated with successful R and D. Qualitative descriptions of such patterns abound in the management literature, but they are generally so broad and so vague that they cannot be used for organizational design or even for rigorous analysis of existing organizations. In the final report of this investigation, we anticipate presenting some characteristics of what appear to be "successful" R and D organizations, in terms of their direct information output [9]. Some data is being collected on ultimate, economic output; however, this study design did not include an evaluation of the economic contribution of the R and D activity to the company. Several other studies conducted in conjunction with the present one have attempted this very difficult task [10].

This study will yield descriptions of the kinds of constraints that we found associated with R and D organizations that appeared to provide the kind of atmosphere that is generally associated wtih successful R and D.

CLASSES OF DECISIONS WITHIN R AND D

In this section we will concentrate on the classes of decisions made *within* the R and D activity which have two general properties:

a) They appear to be strongly influenced by the constraints which members of the R and D activity perceive when they examine the stated policies and behavior patterns of people above them in the hierarchy (see Figure 5).

b) They appear to have significant effects on R and D Behavior—that is, on the R and D Portfolio and on the pattern of Idea Flow (see Rubenstein and Avery [2]). By implication, then, they also influence the ultimate outcome of the R and D process—economic results.

In general, these classes of decisions are non-routine in nature or, in the terms used by Cyert, Simon and Trow [11], they are the relatively "non-programmed" type. Although they occur frequently as a group, they are generally less specific and more unique than the vast majority of day-to-day decisions made in R and D. One might describe them as "milestones" in the sense that they lead to gross changes in activity. Some examples are: "initiating new activities," "intensifying existing activities," "delaying existing activities," or "discontinuing existing activities." In addition, we must add a category of decision which is overtly different from these—"continuing or reconfirming an existing activity."

At this point, a clarification of the term "decision-making" may be necessary. In this investigation, we are not studying in detail the "decision process" as such, since we are primarily interested in the factors which influence decision-making and consequences of that decision-making in a particular situation—R and D. However, the definition of the decision process which guides the design of the investigation includes more phases than are generally included by writers on "decision-making."

Decision-making, as viewed in this study, includes all of the following phases:

—Recognition of problem or need for a decision
—Analysis and statement of alternatives
—Choice among the alternatives
—Communication and implementation of the decision
—Check to see whether decision was implemented as intended.

As a consequence of this view of "decision-making," we are concerned with possible effects of perceived constraints on all phases of the decision-making process—Recognition, Analysis, Choice, Communication, and Check. Hence, it is possible that the perceived constraints in a given situation may have relatively little influence on the actual *choice* among alternatives in a given decision, but they may have a significant influence on the number and kind of *alternatives* which are brought into the analysis prior to the actual choice. For example, researchers may feel relatively unconstrained in their choice of which project to initiate from an existing list of weakly ordered projects (relative to priority). But they may feel very constrained from initiating a project not already on the list before the ones on the list have been completed. Again, they may feel relatively unconstrained with respect to *suggesting* ideas for work in the laboratories; but they may feel very constrained about *advocating* a particular idea which they perceive to conflict with the stated or implicit intentions of their superiors.

We are concerned with decisions about these subjects:

—*Organizational form* (internal organization of R and D)—e.g. organization by "project" or by "function," relations between functions)
—Specific *projects* and major project phases
—*Programs* (groups of related projects)

	Projects	Programs	Fields	Ideas	Transition	Personnel	Organization
Initiate	×	×	×	×	×	(Recruit Hire)	(Change)
Intensify	×	×	×	(Advocate)	×	Promote	
Delay	×	×	×	×	×	Recognize	
Continue (reconfirm)	×	×	×	(Approve)		(Reward)	×
Discontinue	×	×	×	(Reject)	×	(Fire)	(Change)

Figure 7. Some classes of R&D decision-making.

—*Fields* (general technical areas not yet formalized as "programs")

—*Ideas* (suggestions or recommendations for work which have not yet been formally designated as projects or programs)

—*Transition* (progression from the laboratory to market)

—*Personnel* (recruiting, hiring, promotion, recognition, and reward)

The classes of decisions which apply to these subjects yield a large number of specific types of decisions which are of particular interest. Our sample consists of the largest companies in each of our industry groups. Each of these companies does have an R and D activity of some sort in operation. We therefore start our examination of decision-making in R and D with the assumption that there is an existing R and D activity—organized, funded, otherwise constrained, and behaving in a given way. Our attention is focused on the decisions made *about* and *by* R and D which tend to *change* its current behavior or to overtly *reconfirm* its current behavior. Continuing to develop the classes of decisions made *by* R and D, we have categories such as those indicated in Figure 7 for directly observable or reportable decisions by members of the R and D activity.

ASSIGNED MISSION

The mission initially assigned to R and D in an industrial company and the subsequent changes in that mission will have a strong influence on the behavior of people in the R and D activity and on the results of their work.

Subject to their understanding of the mission, their abilities, and the other constraints under which they operate, the company's researchers will attempt to work on problems and in areas which promise to contribute to accomplishment of the mission.

One finding of the investigation to date is that the understanding of mission or scope of the R and D program is very imperfect in many of the companies studied. The research management literature and company documents abound with general statements of mission such as "to ensure the technological future of the company."

Very few statements were found, however, which spelled out in specific terms the relative degree of emphasis to be placed on the various strategies available to R and D in attempting to ensure the technological future of the company.

One possible explanation of this finding is this: although someone in the top management of the company *has* a clear idea of the objectives for which the company supports R and D, he and others in the organization have difficulty in communicating these objectives and phrasing them in operational terms. Another possible explanation is that many or most

A. Over-all Strategies which Describe the General Intent of the R & D Program

1. Service on Current Materials, Processes, and Applications (M, P, A)
2. Minor Improvements One at a Time on Current M, P, A.
3. Continual Minor Improvements on Current M, P, A.

---

4. Major Improvements on Current M, P, A.
5. Intentional Departures from Current M, P, A, one at a time.

---

6. Attempts to Meet a Future Market Mission.

---

7. Coverage of a Technical Field of Current Interest.
8. Coverage of a Technical Field of Potential Interest.

---

9. Search for Knowledge for its Own Sake.

B. Specific Intentions for Individual Projects or Programs

Work Supporting Current Operations

Customer service on current product
Minor improvement of current product
Major improvement of current product
Factory service on current process
Minor improvement of current process
Major improvement of current process

Work Leading to Expansion of Present Product Line

Work on new product not currently made here
Work on radically new product not currently made anywhere
Applied work leading toward an idea related to a new product
Work on new process not currently used here
Applied work leading toward an idea related to a new process
Translation of a research discovery into the prototype of a new product or process or part thereof

Work Not Yet Connected to Any Product or Process

Exploratory work in a field of current interest
Exploratory work in a field of potential interest
Work producing only knowledge for its own sake

Figure 8. Some categories for describing the research and development program (portfolio).

R and D objectives in industry are intrinsically *un*clear and that the communication process only serves to further confuse the issue of what the firm is trying to accomplish through support of R and D. Evidence for both these explanations has been encountered in the study [12].

In order to explore this question systematically, two sets of categories were developed for describing, in quantitative terms, the scope of the R and D program in a company and the relative emphasis placed in each area.

Figure 8, part A, lists a number of categories which might be termed "strategies" for conducting R and D. A company confining itself exclusively to category "1," for example, might be described as following a pure strategy of servicing their current operations—the *Materials* they are currently using, the *Processes* they are operating to convert that material, and the *Applications* of the products or services that result.

Typically, all of the companies in our sample pursue a mixed strategy, combining the categories of R and D work in various proportions. A number of them, for example, intend to conduct work in all of these categories, but place more or less emphasis on categories such as "5" through "9." Some, indeed, do not intend to operate in categories such as "9"—usually considered the province of the university—or "6," which requires a degree of abstraction and forward planning that is not common.

This first set of categories was used in interviews with people in corporate management, division management, and laboratory management. In some cases, direct readings were obtained for each category; in others, the people interviewed were only able to group their responses into three larger categories:

Maintenance R and D—includes strategies 1 through 3
Expansion R and D—includes strategies 4 through 6
Exploratory R and D—includes strategies 7 through 9.

In addition to an analysis of current program intentions, an attempt was made to describe 1) shifts in emphasis that had occurred "over the past three years" and 2) shifts in emphasis that were likely to occur "over the next three years."

This set of data was intended to provide a time perspective for examining changes in the R and D program that had occurred or were impending. An illustrative pattern is shown in Figure 9.

The pattern illustrated in Figure 9 was encountered frequently in companies which had until recently been in a stable situation of supplying a relatively constant market by means of a relatively unchanging technology, based on the same materials they had used for years. In the mid-1950's, however, they began to expand their R and D activities, to

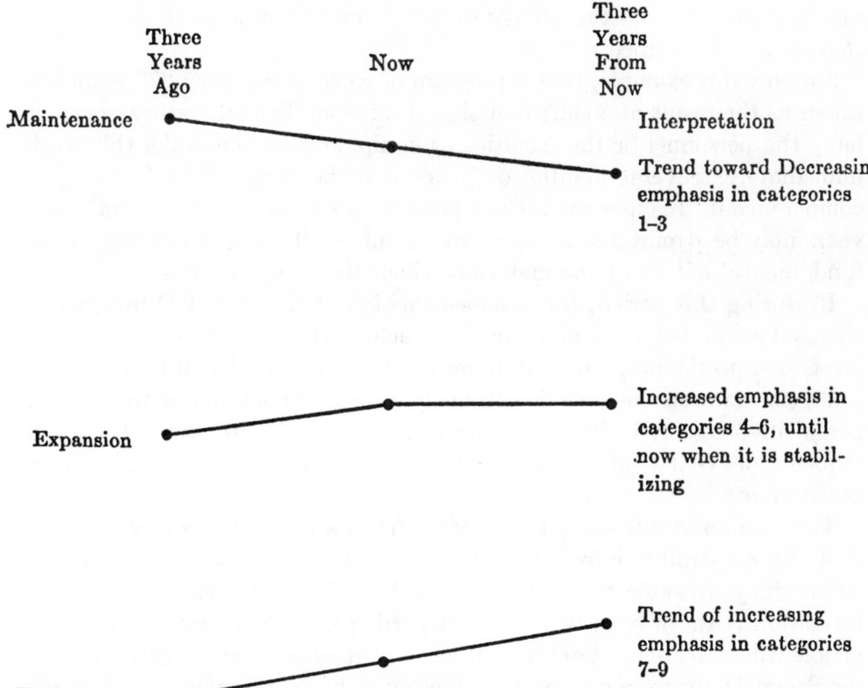

Figure 9. An illustrative pattern of shifting program (portfolio) emphasis over time

re-examine their materials, processes, and applications, and to embark on new programs of expansion and exploration.

This kind of information is very difficult to obtain from most companies, even when they are very willing to supply it. One reason, of course, is methodological—the data may exist, but in forms that are not suitable for transformation into our categories. In this case, rough estimates are made by means of ranking of emphasis, percentage distribution of emphasis, or other means (see Rubenstein and Radnor [14]).

Another reason is related to the remarks above: many companies do not have a clear idea of the relative emphasis they wish to place on these various R and D strategies.

The objective of this aspect of the investigation—the attempt to describe the changing pattern of emphasis (Figure 9)—is to make explicit this very important constraint upon R and D—the changes in management intentions for R and D through time. This constraint leads to one of the greatest sources of difficulty in the relationship between R and D and management. This is the ability of the R and D process to respond to *changes* in the assigned mission.

Suppose, for example, that a program of work in category "7" is undertaken as the result of a shift in assigned mission. The laboratory may not have the personnel or the facilities or equipment to undertake this work immediately. Several months or years may be required to build up a competence in this new area. Once geared up for such work, several more years may be required to achieve any useful results—e.g. a mastery of the fundamental nature of the materials which the company uses.

If, during this period, the assigned mission of the R and D program is changed again, before results have been achieved, much of the effort which has gone into the program to date may have to be written off as lost.

Precise data on this issue is extremely difficult to obtain due to the time period involved. It is difficult to recapture, through interviews, the exact sequence of events and the way they were perceived by the people involved *at that time.*

This is important, since the general framework of the study suggests that the constraints imposed on R and D are subject to transformation before they are able to influence behavior. The first step in this transformation is the way in which an imposed constraint is perceived by the people whose decisions determine R and D behavior. If an assigned mission for R and D, for example, exists in the minds of management, but is never communicated to or understood by these decision-makers, then it may have very little influence on R and D behavior.

Figure 8, part B, gives another set of categories used in the investigation. This set is comparable to the first set, but is more detailed. It has been used for categorizing individual R and D projects or related groups of projects. The major groupings—Maintenance, Expansion, and Exploratory—remain the same.

SUMMARY

The objectives and approach of a long term study of research and development in decentralized companies have been described. The nature of the decentralized company and the patterns of deployment of research and development in such companies were discussed. Some data was presented on the extent of decentralization in a sample of very large companies in 5 industry groupings.

The conceptual framework underlying the study was presented. It emphasizes the potential effects of perceived constraints upon R and D activities at various organizational levels. Classes of significant R and D decisions were illustrated. The assigned mission and ways of describing it analytically were discussed.

REFERENCE

1. For recent listings of "research-on-research" see: *Current Projects on Economic and Other Impacts of Scientific Research and Development*, Annual, National Science Foundation; and the forthcoming "Directory of Research on Research Management" being prepared by the author for the College on Research and Development (COLRAD) of TIMS.
2. The study is now in its 8th year. It involves over 100 large decentralized manufacturing companies in six major industries. *Phase One* traces the historical relationship between corporate decentralization and the deployment of research and development resources and activities in the firm. The organizing principle for operating divisions is examined, as well as the initiation and termination of operating divisions. *Phase Two* examines the dynamics of the relationship between corporate headquarters and the operating divisions with respect to R and D policies and programs, in approximately 25 companies. *Phase Three* concentrates on the investigation of idea flow within and between laboratories of two companies.

   Some reports of various phases of the study are:

   Avery, Robert W., "Enculturation in Industrial Research" *IRE Transactions on Engineering Management*, March 1960.

   Avery, Robert W., "Technical Objectives and the Production of Ideas in Industrial Laboratories," January 1959, Unpublished.

   Cotton, Donald B., "Some Data on the Relation between Divisionalization and Deployment of Research and Development Laboratories in Decentralized Companies, January 1959, Unpublished.

   Rubenstein, Albert H., and Avery, Robert W., "Idea Flow in Research and Development," *Proceedings of the National Electronics Conference*, October 1958.

   Rubenstein, Albert H., "Organization of Divisionalized Research and Development," presented at the Operations Research Society Annual Meeting, November 1957.

   Rubenstein, Albert H., "Organizational Change, Corporate Decentralization, and the Constraints on Research and Development," presented at The Institute of Management Sciences, June 1959. Published in *Chemical Engineering Progress* as "The Constraints of Decentralization."

Rubenstein, Albert H., and Radnor, Michael, "Top Management's Role in Research Planning in Large Decentralized Companies," *Proceedings of the Conference of the International Federation of Operations Research Societies,*" Oslo, 1963. (In Press)

Rubenstein, Albert H., "Organization and Research and Development Decision-Making Within the Decentralized Firm," *The Rate and Direction of Inventive Activity,* Princeton University Press, 1962.

3. International Business Machines Corporation, "A New Pattern for Progress, *IBM Business Machines,* December 28, 1956.
4. "Letting Divisions Run Themselves," *Business Week,* December 19, 1959.
5. Private communication.
6. Simon, Herbert A., Guetzkow, Harold, Kozmetsky, George and Tyndall, Gordon, *Centralization vs. Decentralization in Organizing the Controller's Department,* Carnegie Institute of Technology, August, 1954.

Baker, Helen and France, Robert, *Centralization and Decentralization in Industrial Relations,* Princeton University, Industrial Relations Section, 1954.

Weaver, Adrian G., "The Progress of Decentralization at IBM," Master's Thesis, School of Industrial Management, M.I.T., 1957.

7. See, for example, "The 'Happy Accident' and its Consequences," Chapter 3 in *Science, Servant of Man,* I. Bernard Cohen, Little, Brown and Co., Boston, 1948.
8. Karl Deutsch speaks of "designing for the improbable." Private communication in Columbia University Seminar on Theory of Organization and Management, ca 1952.
9. For the distinction between "direct, information output" and "ultimate economic output," see the author's "Setting Criteria for R and D." *Harvard Business Review,* Jan.–Feb. 1957.
10. Langenhagen, Charles F., Jr., "An Evaluation of Research and Development in the Chemical Industry," M.S. thesis, School of Industrial Management, M.I.T., June 1958.

Miles, William, "An Evaluation of Research and Development in the Textile Industry," M.S. thesis, S.I.M., October 1958.

Ninian, Alexander S., "The Role of Research and Development in the American Steel Industry," M.S. thesis, S.I.M., June 1959.

11. Cyert, Richard M., Simon, Herbert A. and Trow, Donald B., "Observation of a Business Decision," *The Journal of Business,* V. XXIX, No. 4, October 1956.

12. For an interesting discussion of which comes first—"objectives" or "plans" in R and D, see Eric Rhenman, "Research Planning: A Complex Problem." *Proceedings of the Conference of the International Federation of Operations Research Societies*, Oslo, 1963.
13. Avery, Robert W., "Enculturation in Industrial Research" op. cit. [2].
14. op. cit. [2].

THE ROLE OF THE INFORMAL ORGANIZATION IN DECISION MAKING ON RESEARCH AND DEVELOPMENT*

David W. Conrath
Department of Industry
University of Pennsylvania

While an increasing amount of effort is going into the study of the administration of research and development, several facets of the process appear to have gone unnoticed. In particular, we argue that a study of the informal organizations of researchers may offer insights in the administration of such personnel that can lead to improvements in the formal organization. The possibilities explored are presented in the form of four testable hypotheses, which, if shown to be true, have definite implications for the management of research and development. For example, one tentative conclusion indicates a net value in the practice of rotating scientific personnel in and out of administrative positions, appointments being temporary for a fixed duration rather than permanent.

The arguments and evidence presented on behalf of the hypotheses, unfortunately, can be no more than suggestive at this time. Only anecdotes rather than "hard" data are currently available. Hopefully, however, the arguments are sufficiently convincing to encourage further research on the topic.

INTRODUCTION

Research and Development (R&D) is a big business. Howton [14] has estimated that approximately 3 percent of our gross national product (GNP) goes to R&D activities. As our economy becomes more technically complex, this percentage will undoubtedly rise. Because of the increasing importance of R&D, the problems associated with the administration of such activities have been receiving considerable attention.[1] Most of this

* Reprinted from the *IEEE Transactions on Engineering Management, Vol. EM-15, No. 3,* September 1968.

[1] The existence of this TRANSACTIONS is an excellent example. Other relevant examples include [23], [13], and [26].

attention has focused on such things as the design of a hierarchical structure conducive to productive research, the optimal allocation of scarce resources across various research projects, and the proper personnel methods for handling scientists. Little has been said about the effects of informal organizations of scientists, which exist within R&D organizations. We contend that a study of the role of such an informal organization (one that is not recognized as part of the administrative heirarchy), with particular attention to how it affects the formal decision making apparatus, can provide us with valuable insights regarding the management of R&D activities.

This contention has a two-fold basis. Firstly, the evergrowing literature on the economics of R&D provides us with excellent evidence that decision making on R&D, particularly that concerned with project selection, is considerably more than just an economic phenomenon. In an interesting recent article by Mansfield and Brandenburg [17], an explanatory "rational" model, while yielding significant results, proved to be far from satisfactory as a predictor of projects selected and the corresponding levels of effort (budget allocated to each). The authors noted a number of reasons why their model might have fallen short; and virtually all of these concerned behavioral characteristics that can be accounted for by the activities of the informal organization. Furthermore, if we assume that those involved in establishing the values of the variables used in the project selection model knew the cause and effect relationship between the information supplied and the final choice (a not unreasonable assumption since the model was assumed to be reasonable), even the "rational" model was biased in favor of "rational decision making" from the formal organization's point of view.

Secondly, this contention is the product of more than a year's field work observing the decision-making behavior (particularly that involved with budgeting) within NASA and several private R&D laboratories.[2] During the year, intimate contact was made with a number of research personnel. Over 100 persons were interviewed formally, some of them repeatedly. But much more valuable than the formal interviews were the many luncheon conversations and general bull sessions, which arose once the author became accepted by the researchers and the administrative personnel.

Both the literature and the author's direct observations led to the for-

[2] This was done from late 1963 through 1964, while the author was a Research Economist in the Social Sciences Project, Space Sciences Laboratory, University of California, Berkeley.

mation of several hypotheses relevant to the role of the informal organization of scientists in decision making on R&D.

1) The informal organization of scientists (those who view themselves as professional researchers) has a significant impact on the decisions made by the formal organization. Here the presumption is that the formal administrative hierarchy would make decisions other than those they made as the result of the activities of the informal organization. A complete verification of the hypothesis would require the identification of the informal organization apart from the formal and an ability to determine the decisions that the formal hierarchy would have made had the informal organization not influenced the outcome. While the first hypothesis is rather intuitive and appears easy to support from one's experience, the second is not.

2) The effect of the role of the informal organization on decision making on R&D, while contrary to the means desired by the formal organization, is not contrary to the ends of the overall organization. Difficulties obviously exist in the determination of what are "means" and what are "ends." At a rather crude level, we interpret "ends" to be the long-run goals of the organization, such as survival, growth, more-than-adequate profits, prestige, etc. "Means" are the various ways an organization specifies as necessary to accomplish the ends. Means encompass everything from standard operating procedures, to daily directives, to yearly budgeting. In essence, then, the second hypothesis says that the actions of the informal organization, while not in accordance with the desires of the administration, are likely to aid in the accomplishment of the overall organizational goals. This would be particularly true when the goals exist apart from the administration, such as those of owners of private R&D firms or the government in the case of public R&D. This is not to say that all informal activity is to the benefit of the organization in toto, but that this activity is no more likely to be to the detriment of long-range goals than the decisions made by the formal hierarchy unaided. Though the role of the informal organization may not have adverse effects on the long-range goals of the organization by itself, the interaction of this role with the behavior of the formal organization might. This potential effect leads us to a third hypothesis.

3) Recognition of the informal organization without its destruction by the administrative hierarchy of R&D activities is of positive benefit to the latter. Recognition without destruction requires an open acknowledgment of the benefits that accrue to the organization via the behavior of the informal organization, the solicitation and incorporation of these benefits, and the avoidance of formalizing the informal. All of this, of course, would

have to be couched in a more operational form to be implemented, if true. Somewhat implicit in the third hypothesis is the fourth.

4) The formal organization can be restructured to take advantage of the benefits to the overall organization that can be had from informal organization, without incurring costs as great as the benefits.

All of the hypotheses are capable of being tested empirically. Testing them, however, would require a more adequate scheme of measurement than has been given so far. Nevertheless, this problem exists within virtually all of the worthwhile efforts in the social sciences, so that the problem of measurement, by itself, should not foreclose efforts in the direction of hypothesis verification. This paper, however, does not go that far. Rather, it is an initial effort to elicit concern about the role and use of the informal organization of scientific professionals in the R&D organization. The author does not now possess "hard" data, but in defense of the pursuit of such data, descriptive evidence is given to support the hypotheses. Thus, the paper cannot be viewed as conclusive, but rather is suggestive of further potentially useful research.

The paper commences with a brief explanation of what we mean by the "informal organization." We then describe the means used by the informal organization of scientists to achieve its ends. Next, we discuss what the formal R&D organization is trying to do and why the informal organization affects the accomplishment of the formal organization's goals. Finally, we consider the interaction between the informal and formal organizations, and note several ways that the formal organization might take advantage of the positive attributes of the informal organization.

THE INFORMAL ORGANIZATION

The informal organization is just that: an organization that arises without conscious planning [2], initially to meet personal [28] and/or organizational needs that are not met within the framework of the formally recognized structure. The formal structure can be recognized in fact. An outsider could understand it by making reference to charts, written regulations, manuals of operation, and such. On the other hand, the same outsider could not fully understand the informal organization without knowing all of its members, their perceived norms and codes of behavior, their interrelationships, and their like sentiments. The formal organization, the administrative hierarchy, is one that is purposefully designed to accomplish stated tasks. The informal organization, in contrast, is not initiated on the basis of a plan. Instead, it changes over time to meet the needs of its members as an adaptive,[3] rather than preplanned, mechanism.

The informal organization has been a proper topic for research since the well-known Hawthorne studies [24]. Generally the literature has concentrated on the informal "group," such as those studied by Roy [25], and Blau and Scott [3]. Others, Davis [6] for example, have viewed the informal organization as an information network. Sayles [27], in his commentary on work group behavior, is describing the informal organization when he refers to "interest groups." He notes, for example, that the formation of an interest group helps its members "exploit opportunities to improve their relative position" (p. 142). While we do not wish to neglect the importance of the small-group aspect of the informal organization, the focus of this paper is on the interest-group/information-network dimensions of the informal organization. As a consequence, we will use these terms interchangeably.

Finally, the organization as an entity is not necessarily synonomous with the formal organization, the management, the administrative hierarchy, and such. The formal organization may well act in a fiduciary capacity with respect to another part that has the primary vested interest in the organization. Because this dichotomy may exist (and, in fact, is likely to exist in most large organizations), the value structure of those who possess the organization may not be the same as that of those who run the organization. This should be kept in mind, particularly with respect to the second hypothesis.

THE INFORMAL NETWORK IN A RESEARCH ORGANIZATION

To establish an environment conducive to the attainment of their goals, the researchers (scientists) need to have some degree of control over their own work environment. Seldom is the necessary control available without the collaborative efforts of several individuals. No single interested individual is likely to possess the necessary decision-making authority. The vehicle for such collaboration is the informal organization.

Typically, the informal organization has its beginning in what amounts to a social or friendship group [27]. For the scientist, such a group might come into being both for camaraderie and for information-exchange purposes.[4] As the members of the informal network become aware of its

[3] For an explanation of the type of adaptive behavior we mean, see [5], pp. 26–43.

[4] Free interchange among scientists is believed to be a professional norm and necessity [14].

existence, they recognize that coordinated effort gives them the power to control certain aspects of their environment. In particular, they are in a better position to influence the type of research projects on which they will work and the methodology that is to be used. Such power is relatively easy to obtain by individuals who possess a unique expertise [22]. The coordination is not difficult to elicit either, because these groups are likely to be based in common scientific aspirations. The success of one leads to increased prestige for all.

The ability to influence research endeavors can be exercised most effectively by the scientists through their control of the data[5] (information), which must pass through the informal network. Data that are vital to the decision-making capabilities of the administrative hierarchy also have ramifications for the needs of the members of the informal organization. To the degree that the data being processed influence the choice of research, and the methodologies and techniques to be used, there is an impact on the researchers. When the informal organization believes it knows[6] the cause-and-effect relationships between the data and administrative decisions, it may attempt to exercise data control for its own purposes.

The subjects for control differ between the formal and the informal organizations. The administration usually has as its main concern how much is to be spent and how it is to be spent, relative to the goals of the formal organization. The scientists are less concerned with this question,[7] but they are keenly interested in the direction (locus) of effort and the

[5] Data, figures, words, graphics, etc., are only information if they serve a perceived need of the recipient, a need that may exist either before or after the reception. For a more formal definition of this use of "information," see [1] pp. 164ff. Since it is often difficult to make an a priori judgment whether data may be information or not, we will generally use the term "data." "Information" will be used in accordance with the above definition and when discussing literature that makes generic use of the term "information."

[6] Some question whether an organization can "know" anything. We contend that it can. To the extent that there is a collective knowledge on the part of its members, the organization "knows." This is particularly true when the organization in question is primarily an information network. In the particular case we are describing, information that appears to be relevant to the behavior of the members of the informal network is soon the common knowledge of every member. As a consequence, the informal organization "knows."

[7] Many of the approximately 100 scientists interviewed by the author, in both public and private R&D organizations, believed substantial budget variations, particularly for equipment, would not significantly alter their research output, despite public statements to the contrary. The sophistication of their equipment might influence the level of side benefits from their research, such as more suggestions for promising new areas of research, but it was not likely to be significant for the immediate ends sought.

methodologies to be used. The administrative hierarchy seldom attempts to delve into the questions of methodology and technique, since they do not have the capabilities, but the locus of research is a subject for conflict. Both sides feel that they understand this question and both have a vested interest in its favorable resolution.

Most R&D organizations are aware of this dichotomy of interests and have attempted to accommodate this split within the formal structure. The accommodation, however, has seldom been effective. Apparently, a norm of the scientific community is that one is supposed to object to undertaking administrative tasks and will chafe at the constraints imposed by "standard operating procedures" [15]. Due to the dislike of administrative tasks [10] and the general perception of their ineffectiveness, channels that require administrative routine are avoided. Hence, there is great reliance on, and faith in, the workings of the informal organization of scientists.

THE INFORMAL ORGANIZATION AS AN INFORMATION PROCESSOR

Having discussed the nature of the informal organization within an R&D operation, particularly with its unique expertise characteristics, let us turn our attention to the hypotheses presented in the Introduction. The first states that "the informal organization of scientists has a significant impact on the decisions made by the formal organizations." We commence our discussion with an answer to the question "how." We follow this with anecdotal evidence, recognizing that we fall far short of being able to verify the hypothesis.

The informal organization of scientists, since it is essentially an information network rather than an overtly forceful group,[8] has at its disposal three ways to influence the decisions of the formal organization via its control of the flow of data. Firstly, the network can condition the formal hierarchy to view selected segments of data that the latter will receive as viable information. Secondly, it can provide the formal organization with

[8] Many informal organizations (interest groups) have been known to culminate their activities with overt threats and/or actions directed against the administrative hierarchy (e.g., work slowdowns, the formation of unions, the formation of nonunion bargaining units, etc.). Those made up of scientists, however, rarely do. If there is bargaining to be done, e.g., "either I be allowed to spend X percent of my time as I please or I will seek employment elsewhere," it is conducted on an individual basis. Collaborative overt effort appears to be against the norms of the scientific community. Consequently, collective activity is likely to rely on covert, more professionally acceptable techniques.

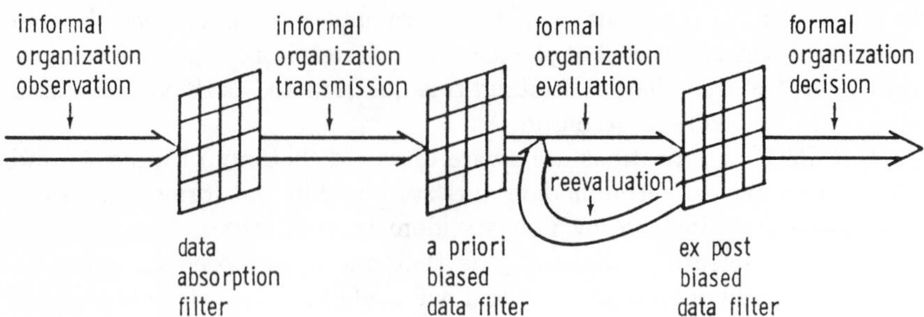

Fig. 1. Data filters.

the means to convert selected segments of stored data into biased information that bears favorably (for the informal network) on a given decision. The first way amounts to an a priori establishment of a biased data filter, the second to an ex post establishment of such a filter. Thirdly, the interest group of scientists can screen the data before they are transmitted to the administrative hierarchy, allowing only that which is not prejudicial to its best interests to pass.[9] Most likely, all three means will be attempted at one time or another. They are represented diagramatically in Fig. 1.

In both the first and second instances, the informal organization acts essentially as a lobby. The network continually provides the administration with a rationale that, in intent, leads the formal organization to view the available data as supporting the position of the informal.[10]

Preconditioning of the administration (the first means presented) may work as follows. The hierarchy faces a choice between one of two basic approaches to a major research endeavor. The researchers have the task of obtaining data that will enable an intelligent decision to be made. In the meantime, on the basis of its supposition about what the data might be like (full knowledge in many cases, since the data may already be available), the interest group provides the administration with testable hypotheses or at least conjectures, which, if shown to be true, support the position of the group. When the data are provided that validate these hypotheses, the choice is obvious. Note that when two different factions

[9] For a discussion of the power that can be assumed via an information or "uncertainly" absorption point, see [18], pp. 165–166.

[10] The formal organization may or may not be aware of the position of the informal. If it is, it usually attempts to institute a counter bias. For an interesting example of such an experimental result, see [5], pp. 67–77.

within the same formal structure play this game, the choice can become quite difficult for the nontechnical hierarchy.

An actual example of this kind of informal activity occurred in one of the research laboratories observed by the author. One informal network discovered that an extraorganization pressure group was forming to lobby for a particular area of research. Members of the network recognized that one of the research efforts they desired to pursue could be proposed so that it might be funded under the guise of fulfilling the wishes of the pressure group. The network quickly proceeded to prepare proposals indicating that one more step ought to be taken in their current research program. The extra step, in addition to being shown as a worthwhile continuation of current research, was described as being capable of providing additional information, some of which was of importance to the pressure group. Thus, when the lobby finally convinced the research hierarchy to undertake research with a specific goal in mind, the informal organization had laid the groundwork sufficiently well, so that it required little effort through formal channels to get support for their proposals.

In this particular case, the informal network had made contact at various levels throughout the formal hierarchy, so the processing of its request received speedy approval. Its position was also enhanced by one member of the formal hierarchy being also an understood member of the informal organization. In fact, he played an important role in the early phases of preparation of the informal organization's case.

The ex post approach to influencing decisions usually takes place when the informal network does not have sufficient insight into the environment to prepare in advance of the data flow. This frequently arises when the informal organization does not have a broad base of contact with the formal. In such a case, the ex post tactic is vulnerable, since the administration can choose to ignore it. It always helps to have at least one sympathizer in the ranks of the formal hierarchy.

An excellent case of the ex post approach was the decision to approve the building of a laboratory facility. For two years, one group within the laboratory sought the construction of a facility in which to conduct their research. For two years, they were rejected, in spite of an elaborate flow of data that they thought adequately defended their cause. Toward the end of the second year, an interest group arose. It decided to change the current tactic. No attempt was made to alter the factual data flow, but the ruling hierarchy was encouraged to see the facility as multiple purpose rather than single purpose, as initially proposed. The hierarchy presumed that the laboratory's activities would expand over time and, since it then appeared that the facility would be capable of suiting several alternative purposes if the need arose, it was approved. Partly because the informal organization was out of touch with the administrative hierarchy, it took two years. Admittedly, however, it was not clear that the hierarchy would have been susceptible to the new interpretation of old data much earlier.

The screening of data before they are transmitted to the formal organization is probably the most common and most effective means of influencing decisions available to the informal network in a scientific organization. When the informal network is in a position to establish such a screen, and if it has knowledge of the cause-and-effect relationships between data and decisions, it is in an excellent position of influence. The primary means for preventing such activity is the establishment of complex checks and balances on the data input. This can work reasonably effectively when the inputs are being screened by distinct subunits of the organization that have little in common and the inputs are sufficiently well understood by these various points of admittance.

The staffing of alternate data inputs, however, entails two problems. One is that few persons in the organization are likely to have the requisite background. The second is that those persons with the necessary qualifications are likely to have a similarity of interests. Consequently, their sentiments concerning the data input are likely to be the same. Only when an R&D activity is large enough (or rich enough) to have the luxury of internal competition will this not be the case. Hence, separate input channels may not cancel out the bias introduced by the informal network.

For single-channel data inputs, the formal organizational hierarchy may be able to construct counter bias filters. This requires that the hierarchy know the nature of the informal organization's biases, so that it can correct for them. This, in turn, requires both a knowledge of the intentions of the informal organization and sufficient technical sophistication so that meaningful counter biases can be established. It is the latter aspect of control that makes tight management of R&D so difficult.

One of many examples of the data absorption filter approach observed concerned two laboratories within the research organization that were doing work in similar fields. Personnel at both laboratories knew that a major effort was going to be initiated in a new area of research, but an area that was relevant to the competence of either laboratory. It was also obvious to all concerned that each laboratory would have to demonstrate its competence in the new area before either (and not both) would be allowed to pursue the research effort in question. The research was a desirable plum, since sizable resources were to be involved and the project would be professionally prestigious.

An interest group at one laboratory, we will call it *A*, recognized that the sooner a proposal for some preliminary research was submitted, the better it would be. If its methodology could be demonstrated to be successful in a pilot study before the other laboratory began its project, the network felt that laboratory *A* would have an excellent chance of being allowed to conduct the entire program. The interested persons in the other organization, let us call it *B*, were slow to start. Consequently, the early start by *A* appeared to be quite significant. Approval of the pilot project, however, had to go through an individual who was a member of the relevant informal network at *B*, even though he was in the administrative hierarchy. He notified *B* of *A*'s proposal and then delayed it's acceptance for over half a year, while *B* prepared its own proposal with the added advantage of knowing what *A* had suggested. In fact, journal articles started coming out from *B* describing its methodological approach as the only viable one to the research problem and belittling the one that was forwarded by *A*.[11]

During this delay, *A* tried to force the proposal through the necessary formal channels using the prescribed procedures. These channels, however, had to make use of the technical competence of the individual delaying *A*'s proposal. Hence, he was in a position to indicate that the proposal had "insufficient scientific merit." Furthermore, the formal presentation was ineffective because speedy approval of the proposal required informal action. Post-budget funding was required and this was nearly impossible to obtain on a formal basis.[12] The only thing that saved *A* from complete rejection was the fortunate selection of a scientist from *A* to a senior administrative position. The best that he could do at this point, however, was secure preliminary funding for both laboratories, explaining that each ought to be allowed to demonstrate its capabilities. The decision of where to locate the new research effort was, in theory, to be based on the results of these pilot studies.[13]

---

[11] This was done to obtain professional, as well as administrative, support for its proposal. *B* realized that the stronger it could buttress its formal presentation by bringing various informal pressures to bear, the better it would be.

[12] The personnel involved at *A* did not perceive the existence of an institutionalized due-process norm to which they could avail themselves, though Evan [9] found that most research personnel did. Either this was because the network at *A* did not believe it had a legitimate complaint, or because the due process appeared to be a function of the informal organization of which *A* was not a part.

[13] Note that though internal competition exists within the research organization, the benefits, in terms of dual data sources, do not necessarily exist. The benefits accrue to the organization only if the disparate data flows reach an unbiased observer. In the example described, this was not the case. Hence, the formal organization had what amounted to a single source of data.

As these examples would appear to indicate, the informal organization does indeed have an impact on the nature of the decisions made by the administrative hierarchy. In each of the three cases presented, it is highly unlikely that the final decisions would have been those made without interest group pressure and, certainly, the timing of each decision was affected. Thus, it would seem that the informal organization is a force to be reckoned with and, as a consequence, its behavior ought to be better understood so that the reckoning can be done on an appropriate basis.

MEANS AND ENDS, FORMAL AND INFORMAL

"The effect of the role of the informal organization on decision making on R&D, while contrary to the means desired by the formal organization, is not contrary to the ends of the overall organization." This, the second hypothesis, is undoubtedly the most difficult of the four on which to gather concrete evidence. We assume that the organization, representing those who have a vested interest in it in proportion to the amount of their interest, has goals of essentially a long-run nature. The organization wishes to survive; it wishes to return a satisfactory profit; it wishes to grow in stature. These goals, we feel, are accomplished as much by the actions of the informal organization as by the dictates of the administrative hierarchy of an R&D organization. It is the nature of the goals of the interest groups of professionals in an R&D activity that leads to this hypothesis.

The means aspect of the hypothesis is almost a tautology. By virtue of the fact that the informal organization does not rely on the procedures established by the administrative hierarchy, the informal organization is using means contrary to those desired by the formal organization. The ends part of the hypothesis, however, is far less obvious. Hence, a discussion of the ends of the scientific and administrative communities is appropriate.

The long-run success of an R&D operation is dependent upon the long-run maximization (or at least "satisficing" [30]) of the utilitarian aspects of its output.[14] Over the short run, however, it is extremely difficult to make meaningful judgments about the expected long-run output of any given R&D operation, at least not directly. Furthermore, the long-run utilitarian aspects may not be capable of being measured along a simple metric, such as dollars and cents. It would be difficult, for example, to

[14] This is the assumption used in virtually all normative R&D project selection models. For example, see [7], [11], [12], and [26].

rationalize the Apollo program on such a basis. Prestige, "the availability of advanced knowledge," and other hard-to-quantify factors also enter into the long-run utility function.

Because of the difficulty in establishing any single basis for the determination of long-run success, simultaneous evaluations of two distinct but interdependent aspects of R&D would appear to be desirable. On one hand, the usual organization attempt to make a direct measure of the operational pragmatics of R&D should be made. Germane questions include the following. How successful has the activity been in producing useful (from the standpoint of the organization's own utility function) outputs? Are the outputs leading to greater profits or greater national prestige, or preventing a relative decline? But this is of necessity based on past and current activities. Only to the extent that answers are relevant to future returns do they satisfy the need to know "how good our R&D activity is."

On the other hand, one might consider a different approach to the expected future returns from the activity. This second measure is of the means rather than of the ends. It involves the researchers' potential, their ability to produce viable new ideas over the long run. Obviously, this potential cannot be measured directly. One indirect measure is the quality of their current output, but, such a quality score must include more than just the current value of their past and current output. It must provide for other measures of ability. The most common questions asked for this purpose are the following. How prestigious are our researchers? What is the standing of our laboratory within the scientific community? How sophisticated are we? How advanced are our methods? How advanced are the problems on which we are working? While answers to these questions cannot reach the essence of the value we seek, they provide the satisfactory surrogate, which hereafter we will refer to as "prestige."

In brief, then, the long-run worth of an R&D operation may be gauged by its current utilitarian aspects and its prestige. Whether R&D administrative hierarchies use such a dual approach, however, is questionable. This is not to say that administrators do not recognize the possible positive correlation between prestige, on the one hand, and valuable output, on the other. Rather, the operationality of the former and the difficulty of making any determination of the value of the latter, perhaps quite rightly, lead to heavy reliance on the former.

The reasons for this are not complex. Definable goals, against which success can be measured, are necessary for the operation (including control) of any organization. The organization must have some viable means for determining how well it is doing. Given that both concrete and abstract goals (such as prestige) exist, the concrete ones command the attention of the administration, because they are more easily understood and operationalized. The less pragmatic goals (as seen through the eyes of the administration) are likely to be attended to only when the operational goals appear to be satisfied. Frequently when this is the case, success in the achievement of the operational goals has been perceived to have elicited the prestige desired. Hence, prestige is often viewed as a valuable by-product of good research, rather than an attribute of the activity that is indicative of future output.

The researchers, the scientists, are much more likely, however, to accept the dual evaluation of the R&D operation. On the one hand, the rewards offered by the hierarchy encourage them to accept the operational goals of the organization. Because they seek these rewards, the need to fulfill organizational goals becomes internalized. The researchers truly believe they ought to accomplish organizational pragmatics. On the other hand, the researchers seek rewards from their professional peer group.[15] They seek a measure of status within that group, and such status is a function of both individual and own-group prestige.[16] The individual seeks to obtain a reputation among the members of his professional peer group on his own, and/or he seeks to identify with a prestigious group, assuming that the prestige of the group will apply to him as well. An example with which most of us are familiar is the desire of a recent recipient of the Ph.D. degree to join the faculty of a "good" university; in part, because it affords him a measure of prestige, which he has not yet had time to earn.

Both individual and collective prestige in an R&D laboratory are heavily dependent upon the level of technical (scientific) sophistication that one is able to demonstrate. That is, prestige is a function not only of the ends achieved in research, but of the methodology used as well. The more sophisticated or advanced the technique, the better it is. Consequently, the nature of prestige is such that it is not always perfectly correlated with the more pragmatic desires of the laboratory. There well may be a conflict between the achievement of the two interdependent goals.[17]

The question that remains is whether the researchers in pursuit of their own goals via informal organization are contributing to the long-run goals

[15] This split has been described aptly by Evan [8], in reference to the role strain of the "applied researcher." It is the author's observation that the vast majority of the scientists in R&D organizations can be so defined. Consequently, this dichotomous dilemma appears to be pervasive throughout the R&D organization.

[16] Using the terms of Maslow's need hierarchy [21], the organization provides the means to meet the more basic physiological and safety needs, whereas the scientific community provides the means to satisfy the higher order social, ego, and self-fulfillment needs.

[17] This conflict has occurred many times. For example, see [16] and [20].

of the organization on the balance. We believe this to be the case, but the problems of presenting proof are substantial. Rather than presenting anecdotes as before, which cannot be satisfactory here since this is more than just an existence hypothesis, we indicate the logic upon which the hypothesis is based.

Three tenets are central to the above position. Firstly, a prestigious laboratory begets higher caliber personnel, both from within and without. The higher the caliber of personnel is, the greater the expected value of the output over the long run will be. Secondly, the basis of prestige, a grounding in sophisticated methodology and the pursuit of significant frontier problems, is also positively associated with the expected value of long-run R&D output. Thirdly, the use of a dual evaluation scheme for the selection of research by interest groups would indicate that these groups consider the tradeoffs between short-run operational pragmatics, and long-range benefits. This should be to the benefit of the overall R&D organization, if for no other reason, because the interest groups are likely to force consideration of the long-run benefits of their position. This forced expansion of time horizon ought to aid the overall organization in reaching decisions more beneficial to those with the vested interest in it.

The first part of the first tenet is not very controversial. It is readily observable that high-prestige R&D activities, such as some of the NASA laboratories, the Bell Telephone laboratories, the General Electric laboratories, etc., have an easier time competing with the universities for high-caliber personnel than do lesser activities. The association between sophisticated input and utilitarian output, however, is not free from controversy. It is easy to give examples where this appears to be true, but the counter arguments are also numerous. Perhaps the primary argument for the position at this point is that the rate of scientific advancement appears to be continually increasing and, if this is so, the incremental improvements, which many organizations have relied upon in the past to keep them solvent, may no longer be sufficient. It will be necessary to occasionally make a significant innovation to maintain market position and such an innovation is dependent upon personnel capable of working on frontier problems.

While the above argument is a rationalization of the second hypothesis, it is no more than that. The hypothesis remains to be subjected to empirical investigation and all we hope to do is to indicate that such an investigation appears worthwhile. Considering the increasing reliance upon R&D activities in virtually all private and public enterprises, we ought to know more about the relationship between the researcher's pursuit of his own goals and how this pursuit reflects upon the goals of the organization of which he is a part.

THE FORMAL VERSUS THE INFORMAL ORGANIZATION

All too often, these two organizations are viewed as engaged in combat with each other and this view is particularly true among the organizations' memberships. While the perceptions are quite understandable, we question the desirability of such a view. To be more specific, we hypothesize that recognition of and circumscribed reliance upon the informal organization is to the benefit of the administrative hierarchy. To gain the benefit, however, administrative hierarchy must cease "fighting" the informal networks that exist within, take advantage of the facilities that the network can offer, and do so without formalizing the informal. Whether this is possible will be treated in the next section. Here we will consider whether the net asset really exists; to do so, we will first consider the basis for the presumption that the two organizations are in conflict. The formal organization, with its rigid structure, provides the opportunities and arouses the needs required for the formation of the interest group network. The organization provides the opportunities by means of its physical structure and the contacts that it provides among its members, particularly those with like interests and needs. It arouses needs by failing to cater to all of those possessed by the individuals within its confines and by eliciting previously dormant ones. Seldom does the formal structure allow adequate socialization and rarely does the administration provide the means whereby the individual members perceive adequate (as they would define "adequate") control over their environment.[18] Hence, the very existence of a formal organization provides the *raison d'etre* for the formation of informal interest groups. Since the basis of existence lies in perceived inadequacies of the formal hierarchy, it usually pits the informal group against the administration. We should add that such a position aids in the recruitment of additional members to the side of the interest group.

The administrative hierarchy recognizes the reasons for the existence of various interest groups. Since they exist to achieve ends not provided by the hierarchy, it is not difficult to understand why the hierarchy views their existence as a threat. Not only is there an implication concerning the inadequacy of performance by the administration, but there is the correct perception that the interest group wishes to assume some of the prerogatives of the formal organization. This is a direct threat to the administrative hierarchy, and typically it reacts by attempting to discredit

---

[18] These are two of the three needs that Barnard [2] feels are served by the informal organization. The third is the need to communicate, but this would appear to be subsumed adequately under the need to socialize and the need for control.

or destroy the informal network. Such a reaction tends to solidify the interest group and reinforce the perception that the two are in direct conflict with one other.

Unfortunately, both the formal and informal organizations usually fail to understand that each is serving a function that, in all probability, cannot be served successfully by the other. This is particularly true for R&D activities. The informal network is in no position to manage the entire organization. Its members neither have the capabilities nor the desires to become encumbered by bureaucratic realities. A need for a well-defined structure exists within all sizable interrelated organizations and a network of interested scientists is in no position to meet this need.

The formal organization can never effectively meet all the needs that lead to the formation of interest groups. In particular, the need to exercise control over one's environment is more of a relative than an absolute concept. Whatever the formal provisions, they are invariably viewed as constraining. More importantly for a research organization, the technical expertise usually rests outside the membership of the administrative hierarchy. Though procedures may be devised to formally incorporate this expertise, its most effective expression is in the hands of the dedicated interest group. Thus, while some semblance of control can be maintained by administrative fiat, the effectiveness of such controls for the goals of the overall organization is highly questionable. Technical decisions in the hands of the uninformed can seldom be justified from a research standpoint.

The one remaining aspect that should be covered is the "without its destruction" phase. This is important because, as implied in the above argument, the formalization of the previously informal removes some of the qualities inherent in the informal. The perceptions of free socialization and of technical control of one's research are likely to be damaged, and the result will be the formation of new interest groups that lie outside the perceived constraints of formal organization. Hence, to gain the benefits of informal organization, formalization can not take place.

The conclusion of the above argument is the statement of the third hypothesis. Data to support it, however, exist only in anecdotal form. Such data exist only where recognition of the benefits of informal organization has taken place and very few such cases can be found. Furthermore, a difficulty exists in making an *a priori* versus *ex post* comparison. *Ceteris paribus* conditions do not hold, hence, the effect of recognition is seldom likely to be separable from the effects of other environmental factors. Nevertheless, the anecdotes we do have will be presented in the next section.

CO-OPTING THE INFORMAL ORGANIZATION

The question that remains is whether the formal organization of an R&D activity can be so structured that it can obtain a net gain from a new relationship with the informal organization. Quite obviously, there would be no point in pursuing this question if we did not believe that our second and third hypotheses will be verified. If they prove to be in error, the suggestions made will be of little value, at least as they relate to interest group activity.

Three ways of revising the relationships will be described. Any one may work to the advantage of the overall organization, but we tend to favor the third for reasons that will be mentioned. Though we can cite a couple of examples of apparently successful accommodation, we are not in a position to make an accurate cost evaluation of the change. The reorganizations can be defended only on the proposition that they have led to better decisions on R&D.

The verb "co-opt" is used to desdribe the action that we feel is desirable on the part of the formal organization to gain the benefits available from informal organizations. Perhaps the semanticist would feel that we are doing an injustice to the word, for we mean a bit more than the dictionary definition. We are referring to the action of bringing elements of the informal network into the formal hierarchy, *without* destroying their identity.[19] We also mean to describe a process that allows the goals of the two distinct organizations to coalesce, without one set of goals completely dominating the other. The implication is that a certain amount of bargaining takes place, whether intra- or interindividual, under conditions where the costs and benefits to both sides of the issue are much better understood than they are currently. To co-opt, then, does not imply capitualtion. Rather, it is an effort to encourage a form of cooperation.

The most common approach, probably because it accomplishes other ends as well, is to bring individuals into the administration who command the respect of the members of the informal network. Generally this involves converting a technically competent individual into a capable administrator.

Almost anyone connected with the scientific community will vouch for the fact that successful conversion (from the standpoint of both the formal and informal organizations) is difficult. As we noted previously, the ac-

[19] Selznick [29] defines "co-optation" as "the process of absorbing new elements into the leadership or policy-determining structure of an organization as a means of averting threats to its stability or existence" (p. 13). We agree with his definition in essence. We only wish to modify it, for the purposes of this paper, by noting that we do not want to include the possibility that the identity of the co-opted organization may be destroyed.

ceptance of administrative chores is counter to the ethos of the scientist.[20] Furthermore, such a conversion may lead merely to a more effective member of the informal network. The convertee is now highly placed; he has access to information of value. His ability to act as a biased data absorption point, however, is limited to the extent that the formal organization knows of his biases and can correct for them. Hence, selection of the proper person is important. In addition, while it is not likely (and not desirable) that the convertee will adopt the seals of the formal organization to the exclusion of those in his network, it is probable that he will introduce modifications to the latter, particularly in the direction of more realistic attainment. This, by itself, may help to eliminate a significant amount of dysfunctional friction between the formal and informal organizations.

The benefits to be obtained from a successful conversion are significant. A better perspective becomes available regarding the balance between the needs of the scientists and the R&D organization. Nevertheless, the administration should be aware of the potential problems involved, including the possibility that the convertee may be excluded from the confidence of the interest group. He may now be perceived to be "on the other side."

If an R&D organization finds it difficult to make successful conversions from researcher to administrator, it might try the reverse method: the conversion of an administrator to one who, at least, can gain the confidence of the researchers. This can be done and was done quite successfully by several persons observed at one laboratory. They all had two characteristics in common, however. Firstly, they demonstrated exceptional competence in their administrative specialty. This would become known to the informal organization through the grapevine. Secondly, they not only gave evidence of a sincere interest in, and sympathy for, the work being done by the members of the interest group, but they made an effort to understand it. This required an exceptional work load. The formal organization did not appear to make appropriate compensation for this, though the hierarchy did recognize the benefits received. Perhaps the real reward for the exceptional effort expended by these individuals was the knowledge that they were in positions of considerable influence, influence vastly exceeded that granted them by their position in the formal hierarchy.

Reliance upon such individuals to bridge the gap between the scientists and the administration, however, should be tempered. Firstly, such ad-

---

[20] Resistance to the conversion might also be based on the general reluctance to disturb any existing social order [4]. But, since a large part of a scientists's social order is based in his professional peer group and much of this is extraorganizational, such a reluctance would not appear to be a significant factor in limiting conversion.

ministrators often begin to identify with an interest group. Consequently, they become, in effect, an adjunct to the network rather than remaining partial to the problems of the administration. This is because the perceived prestige is greater via association with the scientists than it is by means of identification with the administration. This was definitely true in one case observed by the author. Secondly, these persons are often willing to expend the extra effort because of the power they perceive themselves to have as they bridge the gap. It is not unusual, therefore, that they may conduct their affairs strictly for their own benefit and only incidentally for the benefit of either organization.

An alternative to either of the above approaches is being attempted by one large R&D organization. A trial policy is to rotate certain research personnel through one- or two-year assignments as administrators or advisors to the administration. The research organization in question makes a great effort to point out the benefits to the interest group (through the individual involved) if one of its members is willing to temporarily fulfill such a function. Furthermore, the administration emphasizes that it is just a temporary position. This is crucial in order to elicit any interest among highly respected scientists.

Though the researcher-turned-temporary-administrator introduces strong biases into the administrative decision-making processes, these biases are usually identifiable because his associations are known. Consequently, the biases can be appropriately countered, if done subtly. This puts the formal organization in a better position than it would be in if it had little idea how the data was being filtered by the interest group. The administration now has more control over the most likely filter.[21] In addition, the formal organization is in a position to provide the members of the informal network with the necessary sentiments of control over their own environment.

One example of the use of rotation of scientific personnel through administrative positions was given earlier. This was the case where a scientist from laboratory *A* was asked to temporarily assume a senior administrative position. In that position he was able to rescue a proposal submitted by his colleagues that would have been discarded had he not been there. That he would have favored the proposal rescued to the exclusion of the other proposal is a dictinct possibility. In this case, however, the scientist was readily identifiable with regard to his organizational

---

[21] This control must be exercised very carefully; otherwise, the filter might move elsewhere within the informal network, the temporary convertee having been essentially removed from the network.

biases and the administration would have been in a reasonably good position to allow all competing research proposals to come to light. While the individual in question was going to have a voice in the final selection of where the research project was to be located, he now had to consult with a committee of scientists from both the interested laboratories. Prior to his appointment, such a consultation was not presumed necessary.

A second example involves another temporary administrative appointment from the same laboratory. A Research Engineer was put in the position of Budget Coordinator for a period of one year. The administration now had someone with the necessary competence to make tradeoffs on the scientific merits of budget requests. Furthermore, the administration knew precisely the biases of the coordinator and, whenever it was thought that these might influence his judgment, other judgments were brought to bear. This mechanism appeared to lead to a more meaningful budgeting process, especially since there was an indication that the position of coordinator would be rotated among the memberships of virtually all of the relevant scientific interest groups.

SUMMARY AND CONCLUSIONS

Few students of organizations would deny that informal organizations exist within all formal organizations despite efforts to eliminate them. This should be recognized as an organizational fact of life. Such an organization exists because it serves to meet the needs of its members that are not (and often cannot) being met by the formal organization. The need that the administration feels in most disruptive is the need for professional status, a need that the interest group attempts to satisfy through its efforts to control the research environment.

Interest groups usually concentrate their attempts to influence the decision processes through the control of information. This can be done in one of three ways. The informal network can precondition the formal hierarchy to accept only certain data as pertinent information. If this fails, it can provide a new filter for existing data. Thirdly, independently of whether or not the other two approaches are used, the network can screen the data that must pass through it, allowing to pass only that which is not prejudicial to its own interests.

Generally, the formal organization perceives only the negative aspects of the informal organization. Consequently, the hierarchy attempts to prevent activities of the informal organization from becoming fulfilled. But the informal organization in R&D activities does provide a positive service. It is the prime source of technical expertise, so necessary for the well being of the formal organization, and it is an excellent source of extraorganizational information. The problem remains, however, to utilize the benefits of the informal network, while controlling its dysfunctional effects. Incorporating it into the formal structure does not do this.

One possible approach is to engage technically respected personnel in the administrative hierarchy. Since this is not likely to enhance the scientist's position in the eyes of his colleagues, however, it is often difficult to attract the proper individuals. Another avenue is to have a member of the formal hierarchy gain admittance to the informal organization. This can be done, but is extremely rare, primarily because of the effort and intellect required of the individual involved.

A third way to establish the necessary rapport is to rotate members of the informal organization through positions in the formal hierarchy. If done properly and if the participants can be made to see the advantages in such a system for their own peer group, the exchange of knowledge about each others' positions should prove to be exceedingly valuable. Such a rotation should provide the researchers with the recognition that some of the formal organization's goals are pertinent for the informal organization as well.

The above conclusions are built around four researchable, but as yet untested hypotheses. The hope is that the arguments and the anecdotes presented will provide sufficient motivation for further research into what this author feels is a highly relevant area. The R&D organization is somewhat unique in the dichotomy of expertise that exists among its members, the scientists and the administrators. The extent to which organization theory can be used to obtain the greatest advantage from the two bases of expertise for the general welfare of the overall organization should be a subject for more research interest than is presently the case.

ACKNOWLEDGEMENT

I wish to thank my colleagues C. Lundberg and K. Mackenzie, and the reviewers for many helpful comments on an earlier draft.

BIBLIOGRAPHY

1. R. L. Ackoff, with the collaboration of S. K. Gupta and J. S. Minas, *Scientific Method: Optimizing Applied Research Decisions*. New York: Wiley, 1962.
2. C. I. Barnard, *The Function of the Executive*. Cambridge, Mass.: Harvard University Press, 1938.

3. P. M. Blau and W. R. Scott, *Formal Organizations*. San Francisco, Calif.: Chandler, 1962.
4. L. Coch and J. R. P. French, "Overcoming resistance to change," *Human Relations*, vol. 1, pp. 512–532, 1948.
5. R. M. Cyert and J. G. March, *A Behavioral Theory of the Firm*. Englewood Cliffs, N. J.: Prentice-Hall, 1963.
6. K. Davis, "Management communications and the grapevine," *Harvard Bus. Rev.*, vol. 31, pp. 43–49, 1953.
7. B. V. Dean and S. S. Sengupta, "Research budgeting and project selection," *IRE Trans. Engineering Management*, vol. EM-9, pp. 158–169, December 1962.
8. W. M. Evan, "Role strains and the norm of reciprocity in research organizations," *Am. J. Sociol.*, vol. 68, pp. 346–354, 1962.
9. ———, "Superior-subordinate conflict in research organizations," *Admin. Sci. Quart.*, vol. 10, pp. 52–64, 1965.
10. F. Friedlander and E. Walton, "Positive and negative motivations toward work," *Admin. Sci. Quart.*, vol. 9, pp. 194–207, 1964.
11. G. R. Gargiulo, J. Hannoch, D. B. Hertz, and T. Zang, "Developing systematic procedures for directing research programs," *IRE Trans. Engineering Management*, vol. EM-8, pp. 24–29, March 1961.
12. S. W. Hess, "A dynamic programming approach to R and D budgeting and project selection," *IRE Trans. Engineering Management*, vol. EM-9, pp. 170–179, December 1962.
13. D. Hill, Ed., *The Management of Scientists*. Boston, Mass.: Beacon Press, 1964.
14. F. W. Howton, "Work assignment and interpersonal relations in a research organization: some participant observations," *Admin. Sci. Quart.*, vol. 7, pp. 502–520, 1963.
15. N. Kaplan, "Organization: will it choke or promote the growth of science?" in [13], pp. 103–127.
16. E. Mansfield, "Technical change and the management of research and development," in *The Economics of Technical Change*. New York: Norton, 1966.
17. E. Mansfield and R. Brandenburg, "The allocation, characteristics, and outcome of the firm's research and development portfolio: a case study," *J. Bus.*, vol. 39, pp. 447–464, 1966.
18. J. G. March and H. A. Simon, with the collaboration of H. Guetzkow, *Organizations*. New York: Wiley, 1958.
19. S. Marcson, "Organization and authority in industrial research," *Social Forces*, vol. 40, pp. 72–80, 1961.

20. ———, *The Scientist in American Industry*. New York: Harper & Row, 1960.
21. A. H. Maslow, *Motivation and Personality*. New York: Harper & Brothers, 1954.
22. D. Mechanic, "Sources of power of lower participants in complex organizations," *Admin. Sci. Quart.*, vol. 7, pp. 349–364, 1962.
23. C. D. Orth, J. C. Bailey, and F. W. Wolek, *Administering Research and Development*. Homewood, Ill.: Irwin-Dorsey, 1964.
24. F. J. Roethlisberger and W. J. Dickson, *Management and the Worker*. Cambridge, Mass.: Harvard University Press, 1939.
25. D. Roy, "Efficiency and the 'fix': informal intergroup relations in a piecework machine shop," *Am. J. Sociol.*, vol. 60, pp. 255–266, 1954.
26. A. Rubenstein, Ed., "Coordination, control, and financing of industrial research," in *Proceedings of the Fifth Annual Conference on Industrial Research*, June 1954. New York: King's Crown Press, 1955.
27. L. R. Sayles, "Work group behavior and the larger organization," in *Research In Industrial Human Relations*, C. M. Arensberg, *et al.*, Eds. Evanston, Ill.: Harper & Row, 1957.
28. P. Selznick, "An approach to a theory of bureaucracy," *Am. Sociol. Rev.*, vol. 8, pp. 47–54, 1943.
29. ———, *TVA and the Grass Roots*. Berkeley, Calif.: University of California Press, 1949.
30. H. A. Simon, "Theories of decision-making in economics and behavioral science," *Am. Econ. Rev.*, vol. 49, pp. 253–283, 1959.

PRECONCEPTIONS AND RECONCEPTIONS IN THE ADMINISTRATION OF SCIENCE*

Gerald Gordon
New York State School of Industrial Labor Relations
Cornell University

INTRODUCTION

There is an expanded emphasis on R&D in practically every area of activity, which can be ascribed to a general belief that "scientific research is one of the most effective roads toward increased industrial productivity, greater military security, and better health and welfare of the country."[1]

Despite the rise in the importance of science as a daily concern of modern man, until recently factors affecting the conduct of scientific research have not been objectively studied. For example, when we surveyed the literature on the administration of science, we found that between 1950 and 1961 over 80% of the publications were based on speculation rather than on objective evidence.[2] Further, we found that the speculative publications for the most part tended to reinforce, rather than to critically examine, prevalent conceptions of science and its administration.

However, in the past few years, there has been an increase in the number of empirical studies dealing with the administration of science. In fact, enough has been done in the recent past for it to be of value to reexamine some of our preconceptions in the light of recent evidence.

PRECONCEPTIONS OF BASIC AND APPLIED RESEARCH

One of the most entrenched of these preconceptions is the importance ascribed to the differences between basic and applied research. It is my contention that the dichotomy, basic and applied (and such related dichotomies as limited and fundamental, theoretical and action, et cetera), hinders rather than advances our knowledge of the relationship between organizational structure and scientific accomplishment. In the first place, the broad use of these terms offers no clear-cut basis for categorization.

* Originally published in *Research Effectiveness* by B. Yovits, et al., (eds) New York: Gordon & Breech Science Publishers, Inc., 1966.

The dichotomy between basic and applied research refers either to intent of the scientist or to use of the discovery, neither of which is easy to determine. It would take a psychoanalyst to determine motivation and a seer to determine use. But more important than the definitional problems is the fact that these dichotomies are not directly related to the research process. For instance, depending on the motivation or perception of the researcher, the same experiment could be labeled as either basic or applied research.

Thus, if a researcher were doing research on cell reproduction in the hope that such knowledge would lead to a cure for cancer, conceivably the research would be labeled "applied research." But, if he were interested in cell reproduction per se, the very same piece of work would be labeled "basic research." Despite the definition, the research process might be similar.

Not being related to the research process, the distinction between basic and applied research can only be of limited value in research administration. However, the mystique which has grown up around the terms "basic" and "applied" has led to blind alleys and to patterns of research administration based on misconceptions rather than knowledge. For instance, recent findings indicate that each of the following widely held beliefs, in part at least, is erroneous:

1. Most scientific breakthroughs occur in universities while exploitations of the breakthroughs occur in industrial and other applied research settings.
2. Basic researchers tend to be more creative or innovative than applied researchers.
3. As basic researchers are highly dedicated, administrative controls over their work are not only unnecessary but tend to inhibit their innovation.
4. The ideal research setting is the university.

Ben-David's findings, that major breakthroughs often occur in applied settings, calls into question the first two myths. Indeed, referring to the breakthroughs of Koch, Pasteur, Villemin, Devaine, Freud, and others, Ben-David argues that historically breakthroughs tended to occur outside the university.[3]

In regard to the other myths, in independent studies, both Pelz[4] and I[5] have found that certain organizational controls, particularly in regard to resources and evaluation, promote rather than hinder innovation.

From our study of socio-medical research we also found that research conducted in universities was far less innovative than research conducted in hospitals and other settings.[6] Kaplan also questions the assumption that the university is always the most optimal research setting commenting:

However adequate is the research environment in some universities, it is usually the top ten or perhaps even the top twenty that we are thinking about. And even in these top schools there is little question any more that everything is the best in the best of all possible worlds. Yet this . . . is what some observers would have all of industry or government transpose to their own environment.[7]

While the distinctions between basic and applied research may have been valuable in the day of the lone researcher, they are of little value in understanding modern large-scale research. Therefore, I propose that as a first step in the administration of research, we abandon the distinction between basic and applied, which refers to use or intent, and instead that we utilize distinctions that relate to process and organizational imperatives.

In the remainder of this paper I will discuss two distinctions that I think can be of value in research administration—urgency and predictability. Urgency refers to the speed with which the results are needed by the owner of the research resources. This can range from the current urgency of space exploitation to the initial indifference to Goddard's rocket research. Urgency does not refer to the ultimate importance of the research, but rather it relates to the need of the organization for rapid research results. Predictability refers to the extent to which the administrators of a project feel that the steps necessary to achieve their research objectives are predeterminable. The latter distinction is particularly important because we are inclined to think of science almost by definition as the study of the unpredictable. Moreover, the folklore of science emphasizes the importance of the accidental and serendipitous. I do not wish to minimize the importance of the unpredictable in science. But I think it also important to recognize that a great deal of scientific activity consists of exploitation and extensions of the known through traditional research techniques. Indeed, Kuhn states that:

Perhaps the most striking feature of the normal research problems . . . is how little they aim to produce major novelties, conceptual or phenomenal. Sometimes, as in a wave-length measurement, everything but the most esoteric detail of the result is known in advance, and the typical latitude of expectation is only somewhat wider.[8]

Treating the above distinctions as dichotomies, four ideal situations result:

U_- P_- Little Urgency Minimally Predictable Procedures
U_- P_+ Little Urgency Maximally Predictable Procedures
U_+ P_- Great Urgency Minimally Predictable Procedures
U_+ P_+ Great Urgency Maximally Predictable Procedures

Of course research is never completely predictable or unpredictable, and there is always some urgency in regard to research findings. Nevertheless, the use of such ideal types simplifies and, hopefully, clarifies the design problem.

For example, the following findings from group dynamics and from the sociology of science can be used within the context of the above ideal situations to provide guidelines for the design of research organizations.

Findings: In general, groups do better than individuals in solving problems with predictable answers (e.g., solving crossword puzzles), but individuals do better than groups in solving problems when the answers are not predeterminable (e.g., creating crossword puzzles).[9,10]

Guidelines: When research is predictable (P_+), group responsibility for the ongoing research is advisable. When research is nonpredictable (P_-), individual responsibility for the ongoing research is advisable.

Findings: In terms of absolute time, groups tend to solve problems faster than individuals, but in terms of man minutes per hour, individuals tend to solve problems faster than groups.[9]

Guidelines: When urgency is great (U_+), the use of groups for the suggestion of research approaches is advisable. When urgency is not a factor (U_-), individual suggestion of approaches is advisable.

Findings: Specific administrative controls, in regard to resources, seem to stimulate scientific accomplishment.[4] Nonpredictable research is stimulated when administrators actively evaluate research results and is hindered when administrators attempt to specify research procedures.[6] On the other hand, predictable research is stimulated when there is administrative or executive guidance.*

Guidelines: When research is not predictable (P_-), evaluative administrative control is advisable. When research is predictable (P_+), executive control is advisable.

Applying these guidelines to each of the four research situations, the following occurs:

Situation I (U_-P_-)-Little Urgency, Minimally Predictable Procedures

1. Suggestions of research approaches should be made on an individual basis.
2. A number of approaches should be considered, but they should be undertaken sequentially.
3. Research decisions should be arrived at on an individual basis.
4. The organization should evaluate rather than direct the research.

---

* Based on recent findings from our study of organizational setting and scientific accomplishment.

Situation II (U_-P_+)*-Little Urgency, Maximally Predictable Procedures*

1. Suggestions of research approaches should be made on an individual basis.
2. A single approach should be undertaken.
3. Research decisions should be arrived at on a group basis.
4. The organization should assume some directive responsibility for the research.

Situation III (U_+P_-)*-Great Urgency, Minimally Predictable Procedures*

1. Suggestions of research approaches should be made on a group basis.
2. A number of approaches should be undertaken.
3. Research decisions should be arrived at on an individual basis.
4. The organization should evaluate rather than direct the research.

Situation IV (U_+P_+)*-Great Urgency, Maximally Predictable Procedures*

1. Suggestions of research approaches should be made on a group basis.
2. A single approach should be undertaken.
3. Research decisions should be arrived at on a group basis.
4. The organization should assume some directive responsibility for the research.

In addition to aiding in the development of administrative guidelines, structuring research in terms of urgency and predictability leads to a series of hypotheses regarding areas such as tangential research, sources of conflict, and personnel strains.

The pursuit of interesting tangents has long been considered a source of scientific breakthroughs. It is my contention that the tendency to follow a tangent, in part at least, is determined by the urgency and predictability of the research. When research is defined as nonpredictable, research direction tends to be determined by the acceptance and rejection of a series of alternatives. Though the investigation of alternatives may be solely on the level of cerebral trial and error, the process of selecting alternatives can and does stimulate interest in areas tangential to the initial problem. On the other hand, when research is considered predictable, there is a tendency to specify procedures and consequently a reduction in the stimulus to tangential investigation. The degree of urgency with which an organization requires the answer to a problem preconditions the willingness of the organization to support tangential research. The greater the urgency, the less willing the organization is to support tangential research, and the

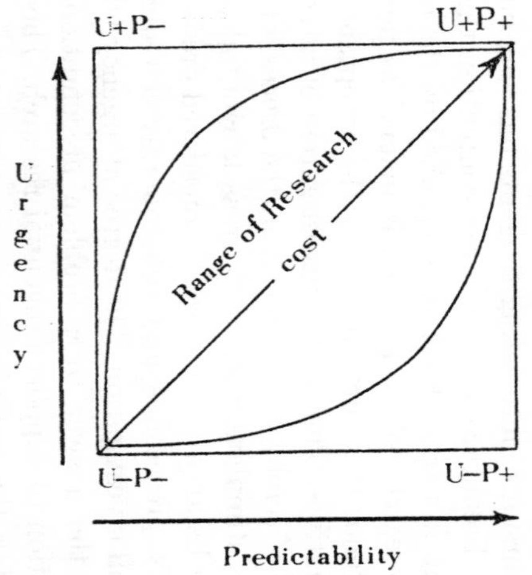

ADMINISTRATIVE GUIDELINES	RESEARCH SITUATIONS U–P–	U–P+	U+P–	U+P+
Suggestion of Approaches	Individual	Individual	Group	Group
Number of Approaches	Multiple Sequential	Single	Multiple Simultaneous	Single
Responsibility for Research Decisions	Individual	Group	Individual	Group
Administrative Authority Pattern	Evaluative	Executive	Evaluative	Executive
INNOVATION				
Toleration of Tangents	High	High	Low	Low
Stimulation to Tangential Research	High	Low	High	Low
PERSONALITY CHARACTERISTICS				
Tolerance for Ambiguity	Needed	Not Needed	Needed	Not Needed
Ability to Tolerate Pressure	Not Needed	Not Needed	Needed	Needed
PRIME CONFLICT AREAS	Resources	Resources Procedures	Innovation	Procedures

Figure 1. Schema for Research Administration

greater is the tendency for it to oppose such research. Therefore, it is hypothesized that in the U_-P_- situation there would be a constraint toward tangential research and that in the U_+P_+ situation there would be a constraint away from tangential research. Further, it is hypothesized that in the U_+P_- situation, where the researcher is stimulated toward tangential investigation and where the organization tends to resist such involvement, conflict between the administrator and researcher over tangential research would be maximal.

Examining other areas of conflict, I would predict that in the U_-P_- situation (where procedures are conceived as nonpredictable by management) conflict between management and researcher over procedures would be minimal. On the other hand, since urgency is not great, support of the project might be limited. Therefore, in this situation I would predict more conflict over resources than over procedures. Conversely, where urgency is great and research considered predictable, I would expect much more conflict in regard to procedures than in regard to resources. In the U_-P_+ situation, conflict would tend to occur over both procedures and resources, and one would probably find a great deal of discontent among researchers.

The last hypothesis concerns the personality attributes required by the research workers. When procedures are not predictable, the researcher would seem to need a high tolerance for ambiguity; when urgency is great, he would need a high tolerance for pressure. Thus, it would be predicated that for research personnel the least psychologically demanding situation would be the U_-P_+ situation and the most demanding the U_+P_- situation.

To conclude, I think that, in attempting to relate organizational structures to scientific accomplishment, it is necessary to critically examine the prevalent conceptions and ideologies of research administration. The approach taken in this paper is an attempt in this direction. The administrative guidelines evolving from this approach are summarized in the schema shown in Figure 1.

REFERENCES

1. Wolfle, D., "Scientific Research as a Responsibility of Government," *Social Science*, **24**, 33 (1949).
2. Folger, A. and Gordon, G., "Scientific Accomplishment and Social Organization: A Review of the Literature," *American Behavioral Scientist*, **5**, 51 (1962).
3. Ben-David, J., "Roles and Innovations in Medicine," *American Journal of Sociology*, **65**, 557 (1960).

4. Pelz, D. C., "Freedom in Research," *International Science and Technology*, **33,** 54 (1964).
5. Gordon, G. and Marquis, S., "Resources and Scientific Innovation," presented at the Annual Meeting of The American Sociological Association, Montreal, Canada (1964).
6. Gordon, G. and Marquis, S., "The Effect of Differing Research Settings and Administrative Authority Patterns on Scientific Innovation," presented at The Annual Meeting of the American Sociological Association, Chicago, Illinois (1965).
7. Kaplan, N., "Organization: Will It Choke or Promote the Growth of Science?" in Hill (ed.), *The Management of Scientists*, Boston: Beacon Press (1964).
8. Kuhn, T. S., *The Structure of Scientific Revolutions*, Chicago: University of Chicago Press (1962).
9. Hare, A. P., *Handbook of Small Group Research*, New York: Free Press of Glencoe (1962).
10. Taylor, D. W., Berry, P. C., and Block, C. R., "Group Participation, Brainstorming, and Creative Thinking," *Administrative Science Quarterly*, **3,** 23 (1958).

THE SYSTEMS APPROACH*

Hendrick W. Bode
Vice President (Retired)
Bell Telephone Laboratories

This paper is intended as an essay on systems engineering, regarded as one aspect of "applied research." Many of the problems confronting the nation, such as urban sprawl and decay, transportation, air pollution, water supply, and so on, involve large systems, and the "systems approach" seems a natural way of attacking them. Systems engineering may also have value for other, smaller, issues, and is frequently urged in such connections also. There seems little doubt that this approach may help us on many fronts. On the other hand, the "systems approach" is sometimes urged, somewhat uncritically, as a sovereign nostrum for all ills. Thus one needs to pay particular attention to aspects of the subject that may make it appropriate or rewarding in some situations but not in others.

Complex situations involving systems-engineering considerations are by no means new. Regional development plans of the past, such as the TVA evidently involved such considerations, just as much as do the environmental projects of the present day. They were, of course, taken care of somehow, whether or not they were identified as systems problems. On a smaller scale, such typical problems as inventory management or the proper scheduling of railroad rolling stock or university classrooms have been with us for a long time, and these must also have been solved, if not always with maximum efficiency.

As a formal discipline, operations research, which can be regarded as a first cousin of systems engineering, developed during the war, especially in connection with bombing and antisubmarine problems. It has flourished ever since, in both military and nonmilitary contexts. Inventory and scheduling problems, for example, would now be undertaken under this heading. In the private sector of the economy, the Bell system has used its own version of systems engineering for many years as a means of

---

* From *Applied Science and Technological Progress,* A Report to the Committee on Science and Astronautics, U.S. House of Representatives by the National Academy of Sciences, June 1967.

planning the growth and extension of communication facilities in an orderly way. In this special area, there is a vast background of relevant experience to draw on. Many of the techniques of present-day systems engineering, such as those related to traffic and queuing, turn out to have been first developed in connection with telephone problems. Some of this experience will be touched on later.

In recent years, the most conspicuous examples of the systems approach have been in connection with large military and space projects. In these applications the "systems approach" may be identified with the initial planning of the project, but it is equally likely to refer to a method of managing a complex technological development so that it can go forward more or less according to a prescribed schedule. In either case, the prestige of the approach is very great. It will be remembered, for example, that the Air Force Research and Development Command, one of the major divisions of the Air Force, was renamed the Air Force Systems Command to give added emphasis to its operations.

Associated with these activities a fairly elaborate formal methodology has been developed. One has only to think of linear and nonlinear programing, game theory, decision theory, queuing theory, and so on, as examples. In general, the techniques tend to be highly statistical or probabilistic and to make great use of computers. A simple but important example of the latter sort is the direct simulation of a complex physical system on a high-speed computer to permit the system response to be explored over a wide range of conditions. It is essentially these techniques, associated with the aerospace industry and related parts of the electronics industry, that are usually thought of when the "systems approach" is recommended for other applications in our technology.

SOME MISGIVINGS

It is simplest to begin by admitting at once that, in the long run, the protagonists of the "systems approach" for other than military applications are no doubt right. There must be many areas, like telephony, in which systems engineering will be useful. On the other hand, it takes only a little reflection to convince oneself also that techniques and methods of thought developed in the aerospace world may not always be immediately appropriate in other contexts. There are simply too many differences between that world and others.

As one example, in military equipment very small margins of performance are sometimes decisive. Thus balances between performance and cost may be quite different from those we would find in other situations. As a second example, considerations of military urgency have only faint counterparts in most civilian situations. This is, of course, important whenever cost-time trade-offs are involved, and is particularly relevant if we try to interpret the "systems approach" as a development-management technique. Finally, although requirements for compatibility do occur, when weapon systems are redesigned it is fairly likely that they can be redesigned from the ground up, with comparatively little regard to what has gone before. They need to be, if maximum performance is to be achieved. In contrast, most of the proposed large-scale civilian systems will probably require plans that will salvage as much as possible of existing equipment and facilities. The design engineer will find himself circumscribed accordingly. Telephone systems engineering has long faced a similar problem in the requirement that any new telephone system must be compatible with all existing equipment in the telephone network. In this respect, as well as in respect to the performance, schedule, and cost considerations mentioned earlier, telephone engineering seems to be closer than most military systems work to the general engineering style required for the putative systems applications of the future.

The impression that the gap between military systems engineering and proposed civilian applications may be greater than most people realize is heightened as soon as one inspects the substantive material with which the systems engineer must actually deal. Thus, one has only to pick up a currently accepted handbook on systems engineering to see how heavily it is larded with reference chapters on such topics as the physics of the atmosphere and outer space, the techniques of telemetry and radar, rocket propulsion, and so forth. The material seems to be well chosen for the purpose in hand, but a similar factual background for an urban reconstruction project, for example, would obviously be quite different. Without going further, one would expect that the urban project would require much stronger inputs from the social sciences. Since social and physical scientists tend to have somewhat different intellectual styles, this might not be entirely easy.

One may also have misgivings of a different sort. Many of the tenets of systems engineering seem pretty obvious and unlikely to contribute anything that would not have been discovered anyway. For example, the systems approach sometimes reduces to a pedestrian enumeration of all possible logical cases. This may occur, for example, in the development of checkout procedures for a missile, or the enumeration of possible failure modes in a space vehicle. As important as such lists may be, they seem to require little more than a decision to do a careful and thorough engineering job. We might have made such a decision without ever having heard of systems engineering.

Another example is furnished by the standard systems-engineering principle that systems effectiveness must be judged with all relevant considerations in mind. Thus, a householder or factory owner may be said to be using the systems approach if he buys electric lights on the basis not only of their initial cost but also of their efficiency in producing light, and still more so if he includes cost of replacement, as measured by expected lifetime, especially for the hard-to-get-at places. (Premium-priced bulbs are available for such purposes.) This is indeed an example of the systems approach, but one might hope to get the same results by the application of ordinary common sense. Moliere's character was impressed by the discovery that he had been speaking prose all his life. Scientists and engineers are less likely to be bowled over by the discovery that they have been practicing systems engineering all this time.

It would be possible to extend this list, but the examples given should be enough to show why one may be pardoned for doubting whether the systems approach is automatic magic, guaranteed to resolve all our most complicated and intractable problems. On the other hand, the examples do not necessarily refute the approach either. The fact that some aspects of systems engineering seem so obvious does not necessarily make the method logically invalid.

Clearly, we must dig deeper to find the distinctive contributions that systems engineering as now understood should be able to make it the areas that now trouble us. The examination of this question is the central topic underlying this paper. Unfortunately, a short paper cannot give very conclusive answers for such a broad question. Too much may depend on individual circumstances. The objective of the paper will be only to describe systems engineering in a sort of broad average sense, leaving questions of specific applicability to be explored as they arise. For this purpose I shall draw on such background as I have in the military field, but the principal source will be Bell System experience, which for the reasons noted earlier seems in some ways more relevant to the country's new problem.

VARYING CONCEPTIONS OF SYSTEMS ENGINEERING

It seems natural to begin the discussion with an immediate formal definition of systems engineering. However, systems engineering is an amorphous, slippery subject that does not lend itself well to such formal, didactic treatment. One does much better with a broader, more loose-jointed approach. Some writers have, in fact, side-stepped the issue entirely by saying simply that systems engineering is "what systems engineers do." In this paper, also, I shall attempt to define systems engineering only indirectly, through a description of some of its principal characteristics.

The most fundamental reason for the slipperiness of systems engineering is probably the fact that the term does not actually mean the same thing in all situations or to all people. Thus there is some built-in "conceptual rubber" that must be identified before we can go ahead with a more specific description of systems engineering along the lines developed later in the paper. To introduce this preliminary discussion here will mean retracing some of the same ground later on, but it seems important to deal with some of the major sources of ambiguity as quickly as possible.

A look at "what systems engineers do," and the intellectual resources they draw on to do it, suggests that there are three important issues that particularly affect the character of the subject. They will be identified in this discussion through the catch phrases, "methodology or technical substance," "early or late," and "staff or line." The first of these was adumbrated in the preceding section. It can be understood by reference to operations research, introduced earlier as a sort of first cousin of systems engineering. Operations research can be described roughly as a study of the best way of making use of existing resources or equipment. It grew up during the war, when for obvious military reasons one carried on as best he could with what he had. Thus, typical questions during the war concerned the best employment of a given total number of bombers, the best ways for arranging convoys with a given inventory of vessels, and so on.

In most cases, adequate substantive knowledge of the properties of the equipment was rather easy to obtain. Thus, the principal assets of the operations analysts have traditionally been methodological. A large fraction of the methodology referred to in an earlier section was in fact developed originally in an operations-research framework. (One hastens to add that "methodological assets" must be interpreted to include experience and an acute mind. For example, Morse and Kimball (1) stress the advantages of a background of scientific research in fostering the ability to pose the right issues.) The operations analyst is thus somewhat in the position of a lawyer who can make a good logical case without knowing a great deal about the substantive aspects of the problem, simply by drawing on a vast background of legal knowledge and experience.

Systems engineering, on the contrary, is frequently described as being like operations research, except that the systems engineer deals with new rather than with existing equipment. In principle, this makes the systems engineer into a design engineer with a somewhat special set of tools. One should visualize the systems engineer as formulating a tentative design for the new equipment, studying it by the methods of operations research, using the results to formulate a new tentative design, and so on. If the operations analyst resembles a lawyer, the systems engineer resembles an architect, who must generally have adequate substantive knowledge of building materials, construction methods, and so on, to ply his trade.

Whether or not this is more than hair-splitting depends on circumstances. There is a continuous spectrum of possibilities. At one end, the issue is of little account. Thus, it would not matter to an operations analyst in a commercial situation whether given equipment was literally in his possession or merely commercially available, so long as its properties were adequately known. The systems engineer is in almost the same situation when he specifies apparatus that may be new but that can readily be constructed by known methods, and with easily predicted final characteristics. The situation is different if the apparatus to be designed is really new either in the sense that it may require the application of new physical principles or that it requires an extension of the state of the art beyond the limits of familiar experience. The physical uncertainties in the situation, or the difficulties of translating theoretically obtainable design advances into quantifiable operational gains must now engross the systems engineer's attention. His job becomes very demanding. An understanding of operations-research methodology may still be important, but unless it is married to a strong base of knowledge of the substantive technology the results are not likely to be optimum.

The proposed new applications of systems engineering can be expected to show many variations in the balance between methodology and substantive knowledge. Thus this is almost the first question one should ask in examining a new situation. Physical scientists, at least, should be especially wary of situations that may involve substantive questions in the social sciences. In the writer's view, the largest and most complicated projects are particularly those that are likely to raise important substantive questions. This is party just because they *are* large and multifaceted and partly because any project involving a large investment and lasting over a long time deserves special attention to make certain that it has the best tools and equipment available. Thus the rest of the paper will be biased toward such situations.

The issues identified by the other two catch phrases represent other aspects of the general question, "What do systems engineers do?" Thus the phrase, "early or late," refers to the stage in the design process in which the systems engineer is supposed to be most active.

In one concept of systems engineering, the systems engineer is most active in the very early stages of the design, where the primary questions are physical feasibility, the over-all design concept, and estimates of ultimate values and costs. In another concept, the systems engineer is most active very late in the design process. It is assumed, in effect, that the physical apparatus has already been designed, and it is the job of the systems engineer to prepare operating instructions, test procedures, maintenance instructions, spare-parts routines, and so forth, to make sure that the "system" will actually operate satisfactorily in practice. There is also an intermediate concept in which it is supposed that the over-all system has been fixed, and that the job of the systems engineer is to provide detailed specifications for subsystems, involving an appropriate balance between cost and performance for these individual components.

All these functions are important and a complete development might need all of them, although they would probably not be performed by the same people. However, this discussion will consider only the early and intermediate stages. The "late" stage seems less critical, both because it cannot come into being at all unless the first two stages are passed and because, as demonstrated in experience, extra effort here cannot fully compensate for bad work at earlier points. On the other hand, sloppy handling of the late stage can negate the results of good work in the early stages. Also it is often important that considerations from the late stage be factored into the planning in the early stages.

The third piece of "conceptual rubber" was identified by the catch phrase "staff or line." It refers to the basic organizational position and function of the systems engineer. More broadly, it is supposed to raise the question of the extent to which essentially management activity, as opposed to purely technical work, is taken to be part of "what systems engineers do."

It is convenient to return once more to the simpler case of operations research. Here we find that the basic conception is clearly that of a staff function (2). The operations-research groups are expected to be small and informal, to report directly to the executive, and to carry no line responsibilities. Since the groups do report to an operating executive, however, and since it is easy to add such specialties as decision theory to the methodological arsenal, the over-all "management flavor" may be quite high. In consequence, operations research is sometimes classified as one of the management sciences.

In systems engineering generally, the situation is more complex. In some cases the systems-engineering groups may be like the operations-research groups just described. In other cases, however, they turn out to be larger and more formally organized, with a character more nearly like that of line organizations themselves. In such cases there may be a variety of patterns for the interaction of the systems areas with other parts of the total establishment. The organizational interplay in the Bell System, as one example, is described later.

In military areas, the drift of systems-engineering groups toward something approaching a line responsibility was stimulated by the military's need to prosecute relatively high-risk technical programs in an efficient and schedule-conscious way. The systems engineers, who had conceived the program in the first place and understood the trade-offs among various performance characteristics, could be expected to be the most resourceful people in dealing with unexpected technical problems as they arose. Thus systems-engineering groups were enlarged and held more directly responsible for final results. The phrase, "systems engineering and technical direction," to describe this enlarged responsibility, especially where a number of contractors are involved, has become common. Specialized project offices, staffed largely by systems engineers and involving a complicated matrix overlay on existing functional organizations, are also common. As a result of this evolution, systems engineering is sometimes regarded as primarily a management technique, suited to keep a complicated program on schedule and budgetary rails. In this interpretation, it thus rests as much on PERT[1] charts and similar devices as on the more classical methodologies described previously.

Management questions of this sort are not considered further in this paper, which is directed primarily to the purely technical aspects of systems engineering. It is important, however, that the issue be canvassed whenever it is proposed that systems engineering be introduced into a new situation. Systems engineers best suited for a project-management role are not necessarily those best suited for purely technical responsibility, and conversely. It is particularly important that the over-all management and organization plan be thought through clearly in advance. To introduce a systems-engineering group into a situation in which these issues are muddy is to invite trouble.

The analogy between the systems engineer and the architect suggests one more point that may be worth making. We have thus far approached systems engineering as though it could be understood entirely by criteria appropriate for any other branch of engineering, or perhaps management. But, like architecture, systems engineering is in some ways an art as well as a branch of engineering. Thus, aesthetic criteria are appropriate for it

[1] Process Evaluation and Review Techniques.

also. For example, such essentially aesthetic ideas as balance, proportion, proper relation of means to ends, and economy of means are all relevant in a systems-engineering discussion. Many of these ideas develop best through experience. They are among the reasons why an exact definition of systems engineering is so elusive.

SYSTEMS ENGINEERING IN THE OVER-ALL ENGINEERING STRUCTURE

These diverse interpretations of the term, "systems engineering," suggest many variations in the way in which systems engineering enters the over-all technological and engineering structure. The complete technological process, as far as engineers are concerned, is classically divided into the three states of research, development, and production. In this classical division, of course, systems engineering does not appear at all. In some of the concepts just outlined it might be represented by a box interpolated between research and development or perhaps after production (and before final use).

In most cases, however, such a scheme is too simple. In the first place, the modern technological process is much more complex than the tripartite classification would suggest, even if we did not have systems engineering to deal with. For example, the Department of Defense breaks up the heading, "development," into three subheadings—"exploratory development," "advanced development," and "engineering development"—in drawing up its accounts. Other people use slightly different words, but the terminology is just as complex. In addition, the actual phenomena do not correspond to a simple linear progression from basic research to production and use. There are various sorts of interactions and feedbacks that may be of great importance for the end result. They are likely to be of particular interest to the systems engineer if parallel paths or interactions between non-consecutive stages are involved. To represent such relations adequately, however, we must think of systems engineering itself as being outside the main structure.

One is reminded of the tripartite division of society into upper, middle, and lower classes with comparatively tight boundaries, in conventional sociology. Contemporary sociologists, of course, feel that they need at least five or six classes to do justice to our world, and that they still must allow for a great deal of social mobility among them. Even so, there are individuals who do not fit well into the scheme; intellectuals and union leaders are the sociologists' favorite examples.

In a similar way, systems engineering can be thought of as having a position somewhat off to one side of the principal engineering structure, but with connections to the main line anywhere from the research area to the final consumer. This is essentially the concept described later for the Bell System. Thus, what we have in view is in some sense an over-all monitoring and/or control function for the complete path from research to final consumption. Whether or not such a function is needed, and the exact form it takes, must, of course, depend on circumstances. There may be no need for it at all if the main development path is sufficiently short and direct. On the other hand, the function becomes increasingly necessary if the path is long and indirect, if it is actually composed of a number of intertwined development paths in parallel, or if there is danger that the ultimate needs of the consumer will be forgotten during the development. From this point of view, the emergence of systems engineering as an important discipline is a natural consequence of the increasing power and complexity of our technology and the fact that we are more and more willing to attempt ambitious, long-drawn-out projects.

CHARACTERISTICS OF SYSTEMS ENGINEERING

We can now proceed with a more specific description of systems engineering by listing some of its most common characteristics. The list is taken from a variety of experiences. It is supposed to describe systems engineering in some sort of average sense if we limit the subject in the ways implied by the discussion just finished. As will be seen, the characteristics range from the near-platitudinous to the fairly debatable.

The characteristics of systems engineering that seem to be most important for the present discussion are the following:

1. To begin with, systems engineering is normally concerned with complex aggregates of simpler components that interact to produce a desired result. Examples are the roads, dams, electric generators, transmission lines, and so forth, that make up the TVA system, or the transmission, switching, and station equipment that makes up the telephone network. It is important that there be significant interaction among the components, at least to the extent that they compete for the same dollar support, since otherwise there would be nothing for the systems engineer to do. He could immediately turn to simpler subsystems. It is also important that the components be essentially under design control, since otherwise again there would be nothing for the systems engineer to do.

The systems engineer's first job is to formulate an over-all systems concept essentially a creative step which governs the relations among the parts in a broad sense and can be taken as the first stage of the over-all design process. Unless the situation is unusually straightforward, of course, a finally acceptable systems concept is likely to be the result of much study and many trials.

The analogy here with the architect's job in planning a new building is obvious. The architect must somehow produce a design concept appropriate to the site, functions, and permissible cost of the building. The various functions that must be accommodated in the building interact strongly with one another at this stage. Later on specific subsystems, like heating, plumbing, and so forth, can be separated out and treated independently. If the architect's job is well done, the final building will have a definite unity and style of its own. It will not, for example, be half Georgian and half modern.

2. The immediate objective of systems engineering is generally taken to be optimizing the output, according to some given criterion, by tradeoffs among the performance characteristics and costs of the individual components. A great deal of the methodology of the subject is concerned with means of making optimization studies. Experience suggests that exact optimizations of this type are likely to be of little direct value. The assumptions on which they are made are too uncertain, or, in any case, the maxima are so broad that the optimum is not critical. The indirect value of such optimization studies, however, may be very great. By performing such computations over and over one gradually gains insight into the considerations that are really decisive, and evolves mathematical models that are accurate enough for the purpose, and yet simple enough to be computable. Particularly sensitive assumptions or parameters should, of course, be given special attention. Thus, such computations are likely to be an essential step in formulating an over-all systems concept of the sort described under (1). We must expect, of course, that the over-all concept may always be subject to feedback from later stages of the study, and cannot be finally crystallized until the whole situation is thoroughly understood.

3. The problem of computing optima is frequently complicated by the fact that the final system may have to meet several logically independent criteria. For example, a new telephone system may be judged by the criteria of cost, quality of the service, flexibility for future growth, and so forth. The TVA system was required to serve a variety of objectives—flood control, power, navigation, improvement in regional living patterns—with the same physical installations. The architect designing a house may have to consider a number of criteria—adequate bedroom space, easy heating, an impressive facade, and so forth.

A balance among these considerations cannot logically be struck by the architect or systems engineer acting alone. He must consult the wishes of the ultimate user of the system. What the systems engineer or the architect *can* do is elucidate the problem by exposing such basic conflicts, by making illustrative computations to exhibit the trade-offs between various characteristics, and so on. In complicated situations, this is one of the most important responsibilities of the systems engineer. He must do his best to see that such issues are thoroughly understood before final commitments are made.

4. In most systems engineering, the statement of the conditions under which the response of the system is to be optimized may also be an important and difficult question. In many complicated situations the inputs are not quite determinate, but are, instead, statistical or stochastic in nature. The random incidence of telephone calls on the telephone system, of enemy intruders in an air-defense system, or of rainfall in the Tennessee Valley are examples. In the case of the telephone system one has to reckon with the predictable heavy calling rates on Mother's Day or Christmas, in the case of the Tennessee Valley with an occasional wet spring, in the case of the air-defense system with the possibility that the enemy may concentrate in one particular area. In fact, in military systems generally one must reckon with the consequences of deliberate efforts on the part of the enemy to negate the system. One must, of course, also allow in these calculations for possible failure or damage modes. Thus, an important responsibility of the systems engineer is to prepare the material so that the weight of all these considerations can be correctly assessed.

5. Many of our present-day systems are so complex that they may take many years to implement. Since we are also living in an age in which science and technology advance with unprecedented rapidity, there is a very great possibility that the system will be unnecessarily behind the times when it is finally built. This is one of the most important as well as one of the most difficult problems that confronts the systems engineer in planning ambitious new systems. On the other hand, unless he discounts the future to some extent, he will emerge with an unnecessarily poor result. On the other hand, such discounts clearly carry with them substantial elements of risk. To deal adequately with such problems the systems engineer must have, or be able to call on, exceptionally sound scientific and technical judgment on possible advances in the state of the art in relevant areas, and he must be exceptionally diligent in planning fall-back positions in case the first hopes are disappointed, or in planning ways of exploiting unusually favorable technical advances if these should occur. These considerations provide perhaps the principal justification for

extending the systems engineer's responsibility from initial planning into some cognizance over participation in the actual management of the project as it goes on.

6. Closely related to this last consideration is another. Many complex projects in weapon systems, regional development, and so on, naturally take place in a series of stages or "bites." The first stage is often the only one that can be planned for concretely, but one must assume that subsequent stages will, in fact, follow. Obviously, the systems engineering for the first stage ought to leave us in as flexible a position as possible for the later stages.

7. One frequently hears it said that systems engineering always deals with interdisciplinary problems. It is true, of course, that large systems projects frequently require contributions from many disciplines, simply because they are so large and multifaceted. It is the business of the systems engineer to recognize such situations and make certain that necessary inputs are secured. However, to make the interdisciplinary character the decisive elements is to miss the point. Systems-engineering problems still occur in comparatively homogeneous environments, such as telephone engineering. Moreover, a satisfactory system is usually not just a composite of heterogeneous elements, any more than a cake is just some flour, some sugar, a few eggs, some milk, butter, and so on. The ingredients still have to be mixed, and the cake must be baked. The baking process is an essential.

One frequently sees interdisciplinary conferences break up in a state of euphoria. Everyone observes that his own discipline is logically relevant, and hopes to make a contribution without extending himself. Except possibly for the very early stages of an investigation, I believe that such hopes are doomed to disappointment. At some point a greater element of intellectual continuity must enter. It seems to be unhappily true that real intellectual progress in any field calls in time for prolonged hard work.

8. Finally, systems engineering is distinguished by the persistence with which it turns to the needs of the ultimate user as the final criterion for planning. Thus, in the initial stages the necessity of establishing that there is a need worth satisfying, and that we know quite accurately what this need is, dominates one's thinking. Later on, the systems engineer must be the conscience of the project, to make sure that immediate engrossmen with the details of the work does not divert attention from its ultimate objective. Here, again, the parallel with the architect who must understand the real requirements of his clients before he can design a satisfactory house for them is obvious.

SYSTEMS ENGINEERING AND THE BELL SYSTEM

To make these observations somewhat more concrete, it is worth while to turn to the special case of the Bell System. Within the Bell System, systems engineering is practiced primarily in Bell Telephone Laboratories. The systems organizations there, working primarily with counterparts in the American Telephone and Telegraph Company proper, assess the present and future needs of the operating system, and from that generate plans for engineering developments to meet them. These activities take up about 10 or 15 percent of the professional manpower of Bell Telephone Laboratories, which is about the same percentage as one finds in the research area proper. Engineering development at various levels, plus related support activities, take up the rest, which is clearly the lion's share of the total. Although these proportions have been arrived at principally by experience, they seem to represent a reasonable balance of effort.

Systems engineering in the Bell System provides a relatively good illustration of the field because the objectives of the activity are comparatively clear and obvious, and because work of this general nature has been carried on for a very long time, so that work patterns are well shaken down. An anticipation of the present concept of systems engineering can, in fact, be traced as far back as 1907, when a predecessor organization to the present Bell Laboratories was established. The situation can be described by quoting a statement about the 1907 organization written by one of the executives of the American Telephone and Telegraph Company some years later:

> The reorganization in 1907 consisted of a consolidation (whose) purpose was to avoid duplication of facilities as well as to get the greater efficiency coming from a closer contact between the staff of the Western Electric Company and our own. (He means the A.T. & T. Company.) It brought to one point scientific study and research, manufacturing experience and operating experience. . . . It simplified and expedited the work of the operating (telephone) companies in that it established one point where all statements of requirements, suggestions of improvements, or criticisms arising out of their operating experience could be considered and discussed from all points of view. . . . It was helpful in the standardization of apparatus . . .
>
> We had at Bell Laboratories the scientists whose work involved labboatory facilities, the men conducting experiments, the shop design workers and the inspectors with suitable equipment of laboratories and model shops available for all. The ideas of our research and development scientists and engineers, worked out on paper or in

rough mechanical form, were there developed into a finished piece for shop manufacture and after manufacture the product was then subject to all the tests necessary to satisfy our engineers that it was worthy of introduction into or continuation in the plant of the Bell System.

Most of this excerpt is concerned with the advantages of an integrated organization in a broad sense. The systems engineer as one of the means of holding such an organization together is not mentioned explicitly. He would hardly have been needed in an organization of the size and relative simplicity envisaged there.

Nevertheless, some of the special characteristics of systems engineering, as they were described in my preceding discussion, come out clearly in the excerpt. It is particularly important to note that the design process starts with a close scrutiny of the needs of the final users—the operating telephone companies who would provide service to the public. Essentially the technological process proper started by matching these needs with the available technology as represented by the research and development men in the organization. Moreover, the technological process ends only with a final determination that the apparatus will be satisfactory to the users, or, as the author says, "worthy of introduction into the Bell System."

Systems engineering was given its explicit charter in Bell Telephone Laboratories in reorganizations that took place soon after World War II. The newly defined systems-engineering charter was described by Dr. M. J. Kelly, President of Bell Telephone Laboratories, in a lecture delivered to the Royal Society in March 1950. After describing the functions of the research and development organizations, Dr. Kelly proceeds as follows:

> One of the principal responsibilities of systems engineering is technical planning and control. In the planning an appraisal is made of the various technical paths that can be followed in employing the new knowledge obtained by research and fundamental development in the specific development and design of new systems and facilities. The determination of the most effective use of new knowledge in the interest of the telephone user is the guiding principle of the planning studies. The most effective use may be the creation of new services, the improvement of the quality of existing services, the lowering of their cost, or some combination of these three . . .
>
> System engineering also maintains close association with our research and fundamental development work . . .
>
> It integrates the knowledge from operations, research and fundamental development, and specific systems and facilities development. With this as a background, it makes exhaustive studies that appraise

> and programme development projects for new systems and facilities. Each study outlines the broad technical plan for a development, its objectives, and its economic service worth. In many of the studies it is recommended that no development be undertaken at the time . . .
>
> . . . Service trials are generally needed during the course of development. It organizes the trials in cooperation with operating engineers and participants in the tests and the evaluation of results . . .
>
> Systems engineering has another important responsibility. It recommends the levels of the various technical standards that are important elements in determining the quality and reliability of telephone service . . .

Since Dr. Kelly made these statements there has perhaps been a tendency to place less emphasis on functions of internal technical control and more on needs and opportunities of the external world. In essentials, however, the charter sketched above is still the one by which our systems engineering operates. The remaining differences are only those that result naturally from nearly 20 years of technological evolution. For example, the rapid growth of technology since the war has generally meant that there are more physical ways in which a given function might conceivably be performed. Thus, the systems engineer has more to choose from and should, if he is conscientious, spend more time in studying possible choices. This situation is compounded by the fact that contemporary systems are generally more ambitious than their predecessors, and thus require more study on this account also.

When there is a large number of possible paths, economic considerations are likely to be paramount. Thus, our contemporary emphasis on finding minimum-cost solutions is perhaps greater than appears in Dr. Kelly's account. Because of the wide variety of situations that may present themselves, it is generally necessary to reduce all economic considerations to an "annual cost" basis in which capital costs, depreciation and obsolescence, repairs and maintenance, and so on, are combined in a single number.

Another problem that confronts the systems engineer increasingly is that of making new systems that are compatible with existing systems. In the telephone network; of course, everything must work with everything else, and some of the apparatus may be 40 years old. There is no possibility of a fresh start. The problem of designing new systems that can be introduced into the existing network without disruption has always been an important one for the Bell System. With the increasing diversity of apparatus in service, and with the radical changes implied in, for example, displacement of electromagnetic apparatus by purely electronic devices, the problem becomes more and more of a challenge to the wits of the telephone systems engineer.

Finally, the rapid rate of technological advance generally, and the desirability of taking technological steps worth making inevitably introduce some elements of technological risk-taking. In addition to some technological risks themselves, one must take risks in the commitment of substantial funds as well as scarce and valuable manpower throughout the technological process. An increasingly important responsibility of systems engineering is the elucidation of the nature and magnitude of the risks involved in such situations.

EXAMPLES

This section will include several examples of systems engineering studies in the past by the Bell Telephone Laboratories. The examples are in some ways rather misleading, since they are all concerned with relatively large systems. The daily occupation of the systems engineer, of course, includes small problems as well as large ones. However, it is difficult to convey the motivation behind the smaller and more specialized studies adequately. The examples may also be misleading because they are all concerned with systems requiring substantial technological advance as well as systems engineering in the narrow sense. This choice was made deliberately, however, since, as noted earlier, these should be the most important as well as the most difficult situations for the future.

Since the studies were so large the systems engineering work cannot be described in detail. The reader should pay particular attention to the interrelation between systems concepts and physical advances, the size of the technological advance undertaken in a single step, the existence of competing systems concepts, the influence of scale effects, and, finally, the approximate time required for a complete systems development.

Microwave Relay Systems

The first example is furnished by microwave radio relay systems, now used extensively for the long-distance transmission of voice and television messages. It was, of course, recognized early in the history of the Bell System that radio, as opposed to wire, transmission furnished one possible means of providing commercial communications. This possibility was in fact exploited to some extent in the years before 1930, using high-frequency (HF) radio signals to overcome especially difficult geographical barriers such as oceans. However, the further exploitation of the radio spectrum in this range was very unpromising. The available frequency spectrum was very small, and had to be conserved for vitally important services; the level of man-made interference was high, the geographically separate communication links still tended to interfere with one another electromagnetically unless they operated on different frequencies, so that the frequency spectrum could not be readily reused, and so on. In the mid-1930's, tentative efforts were made to exploit the very-high-frequency (VHF) region instead, but the improvements that seemed in prospect from such a change were not very exciting.

Near the end of the 1930's, it was suddenly realized that most of the difficulties with early systems could be overcome if we took not a small but a large step in the frequency spectrum. A step of the order of at least 10 or 20 to 1 from the VHF band, to put us squarely in the middle of the microwave range, seemed to be called for. The level of man-made interference here was small, and available spectrum space was adequate. Perhaps most important, at these wavelengths highly directive antennas of moderate size were conceivable, so that non-interfering transmission links using the same wavelength could be constructed.

As a result of these possibilities, some tentative proposals of systems involving relays every 30 or 40 miles were advanced by the Bell research department about 1940–1941, and were given preliminary systems-engineering attention. Short-distance systems embodying the idea were provided the Signal Corps for field use during World War II, and the lead was picked up for commercial use as soon as war pressures permitted. An experimental system was completed in 1947 and the first commercial system appeared a few years later.

In this history one should note the following: Although work on microwave circuitry had gone on all during the 1930's, and the key invention of the klystron had been made, much of the detailed technology of microwave systems was still lacking when the concept of the microwave relay system was first advanced, and we also had too little knowledge of propagation characteristics in the microwave range. Thus, the first result of a systems-engineering examination of the problem was to pinpoint and give direction to further exploratory work needed to supply the missing knowledge. Much of the work of field trials and field tests generally was directed to these ends. It turned out that the propagation characteristics of low-angle microwaves, in particular a propensity to deep multipath fading, was the most critical technical question. It had to be overcome by sophisticated circuitry and the introduction of relatively new modulation schemes to make the system successful.

Moreover, it is noticeable that the system was highly scale-sensitive.

The change from normal radio frequencies to a much higher part of the spectrum was, of course, itself a kind of scale change. It also turned out, however, that the microwave system itself was efficient only for rather broad transmission channels. Moreover, since a large part of the cost of the final system went to the provision of towers, access roads, power supplies to the repeaters, and so on, it paid to provide numerous separate radio links at each site. Thus direct economics also argued in favor of big systems. The system was in fact well matched to the demand for broad frequency bands, which developed at the same time through the advent of commercial television. The clear prospect of such a demand was, of course, the primary justification for undertaking the development.

Finally, it is worth noting that the microwave relay system had a competitor in the so-called coaxial-cable system, on which work was started in the years just before World War II. Here the problems of manmade interference were overcome by a high degree of cable shielding. The coaxial system was also developed and went into commercial use, a few years ahead of the microwave system. For some years, it seemed rather more expensive. However, the principal technical problem associated with the coaxial system is the need for a large number of intermediate repeaters to overcome the high line losses. In recent years, the advent of the transistor, with its low power-supply requirements, permitting the easy introduction of intermediate repeaters powered directly through the line, seems to have reversed this economic advantage. Thus, one sees again the controlling importance of physical and technological advances in systems planning.

Nike-Ajax

The second example is the NIKE-AJAX missile. This is a surface-to-air antiaircraft missile on which design studies began in 1945 and which went into operation about 1953.

During World War II, the principal defenses against bombing planes were, of course, interceptor planes and ground-based artillery. Interceptors were fairly effective, but ground-based artillery was relatively ineffective, at least for reasonably high altitudes, because the target airplanes could too easily avoid the shell by a slight change in course while the shell was en route from the gun. Obviously, a missile was needed that could be guided all the way to the target to counter such evasive maneuvers.

The NIKE-AJAX system represented an effort to provide such a solution, capitalizing on relatively new advances in rocket propulsion and electronics. The system, aside from the missile proper, consisted essentially of two radars, one tracking the target airplane and the other the missile. The outputs of these two radars were fed to a computer that used the information to give a continuously updated estimate of the velocities of the missile and target and the course changes required of the missile to provide an interception. The required course changes were then transmitted to the missile by a data link. This is called a command-guidance system.

The system provided almost endless opportunities for the systems-engineering group to make trade-offs studies among such quantities as missile size, warhead size, amount of propellant, flight time versus trajectory shape, terminal maneuverability versus aerodynamic drag, and so on. These are too complicated to examine here. The most critical systems decision turned out to be the adoption of the command-guidance principle to begin with. There were, of course, other possible guidance principles that might have been adopted. A homing system, using homing apparatus in the missile operating on a radar signal reflected from the target, was perhaps the most attractive.

To the layman the merit of a homing system seems obvious. One gets better and better information as he approaches the target more and more closely. In fact, however, the situation is more complicated than this. A homing head provides really accurate information only in the immediate vicinity of the target, and the missile may or may not be able to make an adequate course correction in the time available before it goes past. Thus, homing is a better principle in a tail-chase, where relative velocities are low, than it is in a nearly head-on encounter, which would be more nearly typical of most antiaircraft engagements. Homing is also relatively better at long ranges, where the radars in the command-guidance system cannot be expected to give accurate information, than it is in close. There are also subsidiary considerations involving the cost of reusable equipment on the ground as compared with simpler equipment in each expandable missile, problems of maintenance and reliability, and so on, which enter into any complete comparison of the two systems.

As it turned out, the choice between the two systems depended in an indirect way upon the question of range. The rocket propulsion readily available at that time did not guarantee very long ranges at best. The problem was particularly serious for a homing system, where typical trajectories lay mostly in dense air, involving high aerodynamic drags. The command-guidance system was superior in these circumstances because it could allow great freedom in choosing aerodynamically efficient trajectories and still lead to an interception. Thus, it could make the most of what propulsion there was. The question of accuracy at extreme ranges was vacuous as long as the ranges were not attainable in any event.

Thus it was determined that we would use the command system, taking advantage of it to eke out all possible range for the missile, and depend upon very sophisticated design in the ground-based radars and computers to provide adequate accuracy for any range we might be able to realize. The alternative path of trying for a substantial improvement in propulsion directly was foresworn as being incompatible with the essential strengths of a primarily electronic organization. In the event, this turned out to be a very fortunate decision. Radar and computer improvements were more than had been counted on, and the system, or its big brother, NIKE-HERCULES, was still effective when propulsion improvements increased the attainable range by several times.

Telstar

The third example is the Telstar satellite. This will be remembered as the communications satellite put up by the Bell System about five years ago. Strictly speaking, it is not an example of finished systems engineering, since it was intended only as an experimental vehicle. However, the experiment accompanied some rather intensive systems-engineering studies in the same field, and perhaps can be introduced here on that basis.

An additional reason for introducing Telstar is the fact that it exemplifies particularly well one of the important aspects of systems engineering, especially in complex new situations. This is the necessity of making sure that one has an adequate and broad enough base of new science and technology before proceeding. Telstar, and other recent communication satellites, are in fact distinguished by the way in which they draw on technology in many directions. The dependence of any of these satellite systems upon the development of launching rockets is, of course, obvious. However, many other elements also were needed. For example, communications satellites like Telstar are frequently described as microwave repeaters in the sky. They operate in the same frequency band as the microwave relay systems described a little earlier, and draw on this whole technique extensively. In the Telstar experiment, a low-noise ground receiver was also important. Thus, the invention of the maser, if not quite an indispensable step, was a very important one. So also was the introduction of the high-precision antenna and tracking system used in the experiment. Even the invention of the solar cell as a means of supplying prime power to the vehicle can be properly taken as a critical step. One has only to see the amount of effort that has gone into power-supply work for other kinds of space vehicles to recognize how important a problem this can be. Thus, the basic lesson to be learned here is that sometimes the best policy for a systems engineer is simply to wait until he has accumulated enough pieces of his jigsaw puzzle to make success reasonably likely. This, of course, does not deny the occasional desirability of going ahead on a modest and tentative basis, as in the microwave relay case, before the physical facts are all in. It does say that there is no real substitute for excellent technical judgment in knowing when to make full-scale commitments and when to wait.

Telstar is also interesting because it illustrates again the existence of competitive systems concepts. Telstar itself was intended as a prototype for a medium-altitude random-orbit satellite system. As an experimental device it was intended primarily to test out the ground-based receiver and tracking systems that such a system would require and the effects of the Van Allen radiation belts on vehicle electronics at these altitudes.

The competing concepts is, of course, the high-altitude synchronous satellite, which appears to have taken the lead at the present time. The high-altitude satellite avoids the problems of a complicated ground tracking system and it can provide continuous service with a very small number of vehicles. On the other hand, the propulsion requirements to put it in place are much greater (from most launch sites it takes more propulsion to get into a stationary orbit than it does to make a hard landing on the moon), a more elaborate antenna system is required to overcome the greater distance to the ground, and there are worrisome problems in connection with propagation delay, particularly for two-way conversations. A scale effect of a sort is also evident when one studies the economics of the problem. A random-orbit medium-altitude system tends to show up best with large amounts of traffic well distributed around the globe and is less well adapted to other situations.

GENERAL REMARKS

The examples just discussed were chosen primarily to illustrate some special aspects of systems engineering that seem to deserve particular stress in any thorough discussion of it. The intended points are the following:

The first is the fact that in all cases the new system involved the exploitation of some definite advances in physics or electronic technology. I believe this is likely to be important whenever a substantial advance is involved. Systems engineering as an isolated discipline, in other words, should not be expected to provide enough advantage in most situations.

It needs new technology to work with. The proper understanding of the implications of technological advances and their effective utilization, on the other hand, are also difficult problems and are, of course, prime responsibilities of the systems engineer. Thus, systems engineering and the basic technology must be coordinated if maximum progress is to be made.

In the second place, in the microwave-relay and NIKE-AJAX examples, at least, preliminary systems planning took place while essential physical knowledge and some needed technology were both still lacking. Thus, one of the important early contributions of systems analysis was the direction of applied research and exploratory development studies to areas of critical importance before a final systems concept could be generated.

In at least the NIKE-AJAX case, the final systems concept involved the tacit assumption that state-of-the-art advances in some critical areas would be made during the course of the development. It is important to note, however, how carefully these areas were chosen. They were, in fact, critical to the system, and they were in fields in which Bell Laboratories was particularly at home. State-of-the-art advances in other directions, however welcome, were not indispensable. The systems engineer who asks for a better result in every direction than the world has yet provided is simply not practicing his trade.

In the third place, scale effects, particularly if the term is broadened to include such considerations as absolute position in the frequency spectrum, turned out to be of controlling importance in several cases. I believe this is still more likely to be true for many of the very broad questions involving environmental control, transportation, and the like, which should be of particular interest to the House Committee. Thus, systems concepts that are appropriate and valuable in one set of circumstances may have no meaning in different situations. It is the business of the systems engineer to understand such questions well, and to have clearly in mind how the scale of the problem may affect the appropriate technology.

Finally, it is important to notice that in each of the examples there was at least one competing systems concept in addition to the concept directly under discussion. The existence of such competing systems can be of enormous value, particularly if they can be studied objectively by the same systems-engineering group. The result is likely to be much better insight into the problem than could be obtained by working with one systems concept alone.

On occasion, of course, competing concepts may lead to the emergence of a third concept, better than either. If the new concept is really valuable, however, it is likely to have its own distinctive character, and not be merely a fusion of the others. Thus, to go back to the earlier analogy, a house can be Georgian, modern, or colonial, but it should not be a little of each. The fox and the rabbit are each biologically successful animals, but a compromise animal would have no natural ecological niche.

The set of examples also brings out one more point that may not be quite so apparent. In each case, the basic systems analysis was done by men who had already spent several years in the same or related fields. They were thus in a sense professionals, qualified through subject matter knowledge as well as systems understanding.[2]

I believe that this is the inevitable pattern for any effective attacks on our well-known problems—transportation, environmental control, and so on. At first, the visiting systems engineer with no substantive knowledge of the field, or the visiting scientist engaged in a summer study, may be able to make a contribution. As the field develops to the point where sustained intellectual hard work is necessary, however, the men who have developed a sort of professionalism because they work in the area continuously will be increasingly the men who count. They may or may not call themselves "systems engineers," but they are in any case the men who understand the field in enough depth to give it structure and continuity.

In the long run, then, the country's future on these problems will depend on finding ways of developing such professionalism. The suggestion made in one of the other papers, proposing quasi-permanent research institutes, is one way of solving the problem. As such it deserves careful attention. On the other hand, the chartering and leadership of such institutes over a period of time is a most difficult problem, and needs to be approached with great care. My point here is that this sort of step, and not pick-up summer institutes or quick systems-engineering studies, is a requirement for serious attempts to address ourselves to the country's largest problems.

REFERENCES

1. *Methods of Operations Research,* p. 10a.
2. Morse and Kimball, p. 2.

---

[2] See, for example, the question of "enduring themes" in the report by J. B. Fisk to the Daddario Committee on December 11, 1963.

A COMPARISON OF A RESEARCH AND DEVELOPMENT LABORATORY'S ORGANIZATION STRUCTURES

Irwin Mordka
General Foods Corporation
Birds Eye Division
White Plains, N. Y.

The four major types of organization structures found in research and development laboratories were investigated. This study, conducted at a large AEC laboratory, recommends how these structures can be most effectively utilized. The structures are broad-span-of-control, projects, project-functional, and functional. They are discussed in terms of the mission, the span-of-control, and the personnel best suited to each structure, as well as the different problems of supervision found in each, such as coordination and encouraging creativity. Each structure has advantages and disadvantages which must be weighed in considering when to use it.

INTRODUCTION

This paper describes not only the circumstances under which each major organization structure commonly found in research and development laboratories is most appropriately used, but also how it can be most effectively utilized. The study on which this article is based was initiated by the management of a research and development company because of its desire to make optimum use of company talent, and its belief that a well-designed and properly operated organization structure is one of the best means of assuring this optimum utilization. The company, under a prime contract with the Atomic Energy Commission, operates two laboratories and a test range engaged in research and development on ordnance phases of nuclear weapons design.

The data for this investigation were obtained principally from interviews with company personnel at all levels. (Supervisory levels are president,

---

* Reprinted from the *IEEE Transactions on Engineering Management, Vol. EM-14, No. 4*, December 1967.

vice-president, director, department manager, division supervisor, and section supervisor. The nonsupervisory levels are staff member, staff assistant, and graded employee.) Other data were obtained from literature on the organization of research-development laboratories and engineering groups, and from company documents and reports.

Classification of Structures

The company, like other research and development laboratories, has four major types of structures. The type most appropriate for a group within a laboratory depends in large part on the mission of the group. The basic structures are

1) *broad-span-of-control,* found among such groups as research, advanced development, and advanced system studies, whose staff members work independently on new concepts and feasibility studies;
2) *project,* found (usually) where different specialists are assigned to a temporary group working on one large-scale project;
3) *functional,* found among groups specializing in particular areas; and
4) *project-functional,* found among functional groups whose personnel each support one or more project groups.

At any one time, a group may be using several organizational approaches. One staff member may be temporarily transferred to a project group. Other staff members may be supporting project groups without being part of them (project-functional organization), while still other personnel may be working on projects under both the technical and administrative supervision of their functional manager (functional organization). The organizational approach of a group depends on its responsibilities.

BROAD-SPAN-OF-CONTROL ORGANIZATION

Missions and Assignments of Broad-Span-of-Control Groups

Missions of broad-span-of-control groups and assignments of their members cannot be defined precisely; whenever work can be defined precisely, it is not appropriate for these groups. For example, an advanced development group may generate a new battery concept and take the idea through the preliminary design stage. A scheduled development group then designs the battery and gets it ready for production. The first function fits the broad-span-of-control structure, but the second does not.

Many assignments in the broad-span-of-control group are generated by the staff members, and short-duration projects may even be undertaken without specific supervisory approval. Assignments which come from supervisors may be based on specific management requests concerning current problems. Journal articles, company reports, discussions with other company organizations and with outside groups—all of these are sources of project ideas for the broad-span-of-control group. After developing an idea to the point where it may be usable by other company organizations, the staff member in this type of group tries to sell the idea.

Characteristics Found Among People Suited to Broad-Span-of-Control Groups

Creativity—The ability to propose and develop new ideas is most important for success in a conceptual group. Characteristically, highly creative people[1] are more apt to stick to their guns when they are in disagreement with others.

A creative person spends more time in the initial stages of problem formulation and in the broad scanning of alternatives, while others are more apt to "get on with it." But a creative person, having disposed of more blind alleys, is able to make a more comprehensive integration. He feels less anxiety to produce. He is confident enough of his eventual success to be able to step back and take a broad look before making commitments.

Tolerance for Ambiguity—Of the many characteristics named by staff members and supervisors as desirable for personnel in broad-span-of-control organizations, a tolerance for ambiguity was one of the most frequently mentioned. By tolerance for ambiguity they meant the ability to work alone with minimum direction in relatively undefined areas; and, of course, such a person has to supply his own motivation, because the work in such groups is not clearly defined. A tolerance for ambiguity is the ability to work on projects whose parameters do not lend themselves to definition.

"Company Experience"—Personnel in broad-span-of-control groups must have enough contact with company organizations to know the current work, including major programs. First of all, a man developing new ideas is more effective when he knows what is needed. Second, he can sell ideas better to people he knows might use them than to people whose work he does not really know; and, finally, in the words of one staff member, "A man working independently needs to know where to go for help and information."

Ability to Take Criticism—A problem in one broad-span-of-control group points up another desirable characteristic needed by staff members working

[1] G. A. Steiner, "The creative organization," Graduate School of Business, University of Chicago, Chicago, Ill., Selected Papers No. 10, 1962.

on unproven technical concepts—the ability to take criticism in large doses. Commonly, members of all such groups discuss their ideas with each other before presenting them to outside organizations. These discussions may yield highly critical evaluations. In one particular group, an engineer generated several worthwhile ideas during his first year in the group. However, when discussion time came around, he just could not take criticism of his ideas, regardless of the merit of the criticism. This supersensitivity made his contribution less valuable than it could have been.

Old hands in these concept groups say an idea rarely gets either completely accepted or rejected. Even when an idea seems to be entirely rejected, it may stimulate other, more fruitful approaches to a problem. Finally, as several people said, a man has to be able to have a large percentage of his ideas rejected without letting it bother him.

Stresses and Frustrations—Besides being creative, having a tolerance for ambiguity, broad company experience, and an ability to take criticism, members of broad-span-of-control groups have to be able to take special kinds of frustration. As one supervisor said, "First you face a long wait from development of your idea to actual use. Then when it is used, you may never hear of it and you may never get credit for having developed it."

A research staff member also noted that the work of his group is generally not appreciated on the outside because it involves long-range projects and does not specifically relate to today's problems. Outsiders may not understand how much time it takes to work out a new concept; and in working on long-range concepts, this staff member has to resist pressure to get him working on current "fads." On the other hand, he must resist the people who think that fulfillment of a particular project will bring the millennium.

Land[2] of the Polaroid Company has summed up in two sentences what broad-span-of-control groups say about the ideal man for their kind of work.

> The inventor must show that the defects in his proposed undertaking are not fundamental but are merely an aspect of the early stage of his development. He must move some group to imagine that the superiority of what already exists represents the maturity of an ancient field for which there is little prospect of future improvement, while the inferiority of his new proposal is a transient limitation of an approach which before long will lead to results far surpassing anything already in being.

---

[2] E. H. Land, "The inventor must be at war with society," *Product Engineering*, vol. 35, pp. 60–62, March 2, 1964.

Special Supervisory Qualifications—What has been said on general qualifications for working in a broad-span-of-control organization obviously applies both to staff members and supervisors. Supervisors in these groups need the same qualities as supervisors in any organization, and most of these qualities were mentioned during the interviews; but one person emphasized that a supervisor in a broad-span-of-control organization needs a special amount of personal security and invulnerability. "Because of the advanced nature of our work, we naturally make more mistakes than people working on well-established ideas. The man with a lot of personal security can allow such mistakes because he knows they will not hurt his strong position or his reputation."

The Practice of Supervision in a Broad-Span-of-Control Group

Levels of Supervision—As mentioned, a supervisor in these types of groups can handle a relatively larger number of men than a supervisor in a group where jobs are interdependent. Thus, ideally, there are fewer levels of supervision (scalar levels) in a broad-span-of-control organization than in other organizations having the same number of people.

Supervisory Responsibilities—A staff member in one advanced development group mentioned two basic responsibilities of his supervisor: (1) anticipating what the company will need in the future, so as to guide and direct the work of his subordinates, and (2) protecting the mission of the group. Staff members and supervisors in almost all broad-span-of-control groups mentioned similar responsibilities. For one thing, the supervisor has to find out what is going on, in the company and elsewhere, that will affect his group. Thus, he is a liaison man for the group.

The supervisor is also a screen. He screens outside requests for consultation and assistance to make sure they are appropriate for his people and that they do not interfere with the group's long-range mission and established priorities. As Eli Ginzberg, Director, Conservation of Human Resources, Columbia University, has said, "The nation is not suffering from a shortage of talented people but of people who know how to preserve and protect their time. For creative work requires time and repose."

Supervisory Style—The type of supervisory style appropriate for a group depends in large part on the group's organization structure and its mission. In the broad-span-of-control groups, seldom does the supervisor *tell* the staff member what he should work on or how he should work. To give direction, then, the supervisor in such groups needs a special style. Suggestions made by staff members and supervisors on how to get people working in specific areas without ordering them to do so, fall into three categories. First, hire people who want to and can work in the desired areas. Second, require regular publication. Third, discuss informally what the company needs and will need, as these needs relate to the group's mission.

The first and last methods need no elaboration. Some laboratories practice the second method. Staff members must publish, say, every six months. This requirement leads them to work on projects that have a reasonable chance of success and are currently acceptable to journals. (There is no conclusive evidence that this practice is either desirable or undesirable. It probably cuts down the time wasted on poor ideas. At the same time, it might hold back or even prevent major breakthroughs.)

Evaluating Performance

Since the product of the broad-span-of-control groups is mainly ideas and concepts, the quality of the product is hard to evaluate and, thus, performance is hard to evaluate. "How do you rate an idea which is ahead of its time?" one supervisor asked. Or how can a supervisor evaluate the success or failure of an idea when, as noted, unusable ideas can generate useful information and even usable ideas are rarely accepted *in toto*?

However, performance in these groups is evaluated; people in this work have proposed several criteria for such evaluation.

Quantity—1) The number of new ideas generated and the number of new applications for old ideas; 2) the number of "decent burials" performed (a decent burial is the presentation of conclusive evidence that an idea is not worth pursuing); and 3) the number of people that come to a person for advice and the number of times they come.

Influence—The extent of influence on the company's technical effort. Are the man's ideas being worked on in other company organizations? Have these ideas resulted in a line item in the company's budget? Have the ideas obtained work for the company?

Presentations—The number of speeches made, the number of symposia participated in, and the number of reports and journal articles written.

PROJECT ORGANIZATION

Missions and Assignments of Project Groups

Project groups are used to design and develop new items and processes, and to prevent and resolve technical problems both on a normal schedule and a crash-program basis.

Crash Programs—On a crash program, two factors are foremost: the goal to be achieved and the available time. Money and other resources expended are secondary considerations.[3] Thus, activities are usually carried out in parallel (concurrently). For example, a recent project group had several alternate designs. While a decision was being made concerning choice of design, models were built for each design. These models were tested simultaneously, and tooling was ordered for each design. Once a decision was made, rejected designs, complete with tooling, were scrapped. Thus money and effort were traded for time.

A task force is an interorganizational project group formed to make changes so that a device may perform its function. These changes may be in design, manufacturing process, or both. A task force is created by members of top management, usually in the late stages of development. The task force normally is in residence at a supplier. It phases out when the problems have been cleared up, as opposed to the project team, which is in existence all through scheduled development.

Regular Programs—To prevent major technical problems from developing on a project, the project group is used on "run-of-the-mill" projects.

Hybrid Products—Combining technologies to develop "hybrid" products is also promoting the project organization. For example, a project group could be used to develop a hybrid timer, combining electromechanical, electronic, and electrochemical principles.

New Processes—Project groups are also being used to develop new processes applicable to a broad range of systems.

Structure and Administration

Company Definition—In the company, a project group:

> is formed when system or component complexity, delivery schedules, or other considerations require that the normally separate development and manufacturing development programs for a component be coordinated into one effort. Each project group is headed by a project manager who is responsible for group actions affecting functions of both the Manufacturing Development and Development technical activity channels. Members are either full-time or part-time consultants. Group membership may change as the progress of the project demands. Full-time members are transferred to that organization of the project manager to which they normally would have reported, if a project group had not been established, i.e., Development or Manufacturing Development organization. They are carried on the pay roll of the organization to which they have been assigned.

[3] T. Moranian, *The Research and Development Engineer as Manager*. New York: Holt, Rinehart, and Winston, 1963.

Organization—Several specialists (representing two or more specialties) are brought together physically and administratively on a temporary basis (usually from six months to three years) to work on a project of sufficient magnitude and/or complexity to require their full-time service and that of a project manager. The number and types of specialists are determined in large part by the nature of the project. These specialists are in continuous contact with each other. Other specialists may be assigned to the project on a part- or full-time basis, but they do not report administratively to the project manager.

The project manager may or may not be a supervisor. Though project managers are usually supervisors, experienced, competent staff members may on occasion also be project managers.

Size—It was emphasized by a number of people that a project group should be small. The tendency to overstaff a project was discussed by a few people and, as evidenced by the literature,[4] this tendency apparently is widespread in other companies. Overstaffing a project does not cut down on the time necessary to complete it, because excess group members tend to get in each other's way.

Characteristics Found Among People Suited to Project Groups

Ability to Work with Others Under Tight Schedules—Two basic traits, in the eyes of many interviewees, are needed by project group members: the ability to work with others on a common project and the ability to work under tight schedules. Also, since group cohesiveness is essential to working efficiency (and meeting the deadline), managers should be careful to assign to such groups people who already know each other and get along together.

Ability to Work Informally—Because of the informality, a project group member must be able to operate in the absence of established procedures. Since he will be assigned several tasks, he must be able to handle a multitude of details at one time. One project manager pointed out that some people can work very competently if assigned to one task, but they do not perform satisfactorily when assigned to work on several tasks simultaneously. Another project manager emphasized that since a project group member is assigned several tasks, he must have broad interests. If his interests are limited, say, he only wants to work on radar, he would not be a desirable project group member.

---

[4] R. B. Kershner, "The size of research and engineering teams," *IRE Trans. Engineering Management*, vol. EM-5, pp. 35–38, June 1958.

Selection and Assignment of Project Personnel

Personnel with necessary talent and experience must be assigned in the number needed. If personnel are strong technically, the project manager does not have to get as involved in training nor in making detailed technical decisions. To the extent practical, the project manager should be able to choose group members.

Personnel who work on the project full time must be assigned both administratively and technically to the project group office. This arrangement prevents possible conflicts because of differences in policies and procedures between the project group and functional groups. Full-time project personnel must be relieved of all responsibilities in their parent organizations.

The number of part-time personnel supporting the project on an "as needed" basis must be limited to personnel in highly specialized fields. Particularly on crash programs, part-time personnel may sometimes detract rather than add to the efforts of the project group. The relationships between the project group and functional groups with these part-time support personnel are more effective when they are clearly delineated and understood.

The Practice of Supervision in a Project Group

Levels of Supervision—Staff members in one project group discussed coordination of a project. Several suggested that when more than one person has responsibility for an area, such as design, one person should be given responsibility for coordinating within the area. This allows the project manager more time for other responsibilities, such as planning. These "lead" group members or "assistant project managers" need not have any formal title or official recognition. However, their coordinative responsibilities should be clear.

Project Manager Authority and Responsibility—The project manager's responsibilities and authorities must be clearly defined and in balance; in other words, he must have sufficient authority to fulfill his responsibilities. And he must have a significant voice in determining project objectives, schedules, resources, and priorities. The authority of the project manager must extend to all aspects of the project. When assignments on a project are split among two or more groups, the advantages of the project approach are negated because no one person can be on top of all aspects of the project at all times, and it is unclear as to who has the final say.

And the project manager must have liaison responsibility. Unless all contacts by company personnel with external agencies are channeled through the project manager, serious communications problems may occur.

AEC Commissioner James T. Ramey, speaking on research management on April 20, 1964, said:

> Line responsibility should be clearly established under a project manager armed with sufficient authority to move ahead without being overwhelmed by red tape and endless project reviews by advisory groups and committees of assorted types.

Variations of the Project Organization

A project group may work on a component, subsystem, or system. It may work on only part or all of the scheduled development life of a project. It may operate as a corporate entity, separate from any established permanent organization. Thus, it may superimpose its own structure on the existing corporate organization. For example, on one task force, the project manager was a division supervisor who reported to a director. Other division supervisors and some section supervisors reported to the project manager while they worked on the task force in nonsupervisory jobs.

Or the project group may rotate from one organization to the next during various phases of the project. For example, a project team at one of the company's laboratories is transferred from one department to the next. It begins as a one-man group, in one division of a department. The team grows in size until it becomes a separate division in the department. It then successively transfers to other departments. Near the final stages, the team is the size of a section and returns to the original department in which it was formed. Finally, a couple of people work on the project part time. The team size expands and contracts at various stages. People join the team when needed and leave it when their services are no longer required.

Comparison of the Project Organization with Other Types

Advantages—As mentioned, the project organization saves time and integrates technologies. Its informality allows quicker decisions and actions. However, these are not the only advantages.

Widespread use of the project organization, according to several supervisors, tends to resist building up and holding on to managerial empires. Projects grow and shrink. Thus, there is no stigma to organizational shrinkage. Also, rotation of talent is built into the system and there is little tendency to hold on to outstanding people.

Morale in a project group is usually quite good. Many staff members interviewed indicated their preference for working in this type of organization. Part of this high morale may be due to the broadening experience received. A person comes into greater contact with people from other specialties, has a better view of project objectives, is assigned a wider variety of tasks, and frequently is working on an important high-priority project that receives much management attention.

Disadvantages—However, certain costs are associated with the project organization. The most mentioned disadvantage of crash programs was inefficient use of manpower, money, materials, and equipment. Besides the unusual amount of rework caused by performing functions in parallel, there is the duplication of facilities, equipment, and material.

Frequent use of the project organization also causes considerable disruption and instability. Permanent organizations must give up men to the project groups; this disrupts their long-range activities and stability. And when a project is over there may be difficulties in reassigning project members. The frequent shifts in personnel make it difficult to time the formation of one project group to coincide with the breaking up of groups whose projects are completed. Disruption is caused by physical as well as administrative shifting of personnel.

This shifting also disrupts the training of specialists. One project member felt he was slowly losing contact with his field of specialization. Whenever he visited his functional group of specialists, he was treated as a guest. Thus, he could not benefit as much from the informal discussions and ideas generated therein.

Further disruption is brought about by the tendency of project groups toward inconsistent operating policies and procedures. The project group working on a crash program, because of the pressure of time, attempts to circumvent established procedures (cutting red tape). This is upsetting to service groups concerned with maintenance of standards and regularizing provision for their services.

FUNCTIONAL ORGANIZATION

Missions and Assignments of Functional Groups

As opposed to the project group which is formed to develop one of a kind (or first of its kind) products, a functional organization works on many projects of the same type.

Structure and Administration

The functional organization is permanent as opposed to the temporary project group. In each functional organization there are specialists in the same field, either a particular subject (e.g., solid-state physics, thin films, explosives), a particular product (e.g., timers, batteries, product testers), a particular function (e.g., design, testing), or a particular process (e.g., welding, encapsulation).

Using the functional approach, when a project enters a laboratory, it is broken down and distributed to the appropriate specialist groups. Each group must see the entire project relevant to its work before starting. This is different from the project group where only one organization has responsibility for the project and that organization works on many aspects of the project concurrently. Thus, each group working on a project must become acquainted with the project, which is different from the project approach where only one group must become well acquainted technically with the project. In addition there is the tendency for functional groups to go over the same work to incorporate their own ideas and ways of doing things. In the functional approach, coordination of the project is achieved at middle-management or even top-management levels. Using the project approach, the project manager coordinates work on the project.

Each functional organization may be working on one or more projects at one time, depending upon the size and complexity of the projects and the size of the group. Widespread use of the functional structure in a laboratory works well when projects are not on tight time scales and when the emphasis is on a thorough, high-quality job.

Comparison with the Project Organization

The functional organization is more efficient and stable, and provides greater standardization of procedures and products. In addition, a person gets better training and experience in his specialty. However, broad technical experience is generally unavailable and it is difficult to obtain an overall view of the project.

Functional Organization Distinguished

As noted in the Introduction, organizational structures are not always amenable to classification. A particular organization may use several organizational approaches at the same time. Then there is the organization whose structure is changing because its mission is changing.

For example, a project group may be set up to work on an electromechanical switch. If, when the project is phasing out, the group becomes permanent and becomes responsible for electromechanical switches generally, it becomes a functional organization. The organization's members may now be considered to be specialists in electromechanical switches rather than specialists in design, manufacturing development, testing and evaluation, etc.

The research organization may have a group of specialists, say, mathematicians, all of whom are in the same area, a particular subject. Yet the mathematics organization is using the broad-span-of-control, not the functional approach. This is because the mathematics department is not concerned with a scheduled program; it is a conceptually oriented group. Jobs do not interrelate.

PROJECT FUNCTIONAL ORGANIZATION

Mission and Structure

Members of several functional groups may be assigned to support a project group full time or part time. *Administratively*, these people report to their functional managers. *Technically*, they report to their project manager(s). The project manager establishes project objectives, plans, and controls. He is responsible for schedules and costs. The functional manager hires and trains personnel, and provides facilities and technical staff assistance. A staff member may appear to have dual supervision under this setup. Actually he is never responsible to the two men for the same thing. The potentiality for conflict under this type of structure is readily apparent. However, there is no evidence to indicate that such conflict exists. Staff members generally are able to decide to which supervisor they should go for particular types of advice, and the supervisors usually do not give advice or direction concerning the same matters.

Advantages

The main advantage is that the project manager is not burdened with administrative and personnel problems of support personnel. Also, staff members can maintain identity with their specialty while obtaining broad experience associating with a variety of projects. And in those organizations where staff members are assigned to several projects at one time, when there is slack time on one project, there are other projects to work on.

SUMMARY

The following conclusions regarding the management of a research and development laboratory were further substantiated by this study.

1) The type of organization structure appropriate for a group depends in large part on the mission and goals of that group.
2) The type of supervision appropriate for a group depends on several factors, two of which are group mission and organization structure. There is no "one best way" to supervise all groups. The type of supervision most appropriate varies from one situation to the next.
3) The type of person who may be outstanding in one type of organization structure may not be a success in another. Some people are successful working under all types of structures, but they are rare individuals. Care must be taken to place an individual in the type of organization in which his personality is best suited and his abilities can be best utilized.

But more important than substantiating these conclusions, this study revealed how these conclusions can best be implemented to assure optimum utilization of a company's talents.

Differentiating Characteristics	Type of Structure			
	Broad-span-of-control	Project	Functional	Project-functional
Mission	To develop and sell concepts usable by other technical organizations in the company.	To work on scheduled programs. Used especially on crash programs and for developing hybrid products and new processes, and preventing technical failures.	To work on scheduled programs.	To work on scheduled programs through the support of project groups.
Span-of-control	Comparatively broad, though subject to same limitations as other types.	Comparatively small.	Maximum number of subordinates (who are themselves supervisors) a manager can effectively handle estimated to be about six.	
Coordination necessary	Very little.	Great deal, mostly handled by project manger.	Great deal, but more coordinative responsibilities handled by many levels of management.	Same as project type, since it supports project manager.
Permanency	Relatively permanent.	Temporary, usually in existence between six months and three years.	Relatively permanent.	Relatively permanent.
Type of personnel needed	Creative. Has tolerance for ambiguity. Able to take (a) criticism of ideas, and (b) frustration of not getting credit for ideas, and long lag between conception and application of ideas.	Likes to work under deadlines. Able to make technical concepts workable and manufacturable. Able to work closely with others in group, informally, and on a crash program under great time pressures.	Likes to work under deadlines. Able to make technical concept workable and manufacturable.	
Specialization of personnel	All specialize in same area.	Includes specialists from two or more different areas.	All specialize in same area.	All specialize in same area.
Applicability of PERT	Not applicable.	Applicable.	Applicable.	Applicable.
Appropriateness of encouraging innovative risktaking	Appropriate.	Not appropriate.	Not appropriate.	Not appropriate.

CHAPTER TWELVE

TECHNOLOGY TRANSFER

The problem of technology transfer exists at two levels. First, between science and technology at the economy-wide or "macro" level which involves a transfer of knowledge between the environment and the innovation. Second, at the firm or organizational ("micro") level, requiring the coupling of research with development, engineering, production, and marketing. Both levels will be discussed in this chapter since both are affecting the administration and organization of R&D activities. Sometimes the organization and philosophy which is most functional for transfer between organizations and environment will be dysfunctional for internal transfer and vice versa. In this case, the R&D manager must balance his needs and develop a compromise solution.

The articles selected for this chapter discusses both the macro and micro levels of technology transfer/coupling. Bode, Kimball, and Bartocha concentrate on the macro transfer process. Allen and Davidson both deal more directly with the coupling and information flow channels within the firm while, finally, Price and Bass deal with both levels and illustrate their interrelationship.

REFLECTIONS ON THE RELATION BETWEEN SCIENCE AND TECHNOLOGY*

Hendrik W. Bode
Vice President (Retired)
Bell Telephone Laboratories

SUMMARY

This paper gives a quasi-historical review of the relation between science and technology. It also attempts to describe some of the outstanding characteristics of science and technology in recent decades. Throughout most of their history the relation between science and technology has been quite loose, and applications of science to technology in many areas have been casual and dilatory. In recent times science and technology have been growing steadily closer together. However, the deliberate effort to apply science to technology on a broad scale and with maximum exploitation of comparatively new science is essentially a phenomenon of the war and postwar years. Since modern science now has more to offer technology that it ever had before, this trend is full of promise, particularly if science research can be kept at a sufficiently high level and in sufficiently close contact with the body of technological activity. However, the systematic application of science to technology on the present scale is a relatively new idea in human affairs, and raises many problems of its own. It appears likely that the benefit to the country from basic scientific research will depend at least as much on the skill with which we manage to solve these problems as it does on the basic research effort itself.

INTRODUCTION

Undoubtedly most of the papers in this collection will begin by commenting on the great difficulty of preparing an adequate answer to the questions posed by the House Committee on Science and Astronautics, and the fact that any one paper can provide only a partial response to

* From *Basic Research and National Goals*, A Report to the Committee on Science and Astronautics, U.S. House of Representatives, by the National Academy of Sciences, March, 1965.

these questions. This paper is no exception. Certainly it has caused the author great difficulty, and it is only in a fragmentary sense responsive to the questions raised by the House committee.

In other respects, the aims of the present paper are still more limited than those to be expected from the other papers in the collection. In particular, I do not attempt to confront the central question raised by the House committee, but instead concern myself with some preliminary issues that seem important. Thus, this may be thought of as a sort of essay that should find its value, if any, as background for the other papers.

The central question raised by the House committee is that of the appropriate level of Federal support of basic research. This question is raised against a backdrop of other considerations: the country's position of world leadership, its activities in science and technology generally, and the beneficial end-effects that stimulation of science and technology, through basic research, will have on the country's cultural, economic, and military positions. Although science and technology are coupled in the statement of the problem, it must be assumed that they may be related to the various end-effects in different ways. Thus, the cultural life of the country should be most closely related to scientific advances, and its economic life to advances in technology, while in the present age our military position may be critically dependent on both factors. Similarly, all these elements may enter in various ways into the country's overall position of leadership.

In posing the issue of basic research against this background, one obviously assumes that the interplay among all these factors is reasonably well understood, so that the impact of changes in the level of basic research on the various end-results can be calculated, at least approximately. This paper is written in the belief that this takes much to much for granted. The interrelations among the various factors are too complex and too little understood for such a computation to be made. The practical connection between basic scientific advances, on the one hand, and technology, on which so much depends, on the other, appears to be particularly uncertain and complicated.

Thus, my fundamental position is simply that a satisfactory answer to question 1 cannot be obtained through consideration of basic research alone. The end-results in which the House committee is interested depend in a complex way on the total technological and economic structure. It is not necessarily true that an increase of basic research by itself would lead to a significant increase in these beneficial applications. The outcome would depend primarily on the overall structure. The primary problem confronting the country, then, is that of maintaining a scientific and technological establishment that works in a coherent and effective way. The central problems in such an establishment may well lie in fields of applied science and technology, rather than in basic research.

My treatment is largely historical. Basic research has been with us at least since the time of the Greeks, and technology for several millennia more, so that there is plenty of material to draw on to show that there has been no unique or necessary connection between the two. At the same time, the historical approach makes it relatively easy to isolate some of the striking new characteristics of contemporary science and technology, and thus to indicate some of the considerations that should be important in a systematic approach to the country's present-day problems. The treatment is intended to be merely suggestive, however; a definitive treatment would be beyond my capabilities.

THE QUESTION OF LEADERSHIP, AND OTHER ISSUES

Before attempting the historical résumé described above, it may be worth while to interpolate one other introductory section. The questions posed by the House committee are about the support of basic science, and they are addressed to a group most of whose members are identified primarily with scientific research. Thus, one might naturally expect a "scientific" answer. In fact, however, the questions imply value judgments and factual backgrounds that lie outside the universe of discourse appropriate for pure science. Thus, one has the choice of a narrow answer that stays within the scientific sphere, or a broader answer with a correspondingly larger seasoning of personal opinion and judgment.

There are two areas in particular in which the issue just raised is important to an understanding of the present paper. The first has to do with leadership, particularly leadership in scientific research. To a professional scientist, research leadership is an end in itself, to be measured by professional judgment, and requires no further justification. In this paper, on the other hand, leadership in any of the areas mentioned by the committee will be related to the international influence of the United States, with secondary emphasis on our domestic well-being. In other words, we shall be concerned with the Nation's ability to shape the world so that it will remain hospitable to western ideas during the present time of troubles.

Obviously, military strength, as mentioned in the House committee's question, is an important element in the United States' international position. In the long run, however, the future must be decided by voluntary acceptance of the basic elements in our culture, rather than by simple force. Thus, strength in science and technology is both an important element in our domestic affairs and an important aspect of our position of international leadership.

The other area has to do with the question of the values of basic research in terms of its economic, cultural, and military applications—the general field of this paper. It is worth noting that this is not quite a fair question to pose to a pure scientist, even if adequate information were available to answer it. All definitions of basic research agree in the statement that the actual motivation for basic research must be simple curiosity about an interesting and challenging aspect of nature. If the work is motivated in any more direct way, it is no longer "basic." Thus the basic researcher is almost necessarily driven to the comfortable, if unexamined, dogma that basic research always pays its own way in the long run. To ask him to examine the issue further is like asking a young lover to give some sensible reasons why the adored person is really so charming.

To stay within the logical confines of basic science, one cannot readily do more than make a more or less detailed exploration of possible lines for basic research, either within some fields of science or in science as a whole. Such an examination cannot furnish a complete answer to the House committee's questions in a logical sense, but it might well furnish an adequate answer for practical working purposes. For example, one might turn up the result that research possibilities in many areas are so promising that the country cannot afford not to pursue them with all qualified workers. In addition, one might find that the number of people in the United States qualified for and interested in doing basic research is in any case so limited that support for them is never likely to be a big item in the Nation's budget. This would make the support of basic research at most a matter of choice of areas to emphasize, rather than one of overall level.

It may help in the understanding of this paper to say that the hypothetical conclusion just stated is essentially what I believe to be true. Of course, one must make qualifications. "Science spectaculars" and "big science" generally must be left out of such a conclusion. Their values must be calculated separately, perhaps in terms of their direct contributions to the country's international prestige, as discussed earlier.

If the support for basic research is to be essentially open-ended, scientists must see to it that quality standards are kept high. The research blanket must not be allowed to cover large areas of plodding, uninspired work, only marginally "publishable" and in the long run merely a complication for the information-retrieval problem. The maintenance of appropriate standards, however, is a job the scientific community should do for itself. They are not readily imposed from without. Subject to these limitations, there seem to be no pressing reasons for trying to restrict budgetary support for basic research. Thus, the fundamental object of this paper is not to suggest limits for pure research but to urge that adjoining areas get adequate attention.

I. Science and Technology in Historical Perspective

A somewhat impressionistic version of the history of science and technology might be imagined as a graph containing two curves representing, respectively, the relative rates of advance in the two areas at various times in the past. The science curve would start several millennia before the birth of Christ, to reflect work, primarily in astronomy, in Egypt and Asia Minor. The first conspicuous feature, however, would be a big bump a few centuries before the beginning of the Christian era, to represent the great achievements of the Greeks during their Golden Age. The Greeks of that period, however, were not noteworthy for technology, and the technology curve would still be at a low level for some time. The technology curve does rise a little later, however, so that for a century or so science and technology flourished together, as the Greek world merged into the Alexandrian. On the other hand, the science curve flattens out rapidly just before the birth of Christ, as the Romans, an eminently practical people, with no particular taste for or interest in science, became dominant in the Mediterranean world. The Roman world, on the other hand—in particular, the urbanized world of the Roman Empire—was quite competent and interested in technology, so that the technology curve continues at a substantial level for some time. After the fall of Rome, western European civilization rapidly decayed and both curves go negative, to indicate that previous knowledge and skills were actually being forgotten at a faster rate than new knowledge and skills were being generated.

The science curve does not rise significantly until the middle of the 16th century with the Copernican revolution, followed in the 17th century by the great age led by Galileo and Newton. This is generally regarded as the beginning of modern science. One need only think of Galileo with the pendulum, the telescope, the elements of mechanics; Newton with gravitation, the calculus, light; Harvey with the circulation of the blood; Levenhoek with the discovery of bacteria, using the first primitive microscopes; and so forth.

The technology curve rises much earlier, perhaps as early as the year 1100. Beginning then and continuing through the year 1500 or later, there was a steady improvement in the arts and skills by which people lived. In degree of advance, it meant as much as the Industrial Revolution meant much later in transforming the United States in the 19th century from the colonial period to a modern industrial state. The inventions and the new skills were numerous. To cite only those of special military value, the crossbow and the longbow were both developed in this time; gun powder and firearms, including primitive artillery, were also invented. So-called "Greek fire" appeared at the siege of Constantinople in the mid-15th century. A more subtle but perhaps more important advance was the development of a better metallurgy. This permitted lighter but stronger armor and much better swords and lances. Advances in shipping and navigation were equally important. The mariner's compass was invented. So also was the decked-over ship, propelled by square or fore-and-aft rigging. Such ships were far more rugged and far more maneuverable, especially in rough weather, than were the earlier light, open boats propelled by oars with only auxiliary sail power. The classic Battle of Lepanto, in which the Venetians destroyed the power of the Turks in the Mediterranean, was a victory for the new ships over the old. So also, in a way, was the defeat of the Spanish Armada, since the Spanish fleet had gone only halfway down the new path. These developments in ships, of course, underlay the great age of discovery that began near the end of the Middle Ages.

Following this burst, there was a coasting period for technology. New inventions were made and new processes found, of course, but they appear not to have had a profound effect on human life until the onset of the modern Industrial Revolution, which can be dated perhaps from the invention of Watt's steam engine about 1765. This led, in the first instance, to the application of steam power to weaving, spinning, and other industrial tasks. The first steamships and steam locomotives followed soon thereafter. It is hard to imagine many comparable developments that could have had such a technological impact, and one must consequently think of the technology curve as first rising to a high peak and then slackening somewhat after the first few decades of the 19th century. However, technological progress was rapid throughout.

Following the Newtonian epoch, there was also a coasting phase in pure science. Although much good work was done in the 18th century, the first notable upturn did not take place until about the year 1800. In mathematics, this was led by Gauss, commonly regarded as one of the three or four great mathematicians of all time, followed by Cauchy, Weierstrass, Riemann, and others. Systematic chemistry, based on Dalton's atomic theory, began. In physics, many fundamental discoveries were made, especially by Faraday and others in electricity. Much was also accomplished in the theory of heat and heat engines, culminating in the enunciation of the first and second laws of thermodynamics about the middle of the century. This work is of particular relevance to our modern industrial age, which depends so largely on mechanical and electrical power.

Even as abbreviated a sketch as this one is sufficient to establish the fact that, until about the middle of the last century, the connection between science and technology was very loose. In general, the times in which science flourished do not coincide with those during which technology was making most rapid progress. When they did flourish together they did not necessarily flourish in the same place. Unless we wish to go back as far as the Alexandrian world, the only real exception is furnished by England near the beginning of the 19th century, and even here it is probable that practitioners in the two fields had little contact with one another.

Another important fact emerges when we review this history in more detail. This is that, in a certain sense, science was far more indebted to technology than technology to science throughout this period. There were, of course, exceptions, but on balance the scientist was in the position of relying on technology, or, more broadly, on the world of practical experience generally, for his tools and much of his information. Technology "was there first." For example, the invention of both the telescope and microscope depended on a flourishing industry in spectacle lenses that already existed. Magnetism was known as an empirical fact, and had been used as the basis for the navigator's compass for centuries before 18th and 19th century physicists got around to studying the phenomenon. Watt's steam engine was invented without the benefit of the Carnot cycle, or Joule's work, and so on.

Thus, the work of the scientist was largely to refine and systematize the knowledge that technology in some sense already had. Of course, technology eventually profited thereby. The scientific understanding gained in the Newtonian epoch led to many advances in navigation, marine and civil engineering, and medicine. However, science was not yet in a position to contribute many actually new things to the world's stock.

II. Science and Technology in Historical Perspective

Science and technology begin to draw gradually closer together, and science begins to take the lead in some areas, as we enter the second half of the last century. Tables 1 and 2 give listings of some of the principal advances in science and technology over a 14- or 15-year period about a century ago.

TABLE 1

Some outstanding contributions to science, 1859–73

Darwin	Theory of evolution	1858
Helmholtz	Basic theories of vision and hearing	ca. 1860–62
Kekulé	Structural theory of chemical compounds	1858–66
Pasteur–Koch	Germ theory of disease	1866–68
Mendel	Theory of heredity	1865
Mendeleev	Periodic table	1871
Maxwell	Electromagnetic theory	1873
Kirchhoff–Bunsen	Spectroscopic analysis	1859

It is sometimes said that the present age of science is an unprecedented one—that man has never before advanced so rapidly. It takes only a brief glance at table 1, however, to show that the 14 or 15 years between 1859 and 1873 were at least equally rich. For example, the year 1859 is the year of publication of Darwin's *Origin of Species*, followed 5 or 6 years later by the *Descent of Man*. These are the equivalent in biology of the Copernican revolution in astronomy, as far as man's understanding of his place in nature is concerned. The year 1873 is the time of publication of Maxwell's *Electricity and Magnetism*. This includes, as an incidental, the whole of the electromagnetic theory of light. Almost more important for our modern age is the fact that it involves the basic theory of radio propagation. The fact that there could be such things as electromagnetic waves—radio waves—was verified with great difficulty 15 years

TABLE 2

Some outstanding technological advances about 1860

[Nonmilitary]	
Beginning of synthetic drug and dye industry	1856
Bessemer process	1856
Industrial dynamo	1860–70
First transatlantic cable (Kelvin)	1865
First plastic	1870
[Military]	
Improved explosives (smokeless powder, dynamite, etc.)	1855–65
Armored ships	1855–62
Machinegun (Gatling, Hotchkiss)	1861–72
Self-propelled torpedo (Whitehead)	1866

later by Hertz. Without Maxwell's prediction, the field might have been undiscovered for many years.

Between the books of Darwin and Maxwell were a number of other only slightly less important advances. In chemistry, for example, Mendeleev enunciated the periodic law and Kekulé laid the systematic foundations of organic chemistry. In other areas, Mendel enunciated the so-called Mendelian laws of heredity, Pasteur enunciated the germ theory of disease—followed quickly by the work of the microbiologist Koch in isolating and identifying many of the most serious disease-causing organisms—Kirchhoff initiated systematic spectroscopy, essential to many fields, and so on. In spite of the richness of present-day science, it would be hard to contend that it has made a better record in any recent 14 years.

Table 2 gives some sample activities in the technological field that were going on at the same time. Here we begin to see some interconnections between technology and contemporary of earlier science. This is obvious, for example, in the chemical fields. The technological application of the dynamo was clearly a dilatory appreciation of the importance of Faraday's pioneer work nearly 40 years earlier. The telegraph cable may similarly be thought of as an outgrowth of scientific work during the first half of the century. The work of Pasteur and Koch was, of course, almost immediately applicable in medicine and public health. On the whole, however, this was an age in which the relation between science and the great bulk of technology was still quite remote.

As a matter of passing interest, table 2 also includes a listing of some of the principal activities in military technology during the same period, approximately contemporary with our Civil War. The idea of applying science and technology in warfare, which has been such a conspicuous feature of recent years, is, of course, not entirely new. It has been given sporadic attention on many occasions in the past, and was the subject

TABLE 3

Some outstanding contributions to science, 1897–1905

Thomson	Discovery of the electron	1897
Curie	Discovery of radium	1898
Hilbert	Foundations of geometry	1899
Planck	Quantum theory of radiation	1900
Einstein	Special theory of relativity	1905
	Quantum theory of photoelectricity	1905
Freud	Psychoanalysis	1904
Pavlov	Conditioned reflex	1904

TABLE 4
Some outstanding technological advances about 1900

Marconi	Radio, practical experiments	1895–1902
Curtis	Steam and gas turbines	1896
Rudolf Diesel	Diesel engine	1897
Wright Brothers	Powered airplane	1903
Fleming	Radio tube	1904

of relatively lively interest at the time of the Civil War. What was involved at that time, however, was clearly the 19th century's technology—not its science.

As we enter the 20th century, the connection between science and technology gradually becomes closer. Tables 3 and 4 give a comparison of representative accomplishments in the two fields near the turn of the century. Several of the items in table 4—notably those related to prime movers—were, of course, quite remote from any contemporary, or near-contemporary, scientific activities, as measured by the other table. However, such engineering work could now rest on properly laid theoretical foundations in pure science, dating, in fact, largely from the first half of the 19th century. It did not need to depend primarily on empiricism or intuition, as it did in Watt's time.

In other items of table 4, notably Marconi's work and the Fleming valve, the advance was obviously an offshoot of a relatively recent scientific discovery. In still other areas, technological applications of earlier scientific discoveries were imminent, but had to wait a little longer for further scientific work. For example, Mendel's pioneering work in genetics, which had been overlooked for a generation, was rediscovered at this time and became the subject of further active research. This led within a few years to the systematic experimental work on new strains of plants and animals that are so important in our present-day agricultural economy. In chemistry, the plastics industry—now so elaborately developed—had made a slow and halting start in the 19th century. It finally began to make consistent progress with the invention of bakelite in 1907.

The decade between 1900 and 1910 was also the period when the large industrial laboratory was first established in this country. (Similar laboratories, principally in the drug and dye industry, had previously existed in England and Germany.) Du Pont, General Electric, and the Bell System all established substantial central laboratories at this time. The individual inventor or engineer of the 19th century was likely to be a man whose primary training had been in drafting or the shop. The new industrial laboratories of the early 20th century showed how much more effective a better knowledge of science and the systematic application of scientific method could be in attacking technological problems. A series of public or quasi-public institutions, such as the Bureau of Standards, the Rockefeller Institute for Medical Research, and the Hygienic Laboratory of the Public Health Service (which later become the National Institutes of Health), were also either established originally or reestablished with broadened charters at this time. They performed a similar function in bridging the gap between pure science and its applications in their particular fields.

The major scientific advances near the turn of the century, as listed in table 3, are, however, interesting not so much for their immediate applications as for another reason. This also was a golden period for science, but it was primarily a germinal period, in which science made new starts whose ultimate implications were great but which lay well in the future. Pavlov's work on the conditioned reflex, which was begun in 1904 and has been a cornerstone of the behavioral sciences for the last few decades, is one example. We are all deeply immersed, of course, in the world of "electronics," ushered in by Thomson's discovery of the electron as a separate physical particle in 1897.

In several instances, new starts began with the discovery that the great achievements of preceding eras could not be taken quite at face value, but were subject to reconsideration or qualification. For example, 1898 is the year of the discovery of radium, which appeared to be a source of infinite energy, thus refuting the first law of thermodynamics so laboriously established in the middle of the 19th century. To reestablish the law, one had to postulate a special atomic world, which led finally to modern atomic and nuclear physics. The year 1899 was the year of the publication of *Foundations of Geometry* by David Hilbert, a German mathematician who is generally regarded as the proponent and formulator of the modern abstract school of mathematics. One of Hilbert's tenets is that mathematics exists whether or not it is in correspondence with the real physical world. Mathematicians were led to this position by the discovery of a number of so-called "pathological" cases such as Peano's space-filling curves, which, in defiance of ordinary intuition, were curves including all the points in a square or a cube. The year 1900 saw the enunciation of Planck's quantum hypothesis, involving the assumption that in some ways nature has to proceed in steps and cannot be continuous.

The period near 1900 was also a time of reappraisal of the theory of light, based on the negative results of the famous Michelson-Morley experiment some years earlier. This experiment, in a sense, left Maxwell's electromagnetic theory of light unchallenged, but without foundation. It indicated, in effect, that light may indeed be a wave motion, but that the so-called ether, which had been postulated as the substance in which the wave traveled, could not possibly exist. Physics was rescued in 1905 with the enunciation of Einstein's first theory of relativity. The theory includes the famous mass-energy equivalence now used to compute ultimate yields in nuclear weapons. Einstein in that same year also gave the quantum theory its first real support by establishing a quantum theory for the photoelectric effect. This further undermined Maxwell by pointing out that, on the atomic scale, light behaved like waves but also like bullets.

There is a consistent intellectual style to all these discoveries. Whereas the universe of Newtonian mechanics was obviously logical and straightforward, these new discoveries indicate a natural world that is in a sense perverse and subjective, that is full of paradoxes and not necessarily straightforward in any obvious way. Anyone who has had to accept the quantum hypothesis, or the relativistic barrier to infinite speed, or relativistic foreshortening, or the equivalence of mass and energy, or Peano's space-filling curve, can no longer believe that nature is made up of simple straightforward elements obviously accessible to the intuition of an untutored mind. Instead, it is subtle, sophisticated, and even deceptive. Freud's enunciation of the principles of psychoanalysis in 1904 is included in table 3 because it represents the same sort of change in point of view. Human behavior is no longer to be understood only through the obvious and rational aspects of the human mind, as the 18th and 19th centuries would have had it, but instead is to be studied by penetrating deeply into a hidden regime with a perverse logic of its own.

In the short run, this change to a more profound and subtle sort of science may have weakened the impact of science for the uses of the ordinary world. In the long run, however, it was full of promise. It meant that by digging deeply enough we could expect to turn up new phenomena and new relationships not readily predictable from ordinary experience. Thus science could play more and more the role of an innovator in technology, a creator of new devices and new ways of doing things. It was less and less confined to improving on and systematizing known technology, as it had been in its early days. The change has, of course, come about gradually, but it is one of the primary reasons for the strong impact of science in the present day.

SCIENCE AND TECHNOLOGY IN THE UNITED STATES

We can conveniently continue this sketch of the relation between science and technology by confining our attention to the United States, the area

TABLE 5

Nobel Prizes in science, 1901–30

Country	Prizes	Country	Prizes
Germany	27	Denmark	4
England	15	Austria	3
France	11	Switzerland	3
Sweden	6	Italy	2
United States	6	U.S.S.R.	2
Holland	6		

of particular interest to us. It is also convenient to center particularly on the years extending roughly from 1930 to 1940—the last decade before World War II. Since the war made vast changes in both science and technology and in their effects, this period is a natural point of departure for any more contemporary problems.

The situation in the United States, at least up to 1930, is of additional interest because it exemplifies so well the rather casual and distant relation between science and technology during most of their history. We have, of course, long been conspicuous in technology. Until recent years, however, the United States has not been a country of key importance in the world of science. We had occasional noteworthy men but they were very few in comparison with the number in older countries.

Table 5 illustrates this. It gives a count of Nobel Prize winners in the sciences (Nobel Prizes are given in physics, chemistry, physiology, and medicine) in the years 1900–30. One notices that scientifically the United States was able to give countries like Sweden and Holland quite good competition, and we actually led Switzerland, but we were hardly anywhere in the major league competition represented by Germany, England, and France.

In contrast, our contributions to technology have been important for many years. A rough documentation of this, using invention rates as an index of contributions, is attempted in table 6. Column A is a listing of the nationalities of the authors of major inventions from colonial times to the present as given in a recent popular almanac. Such a tabulation can, of course, be assailed on grounds both of probable chauvinism in the choice of inventors to whom credit is given and of lack of discrimination in choosing important inventions. As a corrective, column B gives the average annual patenting rate for the years 1930–39 in the countries concerned (*1*). Although the margin is somewhat more modest, this column also shows the United States in a leading role. It should be noted, however, that the result is due in large part simply to the fact that the United

TABLE 6
Invention rates in various countries

	A Total on Selected List 1600–present	B Average Annual Rate 1930–39
United States	203	38,300
Great Britain	58	9,050
Germany	32	14,600
France	29	9,550
Italy	14	3,900
Switzerland		3,130
Sweden	4	1,030

States is a big country. In proportion to population the Swiss invention rate, for example, is much higher than ours.

To describe adequately this period in our history we should make several further remarks. One is that the stature of American science had in fact been growing steadily ever since the late 19th century, when several universities had reorganized their graduate instruction along the lines of the best European models, and 1930 is about the last possible year when one could conceivably ascribe any inferiority to American science. During the 1930's, for example, the United States finished approximately in a triple tie with England and Germany for Nobel awards in science, and since then we have been doing still better.

Another point worth making is that in many areas bridges between science and technology did exist in the United States during this period. These bridges existed in the various industrial and quasi-public laboratories mentioned in the preceding section, the agricultural experiment stations, and the like. The growth of industrial laboratories is perhaps particularly noteworthy. At the onset of the depression there were approximately 1,600 such organizations of various shapes and sizes. With a few notable exceptions, however, this activity was very much on the applied side, with little coupling to advancing areas in science.

Finally, it is worth pointing out that straightforward technological advances, whether brought about by science or by simple invention, were important in this era, but they were not the most conspicuous aspect of the American economy. First in importance were the management and organizational aspects of production. Mass-production techniques, based

TABLE 7
Nobel Prizes in science, 1931–60

Country	Prizes	Country	Prizes
United States	33	Austria	4
England	18	Sweden	2
Germany	14	Italy	2
Switzerland	5	U.S.S.R.	2

on time and motion studies, materials-flow studies, assembly line techniques, and so forth, were the dominant elements of the economy. They tended to lead to production techniques that were fairly similar even among industries producing quite different kinds of goods. We all remember how quickly American industry shifted from peacetime to wartime production under the urgencies of the two world wars.

The years during and after World War II have seen a revolutionary change in American attitudes toward both science and technology. As we all know, they are now very much in the forefront of our thinking, and we aspire to a position of international leadership in these areas that is quite different from the one we had enjoyed earlier.

The shift in the position of the United States in pure science is exemplified by table 7, which gives, in comparison with table 5, a tabulation of Nobel Prize winners for the second 30 years of the Nobel Prize awards. We see here that the United States now has taken a leading role, which would be still more marked if we confined the comparison to the years following the war. The sudden change may be attributed in part to the maturation of our own institutions, as noted earlier, and in part to a very substantial infusion of first-rate European scientists that took place because of the political troubles of the 1930's. As in the case of patents, however, the lead is in large part merely a reflection of our large population. We also benefit from our great material resources; the areas in which we lead tend to be those requiring relatively expensive experimental equipment rather than those that can be dominated by the paper-and-pencil theorist.

In technology, the precipitating cause of the change was clearly our military experience during World War II, confirmed and extended by the military and space program since. The application of relatively new science to military technology was obviously a vital element in many of our undertakings, while the vast scale and ambitious goals of such activities as the Manhattan Project, the ICBM program, and the current Apollo project have led the public to the belief, perhaps unwarranted, that "science" can do almost anything when pursued with sufficient determination and budgetary support.

The success of the Manhattan Project was particularly critical. During World War I, most Americans would have conceded leadership in science and the applications of science to Germany. But the success with the atomic weapon, added to superior performance in radar and other fields, gave the country a quite different view of itself and its potentialities. At the same time, the fact that such a large and complex undertaking could be organized and carried through to completion on a short time scale has lent encouragement to the planning of ambitious projects ever since. "Forced development" has become an established concept, particularly for military purposes. The fact that the Manhattan Project depended on a quite recent discovery in pure physics emphasized the importance of a close coupling between technology and pure science, to permit the rapid exploitation of scientific advances.

On the other hand, a somewhat more gradual evolution toward a science-based technology should probably have been expected even if the war had not broken out. As we have already seen, the pioneer industrial laboratories of the early 20th century were constantly finding more imitators. Moreover, after a long period of gestation, the scientific upheaval near the turn of the century was beginning to bear fruit in many fields. By the early 1930's, for example, it had carried us to the beginnings of modern solid-state physics, so important for contemporary electronics. In atomic theory, it had led us to the point where the basic discoveries about atomic energy could be made. In genetics, the work begun just after the turn of the century had already led by the 1930's to the introduction of commercial hybrid corn. The science that was beginning to emerge by the outbreak of the war had considerably more to offer technology than had its predecessors of a generation or two earlier. It was richer and more diversified, with greater depth of understanding and more lines of attack to offer in any given situation. It produced greater probability of turning up new and unexpected phenomena that might lay the foundation for substantial steps forward in technical method or even totally new areas in technology. Under such circumstances, it seems certain that competitive forces would have produced increasingly close ties between science and technology in any event.

The U.S. position in science and technology is, of course, an important factor in its general position of international leadership for many reasons. Both science and technology are directly involved in our military posture. In addition, technology, through its effects on our economic life, also acts indirectly to help provide the financial support both of our military establishment and of our foreign-aid policy. As we saw in the introduction, however, U.S. leadership in the long run cannot be based upon military strength or even upon foreign aid. It must depend on voluntary recognition by other nations of our culture as a healthy and successful one, worth emulating at least in many of its aspects. Thus our successes in science and technology, as conspicuous elements of our total culture, are important to achievement of leadership.

In reflecting on these questions it is natural to think first of technology. American goods flood the world's markets and carry with them the national image. The fact that they are generally well made is all in our favor. So also is the fact that they increasingly represent advanced technology—that jet transports and data-processing machines, for example, are typical American export items.

It is also important, however, to include leadership in basic science as a vital element in our position. In fact, in the underdeveloped countries, intellectual communication with science on a global scale may be better than it is with technology, if only because science is so internationalized. Thus, Nobel Prize winners in the United States are by no means a negligible factor in influencing the world to follow our lead. Cultural leaderships also helps us in other ways. The fact that foreign students come increasingly to the United States to be educated is a factor in our favor if we assume, as we must, that they generally return home as our friends. Cultural leadership also helps if it means that educated people all over the world must learn to read English because so much that is important appears in that language.

The struggle of cultures is, of course, one that the country must wage on a broad front. Science and technology, however, are important components. Expenditures in science and technology may be indirectly effective for our position of international leadership, in addition to their more direct values. Thus, such expenditures can properly be compared in value with the sums spent for information agencies, direct aid, or other similar means of strengthening our international position.

CHANGES IN THE NATURE OF SCIENCE

With this long background, we can now begin to ask what there is about contemporary science and technology that distinguishes them from the science and technology of past generations, and which poses particular problems for the present day. The writer can hardly claim to make a definitive statement about these questions, but will attempt only to offer some general remarks.

To turn first to science, it is clear that, while we live in a distinguished era, there have been very distinguished epochs of science in the past. In a certain qualitative sense, our era is probably no more distinguished than certain of its predecessors. Nevertheless, it far outstrips them in other respects. Science now is bigger; it covers more fields; there are more interconnections; there are more technical resources on which it can draw so that there are more avenues of useful exploration open to research at any one time. (Of course, there are also more research workers to exploit them.)

These changes seem in a sense to be merely a reflection of the growth in the body of science itself. As the body of science grows, there are relatively more and more interrelations, and in a sense one approaches "critical mass" just as one does as one brings nuclear material together in an atomic bomb.

There are several ways in which the effects of this gradual maturing of science can be discerned. The first is that, as any body of science becomes more thoroughly understood, it is possible to make more imaginative jumps into the unknown to explore more and more obscure effects. The better established the base camp, in other words, the longer the foray one can mount from it. In the early years of science, most of its material came through casual observation. It is only as theory becomes well established that one can make a very specialized and elaborate experiment with hope of success. The discovery of Neptune is the classic instance of a theoretical prediction that led to an experimental finding that otherwise would almost certainly have remained unknown, or at least unrecognized. The prediction of radio propagation by Maxwell, later verified by Hertz, which was referred to earlier, represents another such instance. As we feel more confident in our basic understanding, similar occasions in which one can commit a considerable experimental effort on the basis of a refined theoretical prediction become more and more common. For example, chemical purity in most substances is measured in hundredths or thousandths of a percentage point. In transistors and other semiconductors, on the other hand, the impurity level, at least for critical contaminants, must be of the order of millionths of a percentage point. Such purity is not found in nature or created by ordinary refining. Obviously, no one would undertake the job of finding ways of providing such pure materials without the sort of theoretical understanding that tells him that achievement of such purity would really provide a new kind of performance. Similarly, the modern maser will not "mase" unless conditions are just right. It takes an elaborate deductive process to see that a unique result may be possible if the required conditions are met. In another field, hybrid corn and similar modern plants are obtained from long programs of inbreeding and recrossing, which no practical plant breeder of the past, without the aid of modern genetic theory, would have had the confidence to undertake. Organic synthesis represents still another field in which elaborate and protracted experimental programs can be undertaken only because of the depth and completeness of our theoretical understanding.

A second general fact of our present situation is that, as science grows more mature, more and more areas lend themselves to successful scientific attack. Mathematics and physics, which are perhaps the oldest and best-established sciences, are so because in some ways they are simpler than most other sciences. The problems they confront could be clearly defined at an earlier period. For example, physics is simpler than chemistry. The theory of the atomic nucleus may be complex enough, but the number of kinds of organic molecules is far greater than the number of nuclear species. In turn, chemistry is surely simpler than biology, and biology than the behavioral sciences. Thus, the more complex disciplines necessarily lag behind the simpler ones, and are added one by one to the areas in which really active progress can be expected as time goes by. Lavoisier and Priestley, in displacing phlogiston by oxygen in the mid-18th century, were doing what Galileo was doing to the Aristotelian hypothesis about falling bodies near the beginning of the 17th century. Similarly, Dalton's atomic hypothesis near the beginning of the 19th century did for chemistry something like what Newton's laws of motion did for physics near the end of the 17th century.

More complex areas have had to wait still longer. In certain aspects of biology and the behavioral sciences, quantitative scientific progress perhaps dates from Karl Pearson, who is also one of the pioneers associated with the famous peak near 1900, which I spoke of before. The fact that more and more areas are becoming accessible to scientific investigation, more or less in the style of the physical sciences, is thus one of the outstanding features of our scientific time.

Another major trend is in the growth of interdisciplinary fields. These are fields that lie at the borderline between two disciplines and that make use of the ideas and methods of both. At one time science was becoming more and more fragmented, but the tide is clearly turning. Physical chemistry, the well-known border strip between physics and chemistry, has been joined by another field, chemical physics. Biochemistry has been a flourishing area for many years. Biophysics is much younger, but shows many signs of vitality. There is even a recognized field of biomathematics. This sort of junction, involving the massive importation of the basic concepts of one field into another, frequently yields enormous results. The importation of the ideas of modern physics, particularly in atomic theory and quantum physics, for example, has revolutionized the fundamentals of chemistry.

The final conspicuous aspect of our times is the massive employment of tools (as distinguished from concepts) drawn from one scientific field, or from engineering, in another. The most obvious example of a field that is almost completely dependent on other fields for its tools is astronomy. Ordinary visual observation of the stars goes back, of course, for many millennia, but progress beyond that point had to wait for the contribution of the telescope by physics. The next revolutionary tools for astronomers were photography and spectral analysis. Long time exposures, rather than visual observation, are, of course, the basic observational techniques that astronomy now uses in coping with the dim and distant parts of the universe. Spectral analysis, with its indications of chemical composition, relative motions, physical conditions of pressure, density, and other factors, has been almost equally important.

Spectrum analysis was included in the list of achievements in the golden age between 1859 and 1873 because of its unique value as a tool. In addition to its contribution to astronomy, it has been uniquely valuable to chemists, replacing many of their previous methods of analysis and giving them information not otherwise available. As a tool, it also served physicists themselves in many ways. For example, the long catalog of spectrum observations was the primary source material for the development of the modern theory of the atom.

The history of the use in astronomy of tools from other areas is by no means over. Modern control theory of the highest order is required to position big telescopes with sufficient exactness. Radio telescopes give astronomers a new way of charting the universe. If we succeed in putting a telescope into orbit or on the moon, astronomers will have a new observational tool, independent of the earth's atmosphere, of almost incalculable value.

The importance of this process, by which some of the sciences (or engineering) furnish tools for other sciences, is extremely marked at the present time. One has only to observe what radioactive tracers have meant to chemistry, the life sciences, and many forms of engineering process control, or what the discovery of naturally decaying elements—radio isotopes of various sorts—has meant in historical and geological dating, in periods running from the formation of the continents to the construction of your great grandfather's Windsor chair.

High-energy physics furnishes another example. With respect to experimental equipment, this field is really an exercise in advanced electrical engineering. It could not be attempted without the tools furnished by electrical engineering. Its huge experimental installations represent the classic example of the sort of large-scale expensive resource that scientists of the past did not ordinarily have, and that are indispensable for certain kinds of investigations.

The role of electronics and electronic instrumentation in many other areas is worthy of comment. Comparison of a relatively simple instrument like the electrocardiograph with the old-fashioned stethoscope shows how important even simple new tools can be. Automatic or quasi-automatic electronic instrumentation has revolutionized experimentation in many areas, permitting experimenters to take many times more data in a given time than they could only a few years ago.

While these examples are taken from the natural sciences, the impact of such new tools on psychology and the behavioral sciences is also very great. In many cases, moreover, the contribution is not limited to simple instrumentation. For example, the concepts of information theory, originally developed for communication engineering, have turned out to be unexpectedly fruitful in these fields.

A final example of the widespread application of new tools is furnished by the modern computer. In many cases it serves as a substitute for experiments that could be made only with difficulty, if at all. In others, it provides the only good way of coping with the enormous mass of data produced by the new instrumentation. In the planning of very elaborate experimental situations, involving substantial forays into unknown ground, it provides an almost indispensable way of investigating the situation thoroughly before one starts. In one or another of these ways the computer appears capable of substantially accelerating the rate of progress in many scientific areas.

An analogy between science and mining is a suggestive one here. In the beginning, science exploited nuggets and rich superficial pockets just as primitive man satisfied his small needs for metals. These most accessible deposits of metals were quickly used up, but vastly greater quantities of the world's ores still remained for exploitation through systematic utilization of large-scale equipment capable of exploiting poorer ores or of reaching rich deposits well below the surface. In science, the comparable era of systematic "mining" has just begun.

Since the basic topic of this paper is the relation between science and technology, one further remark may be in order. The instrumentation called for by modern science may be relatively simple, as in recording equipment, or very elaborate, as in space experiments. In all cases, however, it is properly defined as technology, and is the product of essentially technical effort. Thus, the increasing use of instrumentation in science is an important bridge between science and technology.

SOME GENERAL PROBLEMS IN THE RELATION BETWEEN SCIENCE AND MODERN TECHNOLOGY

I have just given a brief account of some of the characteristics of modern science. Logically we should now continue with a similar discussion of modern technology. The discussion of science laid stress on the fact that modern science is increasingly likely to turn up new and unexpected phenomena, which might form the foundation for a substantial step forward in technical method, or even a whole new area in technology. Thus, we might expect the sketch of modern technology to show it in an attitude of passive, though attentive, waiting, ready to run off promptly with any new discovery and exploit it without further ado. If this simple picture were accurate, the application of science to technology would be a relatively straightforward matter, and could be easily discussed.

Unfortunately, the actual application of science to technology is considerably more difficult than this. It is likely, even under the best circumstances, to call for more initiative and active effort in technology than the simple picture would suggest. The subject is a very complicated one, however, because of the great variety of technical and economic situations in which applications of science may take place. An adequate treatment of all these possibilities would be well beyond the scope of this paper. For the sake of formal completeness, however, this section will give a brief sketch of a few of the questions that make the whole matter so complicated, and which must be borne in mind in any final appraisal of our overall progress in the application of science to technology. The logical thread of the paper, then, will be resumed in the following sections with a description of the characteristics of modern technology in limited areas where the interplay between science and technology is most apparent, and reasonably general statements can be made.

The most obvious reason for the complexity of the subject is the fact that the various sciences find their ways to eventual impact on the life of the society through quite different channels. For example, the physical sciences are most closely related to manufacturing and to certain portions of the service industries, such as transportation, electric power, and communications. Thus, a new discovery in the physical sciences is likely to find application, in general, through the methods available in these parts of our economy. The biological sciences, on the other hand, have only a tenuous relation with manufacturing, but they are very closely tied to

TABLE 8

Research and development industry—1961

	Sales $Billions	R&D $MILLIONS Federal	Company	Total[1]	R&D as Percent of Sales
Aircraft and missiles	16.4	3,537	385	3,957	24.2
Electrical equipment and communications	23.1	1,533	861	2,404	10.4
Professional and scientific instruments	5.3	176	208	384	7.2
Chemicals	23.4	224	845	1,073	4.6
All manufacturing industry	246.0	6,313	4,480	10,872	4.4
Machinery	20.0	292	600	896	4.4
Motor vehicles and other transportation	28.0	802	609	192	2.9
Primary metals	20.0	16	143	160	.8
Food	35.0	4	101	105	.3

[1] Includes minor amounts from other sources.
Source: NSF 64–9.

agriculture and medicine. Our methods of capitalizing on scientific advances in these areas, however, are quite different from those in the typical manufacturing industry. The behavioral sciences represent still a different problem, with different channels for application, subject to different constraints.

To simplify our discussion we may restrict ourselves to the single field of manufacturing industry. With related areas in the service industries, as noted above, this still covers the bulk of the Nation's economy, including almost all our activities in military and space fields. This restriction, however, still leaves a great variety of possibilities. Table 8 illustrates the situation. It is an abbreviated form of a standard table giving research and develop expenditures as a percentage of net sales in various sectors of manufacturing industry proper. The four industries—aerospace, electrical machinery and communications, chemicals, and scientific instruments—whose expenditures exceed the average for all manufacturing industry are listed at the top of the table. The rest of the table gives a few samples of the remaining industries whose research and development expenditures are below the overall average. The categories are, of course, quite broad. For example, "Chemicals" includes everything from bulk industrial chemicals to pharmaceuticals, and "Machinery" everything from construction machinery to office equipment.

It takes only a moment's inspection to see that the various industries differ quite widely in terms of research and development. For example, on the average, the first 4 industries spend about 10 times as much for research and development, in proportion to their sales, as do the others. The ratio between the aerospace industry and the food industry is about 80 to 1. Some of this disparity is, of course, a reflection of Government expenditures for military or space purposes. The differences, however, are substantial even when Government funds are subtracted.

The fact that an industry does not spend a large sum on research and development does not, of course, inevitably mean that it is not spending as much as its situation justifies. It is, however, one index to the flexibility and speed with which it is likely to respond to basic scientific advances. It is noteworthy that the four top entries in table 8 have all been recognized historically as "science-based" industries. The chemical and electrical industries, in particular, were pioneers in the establishment of industrial laboratories, and have long experience in the application of new science to technology.

In the rest of this paper, we shall have tacitly in mind science-based industries of the sort found near the top of table 8, possibly excluding bulk chemicals. These are the areas in which the impact of a scientific advance on technology is most clearly evident, and in which the interaction between science and technology occurs under the most favorable circumstances. They are, of course, also critical areas for our defense effort.

The restriction to the science-based industries can perhaps also be justified in part by the argument that they are areas of particular interest for the United States' international position. This is obviously true in the military sphere. It also tends to hold for our normal export trade, since the more technological industries seem to be increasingly the arenas in which advanced industrial nations now compete. As we saw earlier, the most significant exports of the United States are now jet transports and data-processing machines, rather than, say, wheat and typewriters, and ships and transistor radios have tended to replace cotton goods as exports of the Japanese.

The science-based industries are also of special importance because of their indirect impact on the rest of domestic industry. To illustrate, if we look at a random sample of current technological advances in industry broadly, we will probably find that many of them stemmed ultimately from improvements in materials. Thus, they are likely to have been contributed by the chemical industry. A good example is furnished by the use of synthetic materials in the textile industry. In mechanical engineering one is likely to encounter techniques like explosive forming or light-weight actuator and control systems originated or perfected for aerospace applications. The random sample is also likely to include a number of examples of automation, in the form of either automated processing in the factory or advanced bookkeeping and data handling in the office. In either case, there is a fair chance that the advance rests ultimately on modern electronics, perhaps with an assist from the instrumentation industry. The machinery industry—the fifth entry in the list of table 8—is also one whose effect on the technological progress of other industries may be profound, because it creates so many of the tools they use.

To carry this discussion further, we need to turn now to some of the difficulties that may present themselves whenever we consider an actual application of science to technology. These obstacles may arise for the science-based industries as well as the others, and indeed the discussion is intended primarily as a preliminary for the sketch of these industries in the following section. It is included here, however, because it also helps, indirectly, to explain why one must expect such varied results in different areas.

From the technological side, the principal difficulty arises from the fact that many scientific advances are, in a sense, incomplete. They point the way to an advance in technology, in other words, but a great deal more must be supplied both in science and engineering before the step can actually be taken. Frequently the additional advances must be drawn from many fields. The classic example is furnished by the Manhattan Project referred to in an earlier section. Nuclear energy is, of course, based on discoveries in pure physics made even before the war. To make a successful bomb, however, also required substantial contributions from chemistry and chemical engineering, electronics, and mathematics, as well as much more work in physics. The further development of the atomic-energy field has, of course, required continued work in all these technical areas, and more.

The Manhattan Project is an extreme case, but similar situations on a more modest scale are quite common. Further examples are given in the next section. In some cases one must simply wait for concurrent advances in several fields. In others, it may be possible to fill the gaps, but only at the cost of considerable additional effort. When we deal with scientific advances less revolutionary than nuclear energy, the scope and difficulty of this additional effort may overshadow the scientific advance itself, so that the real choice is between expending the effort to exploit one scientific advance or another. Expenditure for applied research rather than pure research, in other words, turns out to be the critical factor (*2*).

Other problems are economic in nature. For example, it is obviously necessary for a technological advance to be justified in terms of the new investment in physical capital than it may require. Again, the Manhattan Project, with its very large expenditures for the Oak Ridge plant and similar facilities, is a good, if extreme, illustration. In normal industry, the weight of such a consideration may depend on the particular activity involved. For example, the question may not be a difficult one in the pharmaceutical industry, where the shift from one drug to another of related sort can be made readily, using substantially the same productive equipment. It is, however, obviously more important in capital-intensive areas such as transportation, power, and communications, mentioned earlier, where capital charges are high and physical equipment may last for many years. Problems of this sort are made much more serious by a high rate of technological progress. When technological progress is slow, it may be sufficient to incorporate technical advances in equipment that needs renewal anyway. As we postulate increasing rates of technical growth, so that technological obsolescence comes more and more before natural wearout, however, this solution becomes less satisfactory. We must debit technical advance with the value of the scrapped equipment.

A related question has to do with the possible incompatibility between a proposed technological advance and the general usages and organization of an industry. This may cover a broad field, including such technically irrelevant considerations as specific building codes, labor union requirements, national distribution networks, and the like. In utilities and transportation it may include such things as standardized hardware and operating practices. In manufacturing industry, it includes the general management and organization of the productive process. The automobile industry, with its elaborate network of suppliers, assembly plants, and service facilities, is an example. Whatever the area, an effective and smooth-working economic organization is likely to be as important for the ultimate efficiency of the system as the basic technology itself. If a technological change is really to be an advance, we must find some way of introducing it without too much disruption of the going system.

The overall competitive structure of an industry is evidently important in all such questions. Broad innovations, whether in usage or in basic technology, are likely to be expensive, and any individual company engaged in such projects is necessarily working, in part, for the benefit of its industry as a whole. Thus the more fragmented and competitive an industry is, the more likely it is that technological advances will be of the limited and specific sort that small concerns, under high competitive pressure, can afford.

All these considerations point in the same general direction; that is, that industry cannot always take advantage of isolated scientific advances as they occur. Exploitation of an advance must be reconciled with all the facts of life concerning capital obsolescence, existing production organization, and so on. In general, technological advance should be easiest in new industries, just as modern cities tend to grow in suburban zones rather than in central areas. It is also easiest when the advance has a limited and specific impact, like the substitution of a new drug, or a new measuring instrument, or a new finish, for an old one, and does not call for a long series of interrelated changes.

When these conditions are not met, we must expect that technological advances may take place in rather large quantum steps, after the accumulation of technological possibilities have provided us with the potential for really significant progress. The "activation energy," in other words, may be quite high. This does not mean that the benefits of scientific progress are lost—merely that they are postponed. To carry through such large changes in an orderly way, however, obviously calls for good planning and the assurance of adequate financial and organizational support.

A final point may be worth mentioning. The application of science to technology does not happen of itself; it has to be brought about through some agency. In many cases, the industrial laboratory type of organization seems to be the natural means. On the other hand, it is not clear that the industrial laboratory fits all situations. To flourish, such a laboratory should be fairly large, with a technical mission that is well defined and yet broad enough to maintain a diversified intellectual atmosphere, with stable financial support, and without overwhelming competitive pressures. These conditions may not be met in all circumstances. Alternative solutions such as trade associations, research institutes, and Government-sponsored laboratories come readily to mind, and evidently need to be considered in any complete survey. They are, however, beyond the scope of this paper.

CHANGES IN THE NATURE OF TECHNOLOGY

We saw in the preceding section that modern technology as a whole is too heterogeneous to admit any simple description. However, if we confine our attention to the science-based industries near the top of the list in table 8, it is possible to paint a reasonably coherent picture.

The science-based industries naturally reflect, to some extent, the characteristics we have previously ascribed to modern science itself. For example, as modern science is becoming interdisciplinary, we may expect its applications to be even more interdisciplinary. Thus in many technological situations we may need substantial teams of scientists and engineers to encompass the required skills. As experimental precedures in a single science are increasingly likely to depend upon a mixture of tools and methods borrowed from other sciences, we can expect a corresponding hybridization of tools and methods in technology. The fact that science frequently takes long steps forward nowadays has its counterpart in the fact that technological projects are frequently quite ambitious. When we look at these characteristics from the technological side, however, they tend to have a different flavor. In addition, we find that contemporary technology has some distinctive aspects of its own.

We can describe the characteristics of the science-based industries most conveniently by contrasting them with the traditional view of the American economy. This was, briefly, that America owed her prosperity in part to the skill of her people and in part to her natural resources. The natural centers of industry were near coal and iron deposits—the principal raw materials—and near good shipping, because of the importance of cheap transportation of bulk products. This meant primarily the northeastern part of the United States, as it meant England and the adjacent parts of the continent for European industry. Mass production of standard items, usually consumer goods, by well-standardized production techniques was the most conspicuous achievement of American industry, and provides a yardstick against which we can set the science-based industries.

It takes only a moment's thought to realize that the traditional picture has very little relevance to much of our present economy. It does not, for example, explain the booming city of Phoenix, Ariz., which has no coal, no iron, no water transportation. Phoenix exists for other reasons. It makes high-value products, based principally on electronics. People like to live there, and transportation requirements for such high-value articles are of minimal importance. The specialized production techniques required by the industry can be practiced there as well as anywhere else. Very similar statements could be made for most other science-based industries. They are located where they are for a variety of reasons—tradition, industry centralization, congenial surroundings, intellectual atmosphere—but seldom on account of any very compelling physical considerations.

We have laid stress on these geographical considerations because they bear so directly on the House committee's concern with the United States' position of international leadership. In the traditional view, we think of the economic and industrial position of the United States as a reflection in part of her generous endowment of natural resources. Obviously, in such highly technological areas, these considerations no longer apply. If an electronics industry can take root in Phoenix, it can take root in Libya, the Congo, Tokyo, Bombay, or anywhere else, so far as objective physical factors are concerned. Thus, the position of the United States in such fields depends entirely on the technical and management skills of its people.

Another contrast with the traditional view becomes apparent when we turn to the details of production processes. Typically, in the science-based industries, one deals with relatively small quantities of (sometimes) very expensive raw materials, and subjects them to a complex fabrication process. The problems of materials and parts handling, production flow, and so forth, which are so conspicuous in normal mass production, are of little importance. Instead, one is concerned primarily with very elaborate process control for a wide range of processes. The "clean room" and the instrumentation center are standard equipment.

The complexity of these processes can be illustrated by a simple look at the range of materials involved in typical cases. The aerospace industry, for example, must deal with a considerable variety of structural materials in addition to the conventional steel and aluminum, for reasons connected with weight, high-temperature strength, dimensional stability, and other qualities. The fact that beryllium, let us say, is perhaps a thousand times as expensive as steel, and raises metallurgical and fabrication problems all its own, is not decisive when beryllium solves a critical problem. Similarly, it turns out that the communications-electronics industry makes purposeful use, in one way or another, of at least half of all the chemical elements, including a number that were little more than chemical curiosities a generation ago. In some cases they are used only in trace amounts, but the traces are important.

The discussion of science given in an earlier section made the point that in relying more heavily on instrumentation and other equipment, experimental science was in some ways drawing more closely to technology. Similarly, in dealing with comparatively small quantities of material in very elaborate and carefully controlled ways, technology begins to take on some of the character of experimental science. As in many areas of experimental science, advances frequently turn on the discovery of clever techniques to deal with hitherto elusive or intractable phenomena.

The development of such sophisticated technologies carries with it two implications worth noticing. First, as such technologies become more specialized and more difficult, they become less and less accessible to traditional mass-production techniques. Thus it is necessary to cultivate them directly at whatever level the country's interests demand. This is especially important because of their significance for defense. One estimate (*3*) puts the fraction of defense material needs currently requiring special-purpose production facilities as high as 90 percent. This is in contrast to the situation in World Wars I and II, where half or three-quarters of military equipment was essentially peacetime goods and most of the rest could be obtained from converted peacetime equipment. It obviously implies that we are not likely to win future wars by World War II's "production miracle."

The other implication has to do with the kind of effort required to develop such technologies in the first place. We took note in the last section of the large and varied technical effort required, in the Manhattan Project, to go from the initial discovery of nuclear fission to a workable bomb. On a more modest scale, a similar history occurs repeatedly in the science-based industries. A good example is furnished by the development of the transistor. The transistor itself arose from a deliberate and aggressive effort to exploit the new field of solid-state physics. To support the work, however, one needed competence in a variety of related areas. Crystallography was one, for example, since crystal structure is basic to the solid state. Methods of growing very large and nearly perfect single crystals was another, since without such units one could not easily know what he was doing. Since very minute impurities of the order of 1 in 100 million have appreciable effects in semiconductors, a separate investigation of the means of making substances to such extraordinary degrees of purity was needed. Once the basic transistor discovery was made, it was still necessary to put it to practical application by aggressive specialized work in many fields. This involved investigations of production techniques for making the necessary materials, for protecting the units, for developing circuit designs and auxiliary devices to permit their particular properties to be used successfully in circuits, and so on. As in the Manhattan Project, the work on supporting technology was not over when the first transistor was operated, or the first bomb exploded. A continuing effort on a wide range of supporting technology has been necessary to carry both fields forward.

A somewhat similar situation exists in the aerospace field. A ballistic missile, for example, is a complex of systems designed to give structural strength, heat shielding, guidance and control, and propulsion. All of these are supported by complex technologies, and the history of advance in the missile field has been largely a history of successive improvements in these technologies. In some cases this effort has been a matter of straightforward engineering, but in others the problems have been so difficult and have required such frequent return to first principles that they are best characterized as "applied research." Military considerations almost always lead in the long run to a large premium for moderate increases in weapon performance. In addition, rocket performance tends in any case to be abnormally sensitive to small changes, especially in propulsion and weight allowances. The inevitable result is great pressure to achieve the highest possible refinement of technology in every aspect of the design.

An industrial laboratory, or similar organization, is the natural means to carry forward the sort of technological effort described in this section. Such a laboratory, if it is of adequate size, can maintain the necessary array of skills to attack either new or old technologies on a broad front, including interdisciplinary problems as they arise. It can also offer the scientific perspective to see what most needs working on in new and comparatively ill-defined areas. Such a laboratory is also able to maintain a close coupling with the world of science, particularly if it is in a position to do a reasonable amount of basic research itself. Thus, it is in a particularly good position to recognize a relevant scientific advance, and perhaps to supply promptly the many bits and pieces that may be called for if the advance is to be turned to practical account.

The fact that so many industrial laboratories find it to their advantage to dedicate a significant fraction of their total effort to basic research (10 percent or so is a representative figure for the larger laboratories) is of special interest for the purposes of this paper. It evidently implies the desirability of very close coupling between basic science and technology in the modern world. The days when the United States could subsist on imported science and homegrown technology are well behind us.

COMPLEXITY AND SMALL NUMBERS

There is one other important way in which the science-based industries tend to differ from the traditional mass-production operations. It has been reserved for a separate section because it leads naturally into a discussion of some related questions concerning large single technological projects. The traditional American economy was an ever-expanding one in which the number of units of any sort increased steadily. This is what "mass production" meant. In consumer goods this still tends to be true. If we look in other areas, however, we find that technological advance often goes in another direction. There is a tendency for greater outputs to be obtained from increase in the size and complexity of individual units and the improvement of utilization factors. Thus, actual numbers of individual units may remain about constant or even diminish.

Most of us are accustomed to the fact that construction machinery, such as earth-moving machinery, seems to grow larger every year. A few large, if expensive, units are more efficient than a larger number of small units. A similar tendency appears to hold in the industries we are talking about here, except that the growth is now not primarily in gross physical size but in speed and in complexity and refinement of design. For example, the total computer capacity of the country has been growing recently by a large factor each year. The growth, however, appears to be due primarily not to increased numbers of computers but to great increases in the speed and working capability of the most advanced types. (A very fast computer must be quite small in overall dimensions, for basic physical reasons, so that working capacity tends to increase, in fact, through the use of larger and larger numbers of very small, but highly refined, components.)

In the long-distance communications before the war, the maximum traffic that could be supported by a pair of conductors was about a dozen simultaneous conversations, or perhaps a few hundred for a cable full of conductors. The corresponding figure that the art would support now is of the order of three or four thousand for the pair of conductors, or some tens of thousands for a complete cable. Of course, both the cable and conductors and the supporting electronic equipment would be much more elaborate, but the overall system nevertheless shows a net gain in efficiency. A comparison of the numbers and performance of our present fleet of B–52's with our World War II B–29's shows the same trend in the military sphere.

The most familiar example, however, is in air transport. In the mid-1930's, the DC–3 was the bellweather of transport planes. The total production, including a very large military production during World War II, was about 11,000 (*4*). After the war these planes continued in use for short flights (about 1,400 are still in service). Their longdistance flights, however, were gradually taken over by larger four-engine planes typified by DC–6's and Constellations. A thousand or so such planes were made in the decade after the war. This seems a relatively small number, considering the great increase in the amount of air traffic. However, each plane could carry several times as many passengers as the DC–3, and was also substantially faster, so that it could provide at least five or six times as many passenger miles per day.

In recent years these propeller-driven planes have, in turn, been displaced for long-distance flights by the modern subsonic jets. This has again entailed a reduction in total numbers. There are about five or six hundred jets of the longest-range types in the country, but each is roughly twice as large and twice as fast as the DC–6's and Constellations, so that they represent considerably more traffic capacity. The supersonic transport plane, if it arrives, will provide a further step in the same direction. It will be still larger, and, of course, significantly faster than a subsonic jet. One estimate places the world market for such planes as low as 200.

Such trends as these have several consequences. With so small a number of articles to be built, the approach to the production problem obviously must differ greatly from the traditional mass-production tack. In some areas, such as electronics, design ingenuity allows us to reclaim some of the savings of quantity production through designs that consist largely of replications of standard subassemblies, and can be automated. However, in other areas, preparation for production consists largely of the preparation of appropriate jigs and patterns. The numbers involved are too small to make it worth while to automate the actual process of fabrication.

Another implication is more important for the purposes of the present inquiry. Obviously, many more engineering hours must be put into the design of these very complex items than were required for their simpler predecessors. As the number of produced items dwindles, however, this greater engineering investment must be supported by smaller and smaller numbers of finished products. Thus, the cost relation between production and engineering development moves farther and farther from the proportions that obtained historically. In some areas of the aerospace industry, for example, there are now supposed to be only five production workers for each research and development employee. In the past, a ratio more like 50 to 1 would have been expected, even in such technologically advanced areas. Where these technological trends obtain, we must expect development costs to be a substantial fraction of overall production costs, and not a meager fraction as they have normally been in the past. This also has an indirect bearing on the desirable scale of support for basic research. It means that when there is a reasonable prospect that the research will benefit development efforts significantly, we are justified in a higher level of activity than we might have been willing to contemplate in the past.

A final point is the fact that the total development bill must be paid before even one unit is available. There is no way of "easing into" the situation. One cannot test the design or the market in a small way. We saw in the last section that the replacement of physical capital by technologically more advanced equipment could be expected to take place in quantum steps, after an accumulation of research results had provided such a large potential for improvement that the costs of replacing still-usable equipment could readily be borne. Obviously, large development charges represent an influence that tends to make the quantum step still larger. In some instances the estimated rate of technical advance may also enter the calculation. In other words, one may elect to defer an attractive development for a few years in the hope of doing still better later on. This makes the quantum step larger yet.

The importance of accumulating an adequate base of new science and technology before proceeding with a development shows itself with particular clarity in systems that depend on advanced technology in several different areas. An example is furnished by a communications satellite like Telstar or Relay. This is cited in one of the other papers as a technological advance that depended on a totally unexpected research result—in this case the discovery of the maser. It is true that the maser, though not quite indispensable, is a very effective contributor to the efficiency of the satellite system. On the other hand, a number of other elements are also important. For example, solar batteries, as the source of power for the electronics in the vehicle, are critical elements. They were also an unexpected result from research, this time from semiconductor physics. Similarly, solid-state circuitry itself is also indispensable, as are many of the technical modulation schemes and other specifically communications aspects of the system. The dependence of the system upon advances in launching rockets is, of course, also obvious.

The success of such a project thus depends on the existence of a full storehouse of interrelated techniques on which to draw. The depth and adequacy of the supporting technology are what count. In this respect, the communications satellite, or the supersonic transport, are at least broadly akin to the atomic bomd and the transistor, which we discussed earlier.

On the other hand, even when such a storehouse exists there may be many remaining problems. The formulation of a suitable system, with the right combination of elements and the best "trade-offs" among the various aspects of the design, may itself be an engineering challenge of considerable difficulty. In a commercial situation, this planning or "systems-engineering" phase must include all the factors of cost, timing, probable markets, and other factors mentioned in the air-transport discussion. Moreover, the full storehouse is a somewhat elastic concept. In normal application it is likely to mean that, while technical approaches to all aspects of the plan are known, we will not always have had actual experience with them on the scale or to the accuracy desired. This, in turn, may call for an estimate of the real degree of technological risk in each aspect of the design, and provision for parallel or alternative courses of action where necessary. This initial planning stage is a much more difficult as well as a much more important activity than it was in earlier times, when technology took less bold steps. It seems impossible to overdo either the quality or the amount of the effort that ought, in principle, to be assigned to it.

This discussion has been at such length because the questions of technical planning and management it raises apply broadly to a whole class of ambitious technical projects. These are, moreover, projects that are especially likely to require Federal support; thus they are particularly relevant to this inquiry. Examples are found in the military and space fields, in "big science," and in various proposals for new types of metropolitan transportation systems, water management, and the like. In detail, projects in these various areas are likely to raise different sorts of questions. In the military area, for example, one is likely to be concerned with balancing technological risk against schedules and military performance; in "big science" one is, or should be, concerned with the trade-off between engineering costs and scientific results; in the other proposals one may be concerned with a whole host of social and economic considerations. However, the basic questions concerning the justification for undertaking a project at a given time, or at all (as illustrated by the supersonic transport)—the adequacy of the technical base and the technical plan erected on it (as illustrated by the communications satellite), and finally the skill of the organization to carry the project through to completion—arise in all fields and are often not easy to answer.

This leads to the final point of this paper. The advance of science and technology often makes the job of technical planning and management much more critical as well as more difficult than it has normally been thought to be in the past. There are two general reasons for this: We are likely to be working in new and relatively unexplored technical areas, where one must make adequate judgments of probable performance and reliability, and of the best ways of realizing them, on the basis of skimpy or nonexistent experience. In addition, we may be dealing with complex and elaborate systems involving a maze of economic and technical considerations, all of which must be thought through in detail and brought into harmonious accord if the outcome is to be successful. Particularly in evaluating complex new projects, these planning and management factors, as well as the intrinsic desirability of the final result, need to be considered.

CONCLUSION

This discussion is intended primarily to be a background for the other papers of this collection rather than a direct response to the House committee's questions directly. To give the paper as much point as possible, however, it seems advisable to add a few words to emphasize points that appear to have at least broad relevance to the issues raised by the House committee.

The first question of the House committee has to do with the appropriate scale of support for basic research. I have not dealt with this question directly. Some incidental remarks about the contribution of scientific success to the international prestige of the United States provide an indirect measure, by inviting comparison with other expenditures to improve our prestige. My remarks on the general rise in research and development costs as a fraction of total production costs in certain areas may also be relevant. In my opinion, there is not much danger that first-class scientific work in the country will be oversupported. No doubt, one would always want to be a bit chary about second-rate work. However, a monetary ceiling on research support does not seem to be a very satisfactory approach to such a problem. It calls instead for internal policing by the scientific community. Any real consideration of such questions must, of course, allow for the fact that research is done in government and industrial laboratories, as well as at universities, and problems of motivation or mission definition, standards, financial support, and leadership may be very different in these various settings.

The Committee's second question, on the areas of science that most deserve support, is not answered very directly either. However, the section on the characteristics of modern science does have some indirect bearing on it. Obviously, the most inviting areas tend to be those in which science demonstrates that it can make the most progress. Thus, the remarks in that section on the gradual diffusion of science into more complex and less tractable fields, on the role of cross-fertilization between scientific fields, and the use of new methods and new instruments in individual fields, are all indicators of potentially rewarding areas for support.

It may be helpful also to recall some of the usual canons of quality in scientific research. Novelty is certainly one; the importance of discovering a new and unpredicted phenomenon requires no argument. Beyond this, the principal criterion can perhaps be described as a sort of intellectual efficiency in getting a great understanding of, and command over, nature for a small price. The generality of the result and the perspective it sheds on a wide range of situations, in other words, are important indices. The fascinating feature of Newton's law of gravitation was the fact that it applied to every particle of the universe. Such a formulation does not rule out the systematic experimental work that constitutes the backbone of science, but it is almost the opposite of defining research as the mere satisfaction of idle curiosity or the indiscriminate heaping up of disjointed facts, without pattern or purpose.

Such criteria as these are too general for routine administrative evaluation of individual projects. Scientific judgment is still required. They do, however, suggest some broad emphases. For example, the criterion of novelty tends to strengthen the role of the individual worker as against the role of "big science." The big scientific project usually exists in the first place only because we think we can foresee, at least dimly, what its results may be. Of course, it may yield something quite new that could not be found by any other means. However, a large fraction of the totally unpredictable discoveries, which furnish the starting point for later important fields, are still made by individuals. Thus, while modern physics advances through multi-million-dollar high-energy machines, it also advances through phonograph turntables in the hands of a Mossbauer. In a copious era, synthesizing and integrating concepts are of particular importance if generality of result is to be achieved. Thus, the same set of criteria suggests special support for areas of work (usually theoretical) that are promising here.

The bulk of my paper, however, is directed not to science but to technology, or rather to the interaction between science and technology. In summary, I have tried to show that, until comparatively recent years, science and technology pursued essentially independent courses. Advances in science affected technology only gradually, and, one might almost say accidentally. There were only a few areas, such as the pioneer industrial laboratories, and public health or medical and agricultural laboratories or experimental stations, in which the applications of science were pursued in a systematic and determined way.

The deliberate application of science to technology on a broad scale is primarily a phenomenon of the war and post-war years. The change has come about partly because science now has more to offer than it ever had before. It is also due in large part to the fact that the public, principally because of wartime experience, now accepts the idea that science is applicable to technology, and looks to such applications as a mainspring for progress.

Since the deliberate application of science to technology in most areas of the country's life is so new, it may not be surprising that it presents a number of problems. The discussion in the section on the characteristics of modern technology, and in particular the later discussion of the problems of technical planning and management of complex projects, were intended to illustrate some of these. Perhaps it is also not surprising that the results in various areas of our society turn out to be uneven.

It is the major conclusion of this paper that these difficulties and unevennesses in the transition from science to technology represent the most critical aspect of the issues raised by the questions of the House committee —the aspect the most needs attention if the country is to maximize the yield from its investment in basic science. There are several ways in which we can think of bettering the situation. For example, since the application of science to technology does not come about all by itself, one way is through a consideration of the possible agencies—industrial laboratory, Government laboratory, or whatnot—that may do the job. The principles of operation that will make any one of these agencies actually successful in its appropriate setting, however, present an important problem in their own right, which goes well beyond the scope of this paper.

Another means of improvement relates to the people required. In my description of technology, I emphasized the need for applied research and for careful advance planning in new areas. The men one would like for such work are easy to describe. They should obviously be highly trained. To work well in interdisciplinary situations, of which they can expect a great many, they should be well enough and broadly enough acquainted with science to understand its structure and motivation. Since they will be close to the research frontier in many cases, they also need direct experience with research. In this respect they should be on the same footing as the typical pure scientist. At the same time, one should surely want men who also have enough engineering background and interest to operate effectively in essentially engineering situations.

Whether or not this ideal is often realized, the country is dependent on the universities for a sufficient supply of reasonable approximations to it, as well as for its supply of pure scientists (*5*). Federal support of research in universities is one of the principal means of assuring an adequate flow of new scientists, and, in gauging the level of support, it is important that needs of both sorts be understood.

A third approach is simply to recognize how much science and technology actually have in common. The descriptions of modern science and technology given in this paper were intended to stress some of these resemblances, including in particular the growing interdependence of the two areas in methods and techniques. In addition to methods, the two fields, when seen from a distance, seem to be growing together in everyday outlook. As we noted a few pages back, the objective of scientific research can be broadly described as understanding nature in an intellectually efficient manner. Similarly, the objective of technology can be described as control of the natural world to bring about prescribed results. But, in the context in which advanced technology now finds itself, understanding and control are inseparable. In very many cases the first and most crucial step is simply to establish a sufficiently thorough and fundamental understanding of a situation by procedures similar to those of pure science. Seen in this perspective, technology appears as a natural extension of science rather than as something essentially different.

REFERENCES

1. Listed are the numbers of patents issued by countries to their own nationals. In European countries, especially, the gross rate of patenting is frequently much greater because of the large number of patents issued to "foreigners" (frequently Americans) who wish to secure patent coverage in countries other than their own. Source: Publication No. 17 of the Subcommittee on Patents, Trademarks and Copyrights, U. S. Senate Committee on the Judiciary, December 1958. The U. S. S. R. is not included in table 6 for lack of comparable data.
2. This is not intended to minimize the ultimate importance of pure research, since the effectiveness of the applied research effort may itself depend on the storehouse of information on which it can draw. It says, however, that in evaluating basic research we should lay stress on broad increases in understanding rather than on specific advances.
3. "New Realities and Old Concepts" by Dr. Peter F. Drucker, *The General Electric Defense Quarterly,* vol. 2, No. 1, January–March, 1959.
4. The number of planes that actually entered commercial service is no doubt very much smaller, but exact figures are not readily at hand. The number given does not include several thousand additional planes produced in other countries. Also omitted from the general discussion, for the sake of simplicity, are designs like the DC-4, which was the actual immediate successor of the DC-3, as well as designs by other makers, which should be included in any comprehensive account.
5. In fact, of course, the two categories are not entirely separate, since many pure scientists eventually migrate into applied fields, thus automatically establishing a bridge between pure science and technology. This, however, does not affect the total number of people needed, although it may imply the desirability of giving more emphasis to breadth of training than is customarily given in modern scientific education.

SCIENTIFIC RESEARCH AND THE INNOVATIVE PROCESS*

William J. Price
Exec. Director Air Force
Office Scientific Research

and

Lawrency W. Bass
Vice President (Retired)
A. D. Little, Inc.

The dialogue between science and technology plays an important, but usually nonlinear, role in innovation.

The process of change is a central feature of the individual and organizational environments of modern man. The creating of new attitudes, new ways of doing things, new forms of social relationships, new products, new industrial practices—in short, innovation in the broad sense of the word—demands our attention, not only because of the results of change but also because of the extent to which the process of change is becoming a way of life.

Understanding the innovative process is therefore of paramount importance. The part played by technology—and we use this term to include product- or process-directed applied science—is generally understood and accepted, but what about basic research which has as its principal goal the discovery and organization of knowledge? Does scientific research play a central role in the innovative process, and, if so, how?

The conventional views based on the idea that innovation usually starts from new understanding give the answer "yes." We also believe that the answer is certainly "yes." It has become increasingly clear, however, especially through several recent studies, that the demonstration of the role of science in innovation requires focus on the nature and intensity of the dialogue between the scientific and technological communities, rather than on a preoccupation with the role of new scientific knowledge as the fountainhead from which innovation springs.

---

* *Science*, 16 May 1969.

INNOVATION, INVENTION, AND RESEARCH

The innovative process includes invention. Invention is the creation of an idea and its reduction to practice; innovation is the bringing of the invention into widespread use.

Scientific research is characterized by the continuous accumulation and ordering of new knowledge. Each research contribution generally builds on what has gone before. Concurrently, ordering takes place through laws and theories evloving within the scientific disciplines.

The process of sophisticated invention is related to orderly arrangement in the continuum of knowledge, because such invention requires the existence of a body of relevant information before ideas can come to fruition. Since the process of invention requires, however, a simultaneous connection of the knowledge with an external situation for potential utilization of the invention, it is a special case of ordering. Nevertheless, the dependence of invention on the relevant body of science means that innovation can be related to the search for new understanding, particularly in radically new technologies, such as the transistor and nuclear-energy technologies.

World War II undoubtedly had a profound influence on conventional views concerning the relationship of science and technology. Many persons who were engaged in scientific research when the war broke out helped exploit scientific knowledge, thus bringing about many important innovations in a short time. Unfortunately, from the standpoint of understanding the role of science in innovation, the fact is often overlooked that, during the war emergency, the vast majority of the scientists involved were working not as basic researchers but as technologists.

It is not surprising, therefore, that innovation is often viewed as an orderly process, starting with the discovery of new knowledge, moving through various stages of development, and eventually emerging in final, viable form. According to this "linear" model, innovation seems to be a rational process, essentially similar to the other, more systematic functions of an organization. The assumption is that it can be analyzed into component parts and controlled rationally—that is to say, planned, programmed, and managed much as other, more routine activities are.

The studies reviewed here indicate that the "linear" model is not typical. One appreciates the nonrational nature of the innovative process when one notes that the more novel the invention is, the less orderly and predictable is the process. The introduction of a new cake flour may be managed rationally. On the other hand, radical innovations often require that the organizations which adopt them undergo major internal changes, many of which cannot be programmed in advance.

William J. Price and Lawrence W. Bass

RECENT STUDIES OF INNOVATION

Several studies of the innovative process have shed considerable light on the role of scientific research. We review three of these briefly and refer to several others.

Materials Advisory Board study

A panel of R&D managers, led by Morris Tanenbaum, director of research and development of the Western Electric Corporation, recently completed a study (*1*) of research-engineering interactions for the Materials Advisory Board of the National Research Council. Each participant selected and documented a case which he believed clearly illustrated productive collaboration between scientific research and engineering. Ten case histories were analyzed. They concerned developments in metals, ceramics, and synthetic polymers. The participants searched the records for patterns of events and circumstances which recurred frequently.

The point which stood out most clearly was that, in nine of the ten cases, explicit recognition of an important need was identified as a major stimulus in bringing about the research-engineering interactions. Basic research by itself rarely produced a technological opportunity which was quickly recognized and developed. Far more frequently, an urgent need initiated a search for a solution from prior basic knowledge. An individual with a well-defined concept of a technological need started the successful research-engineering interaction.

In most of the cases, the science that led to the technological solution was available before the dialogue began. Rarely did the technological need directly stimulate generation of the science used to solve the problem. Also, the fruitful interactions occurred between organizationally independent groups which were often geographically separated.

In only three cases did the majority of the research-engineering interaction events involve in any way individuals whose principal interest was in basic research. However, if consideration was restricted to development of the idea through the invention stage, then in more than half of the events interaction with a basic research finding or a basic researcher was found to be important.

Dow Chemical Company study

A study made by compiling and analyzing the histories of several innovations important to Dow Chemical Company has recently been published by Boyer and his associates (*2*). Members of the company team conducting this investigation found that successful innovations typically involved the complex interplay of concepts and people along a highly branched and unpredictable path. They concluded that "uniqueness cannot be programmed." Their story is concerned with "how different people and different groups interact with each other across substantial barriers (groups, disciplines, geography, etc.) to produce unique results that no individual or no single group is likely to accomplish alone." Important sources of scientific knowledge were research initiated in various parts of Dow because of scientific curiosity, Dow consultants from universities, new employees who had been recently engaged in scholarly research in graduate school, visiting lecturers, technical meetings, journal articles, and input from management.

In summary, the group listed the important sources of uniqueness as access to a large number of original research investigations, however inspired; sustained financial support; means to facilitate communications be tween groups and disciplines; a creative approach to the marketing of unique concepts and ideas; and a desire for uniqueness on the part of management.

Air Force study

Recently the Air Force Office of Scientific Research (AFOSR) made a study (*3*) of the benefits accruing to this service through the support of basic research, primarily in universities, during the last decade and a half. This study, which included material obtained from a large group of persons with thorough knowledge of these investigations—for example, principal investigators—has provided considerable specific information on how the innovative processes pursued by the Air Force have benefited from this support.

The study shows that AFOSR has helped "colonize" many scientific areas which have turned out to have special relevance to important applications. "Colonizing" may be described as increasing the chance of important discovery in an area by accelerating the world's scientific activity in that field. Air Force programs for the support of scientific research and such other activities as symposia, amplified by funding from other sources, have affected very significantly the rate of development of vital areas—for example, hypersonics, magnetic resonance spectroscopy, control theory, visual perception, mass transfer cooling, information theory, cryogenics, and quantum electronics.

This study also found many specific instances in which AFOSR-supported scientific research had provided important inputs to weapons development at all phases of the research, engineering, and production cycle. Contributions were identified with new or improved manufacturing procedures, design techniques, instrumentation, and weapons-systems-component concepts, to mention a few cases. In addition, many of the scientists supported by AFOSR have been helped to achieve and maintain their expertise, and this in turn has made it possible for them to consult and make other direct contributions to the innovative process.

Finally, both in the AFOSR study and in the Department of Defense's Project Hindsight (*4*), the importance of Department of Defense research support of postgraduate education was underlined. For example, at any one time the AFOSR is providing at least partially for the research of more than a thousand doctoral candidates and of many more candidates at the master's level. The overall impact is apparent from the observation that these graduate students rank at the top of the nation's younger generation of scientists and are developing their expertise in areas particularly relevant to Department of Defense interests.

Additional studies

Sumner Myers (*5*), in a survey of 567 innovations in the housing, computer, and railroad industries, placed particular emphasis on the source of externally generated scientific data and on the impact of these data in stimulating technological developments. He concluded that new scientific knowledge seldom starts the process but, rather, that successful innovation comes from the synergistic combination of several ideas, many derived from unrelated R&D.

The Illinois Institute of Technology Research Institute, in collaboration with the National Science Foundation, reported (*6*) a historical tracing of events leading to five major technological innovations (magnetic ferrites, video-tape recorders, oral contraceptive pills, electron microscopes and matrix isolation). Of the 341 distinct key research and development events judged to be important to these innovations, three-fourths came from work believed to be motivated by the search for knowledge and understanding without special regard for application.

Marquis and Allen (*7*), in studying information flow in various R&D laboratories, have been struck with the important role of persons to whom colleagues often turn for technical advice and critiques. These persons, whom they call "technological gatekeepers," are typically heavy readers who also have wide contacts with scientific and technical workers in other organizations, including active researchers in universities.

Rosenbloom and Wolek (*8*) also underlined the importance of information obtained from the external scientific and technological communities.

They reached their conclusion by analyzing the responses of 2000 scientists and engineers from 13 establishments of four corporations and the responses of 1200 members of the Institute of Electrical and Electronic Engineers, who were queried on where and how they received useful information from a source other than their immediate circle of colleagues.

Still another valuable source of information about the interaction of science and technology is the National Academy of Sciences Report for the U. S. House of Representatives Committee on Science and Astronautics (*9*). For example, Suits and Bueche, in analyzing many case histories in the General Electric Research Laboratory, have emphasized the diversity in the types of innovations, the source of the "nucleating event," and the nature of the flow of crucial information.

Several recent articles in *Science* connecting frontier fields of research with developments in technology also give important insights. For instance, Townes (*10*) emphasizes the element of surprise, which could not be planned, in the innovations made possible by quantum electronics. Also, Shirley's discussion (*11*) of the interaction between experimental nuclear physics and the development of instrumentation for chemical research illustrates the synergistic effect in what might appear to be two quite independent fields.

In summary, these studies show three things.

1) Although the discovery of new knowledge is not the typical starting point for the innovative process, very frequently interaction with new knowledge or with persons actively engaged in scientific research is essential.

2) Innovation typically depends on information for which the requirement cannot be anticipated in definitive terms and therefore cannot be programmed in advance; instead, key information is often provided through unrelated research. The process is facilitated by a great deal of freedom and flexibility in communication across organizational, geographical, and disciplinary lines.

3) The function of basic research in the innovative process can often be described as meaningful dialogue between the scientific and the technological communities. The entrepreneurs for the innovative process usually belong to the latter sector, while the persons intimately familiar with the necessary scientific understanding are often part of the former.

MODEL OF THE INNOVATIVE PROCESS

The innovative process may be described (*12*, pp. 21–31) as a complex feedback-type information processing system. One can bring the role of scientific research into focus by looking for the individual science-technology interactions in this information flow. To achieve this focusing, the nature of both the scientific and technological communities should be kept in mind.

Historical and sociological studies (*13*) suggest that science and technology are two relatively independent worlds, each with its own values, goals, and methods. The members of the scientific community pursue the goal of the discovery and organization of new knowledge. New science may forge ahead with relative independence from an ambient technology, although the results of research are made available to both scientists and technologists in many ways. Members of the technological community pursue innovation and related activities. Technological events are usually initiated within technology, in the presence, however, of an ambient, but often important, science.

Thus, the gross picture is that technology usually feeds upon technology and scientific research usually feeds upon other science. It is essential, however, to emphasize the intensity, variety, and effectiveness of the dialogue between the two communities.

This interface is dynamic, varying greatly among different science-technology pairs, and also chronologically for a given area of application. Industries such as communications and computers are much more closely coupled with science than the railroad and agricultural-equipment industries are. Transistor technology was more closely coupled with solid-state physics 15 years ago than it is today.

Any study, such as the Department of Defense Project Hindsight (*4*), which concentrates on isolating the points of origin of technological events will usually reveal that they lie within technology. However, it is invalid to conclude from this finding that "undirected" research—that is, research in the scientific community, not related directly to the technology concerned—was of little help to the innovation which occurred. On the contrary, the other studies cited in this article make it abundantly clear that this research is a highly essential part of the innovative process. It is unfortunate that some people have quoted the first interim report of Project Hindsight, concerning the small identified contribution of "undirected" academic research to weapons system development, without taking into account the severe limitations of the Project Hindsight methodology (*4*) for evaluating the contribution of such research.

MANAGERIAL ASPECTS

Thus it is abundantly clear that any organization dependent on a science-based technology is, in turn, highly dependent on the scientific community.

The discussion of the organization and financing of basic research is beyond the scope of this article. Suffice it to say that the factor of surprise as a characteristic of technological development signifies that the self-interest of mission-oriented organizations requires strong support of basic research throughout the world, and appropriate design of the organizations' own activities in support of science, particularly in maintaining effective dialogue with the international scientific community (*14*). Because the utilization of new scientific knowledge in bringing about innovation increases in proportion to the intensity and effectiveness of the collaboration between the generators and users of information, the nature and mechanisms of these interactions, often called "coupling," deserve exploration (*15*).

Coupling is important to many members of the scientific community, whether they are university scientists seeking closer connection with the innovation being pursued by industry or government, or whether they are industrial or government scientists doing basic research in mission-oriented organizations. Coupling is especially important to technologists, who typically take the initiative by looking for solutions to problems. Specific goals and plans for the use of technology need to be defined, to provide a focus for interaction at the interfaces (*16*). The objectives should be dynamic, because progressive modification is usually required in the light of new knowledge and experience accumulated during the process.

By separating the several aspects or stages of introducing an innovative product, process, or service, one can appreciate the variety of the opportunities for coupling with basic science. Typical major stages of progress, correlated with the functions having the primary responsibilities for each stage, are given in Table 1. The terminology in Table 1 is that of an in-

TABLE 1

Major development stages for the application of criteria for feasibility

Stage	Activity with primary functional responsibility
Product concept	Applied Research
Product formulation	Applied Research
Process definition	Engineering Development
Marketing evaluation	Market Research
Process confirmation	Manufacturing
Market confirmation	Marketing
Comprehensive review	All departments
Decision to implement	Management
Corporate mobilization	All departments

dustrial organization, but a similar sequence of stages occurs, for example, in the introduction of a new weapons system.

As an illustration, let us consider the stage of "process definition." The Engineering Development group has primary responsibility, but needs cooperation and advice, in varying depth, from several other corporate functions. Product specifications should be under review by Applied Research and Market Research to confirm the acceptability of materials made on a pilot scale. The proposed raw materials should be scrutinized by Purchasing, and the process requirements and facilities should be evaluated by Central Engineering and Manufacturing. Preliminary cost estimates and capital requirements should be examined by Finance, while legal restrictions and patent matters should be considered by the appropriate specialists. Management may need to give the project interim approval, and Basic Research should be asked whether new knowledge bearing on the competitive feasibility of product or process has become available.

In industry it is becoming widely recognized that interactions between the specialized skills represented in different organizational functions should be encouraged throughout the course of development and commercialization. To shorten the path between the discovery of new knowledge and its applications, often several types of expertise need to be focused at successive stages. This may be best accomplished through the interdisciplinary team approach. The scientific background required by the team may be provided by a member of the basic research laboratory or by a consultant.

NATURE AND MECHANISM OF COUPLING

The intensity of interaction between scientists and technologists provides a basis for classifying coupling into four main types. The divisions between these types are by no means sharp.

1) "Indirect coupling" denotes lack of direct dialogue between the originators and the users of new scientific knowledge. The technologist, recognizing that recorded knowledge is likely to have an impact on the solution of his problem, conducts a survey of the literature to locate pertinent items. Here, technologists with recent postgraduate education in the relevant science have the advantage. Review articles and up-to-date monographs are of help in locating available sources of information.

It is the consensus in many organizations, particularly in those with a strong basic research component, that indirect coupling is not adequate to support an aggressive program of development in areas where many scientific discoveries are being made. The chances that technologists will comprehend the applicability of rapidly proliferating knowledge and that academic scientists will make the best possible selection of pertinent subjects of research are, it is felt, too limited to provide a sustaining base for the desired rate of innovation.

2) "Passive availability" describes the situation in which scientists are open to approach by technologists desiring their advice, but take no special initiative to stimulate the dialogues. The technologists select the areas in which they believe they can obtain help and then establish contacts with specific scientists in their quest for assistance. This process may be stimulated by establishing joint advisory committees of scientists and technologists, both for selecting research areas and for working on problems of development. If university and institutional researchers are given information about industry's and government's need for scientific knowledge, they are likely to adopt a more positive attitude toward cooperation in problem solving.

3) Direct participation in project work by scientists as consultants or advisors establishes a two-way partnership. Establishment of joint workshop groups promotes knowledge of interface problems on the one hand and of information resources on the other. Organizational and financial arrangements that allow scientists to take part in demonstration phases of projects induce appreciation of the difficulties of practical application. Exchanges of university and government-industry scientists can be productive. Limited support of applied research in universities can catalyze coupling.

One of the most successful techniques for establishing direct participation is the organization of interdisciplinary project teams, discussed by Bass (*17*) and by Hughes (*18*). In this type of operation each problem is assigned to a group of individuals, with different skills and backgrounds, who often apply their expertise on a part-time or interim basis. A team leader coordinates the attack: he determines the degree of effort needed from each member, and the timing of that effort; establishes the pattern of communication and liaison; and has overall responsibility for completion of the task.

The interdisciplinary approach, whether formal or informal, is also a pragmatic technique for information retrieval. Each participant may be expected to have thorough knowledge of his speciality. When his efforts are focused on a specific objective, he can effectively review and select those items that are important to the solution.

4) The "gatekeeper" function is a means used by many organizations to encourage coupling by direct action. A few gifted individuals are assigned responsibility for seeking instances in which an exchange of information between scientists and engineers is thought to be desirable and then for

TABLE 2
Frequency of use of coupling method

Category of coupling	Number of coupling events		
	Suits and Bueche*	Frey and Goldman*	Tanenbaum *et al.*†
1) Indirect	8	5	25
2) Passive availability	28	17	43
3) Direct participation	38	18	40
4) Gatekeeper	14	2	6

* See (*9*).
† See (*1*).

bringing about such exchanges either directly or through stimulation of the appropriate dialogues.

"Gatekeepers" must be competent scientists with broad research interests yet with a bent toward practical applications. This combination of talents is rare, and success in this operation also requires the attribute of being able to communicate effectively and persuasively with both scientists and technologists. "Gatekeepers" may, and often do, act on a part-time basis, continuing direct participation in research projects to maintain their intimate contact with new knowledge in their spheres of interest.

5) The technique of communication used depends on many factors, such as the nature of the problem, the size and type of organization, the physical location, and the personalities of the individuals. When we analyzed 244 coupling events identifiable in 27 of the case histories discussed by Suits and Bueche (see *9*), Frey and Goldman (see *9*), and Tanenbaum *et al.* (*1*), we found passive availability and direct participation predominating (see Table 2). Even though the identification and classification involved considerable subjectivity, the parallel structure of the data suggests that this is a valid conclusion.

SUMMARY

It is certainly true that basic scientific research is an essential part of the innovative process. It is important that we continue to attempt to understand further, and to communicate, the real nature of this role. It is also essential that we use this understanding to ensure that society obtains maximum benefit from scientific research and that the scientific community benefits from these growing relationships.

We believe that in many organizations the scientific and technological communities are quite effectively coupled now, but the growing importance of the process of change requires greater attention to such coupling. The Federal Council of Science and Technology program for improving the relationship between federal laboratories and universities (*19*), the American Chemical Society studies of university-industry relations (*20*), and the strong plea made by Herring (*21*) for additional review articles are important strides in this direction.

REFERENCES

1. M. Tanenbaum *et al.*, "Report of the Ad Hoc Committee on Principles of Research-Engineering Interaction," *Nat. Acad. Sci.—Nat. Res. Council Materials Advisory Board Pub. MAB 222-M* (1966).
1. R. Boyer, T. Selby, T. Tefft, paper presented before the American Chemical Society Symposium on the Innovative Process in Industry, San Francisco, 1968.
3. "AFOSR Research," *Air Force Office of Scientific Research Publications AFOSR 67-0300* (Clearinghouse for Federal Scientific and Technical Information, Washington, D. C., 1967).
4. D. S. Greenberg, *Science* 154, 872 (1966); P. H. Abelson, *ibid*, p. 1123; C. W. Sherwin and R. S. Isenson, *ibid.* 156, 1571 (1967).
5. S. Myers, "Technology Transfer and Industrial Innovation," *R&D Utilization Project, Nat. Planning Ass. Pub. M8961* (1967).
6. *Technology in Retrospect and Critical Events in Science* (prepared by the Illinois Institute of Technology Research Institute for the National Science Foundation, 1968), vol. 1.
7. D. G. Marquis and T. J. Allen, *Amer. Psychologist* 21, 1052 (1966); T. J. Allen and S. I. Cohen, "Information Flow in an R&D Laboratory," *Nat. Sci. Found. Pub. NSF 217–66* (1966).
8. R. S. Rosenbloom and F. W. Wolek, *Technology, Information and Organization: Information Transfer in Industrial R&D* (Harvard Graduate School of Business Administration, Cambridge, Mass., 1967).
9. H. Brooks *et al.*, *Applied Science and Technological Progress* (Government Printing Office, Washington, D. C., 1967).
10. C. H. Townes, *Science* 159, 699 (1968).
11. D. A. Shirley, *ibid.* 161, 745 (1968).
12. J. A. Morton, in "Proceedings of a Conference on Technology Transfer and Innovation," *Nat. Sci. Found. Pub. NSF 67-5* (1967).

13. D. Price, *Technol. Culture* 6, 553 (1965); M. Kranzberg, *Amer. Scientist* 56, 21 (1968); ——, *ibid.* 55, 48 (1967).
14. The growing body of literature on this subject includes the following: L. W. Bass and B. S. Old, Eds., *Formulation of Research Policies* (AAAS, Washington, D. C., 1967); J. Weyl, Ed., *Research in the Service of National Purpose* (Government Printing Office, Washington, D. C., 1966); "The Fundamental Research Activity in a Technology-Dependent Organization," *Air Force Office of Scientific Research Publication AFOSR 65-2691* (Clearinghouse for Federal Scientific and Technical Information, 1965); "Planning Phenomena-Oriented Research in a Mission-Oriented Organization," *Air Force Office of Scientific Research Publication OSR 68-1759* (Clearinghouse for Federal Scientific and Technical Information, 1968); *Basic Research in the Navy* (Report for Naval Research Advisory Committee, prepared by Arthur D. Little, Inc., Cambridge, Mass., 1959).
15. G. Martin and R. Willens, Eds., *Coupling Research and Production* (Interscience, New York, 1967); *Symposium on Interaction of Science and Technology* (University of Illinois, Urbana, 1967); "Proceedings of a Conference on Technology Transfer and Innovation," *Nat. Sci. Found. Pub. NSF 67-5* (1967); "Proceedings MIT Conference on Human Factors in the Transfer of Technology" (MIT Press, Cambridge, 1969).
16. See also J. R. Pierce, *Science* 159, 1079 (1968).
17. L. W. Bass, *The Management of Technical Programs* (Praeger, New York, 1965); ——, in *Handbook of Business Administration* (McGraw-Hill, New York, 1967), chap. V-III, pp. 5–41, 5–57; —— and F. N. Woodward, *Chem. Ind. London* 1967, 1890 (1967).
18. E. Hughes, *Harvard Business Rev.* 1968, 72 (1968).
19. "Education and the Federal Laboratories," *Fed. Council Sci. Technol. Rep.* (1968); *Symposium on Education and The Federal Laboratory-University Relationships* (Federal Council of Science and Technology, Washington, D. C., 1968).
20. M. Harris, *Sci. Res.* 1968, 38 (Oct. 1968); *Chem. Eng. News* 1967, 15 (Nov. 1967).
21. C. Herring, *Phys. Today* 21, No. 9, 27 (1968).

PERFORMANCE OF INFORMATION CHANNELS IN THE TRANSFER OF TECHNOLOGY*

Thomas J. Allen
Massachusetts Institute of Technology

There is rather general agreement[1] that the existing channels for communication both within and between the scientific and technological communities are not performing as well as they should. There is also a great lack of understanding of the way in which these channels actually function.

To increase our knowledge of the communication process in science and technology, a number of research studies have attempted to develop descriptive models of the existing communication systems. An understanding of the manner in which scientists and engineers presently obtain their information, while a major contribution, is not quite sufficient for our purposes. We would like to know more about the impact of various information-gathering practices upon the quality of the research[2] being performed. This would allow us to predict the effects which changes in the information services will have upon the scientist's or engineer's work.

To do this, we obviously require some criterion by which to measure research performance. Satisfactory techniques for determining absolute performance measures on an R&D project have yet to be devised; but the

* Presented at the M.I.T. Conference on Human Factors in the Transfer of Technology, May 19, 1966. The research reported in this paper was initially supported by a grant from the National Aeronautics and Space Administration (NaNsg 235–62), and since November 1963, by grants from the Office of Science Information Service, National Science Foundation (GN233 and GN353). The author gratefully acknowledges the aid of Maurice P. Andrien, Jr., Richard J. Bjelland, Stephen I. Cohen, Daniel S. Frischmuth, Richard H. Frank, Arthur Gerstenfeld, William D. Putt, and Peter G. Gerstberger, who participated as research assistants in various phases of the data collection, and expresses his appreciation to the companies, project managers and engineers who must remain anonymous but without whose help the study could not have been conducted.

[1] See for example: The Weinberg Report [9], [4], [5], and [6]; for a dissenting voice, [2].

[2] The term "research" will be used here in a generic sense, encompassing any and all activities from the basic to the developmental end of the R&D spectrum.

relative quality of solutions to the same problem can be assessed rather easily by a competent judge. This is the technique employed by experimental psychologists in studies of certain kinds of human problem-solving behavior (creative thinking, for example). Several persons are presented with the same problem and a panel of judges is asked to evaluate the relative quality of the answers. The parallel nature of the experimental design allows the psychologist to compare the behaviors observed and relate certain general behavior characteristics to the quality of the solutions produced.

Since we cannot yet afford to hire a sufficient number of scientists and engineers and assign them the same research problem, we must search for cases in which parallelism either occurred adventitiously or was consciously planned. The results presented here come from our first study of parallel research and constitute the third interim report on a continuing research program. The first series of parallel projects studied is made up entirely of government-supported efforts performed in industrial laboratories. All but one set of these projects are quite clearly developmental in nature and can be considered to fall within the realm of technology. The single deviant pair involved a rather fundamental investigation in physics and displays some rather interesting consequent differences in the information-gathering behavior of the investigators. Some of the differences will be pointed out as we go along, but first a word about the methods by which the data were obtained.

RESEARCH METHODS

Once a parallel project has been located, its work statement is obtained from the government laboratory awarding the contracts, analyzed and factored into a reasonable number of subproblem areas (generally subsystems). The breakdown is then checked with the technical person who prepared the work statement, and data collection forms are designed. After all data have been collected from the contractors, the technical monitor is asked to provide a confidential evaluation of each lab's performance on each subproblem. The data presented today were gathered by means of a form dubbed the Solution Development Record and from pre- and post-project interviews with the individual scientists and engineers.

The Solution Development Record is a research tool which provides a record of the progress of an individual engineer or group of engineers (or scientists) toward the solution of a research and development problem. The lead engineer responsible for each subproblem is asked to provide an estimate each week for each alternative approach of the probability that it will be finally chosen as the solution to that subproblem.

Figure 1. Solution Development Record

Manned Uranus Landing in an Early Time Period Study — General United Aerospace Corporation

Date .... Name ....

	Estimate of Probability that Alternative will be Employed										
Subproblem #1: Method of rendezvous at Uranus											
Alternative approaches:											
orbital rendezvous mission with excursion vehicle	0	0.1	0.2	0.3	0.4	0.5	0.6	0.7	0.8	0.9	1.0
orbital rendezvous mission without excursion vehicle	0	0.1	0.2	0.3	0.4	0.5	0.6	0.7	0.8	0.9	1.0
direct mission	0	0.1	0.2	0.3	0.4	0.5	0.6	0.7	0.8	0.9	1.0
____________	0	0.1	0.2	0.3	0.4	0.5	0.6	0.7	0.8	0.9	1.0
Subproblem #2: Design of the electrical power supply subsystem for the space vehicle											
Alternative approaches:											
hydrogen-oxygen fuel cell	0	0.1	0.2	0.3	0.4	0.5	0.6	0.7	0.8	0.9	1.0
KOH fuel cell	0	0.1	0.2	0.3	0.4	0.5	0.6	0.7	0.8	0.9	1.0
Rankine cycle fast reactor	0	0.1	0.2	0.3	0.4	0.5	0.6	0.7	0.8	0.9	1.0
Rankine cycle thermal reactor	0	0.1	0.2	0.3	0.4	0.5	0.6	0.7	0.8	0.9	1.0
Brayton cycle reactor	0	0.1	0.2	0.3	0.4	0.5	0.6	0.7	0.8	0.9	1.0
____________	0	0.1	0.2	0.3	0.4	0.5	0.6	0.7	0.8	0.9	1.0
____________	0	0.1	0.2	0.3	0.4	0.5	0.6	0.7	0.8	0.9	1.0
____________	0	0.1	0.2	0.3	0.4	0.5	0.6	0.7	0.8	0.9	1.0

Figure 1 illustrates the listing alternative approaches identified from the contract work statement, when so specified, or from the responsible engineer when he is interviewed prior to beginning the task. Blank spaces are always provided so that new approaches may be reported as they arise. If at some point in the design the respondent was equally committed to two technical approaches to rendezvous at Uranus, he would circle 0.5 for each, as shown. Eventually, as the solution progresses, one alternative will attain a 1.0 probability and the others will become zero. By plotting the probabilities over time, we obtain a graphic record of the solution history.

The Solution Development Record, by economizing on the respondent's time, provides quite an efficient record of a project history. When the project is completed, each respondent receives a time-plot of his probability estimates and is interviewed at some length to determine causes and effects of design changes reflected in this record.

In considering the sources of ideas, the unit of analysis employed is "messages received" (Menzel, 1960). In other words, each message the engineer or scientist receives which suggests an alternative solution is coded for its source.

A listing of the most frequently cited information channels is shown in Table 1. This does not imply that each idea can be traced to a single channel. More often than not a single alternative will result from messages re-

TABLE 1 **Typical Information Channels Considered in the Study**

Literature	Books; professional, technical and trade journals; and other publicly accessible written material.
Vendors	Representatives of or documentation from suppliers or potential suppliers of design components.
Customer	Representatives of or documentation from the government agency for which the project is performed.
External sources	Sources outside the laboratory which do not fall into any of the above three categories. These include paid and unpaid consultants and representatives of government agencies other than the customer agency.
Technical staff	Engineers and scientists in the laboratory who are not assigned directly to the project being considered.
Company research	Any other project performed previously or simultaneously in the lab regardless of its source of funding.
Personal experience	Ideas which were used previously by the engineer for similar problems and are recalled directly from memory.
Analysis and experimentation	Ideas which are the result of an engineering analysis, test, or experiment with no immediate input of information from any other source.

ceived from several channels; for example, someone on the lab's technical staff might refer the engineer to an article in a trade journal, which in turn leads him to a vendor who provides more complete information. In such a situation, where several channels contribute to a single alternative, equal credit is given to each.

The 19 projects under consideration, involved the following nine general problems:

1. The design of the reflector portion of a rather large and highly complex antenna system for tracking and communication with space vehicles at very great distances.
2. The design of a vehicle and associated instrumentation to roam the lunar surface and gather descriptive scientific data.
3. An investigation of passive methods for transfer of modulation between two coherent light beams.
4. A preliminary design of an earth-orbiting space station.
5. The design of a deep space probe, and appropriate instrumentation.
6. The preliminary design of an interplanetary space vehicle.
7. The preliminary design of a special-purpose manned spacecraft for cislunar missions.
8. The development of a low thrust rocket engine for maneuvering manned spacecraft.
9. An investigation of possible mission profiles for manned expeditions to another planet.

RESULTS

An example of the time plot of solution development records for a typical subproblem is shown in Figure 2. The problem, in this case, is the design of a position feedback subsystem for a very large and complex antenna system. The work statement for both labs suggested approaches α, β and γ. Both rejected these, however, and generated two new approaches each δ, ϵ, ζ and η). In both labs one of the new approaches resulted from difficulties incurred by the currently preferred approach; the other resulted from receipt of new information, and was independent of the state of approaches currently under consideration.

Alternatives such as these can now be evaluated at two levels. First the engineer customer and vendors are used most by engineers, and that the literature is the least used channel. For the scientists, on the other hand, the literature is most often used and no ideas whatsoever originated with vendors or the customer.

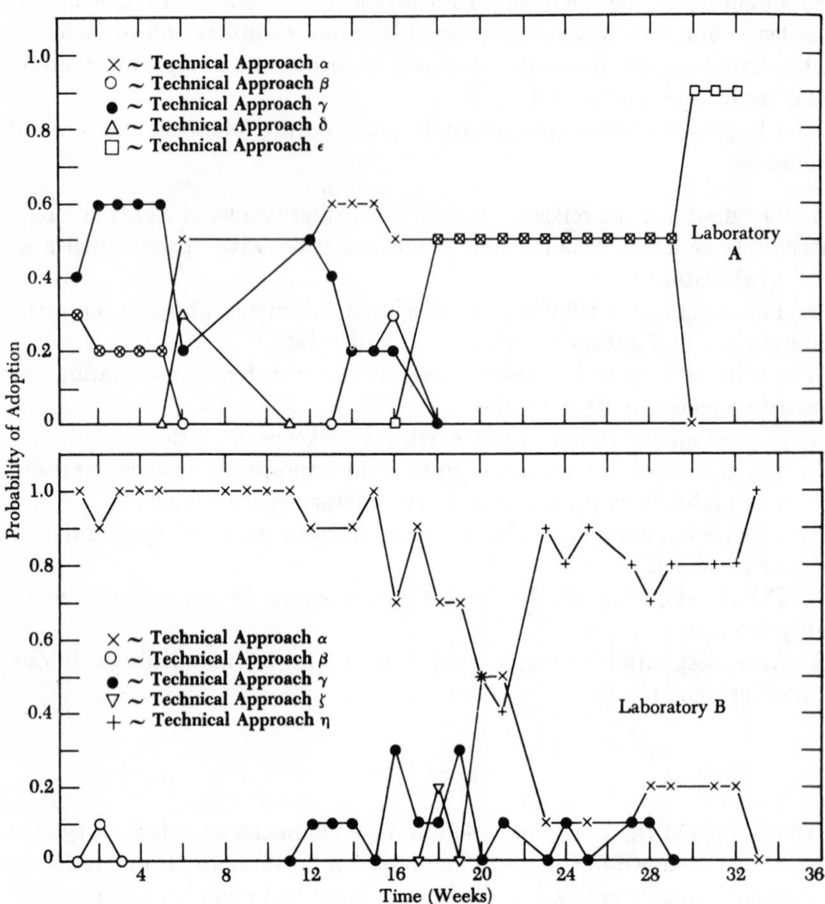

Figure 2. Design of Subsystem to Determine Antenna Position

The most important aspect of this data, however, is that the channels used with the greatest frequency are not the ones which provide the greatest number of acceptable ideas. A chi-squared test performed on the data for both scientists and engineers shows a significant ($X^2 = 19.55$, $p < 0.01$) difference in the allocation of acceptances and rejections among channels.

Relative performance on this basis shows the three channels involving "expert" sources to have the highest performance. These three channels—

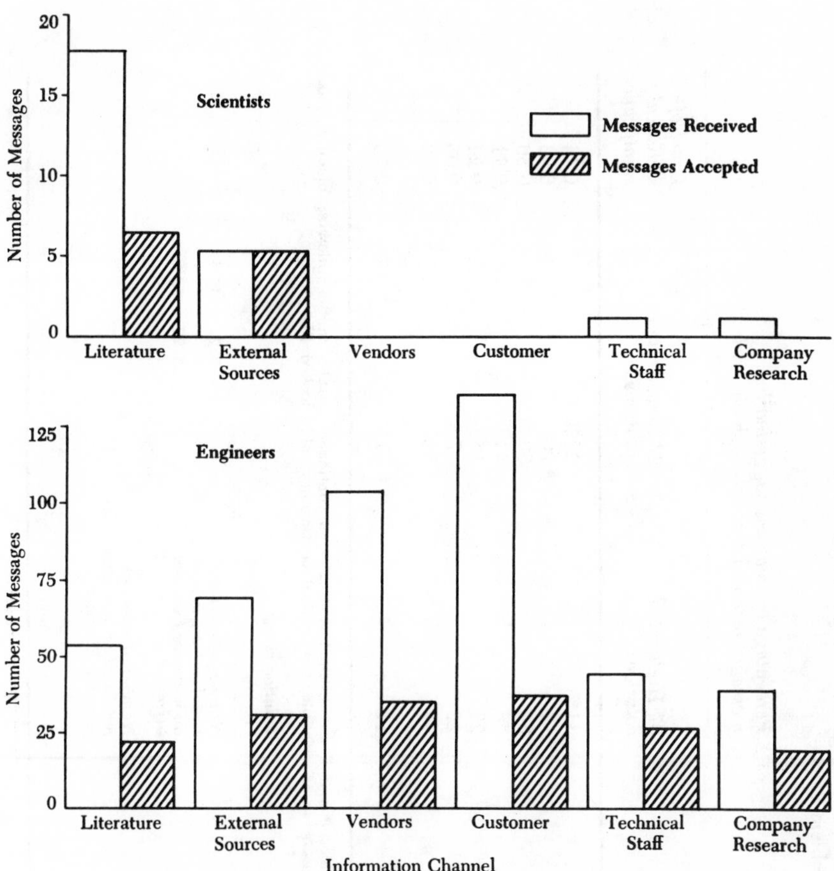

Figure 3. Messages Received and Messages Accepted by R&D Scientists and Engineers as a Function of Information Channel

technical staff, company research, and external sources—all produce very high acceptance rates among engineers. None of the expert channels were used to any extent by the scientists, but the one external source which produced more than a single message had the highest acceptance rate found. This, however, might be spurious since the external source in this case was the scientist's former mentor, which could suggest a distortedly high acceptance rate for his ideas. So, while no hard conclusions can be drawn

TABLE 3 Sources of Messages Resulting in Higher- and Lower-Rated Solutions—27 Subproblem Pairs

Information channel	*Percentage of solutions suggested by messages received through each channel* — *27 High-rated solutions*	*27 Lower-rated solutions*	*Level of statistical significance*
Literature	11%	22%	0.14
External sources	7.4	26	0.03
Vendors	30	30	0.50
Customer	56	44	0.21
Technical staff	22	15	0.24
Company research	22	7.4	0.06
Analysis and experimentation	44	52	0.29
Personal experience	11	11	0.50

The percentages in Tables 3 and 5 are distilled from 2 × 2 contingency tables in the following manner: Taking the first row, *Literature* as an example, the original contingency table looked like this:

Solution rating	*high*	*low*	
Number of solutions based at least in part on messages from the literature	3	6	3/27 = 11% 6/27 = 22%
Number of solutions not based on messages from the literature	24	21	
	27	27	

concerning scientists, it is quite clear that engineers are quite prone to accept ideas from someone they consider "expert." This does not generalize to all interpersonal sources as the very low standing of vendors and customer representatives show. While low acceptance of the former's ideas should surprise no one, the low acceptance rate for the customer's ideas indicates a rather refreshing amount of intellectual honesty on the part of our engineers.

Evaluation by the Customer

For 27 of the 82 subproblem pairs,[4] relative evaluations of the solutions were obtained from responsible technical monitors in the customer agencies. In the remaining 55 pairs, scores were either tied or no evaluation was available. This relative evaluation permits a comparison of the information channels used to arrive at solutions judged superior to those presented by other teams.

Table 3 shows the proportion of both higher- and lower-rated solutions which derived from information obtained through the eight channels. In other words, taking literature as an example, 11 per cent (or three) of the 27 higher-rated solutions were based, at least in part, on information obtained from the literature. Twenty-two per cent (or six) of the 27 lower-rated solutions derived, in whole or in part, from information gained through this channel.

Again, the "expert" channels stand out. Two of the three, external sources and company research, demonstrate significant differences in performance and the differences are in opposite directions. The performance difference for the third "expert" channel is not statistically significant.

The hypothesis to be tested here is based upon the findings of Allen and Marquis (Allen, 1964) for R&D proposal competitions. The use of information sources outside of the laboratory was found in that case to be inversely related to the technical quality of proposals, while use of sources within the lab was weakly but positively related to quality. The hypothesis predicts that poorer performing groups will rely more heavily upon sources outside of the lab, and better performing groups more upon sources within the lab.

In order to test the hypothesis, the actual number of solutions derived from each set of channels is aggregated in Table 4. Since a solution can

[4] Two of the 27 subproblems occurred in the single fundamental science project; the remainder are from the developmental projects. Since the results presented in this section are essentially the same for both of these sub-samples, the data have been aggregated.

TABLE 4 Sources of Messages Resulting in Higher- and Lower-Rated Solutions—27 Subproblem Pairs

Information channel	*Number of higher rated solutions suggested*	*Number of lower rated solutions suggested*
Channels outside the laboratory		
External sources or vendors but not technical staff or company research $(ES \cup V) \cap (TS \cup CR)$	6	10
Channels inside the laboratory		
Technical staff or company research but not external sources or vendors $(TS \cup CR) \cap (ES \cup V)$	7	1
Other channels		
Both or neither $(TS \cup CR) \cap (ES \cup V)$ or $(TS \cup CR) \cap (ES \cup V)$	14	16

$x^2 = 5.63, p < 0.03$

result from several messages, each received over a different channel, those solutions to which internal channels only contributed are compared with solutions resulting only from external channels. To complete the set, a third category has been included. This category comprises solutions deriving from neither internal nor external sources and solutions derived from both in combination. A chi-squared test rejects the null hypothesis of no difference in the performance of internal and external channels at the 0.03 level of statistical significance.

A somewhat more general test of the information gathering behavior of the engineers is a comparison of the sources used in generating all of the solution alternatives. In other words, general information seeking behavior varies as a function of the individual and his particular circumstances. Table 5 shows that a comparison at this level strengthens the conclusions reached on the basis of comparing the sources of solutions alone.

Higher and lower performers again show little difference in their use of the literature, vendors, and analysis and experimentation, and in their reliance upon personal experience in generating solution alternatives. Poorer performers once again rely more heavily upon external sources, and better performers upon sources within their own laboratory, i.e., upon their technical staff and other company research programs.

TABLE 5 **Sources of Messages Resulting in All Technical Alternatives Considered by Engineers Submitting Solutions Receiving Higher and Lower Ratings—27 Subproblem Pairs**

	Percentage of alternatives suggested by messages received through each channel		
Information channel	*85 Alternatives associated with higher rated solutions*	*85 Alternatives associated with lower rated solutions*	*Level of statistical significance*
Literature	8.2	14.0	0.11
External sources	5.9	15.0	0.02
Vendors	21.0	26.0	0.23
Customer	44.0	46.0	0.38
Technical staff	12.0	4.7	0.05
Company research	15.0	3.5	0.004
Analysis and experimentation	48.0	38.0	0.08
Personal experience	11.0	8.2	0.30

DISCUSSION

Three rather striking differences are observed in the performance of the information channels studied. First, there is a wide variance in the frequency with which the several channels are used. Considering only the channels external to the project group, the customer agency and vendors are found to supply almost three times as many suggestions of solution alternatives as do the lab's technical staff or its other research programs. Second, the actual acceptance of these messages is inversely related to the frequency of use. Two of the least used channels, technical staff and company research, yield the highest acceptance ratios. It appears that "expert" channels show the highest probabilities of having an idea accepted.

Finally, comparing the sources of both solutions and rejected alternatives for higher- and lower-rated problems, shows a marked difference in the performance of channels, depending upon whether they originate within or outside of the laboratory organization. Those originating within the lab perform far better than those originating outside.

The importance of this finding to those concerned with promoting the transfer of technology cannot be overstressed. But before delving into its implications in more detail let us marshall a bit more support for its existence.

As we have noted, this is not the first time this phenomenon has appeared. It was first revealed in the study of R&D proposal competitions (Allen,

1964). The proposal competitions studied varied widely in the nature of their problem and ranged throughout the research spectrum from quite fundamental basic research studies to hardware-oriented development and test projects. Across this wide range of problem types, teams which relied more heavily upon outside information sources were found to produce poorer quality solutions. In 14 of 15 cases correlations between the extent to which outside sources were used and rated technical quality of the proposals were found to be negative. The mean rank order correlation for 15 competitions was -0.30 ($p < 0.001$). The data indicate that lack of technical capability within the lab was largely responsible for at least the decision to use outside sources. Inverse relations were found between the use of such sources and both the size of the lab's technical staff and its ratio to the total employment of the lab. Laboratories which do not have the necessary technical manpower resources attempted unsuccessfully to substitute through reliance upon outside technical personnel.

Similarly the study of Shilling and Bernard (1964) shows consistent inverse correlations between the extent to which "paid consultants" are employed by industrial bioscientists and eight measures of laboratory "productivity and efficiency". All of these correlations are statistically significant at the 0.05 level or beyond. Furthermore, the authors found the use of paid consultants to be the only factor "which clearly and unequivocally differentiates [university from government and industrial] laboratories."

The present data (Tables 3, 4 and 5) reveal a similar performance differential. So the evidence which has accumulated is indeed quite convincing, but it does not as yet explain the situation. One clue lies in the finding of an inverse relation between the size (both absolute and relative to total company employment) of a lab's technical staff and the extent to which outside sources are used during proposal competitions. This suggests two factors which must be operating. First, those teams, or more precisely those laboratories, whose research teams rely on outside help possess other characteristics which more likely are the actual cause of the poor performance. The most plausible of these is simply the lack of the required technical competence within the lab. Certainly the use of an information source can seldom be held to *reduce* quality directly. It is, rather, the initial lack of knowledge on the part of the R&D team members which is directly responsible. Some information sources are more capable of counteracting this initial condition than others. This introduces the second factor: sources outside are either less well-informed, which is unlikely, or the flow of information is restricted at the organizational boundary. Why should the organization impose an effective barrier to communication? Before considering the question directly, let us first examine an instance which at first appearance runs counter to the evidence thus far.

Hagstrom (1965), who studied 179 prominent researchers in the formal (mathematics, statistics and logic), physical, and biological sciences found a strong positive correlation ($Q = 0.85$)[5] between extra-departmental communication and productivity in terms of papers published. The correlation between productivity and intra-departmental communication is considerably lower ($Q = 0.42$). Now, how does this relate to the earlier findings and how can the apparent contradiction be resolved? First of all, Hagstrom's measure of extradepartmental communication was restricted to communication within the individual's academic discipline. Furthermore, the organization in Hagstrom's case is somewhat different. It was a university department; all of the other results stem from studies of industrial organizations.

It follows that the differences in the effectiveness of extra-organizational communication in the two situations can be attributed in large part to two factors:

1. The relative commitment of the individual to the organizations or social systems at hand, and
2. The degree to which the boundaries of these organizations are formally structured.

In this context, Hagstrom's scientists confronted a low impedance in communicating across the bounds of their academic departments (but within their disciplines), because the academic department elicits a lower degree of commitment from most academic scientists than does their professional discipline, or "invisible college". Here we should expect to find a higher impedance than at the bound of the academic department, but not so high as at the periphery of a more formalized organization such as an industrial or government laboratory.

At this point our second consideration becomes relevant. As many social scientists in recent years have noted, the difficulty lies in the impermeability of bureaucracy to the influx of information and technology. Bennis, for example (1966), in cataloguing the many criticisms which have been leveled at bureaucracy includes the charge that it, "cannot assimilate the influx of new technology or scientists . . ." Katz and Kahn (1966) provide us with some explanation for this, revolving about two major points:

1. In order to control its intake of information and thereby avert the possibility of being so overwhelmed that the resulting condition is one of

[5] Yule's Q correlation for dichotomous data. No significance level is given.

pure noise, the organization establishes a "system boundary" which defines the appropriate region for organizational activities, and ". . . constitutes a barrier for many types of interaction between people on the inside and people on the outside."

2. Every organization like every individual develops a coding system with which to order its world. This coding scheme, in turn, enhances the efficiency of communication among those who hold it in common. It can, however, detract from the efficiency of communicating with the holders of a different coding scheme.

The two points are clearly complementary. The first is accomplished, in part, through the second. System boundaries are to some degree defined and maintained by a distinction in coding schemes. The boundary, of course, is not intended to be completely impenetrable; the organization must have some exchange with its environment. In order to allow this and yet control the degree, it establishes a limited number of officially recognized channels through which communication must be directed. We have, for example, libraries, purchasing departments and field offices through which information must be funnelled. In the present situation the official limitation of channels probably occupies a secondary position as an impediment to communication. Engineers (often to the dismay of librarians and field office managers) are generally quite uninhibited in short-circuiting such devices. It is rather the development of coding schemes which best explains the evidence we have seen.

Let us now briefly review these results. First, several studies of industrial and government scientists and engineers have shown an inverse relation between extraorganizational communication, contrasting with a direct relation between intra-organizational communication and performance. Second, in Hagstrom's study where the organization (an academic department) appears to occupy a subsidiary position to a more inclusive social system ("invisible college" or academic discipline), and where the communication process measured was external to the first entity but *internal to the second*, a strong positive relation was found between the extent of communication and performance. Third, in the instances in which external communication bears an unfruitful relation to performance, there is evidence that it is not this communication *per se* which degrades performance but other factors, such as lack of the required knowledge by the engineer or scientist seeking information. The internal channels are better able to compensate for this deficiency than are external ones.

The rationale of the shared coding scheme produces a rather simple and straightforward explanation. In industrial and governmental situations the laboratory organization dominates the scene. These organizations demand a degree of loyalty and affiliation far outweighing that required by academic departments. In addition, the members of industrial and governmental organizations acquire through common experience, and organizational imposition, shared coding schemes which can be quite different from the schemes held by other members of their discipline. This is not true of the academic scientists. They generally feel more aligned with scientists in similar research areas than with a particular university or department, and therefore tend to use a system of coding in common with other researchers. In other words, the "invisible college" now becomes the mediator of the coding scheme. Following this line of reasoning a step further, one would predict that were inter-disciplinary communication among scientists measured, the results would show some loss in communicative efficiency. An inverse relation with performance in this case might or might not exist, depending upon other factors, but we would predict some loss in efficiency when compared with intra-disciplinary communication. The problem is compounded when, as is often the case, incompatibilities between the two coding schemes go unrecognized, or when identical coding systems are assumed which do not in fact exist.

There are possible measures which can be applied to reduce the organizational boundary impedance. One which may take place under uncontrolled circumstances is a two-step process in which certain key individuals act as bridges linking the organization members to the outside world. Information, then, enters the organization most efficiently when it is channelled through these individuals, who are capable of operating within and translating between two coding schemes.

The possible existence of such individuals, who in effect straddle two coding systems and are able to function efficiently in both, and perform a transformation between the two, promises their potential utilization in technology transfer. In other words, it appears that information must be obtained by an indirect route. Attempting to bridge the organizational bound directly is not the most efficient path. Rather, the "technological gatekeepers" in the lab must first be reached and it is only through these men that the boundary impedance can be effectively surmounted.

CONCLUSIONS

The study has measured the relative performance of six channels in transferring technical information. The research technique employs the vehicle of parallel R&D projects to provide a control over the substance of the problem and a relative evaluation of solutions. Data are gathered by means of Solution Development Records and lengthy interviews with the engineers. The ideas considered for solution to each problem are thus associated with the channels whence they came, and measures of performance are generated for the channels.

The principal conclusions of the study are:

1. There is a serious discrepancy between the quality of the ideas generated through the channels studied, and the frequency with which these channels are used by engineers.
2. Literature is not greatly used, and is mediocre at best in its performance.
3. Better performing groups rely more than the poorer performers upon sources within the laboratory (the technical staff, and other company research programs) as contrasted with sources outside the lab.
4. A mismatch in information coding schemes appears to be responsible for the ineffectiveness of communication across the organizational boundary. The possible existence of key individuals (technological gatekeepers) shows promise of providing a means of surmounting this organizational boundary impedance.

REFERENCES

1. Allen, T. J., *The Utilization of Information Sources During R&D Proposal Preparation.* M.I.T. Sloan School of Management Working Paper No. 97–64, 1964.
2. Bar-Hillel, Yehoshua., Is Information Retrieval Approaching a Crisis? *Amer. Document., 14,* 1963, pp. 95–98.
3. Bennis, W. G., *Changing Organizations.* New York: McGraw-Hill, 1966.
4. Faegri, Kurt. Science Babel. *Nature, 177,* 1956, pp. 343–344.
5. Fozzy, Paula. The Publication Explosion. *Bull. Atom. Scientists, 17,* 1962, pp. 34–38.
6. Glass, Bently. Information Crisis in Biology. *Bull. Atom. Scientists, 17,* 1962, pp. 7–12.
7. Katz, Daniel and Kahn, R. L. *The Social Psychology of Organizations.* New York: John Wiley & Sons, Inc., 1966.
8. Menzel, H. *Review of Studies in the Flow of Information Among Scientists.* Columbia University, Bureau of Applied Social Research. (mimeo), New York, 1960.

9. President's Science Advisory Committee. *Science, Government and Information: The Responsibilities of the Technical Community and Government in the Transfer of Information.* Washington, D. C., Govt. Printing Office, 1963.

10. Shilling, C. W. and Bernard, Jessie. *Informal Communication Among Bioscientists.* The George Washington University Biological Sciences Communication Project Report No. 16A, Washington, D. C., 1964.

TECHNOLOGY TRANSFER*

Charles Kimball
President
Mid-West Research Institute

The dissemination and transfer of knowledge about scientific and technological discoveries has been a matter of importance since the inception of organized efforts in science and technology in the early part of this century. By and large, new knowledge in science is dispersed in a relatively straightforward manner, with very few instances in which scientists do not get the information they need quite readily. These dissemination techniques are conventional, and have stood the test of time—scientific papers, scientific meetings, and person-to-person communication.

Similarly, the transfer of knowledge concerning new developments in *technology* is not a new issue. The general process for applying new technology—proceeding from basic research through to initial applications—is well understood and widely employed. The steps involve an understanding of the basic phenomena, a clear definition of the mission, applied, or "mission-oriented" research, and the development of relevant designs, processes, and equipment. Such transfer has been carried on quite effectively for many years, expecially within large companies, with many outstanding examples of technological and economic progress resulting from such vertical-transfer activities.

The follow-on process of technology transfer, i.e., communication or coupling between persons who know the new technology and those who need to know, is less well understood.

For some years now, and especially since the advent of very large Federal research and development programs in defense, space, and atomic energy, there has been concern about finding applications in the civilian industrial sector of the economy for the advances in science and technology coming out of the extensive Federal research and development effort. This concern stems from several factors: an apparent distortion or skewing of the na-

---

* From *Applied Science and Technological Progress*, A Report to the Committee on Science and Astronautics, U.S. House of Representatives by The National Academy of Sciences, June 1967.

tional research and development resources; the desire to accelerate the civilian economy through technology; and the need to get the greatest economic benefit from the expenditures of public funds on science and technology.

This paper is concerned principally with the transfer of technology originally developed for defense, space, and atomic energy and its employment in both the public and private sectors, in applications that may be quite different from the purpose for which the technology had been originally developed in such Federal and mission-oriented programs.

There are many useful examples of such "horizontal" transfer of technology from the Federal sector to private and industrial uses, and to other public needs and purposes. Some technology is being transferred as well between nations, between one region of the country and another, and between one industry and other industries. A listing of major technology transfers from the federal sector to the private sector would range from widely recognized accomplishments to many smaller, less obvious incidents.

Technology developed for radar applications during World War II has been extensively applied to commercial TV circuits, air-traffic control, and weather-warning systems.

Military jet-engine technology has been improved and applied to worldwide use in commercial air transport.

Isotopes developed through the Atomic Energy Commission program have found extensive use in industrial processes, agriculture, and analysis techniques.

The computer industries, initially stimulated by defense and space programs, have developed diverse and significant applications in many other fields.

Glass technology was given considerable new dimensions by the need for lightweight, filament-wound, glass fiber rocket casings. These techniques are now extensively employed in the manufacture of storage and pressure vessels, including railroad tank cars, for civilian uses.

Inorganic coatings that change color as a function of temperature, coming out of the aerospace programs, are used as temperature indicators.

Some 50 applications for manufacturing licenses have been filed or granted for new inorganic silicate paints developed for space applications. These are far superior in many ways to epoxy paints, and can withstand a temperature of 4000 degrees Fahrenheit.

A magnetic hammer that causes metals to flow readily is employed to smooth out welding distortions in rocket-fuel tanks and in commercial shipbuilding.

Transfers of management technology, including Program Evaluation Review Techniques (PERT) and Critical Path Method (CMP), have now permeated the major construction companies, and were derived from complex Federal activities such as the Polaris Fleet Ballistic Missile Systems.

The Planning-Programming-Budgeting System (PPBS) is another example of transfer: to State and local governments, and to private industries.

These are a few examples of "horizontal" transfer, as defined above. For the purposes of this paper, they are not to be confused with other, older Government programs that have been both creating and transferring technology for some time. The prime example is the extension service of the U. S. Department of Agriculture. The extractive metallurgy medical technology, and the National Bureau of Standards' services to industry, are other instances of this accepted Federal role.

Technical advances and technology transfers, whatever their origin, can be important factors in the socio-economic growth of nations, regions, industries, and communities. They possess not only quantitative dimensions, but qualitative dimensions as well.

The current interest in technology-transfer opportunities is timely because the Nation is experiencing rapidly accelerating technical, social, and economic change. America must make the best possible use of all its technical resources to enhance our national posture and the quality of our lives. The natural process of technology transfer would take a considerable period of time to assimilate, as would making other uses of Government-financed technical advances if the process were allowed to work itself out naturally. Even the relatively straightforward transfer of the jet engine from military to commercial use took more than a decade. More complex transfers have taken longer. It is possible that the volume of research conducted over the past several decades may have overwhelmed the natural process of technology transfer. There is an implied belief that the natural process no longer works well enough, and that formal intensified transfer programs can bring about broader uses of new technology more quickly and at less socio-economic cost.

For these reasons, over the past several years, certain Government agencies have organized and now operate formal technology-transfer programs. The National Aeronautics and Space Administration is the principal current sponsor of such efforts, and the Atomic Energy Commission has begun transfer programs for non-nuclear technology. More recently, the

Department of Commerce has become involved through passage of the State Technical Services Act. The object of these efforts is not only to move Government-developed technology to the industrial sector, but to State and local governments as well, where the opportunities for transfer application may be appreciable. For example, the systems-analysis techniques developed for military purposes may have value to law-enforcement agencies.

The experience derived from these overt "horizontal" transfer efforts reveals one basic fact—that there is simply not enough known about the transfer process on which acceleration and emphasis are being directed. All the programs to date have been experimental, but they have been so in an operational sense. The measures of success cannot be determined just by the number of transfers accomplished per unit of effort.

In fact, technology transfer is perhaps most significant at the level at which cumulative small bits of new information are recombined and put to new uses. At the present time, it is difficult to manage this process and to measure its profitability. Explicit research into the transfer process is needed. This dimension should be added to the existing operational-experimental scope of these agencies' activities and augmented in other ways.

Those working in the transfer field have come to appreciate the extremely complex nature of this transfer process, recognizing that its successful application and acceleration depend upon many factors. These range from the types of persons involved in the process (the primary issue), the definition of the purpose of the transfer, and the increasing economic relevance of these programs. The process of recognizing a technical advance and establishing its significance in other fields, depending on certain adaptations, has led to the observation that no single transfer technique is suitable for technology of such variety and quantity as is being generated today in the Federal sector. (It is essential here to define *new* technology as that which is new to the person who needs it, or will use it, and not necessarily new to the technical world in general.)

THE CLIMATE FOR INNOVATION

Five general interrelated conclusions concerning the transfer process can be drawn. The first is that there must be a far better climate, more respectivity to innovation and change, if there is to be more effective transfer. There are, for example, appreciable differences in this respect within regions and communities, and within industries and individual companies.

The report on "Technology Innovation: Its Environment and Management" stated that certain cities, such as Boston and Palo Alto, "have an innovation environment that has led to the generation of many new technical enterprises. Chicago and Philadelphia are almost devoid of this type of new business generation." The technological gap between certain agricultural and industrial states may be greater than that existing between the United States as a whole and any major European country.

Many companies, both large and small, are not adequately receptive to employing new technology generated outside their own walls. Exceptions are found most extensively among larger companies that often have specially designed internal apparatus to bring this about. One also finds many smaller companies with highly knowledgeable management who meet this test. Many companies do not wish to make obsolete either existing products or equipment, recognizing as they do the marketing and investment risk implicit in new product development. Perhaps for this reason most transfers have been improvements on existing processes, either improving product quality or reducing production costs. Perhaps more effective transfer and a higher utilization of Government-developed technology would ensue if some additional inducements were provided, such as adequate patent protection and investment tax credits.

THE NECESSITY FOR PROBLEM DEFINITION

The second general conclusion is that the technology-transfer process must be problem-oriented or need-oriented. Overt transfer efforts could, for instance, be directed at one or more specific socio-economic public needs —such as air and water pollution, waste management, traffic safety, improved mass transportation, crime prevention, and improved education and training methods. Many of these, under the proper circumstances, could gainfully employ technological processes developed with Federal funds for different mission purposes.

One example of a specifically targeted mission-directed effort involves biomedical applications of aerospace technology. Its relative success illustrates the value of identifying a group of users with common technical problems, i.e., physicians and medical researchers in several medical schools who uncover and describe quite specific problems. They work with certain independent research institutes who search the supply of federally-derived technical information to help find solutions for these specific problems. Medical-instrumentation problems recently solved by this effort include a special muscle accelerometer to diagnose neurological disorders, employing principles and devices originally developed for a micro-meteorite detector;

a new technique for applying electrocardiogram electrodes to children, originally developed for instrumenting National Aeronautics and Space Administration test pilots; and a modification of the astronaut's helmet for research on oxygen consumption.

RESEARCH ON THE TRANSFER PROCESS

The third conclusion is that the transfer process is not only extremely complex, but that much greater efforts must be expended to understand it, i.e., how a transfer could or could not take place, and how to design future transfer programs to capitalize on this insight. Not enough is known about the "natural technology-diffusion process" for which the acceleration and intensification seem essential, principally because so very little analytical and empirical work has been done to advance knowledge about the process. It lacks a rigorous analytical framework within which the problem of technology transfer can be appropriately analyzed and understood.

The steps that need investigation (concerning their relative importance and interrelationship) are (1) finding the technology, (2) screening for relevance and emphasis, (3) "packaging" for effective use in user terms, (4) bringing the technology to the attention of relevant users, and (5) demonstrating its social and economic value.

Perhaps the circumstance can be illustrated by a chemical analogy. A chemist studies the activities of natural compounds in some known beneficial use. He then correlates this activity with chemical structure and, in this way, in a highly organized fashion that is capable of extrapolation, the method can then be employed to search for new compounds that might act similarly. The same route must be followed in developing transfer programs to promote rapid and valuable applications of new technology. Only then can operations be designed and instituted that support the positive features of the "natural technology-diffusion process" and reduce many identified barriers. To summarize this point: there is now no single "best way" to intensify technology transfer, nor is a "best way" likely to emerge soon.

Too much emphasis has been placed on the mechanism of transfer. More emphasis now needs to be placed on two other, more important, elements. The first of these is the make-up of the supply (information to be transferred) in terms of quality, quantity, and relevance. More must be known about how the supply source works, and how its content can be modified and distilled to make it more meaningful and, if necessary, develop or evaluate alternative mechanisms to bring this about. Secondly, more needs to be known about what causes an ultimate consumer of transferred technology to seek and, then to accept and to employ, that technology. These two elements, if better understood, will give the potential recipient more confidence in the source.

BARRIERS TO TRANSFER

The fourth general conclusion is that there are a large number of "transfer barriers." Some of these will always exist and, perhaps, can only be recognized in the design of future transfer programs. Other barriers, once recognized, can be overcome by designing transfer methods that by-pass or sumount them. The three major barriers are (1) human resistance to change, (2) inadequate skills and narrow viewpoints of people who should be involved in the transfer process, and (3) poor producer-user relationships.

Some of the barriers may not be surmountable under any conditions. One of these, the underlying psychological resistance to change, predominates as a human characteristic at any time and in any period. The two other barriers may be changed only on an evolutionary-time basis, but hopefully more rapidly.

The second and third barriers mentioned have a direct connection with the formal process in our system of higher education. In fact, one could go so far as to say that the entire subject of technology transfer should be dealt with in terms of the "people-transfer process." The problem of information retrieval and transfer of documents is not the main issue. Hundreds of technical reports, sent to a person or organization not capable of handling them, or not interested in their interpretation and reduction to commercial or other mission practice, are useless. Some hope has been expressed in the past that scientists and engineers who are working on Government-financed research and development could be induced to be more concerned with the possible implications of their work for industry, or for other problems of a public nature. This has not been a fruitful source of transfer largely because the type of person whose aspiration is to achieve scientific and technical progress for himself or for his mission is generally not the type who also seeks to effect technology transfers, although there is an encouraging, emerging interest in this matter among some scientists. Technical and management people in the private sector whose sole association has been with Federal research and development programs seldom possess the necessary attributes or viewpoints to develop products or processes for the highly competitive commercial market.

The technology-transfer process is social and economic in form and purpose, rather than scientific or technical. The decisions to use technology, particularly in industry, are economic in nature, rather than technical. Therefore, persons concerned with transfer as their main interest need to be judged on a scale of accomplishment different from that employed to evaluate and reward conventional research and development personnel. The transfer person, for example, must be able to assist the potential user in defining problems and opportunity. Having done so, he must have sufficient technical familiarity to search the supply of new technology to form the basis for a problem solution. This depends, of course, on accessibility and intelligibility of knowledge resulting from the results of "outside" research and development efforts. This same person or persons will then be able to adapt this newly acquired knowledge to specific requirements of the potential user, to whom the new knowledge will be applicable only if it appears to him to be beneficial, in his terms.

To stimulate, accelerate, and promote valid transfer through overt organized programs circumstances must be provided to make it easier for individuals and companies to be innovators: demonstrations that markets exist for a new technology products, that the risk is reasonable, that the cost-benefit ratio is favorable, or that the competition in the area is not excessive. The extent to which this is done for different potential users will vary, but the more this is done by the transfer agent, the easier it will be for the ultimate user to become an innovator in his own right.

The type of person described here might be called an "applier of science" or, preferably, an "applier of technology." He will have two outstanding personal characteristics. He will understand the world in which commercial forces operate, and he will have some broad technical background. It may be advisable to select appropriate generalists and supply them with the necessary technical facts, rather than attempt to convert a conventional scientist through exposure to commercial reality and to the requirements of corporate management in particular. Experience shows that most research scientists and engineers make rather poor transfer agents. Bringing about transfers is not the way they achieve satisfaction. Their education, experience, and general thought pattern do not equip them to deal effectively with the major factors that control transfer. To many persons who generate new knowledge, its transfer to the commercial world or other "practical" purposes is often considered a secondary assignment, one to be concerned with only incidentally or under duress. New technical ideas are transferred and implemented by persons—*not* by reports—and for persons to do this effectively, they must operate in an environment that is conducive to new-enterprise generation.

A number of research scientists and engineers, after a few years of exposure in industry, turn out to be quite capable enterpreneurs and develop intensive interests over the entire spectrum of subjects concerning a business. These persons often make very good "transfer agents," possessing adequate technical background to appreciate the technical implications, with the added incentive of contributing to business interests and knowledge.

THE TRANSFER AGENT IS THE KEY

The fifth and last conclusion is that the time has come now to consider carefully the deliberate development of techniques, university curricula, experiments, and perhaps even new institutions to provide the Nation with many more effective persons who can serve as "appliers of technology." These are not merely persons skilled in the practice of applied research. Rather, they are persons who, when properly selected for motivation, and when skillfully and purposefully educated and trained, will help materially to identify and surmount some of the transfer obstacles.

The technical entrepreneur, the champion of a new idea, is frequently the main force behind technical change. His main strength may be enthusiasm, ingenuity, and a commercial or public purpose, and not a basic-research point of view. He may be more distinguished for these attributes than for his technical expertise. His role is a vital constituent of transfer and innovation. These individuals need to be described, characterized, and identified as early as possible in their professional lives to provide them with significant and relevant educational opportunities, and then to provide working environments that will make their contributions meaningful, such as in independent research institutes, in technical consulting firms, and in certain selected corporate industrial laboratories that have demonstrated multidisciplinary transfer capabilities.

Significant technology transfer can, and will occur only when the right people, markets, and ideas coincide with usable technology at the right point in time. Technology, *per se,* may be the least important element in the over-all transfer process.

Several other approaches are suggested. Our system of university education could be very helpful in developing techniques for retraining the proven entrepreneur who is five to ten years out of school, with updating in his fields, so that his entrepreneurial ability will be enhanced. A few graduate business schools have employed this approach. This effort should be expanded, especially in engineering schools. Special summer institutes for university personnel, including selected graduate students having such entrepreneurial skills, would be useful—especially if the "faculty" were experienced, industrial people with demonstrated entrepreneurial skills and insights of their own.

Such specific curricula directed to increasing the numbers and quality of "appliers of technology" would be helpful in bringing about a more fruitful rapport between universities and industry. This is now limited by the unwillingness of many university personnel to relate their research or academic programs to economic or industrial needs. As such "appliers of technology" become more numerous, proficient, and widespread in the United States, the geographical separation of universities and industries will become less of a limiting factor.

Independent research institutes, many of which have already demonstrated competence in multidisciplinary research and development, should be considered as vehicles to promote interchange of ideas and mobility of people among Government, industry, and universities, to foster and to put into practice the appropriate transfer concepts.

SUMMARY

The economic growth of the United States could be enhanced appreciably with more effective use of new federally-developed technology by the private sector of our economy, and by certain elements of the public sector. Not only would economic growth be accelerated, but many social and community problems could be understood better. Technology transfer fosters more widespread distribution of industrial and commercial activity among the various regions in the country.

The natural process of technical change employing conventional techniques—educational, retrieval, dissemination, and the like—is not adequate in timeliness, quantity, or quality to bring about the necessary accelerated rate of transfer. Research on the entire process of understanding, accepting, and employing technical change, is clearly indicated as a consequence of the growing volume and diversity of technology, and the potential and exciting demands for its fruitful future was.

COUPLING OF RESEARCH AND DEVELOPMENT

Harold F. Davidson
Physical Science Administrator
Army Research Office

"The true and lawful goal of science is that human life be endowed with new powers and inventions"—Sir Francis Bacon

Within the past decade and a half a modern enterprise called research and development has become a major economic activity not only in the United States but in the western world and the Soviet Union as well. This role has been fully accepted by society and shows signs of playing an even greater role in the ensuing years. However to continue its healthy growth or even to maintain the status quo, research and development must show a greater relevance to the needs of its sponsors and to society in general. One of the better ways to increase relevance is improved coupling.

Coupling has many definitions: "Transferring research results to operations," "Accelerating the application of research and exploratory development results to industrial applications," or "Science and technology transfer to the would-be user at the earliest practicable date and in a language he can understand."

All these definitions are good and have one common underlying theme—Let's move research out of the laboratory or the literature and into the hands of the users, be they inventors, innovators or developers.

There are probably other management areas which can be described as coupling, or the transfer process. However, the generally accepted area of application involves research and development, or science and technology, and their coupling to needs. For all intents and purposes, research and development or science and technology can be considered essentially the same.

Coupling of research to development to national needs has come into the forefront of science and engineering management problems with greater emphasis only recently in the United States, and for good reason. The problem has been apparent over many years and is not a new phenomenon. The need for more effective and efficient coupling has become increasingly obvious due to the vast sums of money spent on research and development, mainly by the Federal Government.

In the United States there has been an increasing tempo of congressional, presidential, corporate, and public interest in getting more for the research and development dollar. Monies provided for R&D are leveling off and showing signs of diminishing—at least those funds publicly provided. This situation is something the science and technology community has not had to be concerned with since the Korean War. R&D dollars are apparently to be more scarce, or at least, the utility thereof is going to be subject to considerably greater challenge than previously. Thus, it is most desirable to improve the fruitfulness of corporate and public R&D dollars, and one of the more obvious ways is better coupling.

The reasons arguing for better coupling, or transfer, can be many. In the industrial or military marketplace, none can be so compelling as the drive to stay ahead of the competition. However, and most important, before research or development outputs and other technical data can be converted to useful end products, they must be transferred to the people who can use them—coupling.

Pictorial depiction of coupling is not a simple task. However, Figure 1 can be considered a representative diagram of the phenomenon. The logical sequential progression, from research to development to end item, is not a too frequent occurrence, since there are many pitfalls along the way. For instance, if we reach the late development stage and find we do not understand certain basic phenomena, it then becomes necessary to go back to research and obtain the necessary data to make the development possible.

In the proceedings of the conference on technology transfer and innovation, which was held in Washington in the summer of 1966, Harvey Brooks, Dean of the Harvard School of Engineering, suggested that transfer, or coupling, occurs along two dimensions, vertical and horizontal.

In vertical transfer, the general is transformed into the particular: science becomes technology, and technology finally becomes hardware. Horizontal transfer occurs when scientific or technical information generated in one context is "borrowed" and adapted vertically to meet an organization's needs. Thus, vertical transfer normally takes place within an institution and horizontal transfer takes place among institutions.

Horizontal transfer often involves specific hardware or "frozen information." In the horizontal transfer process, one institution's input is also frequently another institution's output. For example, in the case of the transistor, the research output of Purdue University was horizontally transferred as an input to Bell Telephone Laboratories. Bell, in turn, vertically integrated work done at Purdue University into its own transistor technology. Bell's research output was then horizontally transferred to

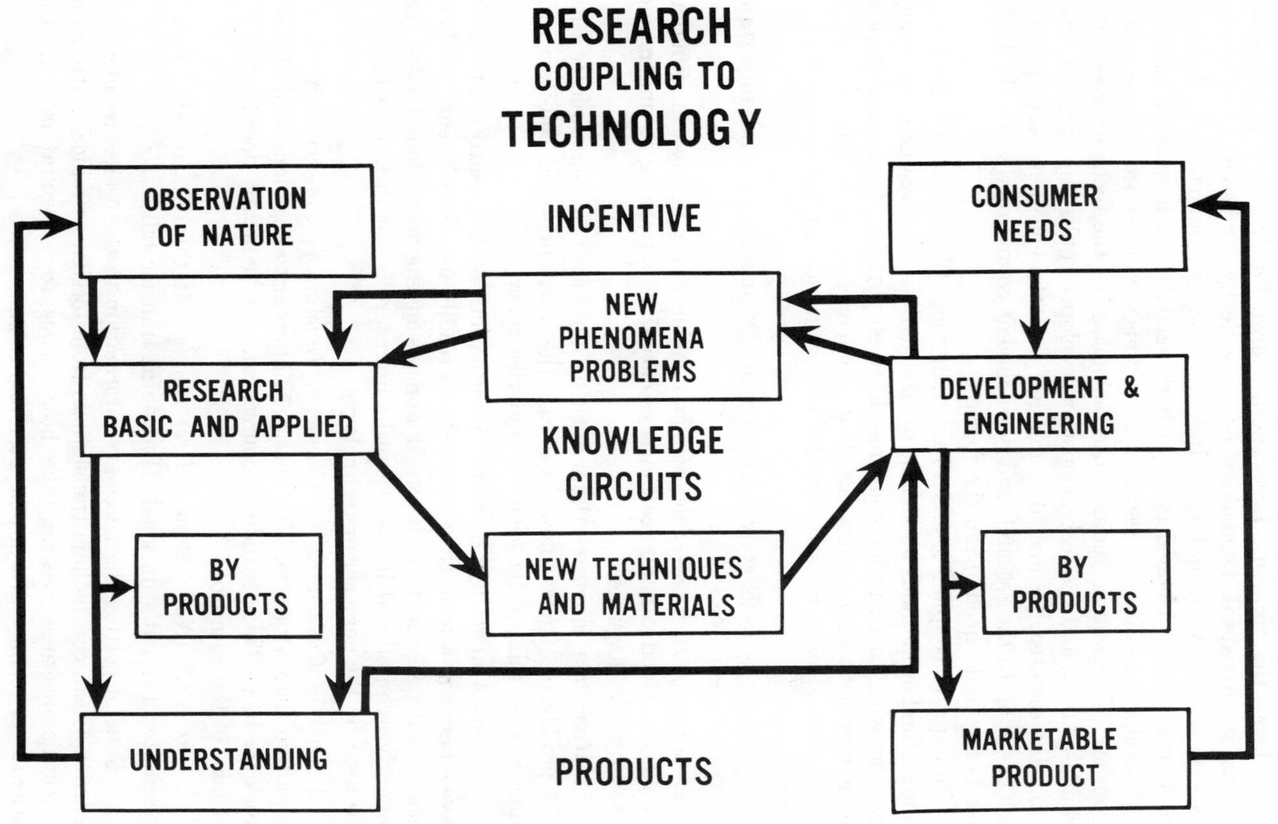

RESEARCH
COUPLING TO
TECHNOLOGY
OBSERVATION OF NATURE
INCENTIVE
CONSUMER NEEDS
NEW PHENOMENA PROBLEMS
RESEARCH BASIC AND APPLIED
KNOWLEDGE
CIRCUITS
DEVELOPMENT & ENGINEERING
BY PRODUCTS
NEW TECHNIQUES AND MATERIALS
BY PRODUCTS
UNDERSTANDING
PRODUCTS
MARKETABLE PRODUCT

other firms, this time in a fairly specific form. Finally, the receiving firms further improved this technology, again vertically. And so we have transistors as we know them today. Industry and government are obviously participants in and beneficiaries of both vertical and horizontal coupling.

Coupling can also be described as a "push–pull" effort. The scientists "pushes" his research findings into technology or the technology oriented would-be user, and the technologist or developer "pulls" the data he needs from the scientist. Or looked at another way, the end item user "pushes" his needs on to the research and development community while the latter tends to "pull" needs from the former.

To improve coupling is easier said than done. Why? Because there is no one method or methods applicable to all situations and because of the many barriers which need to be overcome. Each corporation, business enterprise or government agency has coupling problems unique in many ways to itself. These must be attacked by means unique to the corporation or agency.

The barriers to effective coupling are numerous. Several important barriers are as follows:

a. *Language Barriers*—Scientists and engineers frequently talk different languages. Good communication is essential, as is learning to understand each other's language.

b. *Motivation Barriers*—Users must be motivated to communicate with the producers of new knowledge, e.g., the developers and end-item producers must talk to the scientists and vice versa.

c. *Data Availability Barriers*—Information is frequently not easily available or in a form those in need can readily use. New science tends to lag considerably in time before it appears in engineers' handbooks; frequently as published in the scientific literature is not in a form that can be used by the engineer or technologist.

d. *Lack of Enthusiasm for Change or Innovation*—Conservatism—Let's maintain the status quo. Why change? Things are going along well so don't rock the boat. This attitude, of course, can and frequently does lead to the demise of the enterprise.

e. *The NIH (Not Invented Here) Barrier*—If the data or idea wasn't originated here, it's no good. Horizontal transfer fails.

f. *Costs* of getting the necessary information to the user is frequently a barrier. Costa can include translations from foreign periodicals, attending scientific meetings, visiting the home office for consultation with the scientist or technologist or marketer, and so on.

g. *Size*—The sheer immensity of a company such as General Motors or a government body as large as the Department of Defense, with the attendant communication and transfer difficulties, causes coupling difficulties.

h. *Excess Personnel Layering*—Too many people can be involved in the coupling process with attendant communication, decision-making and other problems. Coupling is almost always best accomplished on a man-to-man basis with no management layering.

i. *Entrenched Ideas and Private Interests* are detriments—obviously they make for tunnel instead of 360° vision and allow little if any room for fresh approaches or ideas.

j. *Geographical Barriers*—Wide physical separation of scientists and the engineers from one another, as well as those who use their output, also causes problems.

Some individuals have disputed the assertion that wide separation of scientists and engineers constitutes a barrier to effective coupling. A National Academy of Science Materials Advisory Board study several years ago did not find geographical separation an effective barrier. But the General Electric Company, Union Carbide Corporation and Bell Telephone, among others, will not agree. Their experience has been that placing scientists and engineers in close geographical, or even better, physical proximity, has a better payoff than having these people widely separated.

Given the need for improved coupling of research and development, what is being done about it?

Civilian agencies of the U. S. Government have recognized the need for better utilization of science and technology results, as have some technical societies. The American Institute of Mining, Metallurgical and Petroleum Engineers held a symposium on research—production coupling problems in the metal industry in October 1966. The Military Operations Research Society held a similar symposium on coupling in November 1968. The National Aeronautics and Space Administration is spending over ten million dollars a year in their technology utilization program. The Department of Agriculture uses its extension program which has been in existence for over fifty years. This program places the county agent as the coupler between the knowledge of the Department of Agriculture and the Universities and the ultimate farmer user. Industry is also beginning to realize the beneficial results of better coupling. Such eminent companies as 3M, General Electric and Union Carbide have recently instituted programs to better couple science and technology. Bell Telephone has long had a program looking to better utilization of research results.

Overseas, several foreign governments have recognized the benefits of better coupling. The French have established a new agency charged with hunting out fresh developments in basic research and finding industrial applications for them. The Russians, in a decree published in October 1968, opted for a better payoff from research and an increase in the productivity of Soviet technology. Several years ago, the British established the Ministry of Technology, a major purpose of which is to move research out of the laboratory faster and to modernize outdated production methods. A monthly publication, "New Technology," carries the message to industry and government. Such importance was attached to this problem that in the early formative stages of the ministry the famous scientist C. P. Snow was second in command.

Knowledgeable Britons have publicly stated that the lag in Britain's economic growth can be explained in large measure by the failure to put research results to profitable work. One explanation is a breakdown in communications between development laboratory and plant. Perhaps more pertinent is a failure to transfer research results from the science laboratory to the engineer, and the limited ability to exercise scientific entrepreneurmanship.

To make the coupling effort more fruitful, many of the aforementioned barriers must be overcome. But there are many needs—also barriers in a way—which require satisfaction.

a. We need more study on fundamental principles, such as the methodology of coupling and the preparation of a reference text on the subject. Also, we need a methodology for evaluating coupling techniques. Work in this area is currently being carried on by a team at Northwestern University.

b. We need to sell the doctrine of coupling to the scientist, the engineer and the production man.

c. We need information on how to motivate scientists, engineers and production people to communicate effectively with each other in a language each can readily understand.

d. We need to gather the limited knowledge and experience in successful coupling and to make the information available to all.

e. We need to evaluate the successes and failures of the recognized coupling efforts under way in industry and government and learn from them.

f. We need to study the role of the academic world in the coupling process, since the academic world is the prime producer of basic knowledge.

g. How do we more effectively close the time gap between research and development?

h. What are the parameters of the communication gap between the research community and the development community?

i. What role do handbooks play in helping bridge a vital communication gap between science and technology, and between technology and production?

j. Are corporate or business coupling directives of any real value?

k. Are technical translators desirable or necessary as communicators between science and technology and production?

l. Are liaison organizations with line authority desirable as "forcers" of coupling?

m. Does coupling lend itself in any way to computerization?

The art of coupling or transfer in the United States is basically in its infancy. Coupling, or transfer, has been referred to as an art rather than a science because it is doubtful it will ever become an exact and mathematical science. The fact that coupling is in its infancy, however, does not mean some of the more pertinent means of accomplishing this goal have not been recognized, such as:

a. Periodically develop a list of corporate or business problems and needs pertinent to the laboratory or research agency, and make these available to the scientist so there can be more relevant research.

b. Periodically evaluate the outputs of each laboratory against corporate or business needs.

c. Add liasion and coupling activities explicity to the goals and missions of organizations.

d. Add liaisons and coupling activities explicitly to the job descriptions of pertinent individuals, such as project monitors.

e. Consider appointing two small groups of liaison individuals—one to establish links between labs and basic research agencies, and another to strengthen the coupling between labs and operations.

f. Provide better opportunities for coupling activities by scientists and engineers, such as special symposia, which bring them together.

g. Insert translators, especially between science and technology.

h. Encourage the creative scientist, where possible, to follow his work beyond the research stage into development, possibly as a consultant.

i. Try to select for both in-house and contract or grant work scientists who are at home with both science and technology—and engineers or technologists who understand and appreciate science.

j. Recognize and otherwise reward individuals for their successful coupling efforts in challenging areas.

k. Consider (with some caution) the possibility of programming a coupling effort.

l. Study good and bad examples. Find out why the crucial differences exist and what they mean in terms of overhauling the present system.

m. Encourage face-to-face conversation between technical people rather than or in addition to going through the chain of command.

n. Minimize the physical space barrier between scientists and technologists—house them together or close by whenever possible.

The list could be extended many times. Even if half of the enumerated ideas are successfully incorporated in a program to improve coupling, a major step forward will have been taken.

Eminent scientists and technologists will agree that not many major advances in science come along in a decade. However, the little bits and pieces haphazardly strewn along the road, when properly coupled to an idea or a need, can make major advances in established areas. These bits and pieces can provide the foundation for new capabilities, even if a basic requirement or market has not yet been established.

More effective coupling will not come by coercion and direction. Rather, it will come by persuasion, education, and constant communication. Scientists, engineers and technologists need to be continually reminded that although research and technology are fine, desirable activities in themselves, to be really useful to society and to the corporation or business, they must as OFTEN and as SOON as possible fulfill a need, as well as fill the fountain of knowledge.

Ideas and opportunities which become technological opportunities and marketable end items are as much a function of competent, aware management and total organizational structure as are the activities of the research and engineering community. This concept, if adopted and understood by both the management and science and engineering community, can only lead to much progress in better and more effective coupling.

REFERENCES

1. Bode, Hendrik W. Reflections on the Relation Between Science and Technology, Basic Research and National Goals.
2. Cetron, M. J. and Davidson, H. F. MACRO R&D, Industrial Management Review, Winter 1969.
3. Harwood, J. J. The Productivity of Basic Research, Presentation at the Mid-Atlantic Regional Meeting of the American Chemical Society, Philadelphia, Pennsylvania, February 1966.
4. Martin, George and Willens, R. H. Coupling Research and Production, Interscience Publisher, 1967.
5. Rubenstein, A. H., et al. Coupling Relations in Research and Development, Second Technical Report to the Army Research Office, May 1969.

6. Olken, Hymen, Spin-Offs: A Business Pay-Off, California Management Review, Winter 1966.
7. Olken, Hymen, Spin-Offs II: California Management Review, Winter 1967.
8. Lesher, Richard L. and Howick, George J. Aerospace Technology Utilization—Bridges to the Future, Astronautics and Aeronautics, November 1966.
9. Myers, Summer. Industrial Innovations and Utilization of Research Output, presented before the National Conference on the Administration of Research, University of Florida, College of Engineering, October 28, 1966.
10. "More Payoff From Research Ordered for Russian Science Establishment" Scientific Research, November 11, 1968.
11. Price, William J."Concerning the Interaction Between Science and Technology" Research Review, Office of Aerospace Research Volume V, Number 10, December 1966.
12. Army Science Conference Proceedings (Supplement) 14–17 June 1966, AD 647010 Clearing House for Federal Scientific and Technical Information, Washington, D. C.

TRACES[1]—Technology in Retrospect and Critical Events in Science

Bodo Bartocha[2]
Francis Narin[3]
Clinton A. Stone[4]

INTRODUCTION

The many commissions, committees, conferences and studies in the area of science policy attest both to the importance of the field and to its inherent complexity. Although these activities provide background information upon which science policy decisions can be based, they are very difficult to correlate because of the lack of well defined, quantiative measures which can be compared from case to case. This lack of an objective understanding of the functioning of the scientific community, at a level commensurate with the scientific content of the disciplines themselves, has been one of the factors contributing to the difficulties faced today by proponents of the public support of science.

We wish to discuss here a study conducted at IIT Research Institute for the National Science Foundation to systematically delineate the process by which non-mission research evolves into innovations of social and economic importance. The study and events analysis are based upon five case histories of the research and development process. These histories, magnetic ferrites, the video tape recorder, the oral contraceptive pill, the electron microscope and matrix isolation were all traced by scientists or engineers working in their own fields of technical competence. After the individual tracings were completed, and the important research and development events identified an analysis of the events was undertaken.

---

[1] The study was carried out for the National Science Foundation by the IIT Research Institute under Contract NSF–C 535.

[2] Deputy Head, Office of Planning and Policy Studies, National Science Foundation, Washington, D.C.

[3] Now President, Computer Horizons, Inc., 7 S. Dearborn Street, Chicago, Ill., formerly at IIT Research Institute and principal investigator for a major portion of the project.

[4] Director, Physics Research Division, IIT Research Institute, principal investigator for the concluding phase of the study and project leader at IITRI.

TRACES

The use of events analysis in studies of this kind is fraught both with promise and with complexity. It is often as difficult to clearly define the categories into which the events are classified as it is to decide the category to which an event belongs. We chose to have the classification of events into the three categories of nonmission research, mission oriented research, and development and application done primarily by the scientists or engineers doing the tracing. This is, of course, a trade off of their technical insight into the subject area against the perhaps more uniform understanding of the definitions on the part of the project leaders.

The three categories of R&D activity were defined for the purpose of this study as follows:

nonmission research—motivated by the research for knowledge and scientific understanding without special regard for its application;

mission-oriented research—performed to develop information for a specific application concept prior to development of a prototype product or engineering design; it should be pointed out that the intended applications are not necessarily those relevant to the particular tracings;

development and application—involving prototype development and engineering design directed toward the demonstration of a specific process or product for purposes of marketing.

It must be recognized that utilization of these classification concepts is sometimes difficult since it depends on knowledge of the motivations of the investigator and/or his sponsor. Distinction between mission-oriented research and development is also sometimes difficult during the late stages of the research to innovation process. Furthermore, it must be realized that both nonmission and mission-oriented research can make contributions to fundamental scientific knowledge. Non-mission research, as reiterated by this study, provides the knowledge base which is used for mission-oriented research; a further function of nonmission research, not as obvious, is that it frequently provides key information which indicates that pursuit of certain lines of mission-oriented research will not be productive at a given point in time.

THE TRACINGS

The tracings were initially chosen by a group of 12 senior IITRI staff members of varying scientific and engineering backgrounds, to have a representative cross section of research and development for study. These suggestions were reviewed by the project staff and NSF personnel to arrive at a final selection. In addition to the previously mentioned problem of making consistent differentiations between nonmission research, mission-oriented, and development and application other rather difficult questions became immediately apparent, including determining when to begin and end a particular historical tracing or lineage. The origins of a historical tracing were selected by the scientists as those research milestones which are recognized as marking the beginnings of the various distinct lineages of scientific specialty that contributed to the innovation. The end of each tracing was taken as the point at which the first generation of acceptable commercial items appear, or the most recent date for which information could be obtained if a commerical device had not yet evolved. In order to demonstrate the methodology used, a simplified tracing is included here to depict the development of magnetic ferrites.

The magnetic ferrite tracing covers the development of a class of materials, widely used today in computer memories, telecommunications and small electric motors, which developed out of a broad base of research activities before and after World War II. Magnetic ferrites have their generic origin in the most ancient known magnetic material, magnetite (Fe_3O_4), and are produced by firing compacted mixtures of iron oxides and one or more other metal oxides such as those of nickel, copper, zinc, magnesium, or manganese. The mixtures can be formed into most shapes and sizes, and through firing they become hard, dense materials. It has become possible to tailor the magnetic characteristics of these ferrite materials over a significant range by varying their chemical composition and processing; herein lies the unique capability that has enabled these materials to find their way into such a great variety of engineering applications.

Hilpert in Germany was one of the earliest experimenters to prepare "magnetic insulator" materials and was granted the first (German) patent in 1909. Yet this ferrite patent expired without having prompted any technical innovations or economic consequences. Helpert's ferrite was unstable and did not have good magnetic properties, and in retrospect, it can be seen that Hilpert failed for a number of reasons. The collateral knowledge at that time in materials processing, crystal chemistry, and magnetic theory was inadequate; furthermore, although some demand for ceramic magnets did exist, the technologies that eventually were to find significant need for ferrites had not developed, and therefore a continued effort based on mediocre results was not considered worthwhile. Thus, direct ferrite development was dormant until 1932 when Kato and Takei in Japan again approached the problem of making a magnetic material with high electrical resistivity. Although they markedly improved the material, their ferrite was difficult to reproduce and its properties changed with age.

Tracing	Date of Innovation	Time Per last 50% Events	No. of Events	Predominant Characteristics of Events	Contributing Technical Disciplines
Contraceptive Pill	1960	1936-1960 (24 years)	80	Nonmission Research Universities and Industry U.S.A. and Foreign	Physiology of Reproduction, Hormone Research Steroid Chemistry
Matrix Isolation	1956	1962-1968 (6 years)	76	Nonmission Research Universities U.S.A.	Chemistry Electrical Discharges Cryogenics
Video Tape Recorder	1956	1927-1956 (29 years)	74	Mission-Oriented Research Industry U.S.A. and Foreign	Control Theory Magnetic and Recording Materials Magnetic Theory Magnetic Recording Electronics Frequency Modulation
Magnetic Ferrites	1955	1946-1959 (13 years)	59	Nonmission Research Universities and Industry Foreign	Crystal Chemistry Telecommunications Ceramic Materials Magnetic Theory
Electron Microscope	1940	1910-1940 (30 years)	50	Nonmission Research Universities Foreign	Cathode Ray Tube Development Electron Optics Electron Sources Wave Nature of Electron Wave Nature of Light

Table I. General Characteristics of the Tracings

In 1933 Snoek at Philips Research Laboratories in Eindhoaven, Holland, began an investigation into the magnetic and electrical properties of binary ferrites.

In 1936 Snoek successfully produced materials which were ferromagnetic and had high resistivities. By 1946 Snoek had laid a firm foundation for improved ferrites.

In the more than two decades between the unsuccessful attempts of Hilpert and the successful work of Snoek, many advances in the basic and widely separated desciplines of crystal chemistry and magnetic theory had led to a storehouse of knowledge by which Snoek could relate crystal structure and composition to magnetic properties. The importance of this broad research base was particularly evident because Philips was an interdisciplinary laboratory of high and broad technical competence, with excellent communications between the research and development people. Philips also provided the link between the telecommunication field's growing need for ferrites and the research in its own laboratories.

Following World War II there was a surge of nonmission research mixed with mission directed research and development and application, leading to the development of the four different classes of ferrites, hard, soft, microwave and square loop, which today are the basis for a $100,000,000 industry in the United States. The simplified tracing does not indicate the name of the innovator, the institution and date of each event as was done in the original report, but it does demonstrate quite clearly the major pattern of the scientific development leading to magnetice ferrites and the disciplines and technologies involved. It also shows several applications of magnetic ferrites.

Tracings for the other four case histories, the video tape recorder, the oral contraceptive pill, the electron microscope and matrix isolation were carried out in similar fashion. Space limitations prevent their reproduction here in detail.

GENERAL ANALYSIS

The research and development activities identified on the five graphic tracings were grouped in terms of category of research, type and location of institution, date of event, etc., to bring out some of the factors which enter into the transition from nomission research to innovation. An "event" is the point at which a published paper, presentation, or reference to the research is made. In most cases this represents the culmination of a number of years of effort and much supporting or related research which is not discussed. In tabulating the events, multiple contributors (as distinct from joint

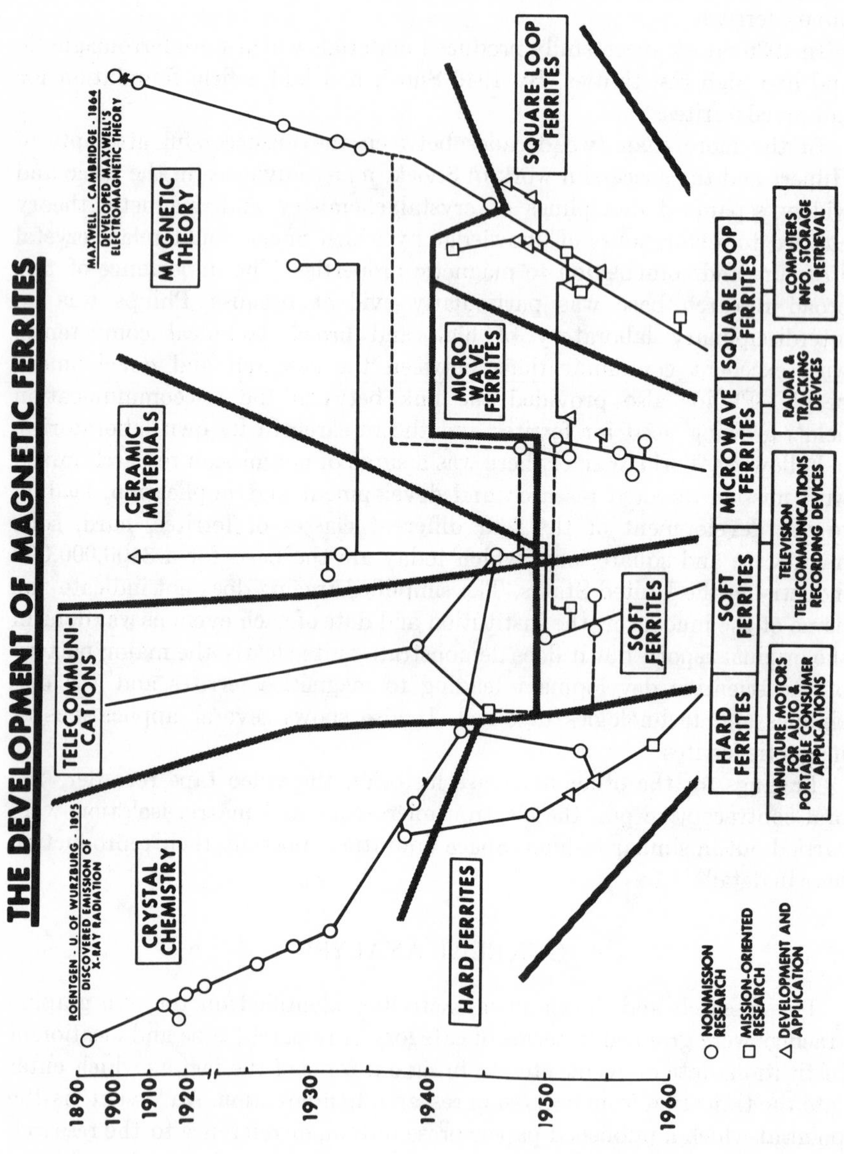
THE DEVELOPMENT OF MAGNETIC FERRITES
MAXWELL - CAMBRIDGE - 1864
DEVELOPED MAXWELL'S
ELECTROMAGNETIC THEORY
MAGNETIC THEORY
CERAMIC MATERIALS
TELECOMMUNI-CATIONS
ROENTGEN - U. OF WURZBURG - 1895
DISCOVERED EMISSION OF
X-RAY RADIATION
CRYSTAL CHEMISTRY
HARD FERRITES
SOFT FERRITES
MICRO WAVE FERRITES
SQUARE LOOP FERRITES
HARD FERRITES
SOFT FERRITES
MICROWAVE FERRITES
SQUARE LOOP FERRITES
MINIATURE MOTORS FOR AUTO & PORTABLE CONSUMER APPLICATIONS
TELEVISION TELECOMMUNICATIONS RECORDING DEVICES
RADAR & TRACKING DEVICES
COMPUTERS INFO. STORAGE & RETRIEVAL
NONMISSION RESEARCH
MISSION-ORIENTED RESEARCH
DEVELOPMENT AND APPLICATION
1890
1900
1910
1920
1930
1940
1950
1960

authors) were counted separately in those cases where they occurred. Events that could not be classified with respect to the parameter being considered were excluded from that tabulation. The zero order approximation, treating all events as if they were of equal value, was imposed.

Table 1 characterizes the tracings with respect to time, characteristics of the events and contributing disciplines. In four of the five tracings the events are predominately nonmission; only in the case of the video tape recorder were there more mission-oriented events than nonmission events recorded. Similarly the research was predominately done at the universities in four of the five tracings, with significant industry contributions in ferrites and the contraceptive pill, and industry predominence only in the case of the VTR. The matrix isolation work was predominately American, while the magnetic ferrities and the electron microscope events were mainly foreign in origin. For the pill and the VTR U.S. research predominated, but there were very extensive foreign contributions.

The diversity of scientific and engineering research becomes quite apparent when one considers disciplines that contribute to innovation. There are 21 different technical disciplines listed as having contributed to the innovations, or an average of four per tracing. There are noticeable technical overlaps between the VTR and the ferrites and these are reflected in the contributing disciplines.

One must realize, of course, that many of the elements of the technological lineages were and will be utilized not only for the application considered here but for other purposes as well. In the interest of simplicity, the authors of the tracings have reduced the number of such lineages by combination of closely related areas and have not shown the related research supporting each event. Thus, the scientific and engineering specialties identified can be considered a minimum.

The tracings identify 339 distinct key research and development events judged to be important to the evaluation of innovation. A very large number of research events of lesser significance to the innovation were part of the total picture but were not documented. Of the 339 events, approximately 70 per cent are nonmission research, 20 per cent are mission-oriented research, and about 10 per cent have been classified as development and application. The relatively small percentage of development events is due in part to the fact that these tracings concentrated on the events leading to the first clearly identifiable commercial utilization and did not considier product improvement and evolution. In that context, however, it demonstrates the diverse background of research on which innovation is based. Inclusion of all of the instrument development, advances in skills and crafts, and peripheral research which underlie the events as identified would serve to further increase the diversity and amount of activity which could be shown as necessary to innovation.

It is interesting to note that several areas of specialization such as magnetic theory and electron physics are common to several innovations. In particular, distinct research events are shown to have contributed to more than one innovation. Indeed, while they were not a part of this study, one knows that other innovations, such as the transistor and synthetic fibers, have utilized research events documented here. This illustrates an important point which, since this study consists of only five tracings, is not fully evident from these data. Knowledge developed by research has multiple application. Thus, it is utilized repeatedly not only for direct innovation but also for the continuous development of new areas of science and technology.

INSTITUTIONAL AND FOREIGN CONTRIBUTIONS

Of all the events tabulated, about 60 per cent occurred at universities, 15 per cent at research institutes and government laboratories, and 25 per cent in industry. In Figure 1, the percentage of contributions from universities, research institutes and government laboratories, and industry were calculated for each of the three categories of research. As one would expect, universities have made the major contribution to nonmission research and industry has provided an even larger percentage of development and application events. The proportion of nonmission research events originating at universities (about ¾) is larger than one might expect based on the distribution of basic research funds. Reports by the National Science Foundation on the distribution of research funding show that typically, universities have been receiving between 50 and 60 per cent of the basic research funding in this country over the past ten years. The larger percentage of contributions reflects in part the influence of foreign universities at a time when U.S. science had not achieved its present predominance. If foreign research contributions are excluded, universities account for less than 70 percent of nonmission events, while research institutes and government are the source of 16 per cent and industry of 14 per cent, which more closely approximates the relative funding for basic research.

This raises the question of the extent to which research and development done outside the United States has been a factor in innovation. Almost half of the research events occurred outside of the United States; the great bulk of these foreign research events occurred in the time period prior to World

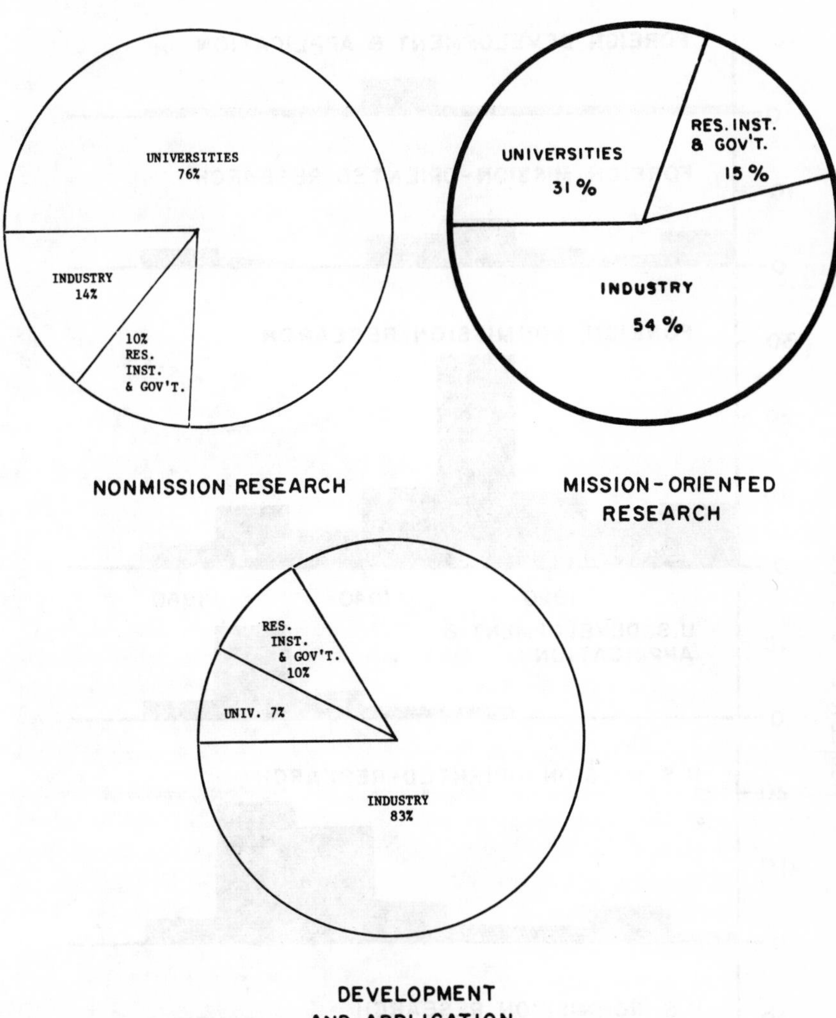

Figure 1. Event distribution among institutions

War II. The events shown in Figure 2 include all the events from the five tracings for this century. An increase in U.S. research is evident throughout the century and a dominating role is achieved after 1940. The continued growth of science in this country, relative to foreign efforts, is clearly reflected in the aggregate history of these specific tracings.

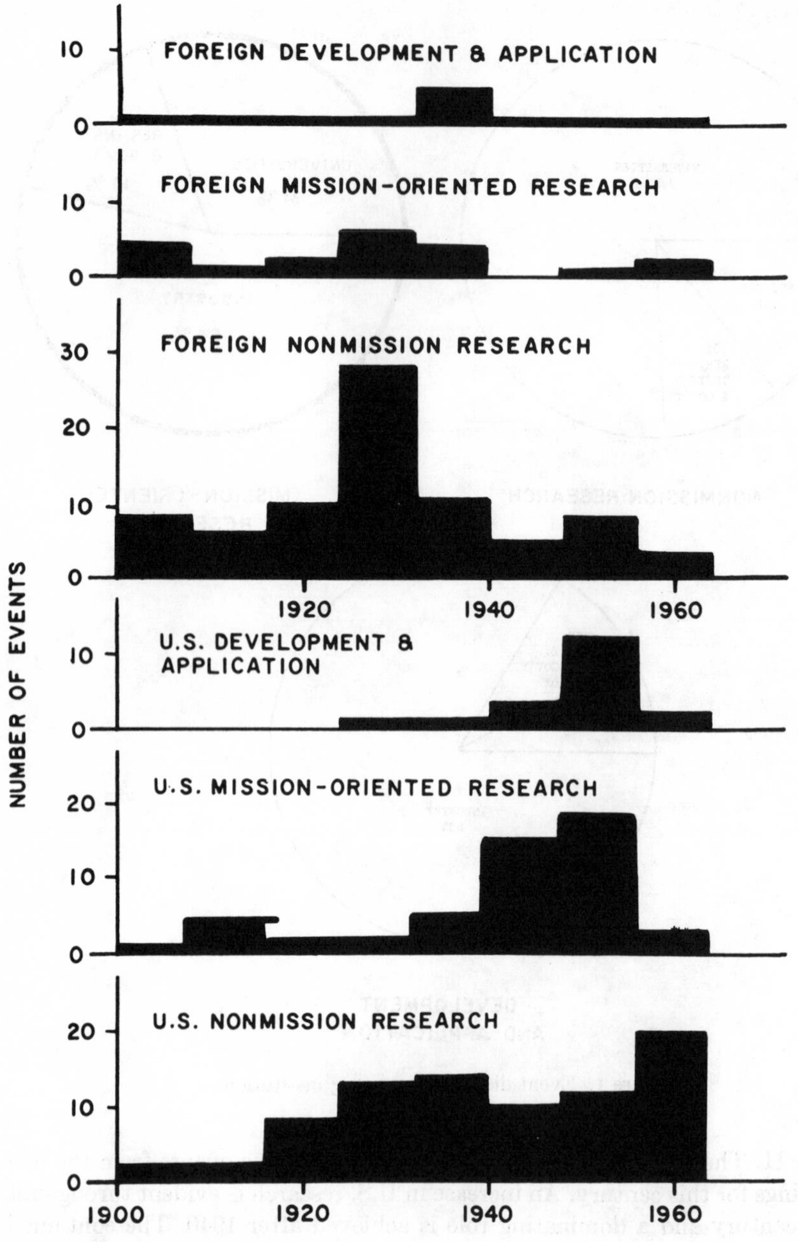

Figure 2. National role in R&D events.

Figure 2 also illustrates that much of the research and development identified in this study took place after 1940. This is indicative of the accelerated activity inherent in the research-to-innovation transition in these tracings. Although the authors have gone far back in history to establish the initial events and the subsequent scientific lineages, more than 30 per cent of all events contribution to innovation occur in the post 1940 period. This is believed to be due to at least two factors. Most of the innovations studied occurred between 1950–60, and as will be demonstrated, an acceleration of effort just prior to innovation generally takes place. Furthermore, there was a very marked increase in R&D activity which took place after World War II.

TIME FACTORS

The transfer of scientific knowledge to technology is an important part of the innovative process. The individual tracings show that the elements of knowledge required and the detailed transfer mechanisms differ among the innovations, ranging from publication to the type of communication in multidisciplinary laboratories. A summary view of the time history of the tracings is shown by the bars in Figure 3 which contain

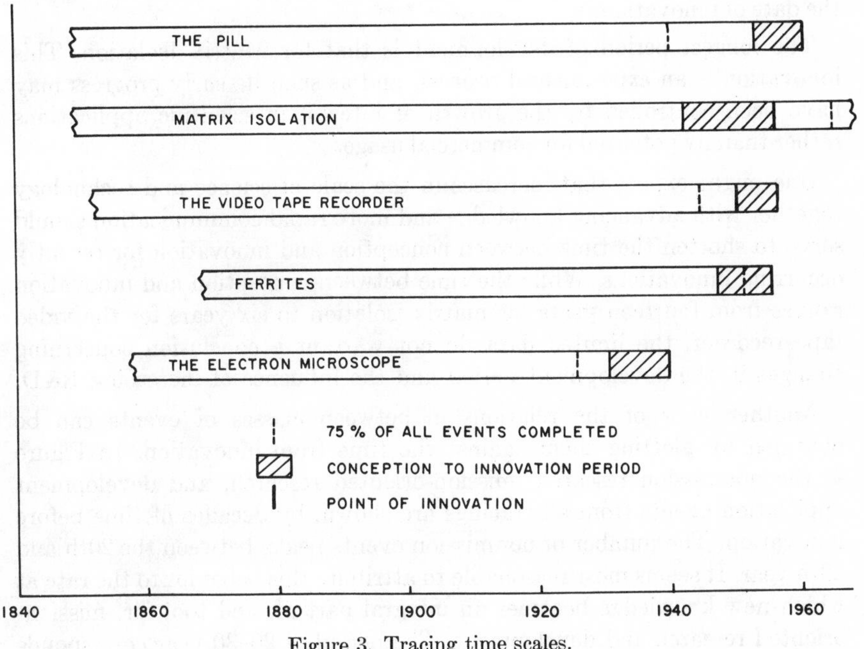

Figure 3. Tracing time scales.

three major time elements: the duration of the history from "origin" to innovation, the period from conception to innovation, and the time at which the knowledge from 75 per cent of the events of all three classifications had been acquired. The 75 per cent level was to represent a point at which the majority of research events had already occurred, but at which a significant fraction of the research and development critical to innovation still remained to be done. Extending the tracings to even earlier origins of knowledge would produce only a minor shift in the position of this point since a relatively few events would be added.

Conception was interpreted as having occurred when a clear concept of the device, process, or effect was apparent. For example, although the suggestion that hormones might be applied to birth control had been made a number of times previously, conception of the oral contraceptive pill is taken to have occurred when Pincus specifically initiated research in this direction using synthetic steroids. Innovation was obviously the approval of a commercial product.

No discrete innovation time exists for the ferrites since the products were produced sporadically over a period of years. The various times at which products were developed late in the ferrite history were used to calculate the arithmetic mean of 1955 which was arbitrarily employed as the date of innovation.

The longest period of development is that for Matrix Isolation. This innovation is an experimental process, and as such its early progress may have been controlled by the growth of interest in scientific applications rather than by potential for commercial usage.

One might expect that increases in the scale of science and technology together with advancing knowledge and more rapid communication should serve to shorten the time between conception and innovation for recently occurring innovations. While the time between conception and innovation ranges from fourteen years for matrix isolation to six years for the video tape recorder, the limited data do not warrant a conclusion concerning changes in the development period and the influence of increasing R&D.

Another view of the relationship between classes of events can be obtained by plotting them against the time from innovation. In Figure 4, the nonmission research, mission-oriented research, and development application events from all tracings are shown, by decades of time before innovation. The number of nonmission events peaks between the 20th and 30th year. It seems most reasonable to attribute this behavior to the rate at which new knowledge becomes an integral part of, and tool for, mission-oriented research and development. The period of 20–30 year corresponds

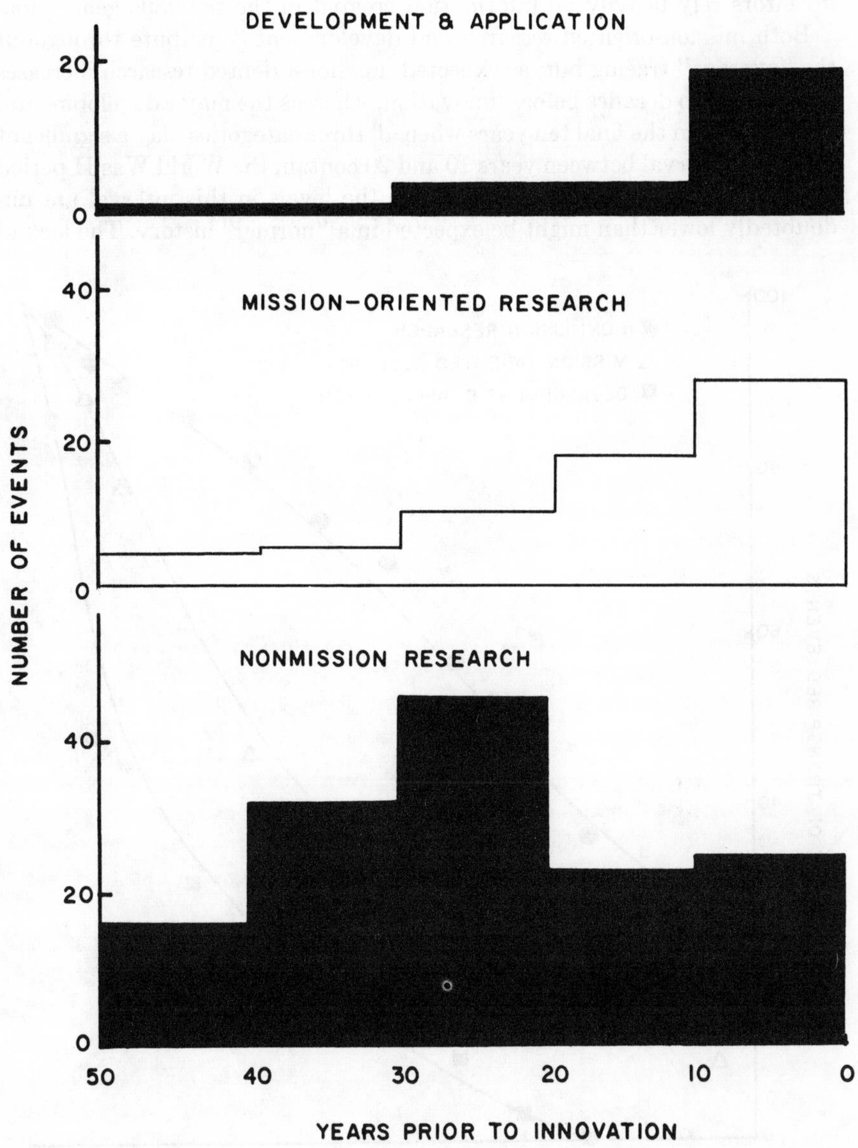

Figure 4. Events by type of research.

roughly to the educational cycle and tends to confirm the fact that most inventors rely heavily on information created in the previous generation.

Both mission-oriented research and development contribute throughout the "average" tracing but, as expected, mission-oriented research increases in the last two decades before innovation, whereas the major developmental inputs occur in the final ten years when all three categories play a significant role. The interval between years 10 and 20 contain the World Was II period for three of the tracings, and therefore the levels in this interval are undoubtedly lower than might be expected in a "normal" history. The lack of

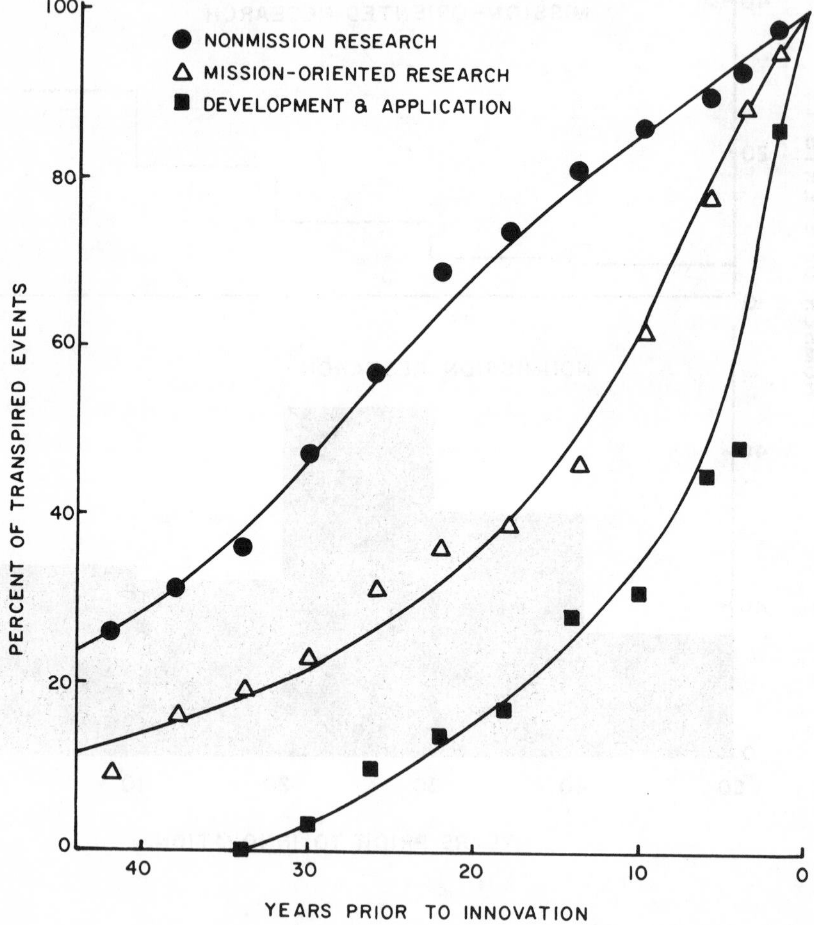

Figure 5. Cumulative activity vs. time.

time detail in the histogram of Figure 4, necessitated by the relatively small small number of events per unit time, limits the degree to which any relationships between research categories can be examined. A plot of the cumulative events versus time partially reduces the statistical problems and, when expressed in terms of percentage, allows a direct comparison of the time histories. These data are shown in Figure 5. Again, the data were normalized to a common innovation date, combined, and plotted in terms of time before innovation. The curves are a nominal fit to the data points but represent a reasonable estimate of the course of progress for each of the categories.

The average time from conception to innovation is approximately 9 years for all five tracings. Ten years prior to innovation, i.e., shortly before conception, approximately 90 per cent of the nonmission research as identified in this study, is found to have been accomplished. Insofar as one can generalize from these curves to most other research-to-innovation transitions, the bulk of nonmission research is completed before the detailed conception of, and decision to attempt, the innovation to which the research will ultimately contribute. Although scientists will often have the foresight to perceive the general area of applicability of their research, the great bulk of the critical research seems to be completed before the direct decision is made to pursue an innovation.

From the previous discussion it also follows that if the history of an innovation is traced only within the confines of its development, the period after conception and before innovation, the resulting picture is indeed incomplete. Thus some of the observations of HINDSIGHT are better understood in the light of Figure 5. Innovation and development are often based in part on science which is 30 years old or older, some 45 per cent of the nonmission research having been completed at the 30 year point. Furthermore, assuming that the date of innovation as defined in this report and the design-decision references point used in HINDSIGHT are roughly comparable, then approximately 80 per cent of the development work remains to be done at year 15, but the 80 per cent of nonmission research already done is completely excluded from consideration in an analysis limited to that short time scale. This built-in bias against long range research results was, of course, recognized by the Hindsight Team.

SUMMARY

This investigation was based on the historical tracing of key events which led towards five major technological innovations. This study produced findings which not only substantiated some intuitively accepted beliefs but which also yielded some interesting points that shed new light on the very involved process which leads from research to innovation.

In all cases studied, nonmission research provided the origins from which science and technology could advance toward the innovations which lay ahead.

Of the key events documented, approximately 70 per cent were nonmission research, 20 per cent mission-oriented research, and 10 per cent development and application. The distribution of performers of key events was as follows: universities performed 76 per cent of the nonmission research, research institutes and government laboratories 14 per cent and industry 10 per cent. For mission-oriented research the corresponding percentages were 13, 15, and 54. For development and application events industry produced 83 per cent, research institute and government laboratories 10 per cent and the universities 7 per cent.

The number of nonmission events peaks significantly between the 20th and 30th year prior to an innovation, while mission-oriented research events and those in the development and application area peak during the decade prededing innovation.

For the cases studied the average time from the conception to demonstration of an innovation was nine years.

Ten years prior to an innovation, i.e., shortly before conception, approximately 90 percent of the nonmission research has been accomplished; insofar as one can generalize from the results of this study, most nonmission research is completed prior to the final conception of the innovation to which it ultimately contribute.

Although nonmission and mission-oriented activities regress during the several years just preceding innovation, it is apparent that the interplay between these types of research activities is important and sometimes even crucial during this terminal period. Innovations in both the near and distant future depend on today's nonmission research.

ACKNOWLEDGEMENTS

The IITRI scientists and engineers who have developed the tracings are:

G. Benn	E. J. Hawrylewicz
J. J. Brophy	S. Katz
H. Cantor	A. J. Mountvala
M. Greenbaum	D. Shefner

Information concerning historical events in the development of ferrites was graciously supplied by Dr. G. W. Rathenau, Philips Research Laboratories, Eindhoven, Netherlands, and by Dr. E. Albers-Schoenberg, Feldmeilen ZH, Switzerland. Dr. Albert Crewe, Argonne National Laboratory, provided helpful discussion of research in electron microscopy. Economic considerations were developed by Dr. E. Burack of Illinois Institute of Technology and Mr. P. Mullenbach of Growth Industry Shares, Inc. The advice and assistance of IITRI personnel—Dr. M. Fisher, Mr. I. Fieldhouse, Dr. E. Sevin, Dr. G. H. Strohmeier, and Dr. T. P. Torda—in the early phases of the project were particularly helpful.

The contributions of Dr. C. E. Falk, Planning Director, National Science Foundation, who maintained unflagging interest and provided incisive criticism, are gratefully acknowledged.

CHAPTER THIRTEEN

MANAGEMENT OF SCIENTIFIC PERSONNEL

Creative people are the prerequisite to innovation and require management styles considerably different from manufacturing or clerical activities. Most discussion among R&D Managers usually ends up on people problems and we suspect that most of an R&D Managers time is devoted to interpersonal leadership rather than planing and decision-making. The three articles selected for this chapter discuss what we consider to be the most important aspects of personnel management in R&D organizations: dealing with creative people, manpower planning, and administrative leadership.

The first article by Harold Guetzkow examines the ways in which organizations influence creativity. He presents several "speculations" which can serve as the basis for the reader's own interpretation of the problem based on his own experience. At the other end of the "abstraction spectrum" Gerd Wallenstein presents the fundamental techniques for manpower analysis and planning applicable to R&D organizations. One important reminder of the need for practical thinking about personnel administration is the real world problems along with behavioral science theorizing about creativity and organization.

Churchman, Kruytbosch and Ratoosh discuss the role of the research administrator. They report the results of long term research on the jobs and characteristics of research managers' and they discuss the points of potential conflict between administrators and scientists. The authors also attempt to characterize a number of role orientations taken on by research administrators. They find no significant correlations, but evidence suggests that there is a distinct development pattern to R&D administrators' role orientations.

THE CREATIVE PERSON IN ORGANIZATIONS*

Harold Guetzkow
Professor of Psychology, Sociology and Pol-Science
Northwestern University

My task is to speculate about the way organizations influence creativity. It is important to remember that people in government and industry are imbedded, always, in their organizations. How do characteristics of these organizations influence the creativity of their members? If we take literally Paul Meehl's remarks about the "creator extraordinary," we argue that the organizational situation has no relevance. All is determined by the creative processes within the individual. The organizational context would not interfere with the creator; vice versa, one could not enhance creativity by changing the organizational environment.

But many of us—and we are psychologists, too—are concerned with more than just the top one-tenth of one per cent of individuals who produce effective originalities, who exhibit newness in their solutions, and who penetrate deeply in the development of innovations. There is reason to believe that creativity is distributed among humans as are most other personal characteristics—many are modestly endowed; some are either generously or miserly gifted; there are a few at the extraordinary extremes. For the large group of mortals, the social context may make some difference in the way their creative talents can be elicited in ongoing social situations. But Paul Meehl's paper also included the notion that one can remove impediments to creativity. It is here that he and I can perhaps find common ground, if we allow that suitable organizational conditions may permit further expression of creativity. But then one no longer focuses on the "creator extraordinary"; rather, one is concerned with increasing in organizations the occasional innovation of individuals who possess considerable or moderate talents.

As was suggested, let me approach a complex problem by being complex. There are two kinds of organizational processes, (1) those which hinder the

---

* Reported from *Creative Organizations* by Gary Steiver (ed.), Chicago: Univ. of Chicago Press, 1967.

development of innovative behavior and (2) those which enhance the creativity of the members of the organization. (It may be that these two sets of processes are simply the inverse of each other, but, because this area of inquiry is quite "data-free," I really do not know.) As individuals engage interdependently in complex undertakings, their organizations provide a way of specializing, as the work is divided among them. The specialization becomes more intense as the members lose face-to-face contact with each other and depend upon third parties for their communications—somehow the participants must co-ordinate their efforts. But, as Max Weber pointed out, one then seeks to regularize the behavior of members of the organization so that their activities may be more easily meshed and controlled. Such development of routines is prized in organizations. In the very heart of the organization, then, are important built-in forces for regularizing—for conformity. One then manages organizations by reducing the uncertainties, by discouraging originalities, by ridding the organization of the unexpected. In the very process of becoming a surviving, thriving organization, the creative innovations of the members are inhibited.

The environments of organizations, however, are not stable. Soon, the very stabilities in behavior which proved so useful at one time become burdensome and inappropriate. Countervailing pressures develop for change—for innovation. Such pressures come not only from external environment; inside the organization itself there are demands for innovation. As the size of the organization increases, as the division of labor shifts, new patterns of communication and supervision are needed. These constitute sources of demand for creative acts, and they allow scope for the creative individual.

In summary: *Organizations exhibit simultaneous demands for routinization and for innovation. The balance of these countervailing pressures determines the organization's climate for the creative member.*

Within the framework just presented, I shall submit six additional variables. It may be that the following three organizational processes, with three features of organization structure, are of consequence in building environments which stimulate the ordinary, as well as the extraordinary, members of an organization to further creativity.

ORGANIZATIONAL PROCESSES RELATED TO PROPENSITY FOR INNOVATION

Three factors in organizational functioning which may be of central importance in determining whether an organizational environment is provocative of creativity are (1) the way the organization handles its distribution of authority, (2) how the organization's slack is used for error absorption, and (3) the manner in which the organization's communication facilities serve the diffusion of innovative ideas. Let us examine each of these facets of organizational process separately.

THE CENTRALIZATION AND DECENTRALIZATION OF AUTHORITY

The authority system provides premises for decision within the hierarchy of the organization. The commands of a superior are taken as "givens," thus decidely limiting the freedom for decision of the subordinates. When there is centralization within an organization, many decisions are taken at the top of the authority structure, so that decisional latitude is narrower for those in intermediate and lower positions, thereby restricting opportunities for non-conforming, creative decisions. A decentralized decisional structure provides scope for innovative behavior through its emphasis upon the development of solutions appropriate to the different environments encountered in the various extensions of the organization. When authority is delegated, full advantage can be taken of broad latitude by those able to develop creative responses to an ever-changing environment in which their organization functions.

Yet decentralized organizations need to possess feedback systems which allow the executives at their top to assess the performance of the quasi-autonomous parts. These may take two forms: (1) There are those feedbacks which monitor the outputs of the decentralized unit, such as financial reports. (2) Then there are those feedbacks which monitor the means used by the decentralized units for achievement of goals, such as "progress" reports which describe the techniques and approaches employed.

When it is possible to evaluate the accomplishment of tasks within a company, the former method is often used, allowing the decentralized decision-makers greater latitude in the means they employ. When it is difficult to co-ordinate operation with goals, there is a tendency in organizations to appraise the unit's performance in terms of the extent to which headquarters' prescriptions of means have been heeded. In either case, when the top executive group finds itself dissatisfied, intervention in the affairs of the decentralized operation occurs, thereby reducing opportunity for innovation. Thus, the requirement that the creative decision be simultaneously practical and innovative imposes a countervailing tendency within the organization to restrict decision latitude. This tendency is less strong when achievement of the company's goals can be easily appraised with some objectivity.

The successful functioning of a decentralized authority structure influences the expression of creativity within the higher levels of management. Because top management's decision-making now is limited within its own organization—inasmuch as many of the internal decisions have delegated successfully to others—these executives turn outward for opportunities to exercise their creative talents. Thus, much energy is focused upon innovation in the acquisition of new organizational components, as through mergers, or by extensions of the company's capital resources. At times service in community organizations—such as the Chamber of Commerce—is exploited by top management as an occasion for creative self-fulfilment, when the scope of decision-making within the company is restricted because of decentralization.

Within those organizations in which there is much technical specialization and within those exhibiting much diversification, one would predict the tendency to intervention by top management in day-to-day operations to be less. In such situations—regardless of formal administrative policy on the distribution of authority—it would be likely that occasions for innovation by lower management would be greater. Such circumstances induce a *de facto* decentralization of decision-making, inasmuch as members of the upper echelons of management do not possess the technical competence required to assert premises for decisions by those working in constituent units of the firm.

Thus one speculates: *A dispersed distribution of authority within a firm provides more occasions for innovation, creative decision-making, especially when the decentralized unit exists within a diversified firm and possesses relatively objective criteria in terms of which its output may be apraised.*

Organizational Slack and Innovation

Creativity pushes thought into unexplored areas, and thus is fraught with potential for error. Because new ideas, by their very definition, have not been tried before, the chances that they are impractical are great. Yet it is difficult to know whether innovations are contributions or sports, until they have been winnowed by further research and development; but to avoid premature judgment, one needs time and resources. Does the organization have sufficient slack to absorb the costs involved in innovative errors?

When an organization has little slack—when the ship is tightly run—the climate is unfavorable for innovation. Immediate assessment must be made of the short-run payoff of new ideas, for the organization is not able to survive, in the long run, if it fails to eliminate its short-run errors. Managers are forced to introduce impediments to creativity, as described by Meehl: The individual becomes anxious, he restricts the depth of his exploration of new paths, he centers his attention upon items closely related to the company's immediate output. If there is little organizational capacity to absorb the consequences of errors, one bets only on sure things. I wonder whether the increased pace in innovations of American industry has not come from the displacement of the smaller organization, fashioned around one or two potential inventions of the creator-enterpriser, by the larger organization, quite able to absorb unproductive, bizarre ideas.

Coupled with organizational slack, one finds an ethos within the organization that is conducive to change. Risk-taking is legitimate, and expected. The norms within the organization are so set that one may properly talk about one's failures as well as one's successes in innovation. In fact, managers within such enterprises internalize the query: "Come now, how can this be done better, were we to take a fresh look at the whole problem?"

One speculates then: *The greater the organizational slack, with its increased capability of absorbing errors and ethos for risk-taking, the greater the propensity for innovation.*

Inasmuch as organizations must survive in the short run in order to be permitted to benefit from creativity in the long run, pressures often develop to remove organizational slack when the organization encounters immediate rough going in an adverse environment. Yet, it is then that innovation is needed. Thus, again, a paradox obtains: During times of stress, just when creativity is needed, some of the slack conducive to innovation is taken up. One way out of the dilemma is proposed below, in the utilization of special *ad hoc* group structures for innovation, such as the task force. Thus, although organizational slack is reduced in general, special innovative groups may be able to handle the immediate crises confronting the organization.

Communications as Catalysts for Innovation

The creative individual has contact with his organizational environment by means of its communication system. The employee talks with others; he reads and writes messages. The very problems he tackles often are called to his attention by the communication system—and unless they are the more fundamental ones confronting the organization, the individual's creativity is brought to bear upon trivia. In some companies, an attempt is made to alert upper management to occasions for innovation by communicating directly when programmed routines seem inadequate. If the communication system filters out the unpleasant and distorts the realities so as to present, by and large, images of integrated, successful operations, managers throughout the communication net will not have the disjunctive components with which to create new solutions; they will be lulled into acceptance of things as they are.

To increase the relevance of the creativity of the individual, the communication system must work well in both the vertical and the horizontal dimension. Each person in the organization must be heard as well as talked to, and the communication net must not be so overloaded as to drive out the half-formed thought which needs sharing, so that only the hard-sell, well-formulated notion survives. The need is not merely to increase the flow of ideas upward; equally important is the need to share ideas sideways and downward.

An executive situated at a peculiarly fruitful junction within the communication system may bubble with "half-baked" ideas. He must be able to relay these ideas to associates, both peers and subordinates, for further creative development. The functional specialities like sales and engineering must have an adequate language for communication of their problems to each other, so that the bonds of assumed constraint may be broken and innovations achieved. When there is geographical dispersion, counterpart persons in different sites need opportunities to spark each other's ideas, so that adaptations of solutions to similar problems may be creatively molded to fit widely different regions—a need of special relevance, for instance, to those involved in international operations.

To this point, emphasis has been placed on communication processes within the organization which might enhance creative work by its members. But communication systems can also inhibit innovation, especially by overlooking the communication burdens of participants in the system. When the channels are crowded with routine paper flows—when there is emphasis upon the empty "In" basket—then not only will there be less time for innovation, but creative ideas will be drowned in the seas of programmed trivia. As is so often the case in the operation of organizations, the communication process must be balanced and timed, so that one does not make "too much out of a good thing," thereby defeating the original purposes.

It seems clear from studies that individual creativity is often a "lonely" process, with the innovator at times needing isolation and seclusion. Just as it is quite legitimate in business practice to hold telephone calls because an executive is "in conference," some day it should become as acceptable to block communications because a man is "in creative thought."

Thus one may speculate: *The communication system of an organization may be tuned so as to provide materials for creative activities without depriving members of the organization of time for creative work.*

In this discussion of the organizational processes related to propensity for innovation, only three processes were treated: authority, slack, and communications. This means that such important components as the organization's status system, its recruitment and internal promotion procedures, and its purposes and goals were neglected. Yet these latter factors are worthy of exploration, too.

Organizational Structures as Vehicles for Innovation

It is useful to consider a more static way of inducing innovation, by rearranging the division of activity among the participants in an organization, either temporarily or permanently. Three such structural arrangements will be discussed: (1) *ad hoc* devices, which provide for rearrangements on short-time bases, (2) role differentiations, and (3) subgroup specializations, of which the two later arrangements establish divisions of labor with respect to the creative function in organization for longer periods of time.

My earlier analytic distinctions between process and structural ways of increasing innovation in organizations are arbitrary, for the effectiveness with which the structural devices operate will depend importantly upon the organizational processes which exist within these various structures. As one cannot consider all factors simultaneously, distortion of reality can be avoided if we bear in mind the intimate interrelations which hold between process and structure.

Ad Hoc Devices

It is feasible at times to establish special devices on an *ad hoc* basis to tap the innovation reservoirs of the organization. For many years now, suggestion systems have been signals for the flow of ideas from all members of the organization, even those involved in the most routine work. Based on the premise that each individual in the organization is potentially able to develop innovations for the improvement of the organization, the suggestion systems provide special occasions on which creativity is expected from all, with opportunity for special rewards. In one company, special creativity training has been found most useful in raising the productivity of the suggestion system, demonstrating that more innovations and innovations of higher quality emanate from this attempt to capture the creative impulse of all members of the organization by providing a special structural device to elicit and screen suggestions for improvement. Or, in communications terminology, increasing the quality of input in this fashion improves the quality of output.

More elaborate, perhaps, in the way of providing for *ad hoc* techniques to elicit innovation is the special conference called to solve particularly difficult problems—the "brain-storming" group. By attempting to separate evaluative activities from those fluency processes needed for the production of fresh ideas, the "brainstorm" session provides a seedbed for potential innovations. This device may be invoked at any time by any individual or co-operative set-grouping within the company. For the hour or two of its existence, it provides a structure within which there is opportunity for innovation. Grotesque and outlandish ideas are legitimized, even though, under ordinary conditions, such ideas would be ruled out of bounds.

Sometimes the *ad hoc* group is placed upon more permanent footing, as when junior members of management are constituted into a "shadow board," convening regularly just before each company board meeting on an identical agenda. Such "junior boards" have proved productive of innovations, often outside the ken of seasoned directors, whose long years of experience limit the founts of their creativity. Or, within the heart of the company, two or three persons may be freed for a month or two from regular duties to constitute a "task force" for the development of special insights on particularly vexing problems. These teams may be of special usefulness in spanning existing departmental structures in which rigid boundaries restrain the innovations of solutions which cut across previously established borders. The "task force" has been used constructively in the innovation of solutions in government, as witnessed in the work of the two (Hoover) Commissions on the Reorganization of the Federal Government.

Creative Roles

The society in which organizations are imbedded often provides norms prescribing special roles to the creative individual: He is given a tolerance and at times even a license to which more ordinary souls dare not presume. Sometimes the productive person gains such freedom by merely being different. These role prerogatives for the artist and "mad scientist" exist within the industrial and governmental organization, as well as within the society at large.

Most organizations have their "geniuses." These "oddballs" are allowed, even expected, to "get away" with much, as their transgressions are overlooked. They serve as gadflies, asking impertinent questions. Wise management cherishes men who plug unusual solutions into ongoing routines. Although I have never heard of a company that formally prescribed positions for the "ViceP-resident of the Offbeat," much can be done informally to take full advantage of rare creative talents.

The authority patterns may be so arranged as to legitimize such creative roles; in fact, I know of one company which requires that the vice-president of each division periodically identify its "idea men," so they may be placed in work positions possessing slack and located at frequently used communication junctures within the organization. Should the creative individual tend to isolate himself, efforts can be made to place him at points of access, so that the organization as a whole can tap his inventiveness. In fact, it is possible that the sheer fact of identifying the innovator will accentuate his propensity for creativeness—because roles usually involve reciprocated expectations.

Group Specialization

Within organizations, one may establish on a more or less permanent basis groups of varying size whose central function is innovation.

These are small teams, such as a research group, which may be attached to a product division of a larger company. Its focus may be narrow, attention being given only to product improvement. Or the team may be attached to upper management, as in the case of an operations research unit, with authority to tackle the entire range of management problems, from accounting to maintenance.

There are larger groups, too. A whole division of a company might be devoted to "Research and Development." Or a special pilot plant may be constructed for purposes of innovation. Planning departments attempt to look ahead, and then to devise creative adaptations to predicted changes in the company's environment.

But, be the unit small or large, it must have adequate authority for its operation—it must be given slack—and it must communicate its output to other parts of the organization. Specialized groups for creative work within organizations are beset by many of the same organizational problems as are more routine operations. In fact, the organization as a whole will often attempt to encyst the disturbing, innovating unit within its midst.

This description of the way organizational processes capture the innovating groups is familiar to us all: Too many ideas are produced for development, so one must sit in judgment on which ideas will be allowed to move forward. Then, resource allocations must be made. And soon one has a decision apparatus of some magnitude for processing (in a somewhat orderly, bureaucratic way) the fruits of innovation.

Consider the problem of organizational slack: At first, there is ample free time, and the innovators roam far and wide. But only those ideas which are practical tend to be rewarded. As time goes on, the innovators identify more and more closely with the organization's goals. They then prohibit themselves from tackling problems with solutions that are remote, since the risks now seem hardly justified. In one "think company," the creative scientists have become too involved in their pressing tasks even to take vacations—and now the company purchases slack for its own employees by paying bonuses to those who are willing to take vacations, thus attempting to maintain their readiness for innovation year after year.

So one may speculate: Ad hoc *and permanent rearrangements of the group structures of organizations may be used to induce increased propensity for innovation.*

Just as each process may be used to enhance creativity—be it the way authority is exercised, the way organizational slack is utilized, or how the communication system functions—so both structure and process changes may serve as vehicles by which innovations are suppressed and reduced. As my remarks have indicated, the development of organizations to provide seedbeds for innovative activity by ordinary and extraordinary members, is a thoroughly complicated process—and I am sure that my speculations constitute but a bare beginning toward improved understanding of these fascinating problems in the organization of human behavior for creativity.

FUNDAMENTALS OF TECHNICAL MANPOWER PLANNING*

Gerd D. Wallenstein

Planning for business purposes is coming of age. Financial planning, marketing planning, product planning: these are widely accepted planning activities of the post-World War II era. Manpower planning has been less conspicuous in public meetings, studies, and writing. But people are a business organization's most valuable asset. Manpower planning should command the manager's attention for a good part of his time.

Acceptance of manpower planning by managers probably had to await several other favorable developments:

The acceptance of planning for any business aspect. This required a change from the free-wheeling entrepreneur tradition, which until recently was seen in complete opposition to planned action. Today's managers no longer identify planning with socialism or, for that matter, with any type of restraint of business.

The ascendancy of the beahvioral sciences and of those who apply them in management situations.

The growth of monumental organizations and projects, in government and industry, involving tens of thousands of people.

The phenomenon of periodic shortages in skilled personnel in the midst of man-hour-reducing automation, increased educational opportunities, and greater mobility.

Manpower planning in a free enterprise society as we understand it must pick its way along the narrow road between excessive methodology and too much psychology. In the extreme, methodology can dehumanize the business process and depersonalize human relationships within it. Such excess would reduce the individual to a faceless commodity—*a thing*, not a person. This is a condition incompatible with the goals of today's enlightened free enterprise.

On the other hand, an excessive psychological concern with each individual's personality and his right to be different can obstruct the disciplined, orderly conduct of business in large organizations. Particularly in tech-

* Portions of the American Management Association, Management Bulletin No. 78.

nically oriented companies, the search for compromise between individual freedom and methodical action becomes a daily managerial task.

In this search, understanding of the business philosophy which affects the individual may be more important than any methodology whatsoever. So this publication attempts to develop such understnading as a prerequisite for technical manpower planning. Planning is here defined as thought *before* action, including the strategy required to transform thought *into* action.

This survey of planning philosophy is broader than the terms applicable to any one specific company. Certain assumptions are reasonable for one company while others are not. A single correct company image should not be sought. The range of possibilities should be examined with an open mind, and only that which matches the particular company personality should be selected.

ANALYSIS: BASIS FOR MANPOWER NEEDS

Manpower planning cannot be done in an information vacuum. The characteristics of the company and its people, products, nad business environment must be known—either as the result of other planning or by a special analytical effort. The analysis must attempt to answer these questions:

Who are we?
What do we do?
Where are we?
Where do we want to go?
What money will we have to get there?

The answers will provide a basis for manpower needs. The questions may be regrouped in the following three categories, which lend themselves to fruitful investigation:

1. Interpretation of the company character.
2. Interpretation of the plan for products, processes, services.
3. History and trend of research and product development expenditures.

Interpretation Of The Company Character

Understanding the company character is one of the most elusive of tasks; yet company character is more clearly attributable to a few individuals and governs the company's human relations more effectively than any statistical characteristic, such as sales volume, product catalogs, or employee statistics. A company acquires the character of its dominating managers-often one or two men who may be the founders or, later, career executives. Technical manpower should be planned and cared for with a good understanding of this character. If this is not recognized, many human mismatches will result, with attendant high turnover rates: those who stay will include many frustrated professionals and ineffectual managers.

What is this character made of? It is a composite of business alternatives adopted by the pace-setting executives, in accordance with their personal character and the type of business they have chosen. This composite may be defined as the dominating set of ethics, objectives, contributions, venture spirit, and decision-making policy by which the majority of the company managers are guided.

Ethics is considered to be a loaded word by many people, but there is no substitute for it in the dictionary. One may agree to view ethics as a relative thing, without the customary association with good or evil. It is then possible to observe important differences among companies. These differences exhibit themselves in three areas: customer orientation, product orientation, employee orientation.

Customer orientation, to some individuals, means customer satisfaction above all-if necessary, assured at considerable financial sacrifice. Some businesses are conducted under a policy of buying back the customer's order rather than leaving him dissatisfied. Other business managers, not necessarily less ethical, may take a rigorous literal interpretation of their obligations to the customer. They tend to go by the book. In their opinion, the customer receives fair value; it may be *his* exaggerated expectancy that causes dissatisfaction. This interpretation of ethics may be most appropriate in a contract specification type of business. Yet another type of manager operates on the assumption that everybody wants something for nothing. He therefore develops protective ethics which cause him to give the customer the minimum value which he can get away with. In some very fast-changing, perishable-nature types of consumer business, such ethics may be a prerequisite for survival.

Product orientation cannot be divorced from considerations for customer orientation, but it is useful to consider its aspects separately. Certain product ethics may be a sine qua non for certain products. For example, in the pharmaceutical field one may assume a deeply responsible ethical attitude connected with the oath of Hippocrates, while in the plastic toy field product inaccuracies and fragility are taken for granted. The demands made on product reliability in the electric and electronic public utility fields exceed those for the most exalted consumer electronic product by some order of magnitude. Quasiethical business characteristics go with the product. But no such inherent relationship forces a businessman or manager to devote his personal life to a particular product field. Therefore, one may reason, a man chooses or, at least, stays in a product field which enables him to find compatibility of prevailing ethics with his own.

Employee orientation is the most readily recognized part of the company character. While any company is described as a good place to work by its pace-setting managers, there is a wide range of interpretation of the ethics which make it so. The range encompasses extremes of paternalistic benevolence to opposite extremes of almost complete disinterest in the individual. Most managers' employee ethics fall between these extremes, but with sufficient differentiation to create many distinct types of company character. Are top managers ethically motivated to devote part of their time to employee welfare and personality problems, or will they do so only in exceptional cases of serious pressure? When a long-term employee is laid off, is there a feeling that the man was fairly considered for other alternatives? Is it generally understood that the layoff was inevitable because of decline in business, obsolescence of skills, or similar understandable reasons; or is the reason incomprehensible to most of the employees and hence considered arbitrary? Are company managers taking some part in community affairs which may be a source of reflected pride for the individual employee? All these characteristics may be relatively intangible, but companies acquire a reputation for them. In their totality they may bedescribed as employee orientation ethics, not to be valued as good or bad but as representing a specific ethical climate in which some employees will thrive while others are mismated.

Astute, self-appraising managers are able to assess their own ethics in customer, product, and employee orientation so that they may set the keynote for the "type of man we want around here." Since it is not likely that these ethical characteristics will be stated in writing, manpower planning should be performed under close personal contact with the keynote-setting managers. Only thus can the managers of detail planning and performing departments proceed in the spirit most compatible with the company character.

Objectives, value contributions, venture spirit, and decision-making policy are considerably more tangible then ethics. A typical listing of alternatives for defining company character is given in Exhibit 1.

Company objectives may be subdivided into profit and growth objectives and specific market and product objectives. Business goals always include profit and growth, but the particular combination of the two can make a striking difference in company character. In some companies, growth is the magic word. The managers make decisions with a bias for growth which extends far beyond the sales force. New business is continuously solicited

SOME ALTERNATIVES TO CHOOSE IN DEFINING COMPANY CHARACTER

Growth and Profit Objectives	1. Growth is the magic word. 2. Profits as we go—growth may come later. 3. Cannot seem to choose—grow fast and profitably always.
Product and Market Objectives	4. Aspire to be one of the five largest suppliers of wicked widgets. 5. Beat every competitor in price on unmanned Venus gondolas. 6. Obtain at least 10 percent of the Navy airborne dogfood market. 7. Expand internationally, selling at factory cost, etc.
Value Contributed	8. Scientific-invention-orineted. 9. Manufactured-volume-product-oriented. 10. Contract-job-and-service-oriented.
Venture Spirit	11. Very aggressive: will risk substantial funds to gain new markets. 12. Very cautious: will stay in its field—unless a customer prepays new venture. 13. Moderately aggressive: will consider new fields subject to carefully presented plans.
Decision Making	14. One man makes all the decisions. 15. Most decisions are arrived at in committees. 16. Managers have delegated responsibilities—and use them.

Exhibit 1

without much regard for its suitability and profitability, people are hired at a fast rate, buildings are forever rearranged and expanded. Although these managers may not be conscious of it, they are subordinating profits, and possibly product success, to growth. This can become a way of life and thus develop into a distinct personality trait, if the business environment is favorable for many years in succession and if the company operates in fields where profits are not essential for survival.

Such may be the case with some companies primarily engaged in supplying custom-built military items. As long as the military purchasing budget remains high, such companies might inflate their capabilities, obtaining large orders by a mixture of unbridled enthusiasm and low pricing. The financial confusion resulting from a large number of military contracts in the house at various stages of completion and negotiation, may enable the managers of such a company to escape from profit responsibility. They may be aided in this attitude by a high score in social standing which accompanies the excitement of climbing sales and the bustle of activity engulfing the employees. Such a growth-dominated company is, for the same reasons, very vulnerable to changes in business conditions. One astute competitor can puncture the happy bubble, and shifts or decline in military buying can dry up the source of future orders. When that happens, the company not only faces an economic crisis, it loses its personality.

In other companies, some specific profit percentage is the measure of all decisions. Such companies may lose out on many otherwise promising opportunities which do not look quite as profitable as the standard objective. While these companies may have slow growth and are in little danger of losing their personalities, they may lose their personnel.

Most company personalities are to be found somewhere between these extremes, for there is room for individual differentiation in the wide middle ground. An average annual growth objective of, say 10 percent with an average net profit on sales objective of 3 percent, represents a personality different from the one represented by the same figures in reverse order. The company with the 10 percent growth objective may appear much more vibrant than the one with the 10 percent profit objective. It is difficult to be a battle-scarred hero and a thrifty planner at the same time.

However, the profit-growth mix in a company's personality may be changed with relative impunity, as long as the extremes are avoided. Some alterations in company character are made inevitable by the change of the chief executive. They are costly in lost motion as key personnel try to reorient themselves; some personnel are unable to do so and quit. Nevertheless, a viable company personality will survive.

Market and product objectives may be on record if the company does have a formalized long-range plan where *objectives are identified.* If not, it is possible to analyze these objectives from the company's past performance and present posture. Is the product field well defined; and if so, what major categories can be discerned? Must fairly widespreda diversification be considered, including acquisitions and mergers? Conversely, is the company already overextended, making retrenchment, loss of markets, and divestment of subsidiaries likely? Is the company selling technical capability per se and not only through the medium of products or processes? Are technical operations confined to one country, or are some international? Is the company approaching a multinational make-up? In its defined markets and with its defined products, what are the company's market-capture objectives? In which market sectors is it expected to be the leader? What relative capture of total market potential is considered good performance? These objectives will have a strong bearing on the manpower requirements.

Value contributions, interrelated with product and market objectives, warrant a separate appraisal. In this category, one may distinguish these types of contributions: scientific innovations; volume manufacture; contract projects, such as construction and public works; and service operations.

A company is founded and developed around the type of business in which its founder has value to contribute. If over a period of time the company attempts to contribute value in several of these types *under the same management,* it does so at the risk of tampering with its personality. In most cases, equally contributed value in volume manufacture *and* service for sale, or in scientific innovations *and* contract projects, is no more feasible on the part of a group of people than it would be by one individual. These incompatibilities can be remedied by conducting each type of business in a separately managed subsidiary under a common corporate cover.

This personality principle is not black or white. A modest amount of service business may be successfully conducted by a company whose principal business is volume manufacture. The same is true for most of the other possible combinations. The important point is, however, to recognize that the company personality is identified only with the principal line of business in which its value contributed is clearly perceived by insiders, customers, and the general public alike. Whatever other types of business may be included must be clearly subordinated. The best assurance that the managers will not lose their awareness of this restriction is to require secondary business activities to be justified as essential additives to the principal business with the principal customers.

Company venture spirit is a very distinct characteristic–one which derives directly from the chief executive. Companies may be known as very aggressive or very cautious (omitting intermediate positions) because of the image of the top man. Thus this characteristic is subject to change with a change of top executives. If the new man, or group of men, brings about this change abruptly, the company's identity may be put in jeopardy. Perhaps this is so because the venture spirit is felt not only inside the company, but its customers as well. They will be quick to sense that the previously aggressive, fast-moving company has lost its momentum; or, conversely, that the staid, reserved company has gone off into a frenzy of activity. The gamble in such drastic personality changes is that enough new customers will be gained to offset the loss of those who refuse to deal with a company of changed personality.

The venture characteristics, together with the ethics, of a company are directly identifiable with those of the founder or long-time chief executive and remain more clearly so than the more flexible targets for profit, growth, and product success.

Decision-making policy also has considerable effect on company personality. Even a casual visitor will notice who runs the place in a company where all important decisions are made by one man. Similarly, a company run by committees exhibits striking characteristics of its own. Perhaps least striking–and therefore most likely to radiate a balanced, relaxed atmosphere–is the company where most decisions are handled by managers who have well-defined, delegated responsibilities.

As with most other characteristics, company personality traits are not absolute but appear in certain combinations with the type of business the company is engaged in its size, age, and market position. Specific decision-making character is, therefore, not readily evaluated as good or bad, but must be understood in the context of the company's total personality.

Interpretation Of Company Plans For Products, Processes, And Services

This part of the analysis is concerned with the company's technical plans which are sufficiently definite to appear on budgets and forecasts. The technical activities may include several or all of the following:

Planned product improvements.
Planned new products to be developed.
Expanded or new technical services.
Planned research projects.

The technical manager will need to interpret these plans for guidance in his manpower planning.

What general technical involvement do the *planned improvements* represent? Will the resulting workload demand mainly supporting personnel, or will it, by contrast, demand advanced skills? What market timing is expected for these improvements? Will some of these planned projects be abandoned when reasonably accurate cost estimates can be made? If so, should the manager prepare for a possible cut-back in these plans in the midst of his work force buildup?

Planned new products pose the same questions; but, because of the greater magnitude of the projects, the tecnhical manager may plan for them with more certainty if these plans have matured from a preceding screening and study period. Even then, only he can interpret the significance of the new product development in terms of known or new technology and numbers of technical people in different assignments. He will have to plan these activities within the arbitrary constraints of annual budgets. And he will be under pressure from marketing people to meet or improve the schedule of releases, against the forever looming threat of design failures, redevelopment, and technical procrastination.

From the technical manager's standpoint, each new product development project is unique–no matter how well established the technology and the market parameters may be. This is so because no two developments are of exactly the same magnitude, degree of difficulty, market pressure, and coincidental budget conditions. Nor is the relation of the individual project to all other simultaneous projects predictably typical. Often, but not always, one major project is given overriding priority; but several others are nevertheless expected to progress at the same time. Only when the exact identity of all projects is known can technical manpower be deployed with optimum effectiveness. Personal study and interpretation of the product plans by the responsible technical managers is therefore essential for good performance in their jobs.

Planned new processes are usually associated with the manufacturing function. In the electronics industry, for example, manufacturing processes are dependent on corresponding engineering planning and support by the product development people. Basic product design approaches may be affected. Such plans for the factory floor may have a considerable repercussion on manpower in the product development departments. In some other industries, new processes may in fact take the place of a new product. A new process, then, often means construction of a new plant, including long-term investment decisions, and plans for technical personnel of new skills in new locations. It is obvious that the technical managers involved must be in a position to share and interpret these plans in their own way, so as to prepared for the added or new responsibilities.

Expanded or new technical services can cover a wide range, depending on the industry and on the definition of the term "service." For many manufacturers, customer-contracted engineering is a service offering. Such engineering may include customer product development to specification, special product modifications, installation, training, and maintenance projects. For the manufacturer principally engaged in volume production, such service offerings can be attractive to the extent that they broaden the scope of technical work and spread the cost of common internal support functions such as drafting. To the customers, these offerings may be equally attractive, because of their belief that the manufacturer derives profitable return from production and may therefore be prepared to price the services as "leader items." Plans for expanded and new service offerings are therefore a natural happening in technically oriented manufacturing organizations. Because of their almost transparent orientation toward individual customers, service offerings may be subject to more gyrations–and thus less firm planning– than the company's product offerings. Technical managers have a direct hand in shaping these gyrations; they should therefore have prime responsibility for the manpower effects. But general management will need to establish a policy for the maximum tolerable manpower disturbances in order to preserve the integrity of needed basic product development plans.

For companies which offer engineering project time as a principal line of business, planning for new service offerings takes the place of new product planning in the manufacturing company. It should thus be more amenable to rational prediction within the company's growth and profit objectives.

Planned research projects may be treated differently from product development projects. While any generalization about research can be controversial and sometimes explosive, it does appear to be generally accepted practice to budget for research by lump sum or percentage of sales volume rather than by individual planned projects. Therefore, research manpower planning should be relatively stable and orderly. The often-discussed difficulties of evaluating research achievements on one hand, and of motivating research people on the other, are not lessened by this stability. But, as a general rule, these difficulties occur within a known frame-work of budgets and facilities. The technical manager can concentrate on the problems of allocating the available funds and of staffing the department with people of skills suited to his interpretation of the research goals. The uncertainties of the research activity are thus offset by the relative immunity from external distuprion and interference to which product development and service engineering organizations are exposed.

History And Trend Of Product Development Expenditures

For a meaningful analysis of company expenditures associated with technical manpower, the widely used catchall term "R&D" is not useful. Research in technically oriented manufacturing and service organizations encompasses the exploratory, scientific investigation work identified by disciplines, technologies, and skills rather than by markets and products. The objective of research is to assure future proprietary innovations or to make defensive appraisal of other people's innovations. Funded by current expense budgets, research is nevertheless a long-term investment in character. Planning of research manpower and facilities is therefore only indirectly related to product plans and market performance.

Not so with product development. In any manufacturing company, there is a direct relationship between growth and new product development. In the fast-moving technical fields, a certain minimum of new product development is necessary to assure the survival of the company.

Over a period of time the company management develops an experience value for the product development effort required for survival. This value is commonly expressed in terms of the percentage of sales volume dollars plowed back into development. Most technical product manufacturers use between 4 percent and 10 percent of sales for product development.

For planning purposes, a generalized percentage figure is quite inadequate. In the first place, accounting practices change, as a result of which one year's percentage may include more–or less– of the development-related engineering expenditures. Even where the same departments report expenditure consistently to the same accounts over several years, actual work may shift from new development to repair, evaluation, and support activity. In the last case, a seemingly sustained percentage of sales dollars is in reality declining for *new product* development in contrast to development engineering activity overall.

For these reasons, and for convincing market strategy reasons, product development funds must at any given time be allocated to definitive new product projects. Thus total expenditures for new products are the sum of known and needed projects, within the constraint imposed by budget limitations. The overall development budget will average some reasonable annual percentage of sales. But actual expenditures under it are made on new products, each of which has its total project budget spread over several years. Analysis for manpower planning purposes therefore concerns individual products, the development time and cost required for them, and the ratio of development cost to resulting lifetime sales.

The analysis may be improved by grouping products into closely related product families, particularly if each family represents a long-term commitment to established markets. A further consideration important for manpower planning is grouping by technological specialties.

Such an analysis of the company's product development history can yield the following information:

1. The typical or average length of the development cycle.
2. A numerical indicator of the sales earned by product development action Growth;[1] multiplier M equals product lifetimes ales volume divided by total product development expense.
3. The history of the multiplier M for major products, as a measure of contribution to company growth.
4. An indication of the approximate break-even multiplier M, where new products developed and sold just offset the proportionate decline in sales of old products.

---

[1] Multiplier concept, as developed by author's staff, is described by A. J. Lipinski, "Planning for the Company Growth," *NAA Bulletin,* November 1964.

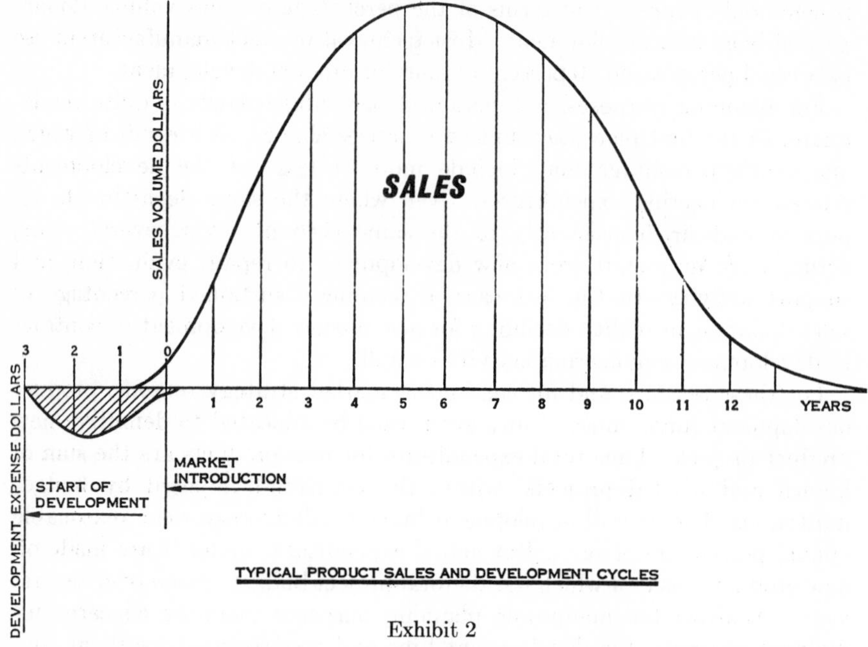

Exhibit 2

5. The range of multipliers by products and product families, indicating the highest growth potential products as well as the leader items.

If company administrative and accounting practices permit, the expense figures used should preferably include all contributing departments' expense burdens. Included would be the cost of directly supporting machines, such as engineering computer costs. If this is not done, figures covering periods of five years and more may not be comparable because of displacement of man-hours by machine-hours, and of one type of man-hours by other skill types. Also, to arrive at a meaningful historical analysis, some retroactive reallocations of expenditures which had been reported under different accounts may be necessary

One of the most common obstacles to product development planning for growth is the inability of many managers to grasp the significance of the time delay involved. An expenditure is approved in one year and incurred in a later year–and resulting sales materialize still later. In a typical example of the industrial electronics industry illustrated in Exhibit 2, an average product development cycle of three years is followed by a product life cycle of 12 years. The buildup of development effort prior to and during the three years can be further examined ,as illustrated in Exhibit 3.

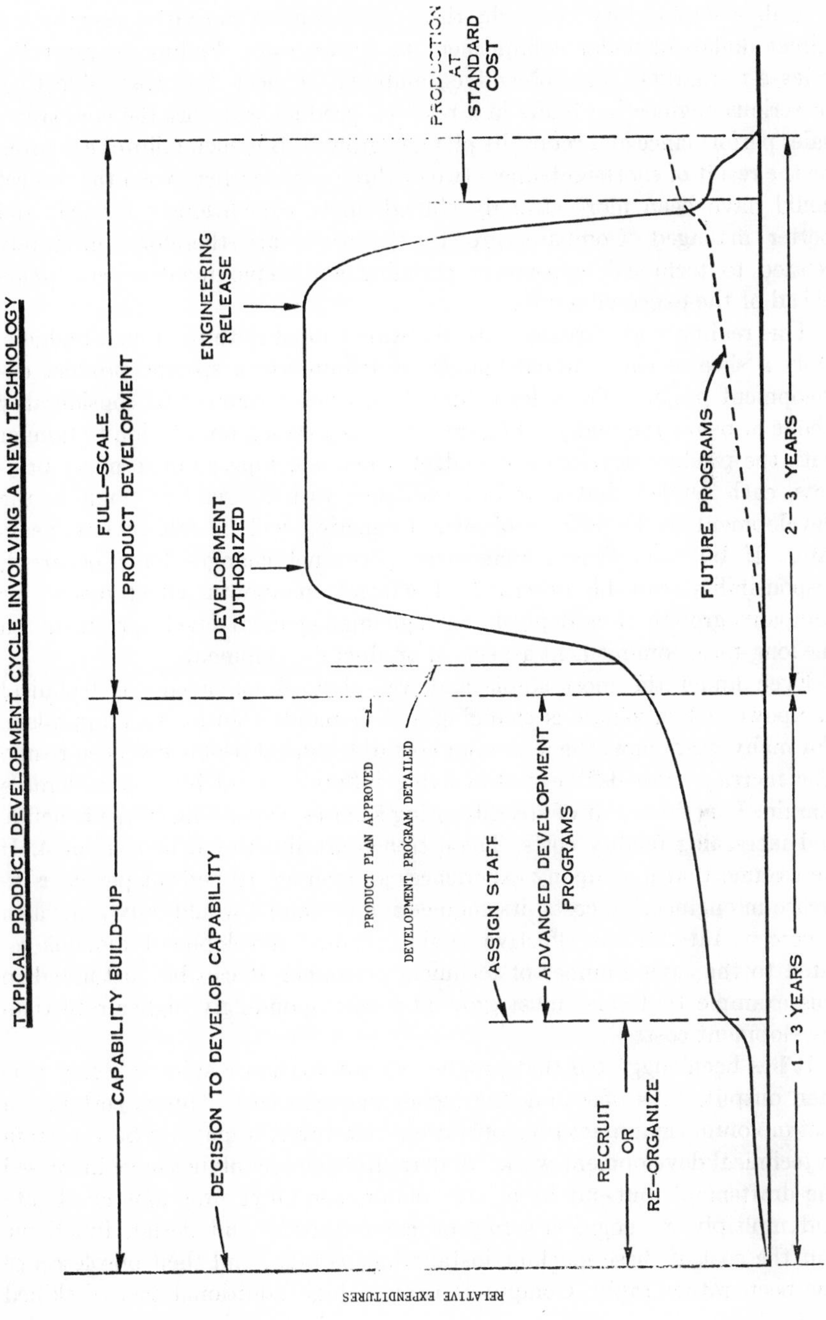

TYPICAL PRODUCT DEVELOPMENT CYCLE INVOLVING A NEW TECHNOLOGY

CAPABILITY BUILD-UP

FULL-SCALE PRODUCT DEVELOPMENT

DECISION TO DEVELOP CAPABILITY

DEVELOPMENT AUTHORIZED

ENGINEERING RELEASE

PRODUCTION AT STANDARD COST

PRODUCT PLAN APPROVED

DEVELOPMENT PROGRAM DETAILED

ASSIGN STAFF

ADVANCED DEVELOPMENT PROGRAMS

FUTURE PROGRAMS

RECRUIT OR RE-ORGANIZE

1 – 3 YEARS

2 – 3 YEARS

RELATIVE EXPENDITURES

Exhibit 3

Unlike exploratory research, these development activities represent a direct dollar-for-dollar commitment to future sales. Failure to meet the release-to-market time objective, inability to meet the cost objective, or serious engineering faults in a released product will hurt the company's sales performance and retard its planned growth. But such failures can often be the result of shortsightedness two or three years earlier, when the project could have been more strongly staffed, more expeditiously funded, and better managed. Company growth objectives are therefore intimately related to technical man-power planning and deployment several years ahead of the expected results.

This reality is at variance with the wide-spread faith in annual budgets. Only a slice of each annual budget contributes to a specific product development project. The sales volume in a given year may be considerably above or below the budgeted figure. There is a strong temptation to tamper with the product development budget which is composed of so many projects, each funded that year in accordance with its relative point in the development cycle. Effects of such tampering will be felt several years later. If by that time management personnel changes have occurred, responsibility can be obscrued. Technical manpower effectiveness for company growth thus depends on high management level agreement on the long-term commitment aspects of product development.

Even under the most stable and well-planned management, technical manpower effectiveness is changing and demands continuous reappraisal. For many years now, the man-hour cost of technical people has been rising. The increase exceeds the cost-of-living inflation trend by a considerable margin. It is the result of steadily rising salaries, expanding fringe benefits, and increasing facility costs. These trends are illustrated in Exhibit 4. If we assume that a company experiences an average 10 percent per year increase in engineering costs, its engineering personnel would only grow at a 7 percent rate. If the effective salable product development remains related to the same number of technical personnel, it can be postulated in this example that sales must grow at a correspondingly higher rate than development costs.

It has been suggested that progressive automation results in higher per-man output, thus offsetting the higher per-man cost. This is certainly a fact in volume manufacturing operations. However, it may not be so certain in technical development work. Modern drafting techniques have increased the draftsman's out-put by a large factor; computer programs accelerate and multiply an engineer's routine computations and design functions. But the cost of these machine installations is high, and their obsolescence has been rather rapid. Computers carry a high additional cost of skilled

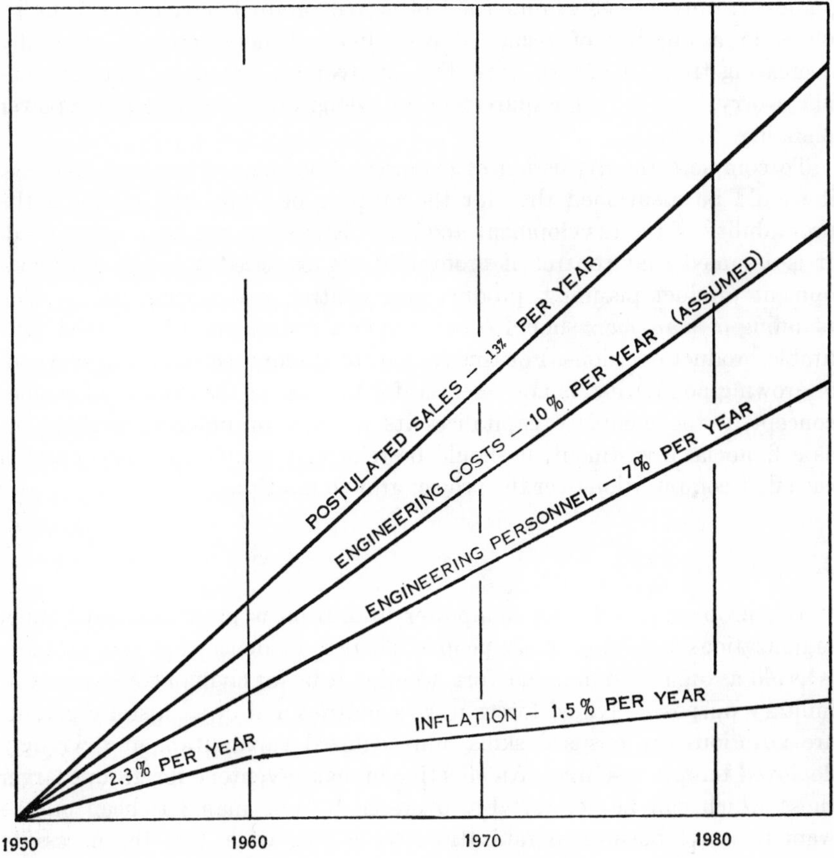

ENGINEERING COSTS VS MANPOWER TRENDS

(1) COSTS RISE FASTER THAN TECHNICAL PERSONNEL

(2) SALES VOLUME MAY NEED TO RISE FASTER THAN COSTS

Exhibit 4

specialist programmers. Moreover, the complexity of the typical technical product has been increasing, so that more specialized design and parts development, test-procedure writing, and environmental testing may be associated with equivalent dollar value of product. This is a very complex problem, one to which different answers may be found in different companies. In any event, examination of actual product development multipliers in a number of technical companies demonstrates a gradually decreasing trend. Concern with this unfavorable trend is therefore no-idle worry, but a real requirement for along-range technical manpower planning.

To complete the discussion of historical development expense analysis, it should be mentioned that for the purpose of manpower planning the profitability of the development and sales figures has not been questioned. It is assumed that control of profitability is exercised through predevelopment product planning, product cost control, and pricing policy. The planning of *manpower* should occur within a framework of assumed profitable product decisions. For this reason the discounted cash flow method, of growing popularity, is not essential for this use of the growth multiplier concept. If the company capitalizes its product or process development as a financial investment, it should be relatively simple to superimpose a cash flow computation over the project growth multiplier.

Manpower Inventory

The problem of efficient manpower utilization is present in all human organizations involving many people. There is evidence that this problem is as old as organized human effort, whether it be for civilian government or military purposes. Armed forces in all countries and of all historic periods are notorious for misused skills, unrecognized capabilities, and wrongly deployed human resources. An effective human inventory for groups larger those which can be comfortably overseen by one man has been on the wanted list of business organizations for a long time. But the necessary interchange of information between many small departments, even when aided by a large personnel staff, is cumbersome and has been too slow to register continuous personnel changes.

The very rapid expansion of modern technical business has at last provided an overwhelming impetus as well as a competent tool for this purpose. In business organizations with personnel strength in the 100,000-and-over category, spread over a number of locations, some kind of accurate, fast-moving, employee inventory becomes essential. Without it, people possessing desired qualifications in one location may be poorly utilized or perhaps coincidentally terminated in another. Likewise, the qualifications of job applicants cannot be conveniently compared with the specific needs of the various locations, or even with the needs of widely separate departments at the same location. Very large organizations are beginning to program their computers for such purposes.

That the beginning is always difficult is a proverbial truth. Computerized manpower inventory is no exception. One prominent company has actually started with a 50-page booklet in which its engineering and scientific employees were to record their skills, education, and experience. As in all new computer applications, the reduction of standard human long-hand information to computer language is a costly, time-consuming programming job. But once the programming and learning period has been completed, the built-in self-propagation of automated processing makes even the human interface "automatic."

Such a smooth-running state of the man-power inventory is evidently about to be attained by the IBM approach. In 1965 IBM began using its IRIS (IBM Recruitment Information System) for new applicants. On an eight-page folder, the job applicant fills in the type of information usually requested on application forms, *plus* specific data about his experience in many fields, ranging from aeronautical-astronautical technology through industrial design to tool die and model making. Archeology, public relations, and zoology are not neglected. Foreign language skills are included. All this information is fed into a central computer where it is stored. As job openings occur (the requirements for which are also stored in the computer memory), suitable applicants can be machine-matched. The data for all applicants responding to a specified job opening are then printed out by the computer and made available to the location where the opening occurs.

Meanwhile, IBM and some other large companies have been seeking the same information from their present employees. Reportedly, a computer memory for all 110,000 IBM employees in the United States has been completed. Ther egister includes skills; experience; age; salaries; and "secondary" knowledge not required on the employee's present job, such as languages. Its usefulness is ostensibly for speedy, optimum application of available talent to changing job requirements. Particularly in project-oriented organizations, such as Lockheed Missiles and Space Company, large numbers of highly skilled and educated people are affected by the cyclic nature of project work. The computer inventory can contribute to increased effectiveness and eliminate many of the otherwise inevitable inequities in personnel reassignments. As an extra benefit, the call for unusual interdisciplinary skills on foreign field assignments and specific research projects can now be answered immediately if such a person exists somewhere in the company.

But this is not the limit of the computer inventory's usefulness. Routine programming of promotion and salary increases becomes practical. Such expanded use may be controversial. Traditionally, an employee considers his progress in rank and salary a matter of great emotional as well as practical concern. Whether or not he prefers the programmed impartiality of the machine to the idiosyncrasies of the traditional person-to-person relationship with his immediate supervisor remains to be seen. The tools are now available.

Not every company may be of a size warranting its own computer memory on the premises. For those that are not, leased computer services may be the answer. However, permanent storage of such highly personal, confidential information by an independent service organization raises questions of information security. It may be recalled that in the early days of telegraphy, misappropriation of their clients' confidential business telegrams discredited the private telegraph companies in England, with the result that a government monopoly was established to guarantee privacy of the messages. Perhaps such occurrences would be unthinkable today. But a company's managers may think long and hard before they release all their employee data to the care of a separate enterprise over which they have no control.

Whether on the premises or leased, computer manpower inventory seems assured of rapid ascendancy. Wherever computers with suitable capacity are already in use, this technique for improved personnel utilization is to become the hard core of manpower administration.

Pending comprehensive computer coverage of this territory, manpower planning requires an orderly system of experience and seniority rating, salary progression records, and periodic reviews. For the more highly skilled people, personnel departments will be required to provide increasingly sophisticated services. The days of the less intimate relationships between employer and employee are gone, and managers of highly educated people spend a good deal of their time dealing with personal problems of employees. They rely to an increasing degree on the personnel specialists for those portions of employee administration which can be taken out of the hands of the immediate supervisor. Thus the personnel department is a vital part of any man-power planning program.

SYNTHESIS: MEETING FUTURE MANPOWER NEEDS

It has been shown how by analysis a company's past and present technical achievements, market position, personality, and technical manpower strength can be evaluated to provide a basis from which to plan the future. This is not a one-time task, but an analysis which must be brought up to date in periodic intervals.

On this basis, the synthesis of planning for future manpower needs can be undertaken with confidence. Synthesis raises these questions:

What people will we need and when?
How do we keep the best we have?
How do we get new people?
How can we combine personal and company goals?
How do we adapt to changes?
How will we get best performance from all?

To answer these questions we must define our future needs in specific terms and make adequate provision for filling them. Leadership must be developed and a group environment brought in tune with the times.

Defining Technical Manpower Needs

The analytical exercise now comes into its own. With plans available for product development objectives, market expansion, and technological progress, each technical department can prepare a plan for its anticipated needs. A central tecnhical liaison staff providing interdepartmental guidance and interpretation of each department's likely role in specific future programs is a prerequisite.

The individual department may then forecast its manpower needs in a format similar to the sample shown in Exhibit 5. This type of format is

GENERALIZED ENGINEERING MANPOWER PLAN FOR PERSONNEL PROJECTIONS

Basic Assumptions

- Budget forecast or trend: for example, 15 percent increase in three years.
- Attrition rate: for example, 1 percent per month.
- Assistant engineers recruited from colleges.
- Assistant engineer promoted to engineer in two years.
- Engineer promoted to senior level in five years.

Personnel Projection—Three Years

	Present Number	*Attrition*	*Promotion*	*Total Loss*	*Level in 3 Years*	*To Be Recruited*
Section manager						
Supervisory engineer						
Senior engineer						
Engineer	25	8	10	18	25	18
Assistant engineer	10	5	11	16	15	21

[Note: The figures above have been filled in for demonstration purposes only]

Exhibit 5

strictly numerical; it may be supported by a narrative explanation illuminating the finer assumptions which need to be considered.

Of particular significance is a projection of the anticipated decline of old skills and the buildup of new ones. For example, the displacement of the vacuum tube ty the transistor made many good tube-circuit designers relatively obsolete. However, many established companies were able to anticipate the trend and plan for retraining and other gradual adaptations to the new transistor skills. Similar technological changes are at work in many fields, so that planning for changing skills–or at least changing emphasis on existing skills–becomes a continuous job. Department by department, these changes should be estimated, and the present personnel should be evaluated by skills to detect the future surpluses or deficiencies in good time for remedy. The need for optimum use of the existing people and the requirement for maintaining balanced skills in spite of changing budgets suggest an interdepartmental skill exchange. This is one of the few legitimate applications for committee management of a common problem. In the committee, information about people with specified skills can be exchanged between department managers, to the better job satisfaction of of the individual employee and his manager alike.

Similar committee activity may be the best approach to planning for changing needs of supporting skills and functions, many of which are frequently set up to serve a number of technical departments.

It should be mentioned that these specific manpower projections by departments should include all the marketing and manufacturing operations with coordinated technical skill problems. If such coordinated planning lags behind, new technology cannot be adsorbed at the right time by the selling and producing departments. This would result in sidetracking development engineering talent for help in the factory and field and in slowing down the buildup of sales. The company would probably fail to meet its growth and profit objectives on this technologically new product.

For planning purposes, definition of product development manpower should there be broad enough to include the contributing people in several functions.

On Reading For Manpower Planning

It has been said that most managers do not read books. Presumably, in their off hours they are too busy reading company reports, *Wall Street Journal* financial pages, and bleeding ads in *Fortune* magazine. This is a myth perpetuated by managers who feel safer with the "no-nonsense, doer" stereotype of traditional business-tycoon folklore. In reality, many self-made men are voracious book readers, and a new breed of educated, inquisitive managers is taking over. There is a constant danger that the myth will be made a reality by a stream of dry, tasteless, nuts-and-bolts types of business publications–books which seem determined to prove that there shall be no fun, no enlightenment, no stimulation in book reading.

For all those ready to defy the stereotype, a short reading list appears below. These writings are eminently readable. In the methodology category, J. Wright Forrester and Edward B. Roberts have written books which offer insight into the mechanism of modern technical company decision making and management of people. The hurried reader may skip the purely methodological chapters; there is more than enough value in general parts. Mason Haire's *Psychology in Management* is a worthy companion, with practical advice on how to get the best results from people, The March 1963 issue of the *I.E.E.E. Transactions on Engineering Management* contains three excellent short articles; the titles as listed are self-explanatory. Unfortunately, other issues of this publication series overflow with involved mathematical computations, with little management pertinence in evidence. The AMA Management Report, *Optimum Use of Engineering Talent,* includes the very readable paper by Robert Shank and several other papers of timely value written by practicing managers.

The philosophical listing has been kept to four short books. A particularly readable version of an otherwise heavy subject matter is *Introduction to Jung's Psychology.* Siu's book comes from the experience of a successful scientist-manager. The late Nobel-prize winning scientist, Alexis Carrel, has written a critique of our civilization with great significance for managers. Crawford Greenewalt of Du Pont needs no further introduction.

ANALYTICAL AND METHODOLOGICAL

Blood, Jerome W., ed., *Optimum Use of Engineering Talent,* Management Report 58, American Management Association, New York, New York, 1961.

Covner, Bernard J., "Engineers in Midstream," *I.E.E.E. Transactions on Engineering Management,* Vol. EM-10, No. 1, March 1963.

Dunlop, Robert A., "Developing an Experience Register for Engineers," *I.E.E.E. Transactions on Engineering Management,* Vol. EM-10, No. 1, March 1963.

Evan, William M., "The Problem of Obsolescence of Knowledge," *I.E.E.E. Transactions on Engineering Management,* Vol. EM-10, No. 1, March 1963.

Forrester, J. Wright, "Common Foundations Underlying Engineering and Management," *I.E.E.E. Spectrum*, Vol. 1, No. 9, September 1964.

————, *Industrial Dynamics*, M.I.T. Press, Cambridge, Massachusetts, 1961.

Haire, Mason, *Psychology in Management*, McGraw-Hill Book Company, New York, New York, 1964.

Roberts, Edward B., *The Dynamics of Research and Development*, Harper & Row Publishers, New York, New York, 1964.

PHILOSOPHICAL

Carrel, Alexis, *Man, The Unknown*, MacFadden Books, New York, New York, 1961.

Fordham, Frieda, *Introduction to Jung's Psychology*, Penguin Books, Baltimore, Maryland, 1953/1964.

Greenewalt, Crawford, *The Uncommon Man*, McGraw-Hill, New York, New York, 1959.

Siu, R. G. H., *The Tao of Science*, M.I.T. Press, Cambridge, Massachusetts, 1959.

THE ROLE OF THE RESEARCH ADMINISTRATOR*

C. W. Churchman
School of Business Administration
University of California
Berkeley, California

C. E. Kruytbosch
State University of New York
Buffalo

P. Ratoosh
University of Rochester

INTRODUCTION

Every organization, whatever its activity, tends to develop means for measuring its performance. In many cases the need for performance measurement is excessive and reflects an obsession with control. Establishing quotas for salesmen is often an example of satisfying an obsession rather than a function in that it represents some decision-makers' illusion that they have more control over the organization than they actually have.

An industrial organization with a tangible product meets with comparatively fewer difficulties in assessing its performance, complicated as the task may be, than an equally complex research organization. Because they may be unaware of the difficulties of the concept, it seems to many administrators that the idea of "profit" is hard, objective, and well-defined. But the goal of a research organization is long-range, the value of a piece of research often cannot be accurately estimated for a long time after the research is accomplished, the results of research are frequently unforeseen. These facts create difficulties for research organizations and anxieties

---

* Reprinted from *Research Effectiveness* by B. Yovits, et. al. (eds); New York: Gordon & Breech Science Publishers, 1966.

for research administrators. How can a research organization justify its exixtence?[1]

These problems have detailed consequences for the research administrator. In an organization whose product is something other than research, it is generally held that the administrator plans and coordinates activities leading to predictable goals and that whatever subordinates may do might be performed more competently by the administrator if he had the time. But in a research organization no one can foresee consequences of research activities, and specialists understandably know more about their work than their supervisor. The research administrator's task, then, is a contradiction in two senses: to coordinate the unpredictable and to pass judgment on work of those more expert than he.

Some empirical approaches to both of these paradoxes have been attempted. There are several general studies of the relationships between risk-taking behavior and personality [(10)] but there are very few investigations of personality differences among administrators.[(13)]

On the level of social psychology and small group behavior, a study of scientist-supervisor interaction by Baumgartel[(2)] distinguished several styles of supervision in terms of the mode of exercise of authority and further related these styles to performance among the subordinates. However, no attempt was made to examine the conditions producing these styles. A step in the direction of regarding supervisory style as taking place within a larger organizational context is the tentative finding that the degree to which the supervisor is considered to have a voice in departmental decisions made by his superior is positively related to worker attitudes and performance. A study of a public utility company over a decade ago[(8)] found this to be a more important determinant of employee attitudes than conventional management practices. In view of a prevalent conception of the research administrator as a "buffer," one might expect this to be especially important in research organizations.

The problem of the relation between expert authority and bureaucratic authority has concerned sociologists and other organization theorists since Max Weber's theory of bureaucracy began to be applied in empirical

[1] One of the persistent themes in the literature is the question of whether scientists can or cannot be managed (see Reference (1)). One of the strongest pleas for "strong application of *existing* management knowledge and techniques to the R&D area" is made by C. Wilson Randle (Reference (2)). He claims "the laurels will go to those who actually manage research instead of just wishing they could." Though the precise positive functions of management in research productivity and creativity remain controversial, it is at least clear that bad management will cause researchers to quit. (See Reference (3)).

studies. For example, the staff-line system of organization is one mode of bringing professional expertise to bear upon line problems. However, this mode also creates problems of identification, competition, and information flow within the organization.(3) The experts' primary reference groups often lie outside the organization, whereas line managers are more completely identified with the organization.[2] These observations are clearly relevant to the research bureaucracies that have emerged in the last two decdaes; yet 20 years of shifting educational patterns have served to modify, and in some cases obliterate, the staff-line distinctions.[3] The current assumption in the literature is that line administrators in research organizations generally emerge from technical work, but in fact very little is known about the characteristics and careers of research administrators.(14,7) Similarly, very little is known about their administrative orientations and practices.

CONCEPTS AND PROCEDURES

This paper reports an attempt to develop a method of describing styles of research administration in various organizational contexts. From the points of view of acadmeic sociology, psychology, and organizational design, it is important to obtain this descriptive material. Sociologically, we are concerned with the ways in which apparently conflicting requirements of scientific and technical activity and organizational control are reconciled. The psychological interest focuses on intrapersonal conflicts engendered by inconsistencies between organizational constraints and personal defenses. Information on existing patterns of work and attitude is essential to any attempt at improving the conditions under which research adminsitrators labor.

Two general types of information were deemed pertinent to these aims—accounts of the activities of research administrators (job content and time spent on sub-tasks) and indicators of attitudes toward these aspects of their work (relative importance of sub-tasks, ideal conceptions, and individual satisfaction). We rejected the case study method because there is already a surfeit of qualitative case study material on the problems of research administrators. Our interest in organizational determinants indicated the

---

[2] For an extensive treatment of the "specialist" versus "institutionalist" orientations see Kornhauser, Reference (6). This book explores the built-in strains between work establishments and professional institutions.

[3] Almost a decade ago Herbert Shepard, Reference (11), made some acute observations on how the meeting of traditional theory of industrial organizations and organizational traditions in science were producing a new direction of industrial organization theory, incorporating a great deal of human relations.

need for a wider sample "coverage" in breadth and depth than a case study would permit—information from administrators in varying organizational contexts and at several levels within each context. Finally, a detailed case study is most appropriate when there is a good body of theory that lends itself to a "critical test." The field of research administration, however, is distinguished more by the quantity and variety of theories and approaches than by their quality.

The desire for wider coverage suggested use of a questionnaire instrument of some kind. Such an instrument seemed promising especially because it offered a future tie-in with the several on-going survey research approaches to the social and social-psychological correlates of productivity and creativity in R&D environments. We hope at a later date to perform sociometric studies in some sample sub-organizations in order to relate the perceptions of colleagues and subordinates to the research administrators' self-perceptions.

Our problem in developing a questionnaire was to reconcile our requirements for "measures" of various orientations with our desire for descriptive material on the kinds of concerns research administrators have. We compromised with an open-ended list of 11 classes of activities or functions (drawn from the literature and discussions) likely to be carried out by research administrators. The questionnaire was supplemented by a series of unstructured interviews of a subsample of respondents. The questionnaire also elicited information on selected attitudes, social background and career factors, and perception of the relevance of organizational groupings to their work. These findings will be reported elsewhere.

In the pretest interviews the list of functions was discussed and respondents were asked to rank each class of activities:

a. "*The order of importance* you assign the functions for getting the job done under present conditions;"
b. "*The amount of time* you spend performing these functions under present conditions;"
c. "Given greater freedom from various pressures and greater control over demands upon you, how would you rank the importance of the functions in order to do the best possible job? In other words, what *ought to be the order of importance* to achieve maximum effectiveness?"; and
d. "The functions you personally find *most satisfying to perform.*"

For purposes of analysis we grouped these functions into four categories:

a. Scientific and technical activities, in the sense of personal participation in the research work and keeping up with the literature and developments in the field;

b. Planning activities, such as selection of projects and development of new programs;

c. Maintenance of the research environment in the laboratory through cultivating good interpersonal relations and criticism and encouragement of good ideas; and

d. Activities relating to administrative control, such as budgeting, accounting, and securing adherence to schedules on projects.

The results of submitting questionnaires to a selected group of subjects, and grouping the data as indicated above, are shown in Table 1.

THE ROLE ORIENTATIONS

Analysis of the results depicted in Table 1 follows two main areas of interest. The first is identification of styles among the respondents in terms of the patterns of emphases they gave to these aspects of their work; and the second is examination of some of the consistencies or inconsistencies among the rankings of importance, time spent, ideal situation, and satisfaction.

Let us first turn to the styles. We measure "style" by the weights given to the sub-tasks by the respondents. We did not initially anticipate that there would be much variation in the rankings, but the data proved otherwise. The rankings in Table 1 show the emphases the respondents placed upon various aspects of their work. For instance, in terms of importance in getting the job done, respondents Nos. 4, 7, and 12 and the defense contractor bench supervisor rated their own research work high or medium, whereas all the rest rate this low.

Though all the researcher-oriented respondents had administrative positions with supervisory responsibilities, they were all uncomfortable with the term "supervision" and preferred to use terms such as "consultation with colleagues." Their significant reference groups were universities and professional societies. The defense contractor bench supervisor—an engineer—had recently received a coveted technical award from his company; and he was being considered for a senior non-supervisory post. Government laboratory respondent No. 12, a young physicist with clear research ambitions, had recently accepted a junior supervisory post on a trial basis but maintained he was extremely unhappy with the demands

TABLE 1

Research, Managerial, and Administrative Orientations Among R&D Administrators
Part A. Scores of Respondents in Selected Organizations on Rankings of Functions

Respondents	Actual Importance a	b	c	d*	Actual Time Spent a	b	c	d	'Ideal' Situation a	b	c	d	Personal Satisfaction a	b	c	d
Government R&D Lab.																
Respondent No. 4	H	L	H	L	H	M	H	L	H	L	H	L	H	L	H	L
Respondent No. 7	H	M	M	L	H	M	L	L	H	M	L	L	H	L	M	L
Respondent No. 12	M	H	M	L	L	M	M	L	M	H	M	L	H	M	L	L
Respondent No. 6	L	L	H	L	L	H	M	L	L	H	H	L	M	H	H	L
Respondent No. 8	L	H	H	L	L	M	H	M	L	M	H	M	M	M	H	L
Respondent No. 9	L	H	M	L	L	H	M	H	L	H	M	L	M	H	H	L
Respondent No. 11	L	H	M	L	L	H	M	M	L	H	H	L	L	M	H	L
Respondent No. 10	L	H	H	M	L	H	H	M	L	H	H	L	L	H	H	L
Respondent No. 1	L	H	L	M	L	H	M	H	L	H	M	M	M	H	M	M
Respondent No. 3	L	H	M	H	L	H	M	H	L	H	H	M	M	H	H	L
Respondent No. 2	L	M	M	H	L	L	M	H	L	M	M	H	L	L	M	H
Non-profit Research Org.																
Research Director	L	M	M	H	L	M	H	L	H	M	H	L	H	M	H	L
Large Defense Contractor																
2nd level sup. (A)	L	M	H	M	L	M	M	H	L	M	H	M	M	H	H	L
2nd level sup. (B)	L	H	L	H	L	H	L	H	....				H	M	H	L
Bench level sup.	H	M	H	L	H	M	M	M	H	L	H	L	H	L	H	L
Large British Industrial Org.																
Mgr. Research Div.	L	M	M	M	L	M	M	M	L	M	M	M	L	M	M	M
2nd level sup.	L	H	L	M	M	H	L	L	M	H	M	M	M	H	L	L

* Description of Functions (See also Table 1, Part B.)

a = Own research (10 + 11)
b = Planning (3 + 4)
c = Morale and criticism (6 + 7)
d = Administrative control (1 + 8)

Scores

H = 0 – 4.75 (High)
M = 5 – 7 (Medium)
L = 7.5 – 11 (Low)

TABLE 1 (cont.)

Part B. Categories of Functions of R&D Administrators

1. Budgeting
2. Assessment and evaluation of personnel—hiring and firing
3. Long-range planning of important areas of R&D; development of new R&D programs
4. Short-range planning—selection and approval of specific projects and work assignments; review of ongoing work
5. Coordination of plans and projects with objectives and policies of the organization and funding sources
6. Creation and maintenance of good morale and human relations
7. Criticism of scientific and technical ideas; encouragement of development of good ideas
8. Maintenance of adequate work levels on projects and adherence to schedules
9. Dissemination of the R&D activities and accomplishments of your organization
10. "Keeping up" with scientific and technical events in the field
11. Conduct of research or development work himself—personal projects

this made upon his research time and his relations with his former colleagues.[4]

A further feature of the ratings of the researcher administrators was a tendency to minimize the importance of planning functions—"You can't plan basic research," one of them commented. Though planning was discounted, the "researchers" acknowledged the importance of creating and maintaining a favorable research environment. Finally, all the respondents high or medium on research rated the administrative control function low.

This apparent opposition between a scientific-technical orientation and approval of traditional organizational control mechanisms naturally also appears in reverse. Government laboratory administrators Nos. 10, 1, 3, and 2, and all the men in the other organizations (except the defense contractor bench level supervisor) rate the functions of administrative control high or medium. Planning functions loomed important in the scheme of the administratively oriented respondents, with comparatively great importance attached to short-range planning. It is suggestive of this style that all three of those respondents who minimized maintenance of

[4] These two men were clearly at a significant turning point in their careers in terms of remaining in scientific work or committing themselves to administrative careers. The literature seems to be fairly unanimous in stating that the greater rewards lie in management careers. A fruitful area of inquiry might be to investigate the consequences of holding research, managerial, or administrative orientations for the career development and promotion of lower-level research supervisors.

research environment functions also responded high or medium on administrative control. Among some technical supervisory people there is a complete rejection of such "human relations" concepts as "prestige" and "status symbols," and a strong belief in an autonomous technical logic that works best when not interfered with. For example, one of our interviewees replied to a question about the recent increase in prestige among scientific workers:

"This prestige thing—by definition it means that you're trying to put something into it that does not really exist in the position; so, it being artificial, it is something I care very little about."[5]

A number of respondents rate both research and administrative control low, putting greater emphasis on the planning and maintenance of research environment aspects of their role. These "managerial" orientations clearly emerge as a type—for example, government laboratory administrators Nos. 8, 9, and 11, with No. 10 and the defense contractor 2nd level supervisor (A) as marginal cases. Significantly, none of these is a lowest-level supervisor. A striking feature of these respondents was their penchant for openly playing down their own technical role, easily admitting, "Supervision doesn't make much sense when they are smarter than you are." They characterized their technical function as primarily one of veto of poor proposals: "If one of my division heads doesn't want to do what I told him, I say, 'What do you want to do?' He tells me, and if I don't see anything stupid with it, why, that's what he does." On the other hand, they pointed out that one of their basic responsibilities involved shaping the research goals of their group. "I feel that an administrator in the research area should participate in helping to chart the goals of the group, especially in an applied area of research. And even in a basic area I still feel that way, maybe to a lesser extent; but I think the administrator should take an active lead in shaping the group. This may be done by selective recruiting. If you want to go into a new area, all right—you recruit in that area—as well as redirect people who are already established in areas of research, in other words, redirect their programs."

In guiding the efforts of subordinates, respondents stressed the crucial importance of the creation and maintenance of a good research environment. "Depending upon the man and the work, you may influence him just by showing a greater degree of interest in something that he's doing along the lines that you want him to. Let him know you're interested in this area and

---

[5] This is similar to the embarrassed rejection by the directive and organic oriented group of psychiatrists of questions about social class position, as reported in Hollingshead and Redlich's study, *Social Class and Mental Illness*, Reference (4).

that you think his work is intersting and promising. Certain people will start bending and going around into a new direction. Or you can just simply find an area that you think needs attention, and you have some people that you think are competent enough to go into the area, then just by describing the problem to them and emphasizing the need in the area, you can get a few more to go . . ."

Unfortunately, our attempt at defining a "political" function for managers turned out to be a too-inclusive category—interpreted in too many senses by the respondents. Our conception of this set of activities nevertheless is worth mentioning. This conception is of the research administrator as a maker of policy about the uses and direction of scientific and technical work, primarily through his influence on the funding process. He plays a role in pushing certain areas of work; in steering given projects to certain funding sources; and in persuading existing and potential funding sources of the use, desirability, or necessity of supporting given areas of work or specific projects.

INCONSISTENCIES IN THE ROLE ORIENTATIONS

The other area of interest concerns the consistency, or lack of it, among the rankings. Patterns of strain or dissatisfaction can be inferred from these data. Government laboratory respondents Nos. 4 and 7 ("researchers") and 10 and 2 ("administrators") showed very little variation from ranking to ranking. They were consistent; i.e., they appeared to gain personal satisfaction from spending much time on performing functions they considered to be very important for getting the job done, as well as feeling that their present lot conformed in major outline with their ideal conceptions. Government laboratory respondents Nos. 12, 6, 9, and 3, on the other hand, showed significant discrepancies among their rankings. No. 12 felt he could spend little time on the work he liked most; No. 9 felt he spent inordinate time on administrative matters; No. 3 received little satisfaction from performing administrative functions, which he nevertheless considered essential to getting the job done. The major difference between the consistent and inconsistent rankers appears to be the length of tenure in the present position: the more recent the assumption of the position, the less likelihood the man has worked out a consistent image of himself in his role. These remarks must be qualified by the comment of the British research manager who said that he could not very well admit discrepancies among his rankings of importance, time spent, and satisfaction without also admitting his failure as an administrator.

In summary, the rankings of activities performed by the administrators revealed a surprising variety of role conceptions. Further, inconsistencies in the rankings indicate dissonance between what the administrator feels obliged to do and what gives him most satisfaction.

REFERENCES

1. Ahlberg, C. D. and Honey, J. C., "The Scientist's Attitude Toward Government Employment," *Science*, 113, 505 (1951).
2. Baumgartel, H., "Leadership Style as a Variable in Research Administration," *Administrative Science Quarterly*, 2, 344 (1957).
3. Dalton, M., "Conflicts Between Staff and Line Managerial Officers," *American Sociological Review*, 15, 342 (1950).
4. Hollingshead, A. and Redlich, F. C., *Social Class and Mental Illness—A Community Study*, New York: John Wiley & Sons, Inc. (1958).
5. Kaplan, N., "Organization: Will it Choke or Promote the Growth of Science?" in Hill (ed.) *The Management of Scientists*, Boston: Beacon Press (1964).
6. Kornhauser, W., *Scientists in Industry: Conflict and Accommodation*, Berkeley: University of California Press (1962).
7. Mainzer, L. C., "The Scientist as Public Administrator," *The Western Political Quarterly*, 16, 814 (1963).
8. Pelz, D. C., "Leadership Within a Hierarchical Organization," *Journal of Social Issues*, 7, 49 (1951).
9. Randle, C. W., "Problems of Research and Development Management," *Harvard Business Review*, 37, 128 (1959).
10. Scodel, A., Ratoosh, P., and Minas, J. S., "Some Personality Correlates of Decision-Making Under Conditions of Risk," *Behavioral Science*, 4(1), 19 (1960).
11. Shepard, H., "Superiors and Subordinates in Research," *Journal of Business*, 29, 261 (1956).
12. Shepherd, C. and Brown, P., "Status, Prestige, and Esteem in a Research Organization," *Administrative Science Quarterly*, 1, 340 (1956).
13. Tagiuri, R., "Value Orientations and the Relationship of Managers and Scientists," *Administrative Science Quarterly*, 10, 39 (1965).
14. Uyeki, E. S. and Cliffe, F. B., "The Federal Scientist Administrator," *Science*, 139, 1267 (1963).